The Law on Financial Derivatives

In heaven there was a discussion between the recently deceased as to which profession had existed first:

Doctor: *"Eve was made out of Adam's rib, therefore a doctor must have been needed from the beginning."*

Engineer: *"The world was manufactured out of chaos: that required an engineer."*

Derivatives trader: *"Who do you think created the chaos?"*

AUSTRALIA
The Law Book Company
Brisbane ● Sydney ● Melbourne ● Perth

CANADA
Carswell
Ottawa ● Toronto ● Calgary ● Montreal ● Vancouver

AGENTS
Steimatzky's Agency Ltd., Tel Aviv;
N.M. Tripathi (Private) Ltd., Bombay;
Eastern Law House (Private) Ltd., Calcutta;
M.P.P. House, Bangalore;
Universal Book Traders, Delhi;
Aditya Books, Delhi;
MacMillan Shuppan KK, Tokyo;
Pakistan Law House, Karachi, Lahore

The Law on Financial Derivatives

By

Alastair Hudson
LLB LLM (Lond)
Barrister, 2 Paper Buildings, Temple
Lecturer in law, King's College, University of London

LONDON
SWEET & MAXWELL
1996

Published in 1996 by
Sweet & Maxwell Limited of
South Quay Plaza, 183 Marsh Wall,
London E14 9FT

Typeset by Selwood Systems,
Midsomer Norton
Printed by Butler and Tanner Ltd,
Frome and London

No natural forests were destroyed
to make this product:
only farmed timber was used
and re-planted

ISBN 0 421 54610 7

**A catalogue record for this book is
available from the British Library**

Preface

The derivatives markets have become more and more newsworthy in the 1990s. The Barings collapse was the most straightforward disaster to strike the image of the marketplace. It has also reminded the markets of the problems which still face it; awakening in the minds of regulators and legislators the spectre of regulation of the OTC ("over the counter") derivative markets. There have been a plethora of derivatives-related farragos since the Hammersmith and Fulham litigation. Metalgesellschaft, Orange County and Proctor and Gamble have reinforced the need for lawyers to understand these volatile and complex new products, to protect their clients from the risks the markets present and to maximise the available benefits.

The "Law on Financial Derivatives" aims to provide the first comprehensive guide for the lawyer (and the non-lawyer) to the legal complexities of the derivatives market and to understand the structure of the products.

This book is based on a number of basic assumptions. The first assumption is that the lawyer is a manager of risks in the context of the financial markets. The financial institution looks to the lawyer to control legal risk and preserve means of terminating unwanted transactions.

The second assumption is that the innovation which has characterised the derivatives markets, will continue. This book is therefore expected to appear out-of-date over a five year period with respect to its descriptions of the *full range* of derivatives products. However, it is also assumed that the *form of innovation* in the derivatives markets will continue to centre on those few basic structures discussed in this book. Therefore, the legal analysis will continue to hold good.

The third assumption is that the risks involved in the derivatives markets will lead eventually to the introduction of regulation to cover these products. Therefore this book attempts to plot some of the ways in which regulation might be introduced and the economic considerations that would have to be taken into account by any regulator.

I would like to express my thanks to Edward Murray of Allen & Overy and to my editors at Sweet & Maxwell, whose patience and support have been invaluable. My thanks also go to my parents, brothers, close friends and family dog who have put up with my incessant babble about this subject. However, in time-honoured style, any mistakes are entirely the fault of unexpected movements in interest rates.

Alastair Hudson
November 22, 1995
2 Paper Buildings, Temple

Contents

v   Preface
xi   Introduction
xv   Acknowledgment
xvii   Table of cases
xviii   Table of statutes

Part 1: The Products

para.
1.1   Introductory
1.2   Derivative Strategies
1.3   Swaps
1.4   Debt Options
1.5   Equity Options
1.6   Warrants
1.7   Forwards and Futures
1.8   Hedging

Part 2: The Markets and their Documentation

2.1   Exchange Traded Products
2.2   The Primary Markets
2.3   OTC Derivative Contracts
2.4   The Confirmation
2.5   Master Agreements
2.6   The Schedule
2.7   Tax Representations
2.8   Pre-contractual Undertakings and Procedure
2.9   Set-off
2.10   Transferability of Obligations
2.11   Termination

Part 3: The Legal Issues

3.1   Interest Rate Swaps
3.2   Netting on Insolvency
3.3   Automatic Termination
3.4   Restitution
3.5   Capacity

3.6   Conflict of Laws
3.7   Capital Adequacy
3.8   Political Risk
3.9   Agents and Fund Managers
3.10   Trusts and Fund Managers
3.11   Transfer Clauses and Novations
3.12   Gaming
3.13   Breach of Warranty
3.14   Suitability
3.15   Regulation

Part 4: Taxation

4.1   Tax Provisions in Master Agreements
4.2   The Taxation of Financial Derivatives

Part 5: Credit Risk and Collateral

5.1   Introduction
5.2   The Credit Aspect of Derivatives
5.3   The Credit Profile of OTC Options
5.4   The Credit Exposure of Swaps
5.5   Collateral

Part 6: The Regulation of the Derivatives Markets

6.1   The Derivatives Revolution
6.2   The Foreign Exchange Market
6.3   The Derivatives Markets
6.4   The Products Involved
6.5   Types of Institution Involved
6.6   What are the Risks Involved?
6.7   What are the Policy Motivations?
6.8   Possible Solutions
6.9   Regulation
6.10   Taxation
6.11   Overseas
6.12   Conclusions

Appendices

page
233   ISDA Master Agreement
259   Schedule to the Master Agreement
264   "Non-standard" OTC Options Confirmation/Master Agreement

CONTENTS

271   Short form "Non-standard" OTC Options Agreement
274   Long form "Non-standard" OTC Options Confirmation
277   Pro-forma "Non-standard" Equity Index Swap Confirmation
281   Pro-forma Mark-to-Market Collateral Agreement
285   Confirmation of OTC Bond Option Transaction
295   Confirmation of OTC Equity Index Option Transaction
303   Confirmation of OTC Single Share Option Transaction Physical
       Settlement
318   Section-by-section Derivatives Supervision Act of 1994
323   A Bill

333   Glossary

343   Index

Introduction

This book deals specifically with the Over the Counter ("OTC") derivatives markets, their documentation and regulation. The literature on derivatives dealt on exchanges is comprehensive enough to make its repetition here unnecessary. The OTC market is of far greater interest to the legal advisor and the financial professional and has yet to be the focus of legal literature. The primary difference between exchange-traded derivatives and OTC derivatives is that the OTC market operates, for the most part, without rules. The lawyer does not have reference to exchange regulations, rather the lawyer must become well-versed in the commercial and financial aspects of the derivatives markets. The derivative is a creature of market innovation and continues to be subject to rapid change. The lawyer must be conversant in the basic building blocks of the OTC derivatives products to be able to deal with further product development. The extent to which there is a cadre of settled legal principle is provided by the standard market documentation. Therefore, a familiarity with the construction of standard market documentation is vital.

Lawyers play an important, but strictly-defined, role in the derivatives markets. The most involvement lawyers have in financial transactions, is in risk management. The lack of explicit, systematic regulation of the OTC derivatives markets generates a new dimension of risk. Whereas the financial professional deals with the commercial risks of market movement, client failure to pay, and so forth, the uncertainty of the legal construction of the products involved adds a new species of risk. Therefore, there is a need to focus attention on the nature of the risks involved in OTC financial derivatives. The role of this book is to examine the legal risks involved in derivatives transactions and the means that market practice uses to circumvent or minimise (as appropriate) those risks. Derivative product strategies seek to manage financial risk, credit departments seek to manage credit risk and therefore lawyers seek to manage legal risk.

There is little decided or settled law involved in this area. Therefore there is room for speculation as to the effect of settled law and legal analysis on the derivative products that exist. The concentration on legal risk management requires exploration of these issues. This book is therefore an introductory and, in some respects, exploratory venture. The importance of such an undertaking is to set out for the banker, the lawyer advising and those coming new to the markets, the parameters within which risks currently appear to lie.

The reader may therefore benefit from an explanation of the lay-out of the book.

Part 1

The opening section of the text attempts a concise explanation of the products which are involved in the OTC derivatives markets. Definition of the products is usually dealt with in market-orientated terms. What is attempted here is to set out those financial market definitions and then to translate them into a legal analysis. The underlying argument of the book is that the products, while they are the result of enormous innovation, are composed of well-understood legal structures and will continue to be so.

The derivative markets are primarily client-led. The banks develop products to sell to their client-base and therefore are reacting to the same set of client requirements. The intensification of product complexity is based on the same basic products and the same market requirements: increased funding at lower rates, financial risk management and greater speculative return on standard market products.

Part 2

The use of standard market documentation is considered in this section. The proliferation of market documentation means that the chapter is constructed around the typical features of market documents. The purpose and drafting of particular provisions is dealt with in the section. Its aim is to explain the role and effect of each contractual provision on the range of derivative products considered in Part 1.

There are three stages in the documentation process which are considered in detail: the confirmation of the particular transaction, the market standard master contract governing the range of transactions effected between two parties, and the customised form of schedule attached to the master contract. Examples of the market documentation is attached in the Appendices 2 to 9.

Part 3

The third part deals with the legal issues which are thrown up by OTC derivative products generally. The derivative markets have yet to benefit from definitive judicial comment on either the products themselves or on the efficacy of the standard market products. The primary legal issues are generated by the commercial concerns of the parties. For example, much discussion has centred on the attitude of insolvency law to provisions in the standard documents to the automatic set-off mutual obligations on the insolvency of one of the parties. This issue is generated by the parties' credit risk management concern as to the counterparty's failure to pay under its obligations. The Legal Issues section is therefore a collection of the questions which have appeared to the market participants as the main risk management problems identified by the lawyers.

The primary areas of legal difficulty are insolvency, the difficulty of dealing with special purpose vehicles as counterparties and the effect of principles of contract law on the market standard documents. The main issues covered are: Netting; Capacity; Capital Adequacy; Trusts and Fund

Managers; Agents and Fund Managers; Transfers and Novations; Gaming; Insurance; Cherry-picking.

Netting deals with the problem of setting off obligations of one of the parties where they become insolvent. Similarly, Cherry-picking is the concern which arises out of the insolvency issue, where the one of the parties seeks to give effect to profitable contracts and to repudiate unprofitable ones. Capacity of the parties to enter into OTC derivatives transactions has been the primary subject of legal analysis in this area in the headline cases. Linked to the notion of capacity is the question which has arisen in recent American litigation of the 'suitability' of particular products for corresponding counterparties. Capital Adequacy regulation is a growing area of importance for banking institutions in motivating and controlling the use of OTC derivatives products. The role of fund managers and hedge funds in the markets is a vexed issue caused by difficulties of identifying the relevant counterparty. Trusts and Fund Managers deals with the issue of trust funds which are involved in the derivatives markets as counterparties. Agents and Fund Managers look to the role of the fund manager who acts as a market party for a disclosed or undisclosed counterparty. The Transfers and Novations section deals with a number of provisions in the standard form contracts which provoke legal difficulties. There have been concerns about Gaming laws and the status of many derivatives products as enforceable contracts for differences.

Part 4

This section deals specifically with the new species of tax regulation introduced by the 1994 Finance Act. The growing use of tax derivatives and the focus of tax regulation on the derivatives market, requires a specialist analysis of the area. The tax analysis of a financial derivative will clearly have a large impact on its profitability – the proper tax analysis is therefore an important component of derivative strategy.

Part 5

Credit Risk and Collateral deals with the essential commercial problems of controlling credit exposure in an increasingly volatile marketplace. A number of different entities will use derivative instruments in the current market place. Derivatives are used by dealers as a hedging tool and a means of speculation. Issuers of commercial paper and equity stock use derivatives as a means of hedging exposure, providing access to a lower cost of funding and providing access to particular types of funding in the first place. Investors who enter the derivative markets use the products as a method of portfolio management, as hedging tools and as a means of speculating.

The central purpose of the derivative instrument is risk management. The use of the derivative enables the treasurer to minimise the company's exposure to the risk of movements in underlying rates and prices. For the banking institution, the risks faced cover a broad spread of issues from the economic movements in the marketplace to credit risks on counterparties' default, insolvency, the failure of management systems and procedures to facilitate complex derivatives transactions.

Credit risk itself sub-divides into settlement risk and counterparty risk. Settlement risk is concerned with the risk that the counterparty will default or fail to perform its obligations under the contract.

Collateral is a distinct form of credit protection which throws up a plethora of legal problems of its own. The growing market practice of using collateral has prompted the desire to deal with the subject separately from the credit risks as such. There are a number of different ways of managing credit and other risks which are discussed. The market has begun to favour collateral over the others for reasons which are developed in the Risks section.

Part 6

The final section is concerned with the likelihood and form of future regulation of the OTC derivatives markets. The chapter is culled from a number of academic papers and conference discussions which have taken place over recent years. Political pressure in the USA has sought, already, to introduce legislation to control the derivatives market. The aim of this section is to introduce that discussion to the UK legal audience and enable consideration of long term strategy to develop.

The bulk of this book is concerned with the efficacy and structure of the standard form contracts and their standing with respect to English law generally. As such, this book will deal with issues of financial concern and begins with an analysis of the different products that are involved before dealing with the standard form contracts and their relevance to each form of product.

What it does not do is examine the pricing issues involved in these markets, although it will deal with matters to do with structuring of the more complex OTC derivative products. The final section deals with the tax treatment of these products in the UK and attempts to offer a coherent analysis of those issues.

Acknowledgment

Grateful acknowledgment is made to the *International Swaps and Derivatives Association Inc.* for permission to reproduce the following in the appendices:

ISDA Master Agreement
Schedule to the Master Agreement
Non-standard OTC Options confirmation/master agreement
Short form non-standard OTC Options Agreement
Long form non-standard OTC Options Confirmation
Pro-forma non-standard equity index swap confirmation
Pro-forma mark-to-market collateral agreement
Confirmation of OTC Bond Option Transaction
Confirmation of OTC Equity Index Option Transaction
Confirmation of OTC Single Share Option Transaction Physical Settlement

Table of Cases

Astor Properties Ltd v. Tunbridge
  Wells   Equitable   Friendly
  Society [1936] 1 All E.R. 531 19,
                                    122, 131
Bank of India v. Trans Continental
  Commodity Merchants & Patel
  (1982) 1 Lloyds Rep. 586 16, 24, 119
Barclays Bank v. Sims (W.J.) &
  Cooke (Southern) [1980] Q.B.
  677; [1980] 2 W.L.R. 218;
  (1978) 123 S.J. 785; [1979] 3
  All E.R. 522; [1980] 1 Lloyd's
  Rep. 255 81
Bell v. Lever Bros [1932] A.C. 161 . . . 81
British American Continental Bank,
  Re (1922) 2 Ch 575 . . . . . 16, 24, 119
British Eagle International Airlines
  v. Compagnie Nationale Air
  France [1975] 1 W.L.R. 758;
  [1975] 2 All ER 390; 119 S.J.
  368; [1975] 2 Lloyd's Rep. 43,
  H.L. 20, 122
Castle, Re [1917] 2 KB 725, [1916]
  W.N. 195 . . . . 20, 123
Charge Card Services, Re [1989]
  Ch. 497; 1988 Fin. LR 308;
  (1989) 8 Tr. L.R. 86; [1989] 6
  I.B.F.L. 254, C.A. 190
Collins v. Association Greyhound
  Racecourses Ltd [1930] 1 Ch 1 . 143
Cooke v. Eshelby (1887) 12 App
  Cas 271 143
Furniss v. Dawson [1984] A.C. 474;
  [1984] 2 W.L.R. 226; (1984)
  128 S.J. 132; [1984] 1 All E.R.
  530; (1984) 55 T.C. 324; [1984]
  S.T.C. 153; (1984) 81 L.S. Gaz.
  739; (1984) 134 New L.J. 341;
  [1985] S.L.T. 93; (1985) 82 L.S.
  Gaz. 2782 . . . . 160, 161
Gee v. News Group Newspapers
  The Times, June 8, 1990 81
Hazell v. Hammersmith & Fulham
  [1992] 2 A.C. 1; [1991] 2 W.L.R.
  372; [1991] 1 All E.R. 545; 89
  L.G.R. 271; [1991] RVR 28;
  (1991) 141 New L.J. 127; (1991)
  155 J.P.N. 527; (1991) 3 Admin
  L.R. 549, H.L. 12, 14, 15, 117,
                              118, 122, 134,
                              136, 139, 209

Kelly v. Solari [1841] 9 M&W 54 81
Kleinwort   Benson   v.   Sandwell
  Borough   Council   [1994]   1
  W.L.R. 938; [1994] 4 All E.R.
  890; 92 L.G.R. 405; (1994) 138
  S.J.   (LB)   26;   The   Times,
  December 30, 1993; The Inde-
  pendent, January 5, 1994, C.A. . 146
Knightsbridge Estates Trust Ltd v.
  Byrne [1940] AC 613; [1939]
  Ch. 441 65
Langton v. Waite (1868) LR 6 Eq
  165; 37 LJ Ch 345; 18 LT 80; 16
  WR 508 143
Lisser & Rosencranz's Claim (1923)
  1 Ch 276 . . . . 16, 24, 119
Morgan Grenfell v. Welwyn Hat-
  field DC [1995] 1 All E.R. 1; The
  Times, June 1, 1993, D.C. 14, 16,
                          117, 118, 137, 145
N.V. Slavenburg's Bank v. Inter-
  continental Natural Resources
  [1980] 1 W.L.R. 1076; (1980)
  124 S.J. 374; [1980] 1 All E.R.
  955 188
Ogdens v. Nelson [1905] A.C. 109 . . 20
Pearson v. Scott (1878) 9 Ch D 198 . 143
Pratt v Willey (1826) 2 C&P 350 . . . 143
Shipton Anderson & Co (1927) Ltd
  v. Micks Lambert & Co (1936) 2
  All ER 1032 . . . . 20, 123
Smith v. Harrison (1857) 26 L.J. Ch.
  412; 29 LTOS 11; 3 Jur NS 287;
  5 WR 408 81
South African Territories v. Wall-
  ington [1898] AC 309 . . 19, 122, 131
South   Tyneside   Metropolitan
  Borough Council v. Svenska
  International plc [1995] 1 All
  E.R. 485 122
Stewart v. Aberdein (1838) 4 M&W
  211; 1 Horn & H 284; 7 LJ Ex
  292; 7 LT 46; 150 ER 1406 143
Westdeutsche Landesbank Giro-
  centrale v. London Borough of
  Islington [1994] 1 W.L.R. 938;
  [1994] 4 All E.R. 890; 92 L.G.R.
  405; (1994) 138 S.J. (LB) 26; The
  Times, December 30, 1993; The
  Independent, January 5, 1994,
  C.A. 87, 146

Table of Statutes

1845 Gaming Act (8 & 9 Vict., c.
    109) 15,115,136,147
1977 Unfair Contract Terms Act (c.
    50) 146
    s. 11 147
1982 Insurance Companies Act (c.
    50) 138, 147
    s. 16(1) 138
    s. 36 .... 138, 139
    s. 58 139
1985 Companies Act (c. 6) 65, 164
    s. 35 135–136
    s. 35(1) 135
    s. 35A 135–136
    s. 35A(1) 135
    s. 35A(2) 136
    s. 395 188
    s. 396 188
    s. 744 .... 65, 66
1986 Building Society Act (c. 53) .. 137
    s. 23(1) 137
    Financial Services Act (c.
    60) 144, 147
    s. 43 148
    s. 48 148
1988 Income and Corporation
    Taxes Act (c. 1)
    s. 468 164
    s. 469 164
1989 Companies Act (c. 40) 134
1992 Taxation of Chargeable
    Gains Act (c. 12) 156
    s. 149(1) 156
    (2) 156, 157, 158
    (3) 158
    (6) 158
    s. 170 156
1993 Finance Act (c. 34) 154, 155
1994 Finance Act (c. 9) 154
    Chapter 11 ....154, 163,
                    164, 165
    ss. 147–177 154
    s. 147(1) 155, 156
    (4) 156
    s. 148(1) 156

    (2) 156
    (3) 156
    (4) 156
    (6) 156
    s. 149 163
    (5) 162
    s. 150 ....159, 160, 163
    s. 150(1) 159
    (2) 160, 161
    (3) 161
    (4) 160, 161
    (5) 160
    (7) 162
    (8)(a) 162
    (8)(b) 162
    (9) 162
    s. 151(1)(a)(b) 162
    s. 152 164
    s. 152(1) 163
    (2)(a) 163
    (b) 164
    s. 154 155
    s. 154(1) 164
    (2) 164
    s. 155 .... 164, 166
    s. 155(1) 164
    (2) 164
    (4)(a) and (b) 164
    (5)(a) and (b) 164
    (6) 164
    (7) 165
    (8) 165
    s. 156 165
    (1)(a) 165
    (b) 165
    (3) 165
    (7) 165
    s. 157(3) 165
    (5) 165
    (6) 165
    s. 165 166
    s. 165(9) 166
    s. 166 166
    s. 167 166
    s. 167(2) 166

Part 1

The Products

Contents

1.1 Introductory
1.2 Derivative Strategies
1.3 Swaps
1.4 Debt Options
1.5 Equity Options
1.6 Warrants
1.7 Forwards and Futures
1.8 Hedging

Introductory   1.1

This section is based on a number of basic assumptions which it seems
prudent to air at the outset. The first assumption is that, in the context of
financial instruments, the lawyer is a manager of risks and nothing more.
The financial institutions only require legal input to prevent them from
transgressing regulations and to ensure that, in the event of a dispute, the
form of the contracts and the conduct of business documentation will
enable the damage to be limited.

The second assumption is that the innovation which has epitomised
the derivatives markets up to now will continue such that it will be
impossible to write a book which claims to discuss all the derivatives
products in existence but that will not be obsolete by the time it is
published.

However, this second assumption is tempered by the conviction that
the form of innovation in the markets centres, and will continue to centre,
on a few basic building blocks and that a legal analysis of these blocks
will form the basis of an analysis of any derivative product in the future.

The third assumption is that the risks involved in the derivatives markets
will lead eventually to the introduction of regulation to cover these
products. Therefore this book attempts to plot some of the ways in which
regulation might be introduced and the economic considerations that
would have to be taken into account by any regulator. As such, it is
thought that this book will continue to be of enduring use to the inquisitive
and the practitioner alike during the flux in the global derivatives market.

While the book aims to be a text that considers the standard form
contracts and the attendant legal issues, the lawyer coming fresh to this
subject will benefit from a discussion of the financial products involved.
The financial derivatives involved are clearly growing at speed and therefore consideration of the products in place at any one time is subject to
change. However, it is possible to identify the basic roots of all derivative
products and give an idea of the generic issues that are likely to emerge
from any future product innovation.

It is often said by those in the markets that there are only three forms of product, the swap, the forward and the option, and that all else is embroidery based on these building blocks. Therefore, this homily shall be the starting point. This chapter will consider the structure of swaps, forwards and options as financial products and then move on to consider the extrapolations made by some of the mature bond and warrant markets on them. The aim is to show the ways in which they have developed.

Historical development

The currency swap, one of the earliest of the modern derivatives, first emerged as a method of eluding national exchange controls. Where companies sought to conduct business in another country from their residence, they had to contend with restrictions on the amount of a foreign currency which they were allowed to borrow. The banks developed a means of finding a company resident in the target jurisdiction which could borrow the currency without the strictures of exchange control. The currency was then made available to the original client by swapping entitlement to the cash. This required the banks to locate two companies with exactly reciprocal currency requirements.

The currency swap continued to be a useful instrument even after the abolition of UK exchange control in 1979 because it enabled domestic borrowers to make use of more advantageous loan terms available to borrowers in a different currency. The factors to be taken into account were whether more advantageous loan terms would still confer an advantage after the costs of putting the swap transaction into operation had been met. For example, a German company could borrow Deutsche marks in Germany more cheaply than an American company. Where the German company required US dollars, it was easy to have the German company borrow Deutsche marks and the American company borrow US dollars and then simply swap the sums of money. As the markets have progressed, the effective cost of these transactions has reduced and therefore conducting such a deal is now a cost-efficient means of reducing the way in which foreign currency debt is obtained.

To attempt a legal analysis, or to consider the variety of legal analyses that are available, understanding the structure of these complex instruments is vital. The structuring of a currency swap transaction may differ where the commercial aims of the investor differs.

Example
The early swap transactions which sought to avoid exchange controls, had the regulatory framework as their prime aim. When exchange controls were removed from most foreign exchange transactions, the prime aim became lower cost of funding. In the modern market the investor might be seeking to speculate on the interest rate attaching to a particular currency rather than to obtain a quantity of the currency. A transaction where a German company seeks to borrow US dollars, will have the physical delivery of the currency as an essential

part of its structure. However, a currency swap which centres on interest rate movements, will be differently structured because the parties are not required to enter into the money markets to deliver currency.

Therefore, the obligations, their tax and regulatory effects may differ greatly. Alternatively, the investor may seek to elect whether it wishes to take delivery of a quantity of the currency itself or simply receive the cash equivalent of the market movement.

The commercial structure therefore dominates the legal analysis of the transaction and also the way in which the lawyer gives effect to the transaction. It is possible to use a commercial structure to deliver a different legal conclusion and vice versa. Much of the innovation in the marketplace revolves around this attempt to deliver solutions in a form which is commercially acceptable.

Much of the legal analysis that is entered into in the following sections will return to this point of inter-changeability of these products. However, this approach is entirely justified. For the lawyer to appreciate the derivatives markets' fluidity and complexity, it is first necessary to understand the similarity of the analysis between one product with the possible analysis of another. Market forces require innovation to achieve ends which are well-understood. The client requires structured solutions and the banks require new products to provide satisfactory profit margins in a highly competitive marketplace.

The solutions are therefore based on classical formulae but window-dressed for regulatory or marketing effect. There are entities that can enter into swaps but not options[1], for example. Therefore, while the client might require a swap to satisfy its cost of funding needs, a product which was designed as an option may have to be re-interpreted as a swap to achieve the desired commercial effect and meet regulatory rules.

To understand how one product can be interpreted and constructed as another is therefore vital to the strategic derivatives planner. The aim is to move from one financial structure to another while remaining within the requirements of the relevant regulations. Similarly, regulations may change over time and old deals might become unlawful as a result of supervening legislation. Therefore, the lawyer's approach to derivatives structures must remain flexible enough to move between the different types of product and re-characterise the transaction while retaining the same commercial effect and pricing structure.

The first chapter explains how this commercial goal can be achieved by the manipulation of legal concepts. Later chapters consider the detailed analysis of the legal issues and the structure of the legal documentation necessary to give effect to this variety of analysis.

---

[1] See, e.g. Italian central banking regulation of investment funds.

1.2 Derivative Strategies

1.2.1 What is a "Derivative"?

Before attempting to define and explain each product in detail, it would be as well to attempt a definition of the term "derivative". The term is not susceptible of precise definition: it can be considered to be the collective term for the range of products discussed in this book, which have grown in the late 1980's and 1990's. A derivative product is a financial product that is *derived from another financial product.* For example, an option to buy a share at some point in the future is a financial product derived from the underlying share. Similarly, a swap on an interest rate is a product derived from the underlying loan. Hence the term "derivative" as a collective definition.

Why enter into a derivative?

The fundamental question is to explain why a derivative product is necessary in any event. The goal of all derivative products is to obtaining funding at a preferential rate or to take speculative advantage of a movement in a financial market for the investing institution. There are four basic forms of activity:

1. Speculation
2. Hedging
3. Asset liability management
4. Arbitrage

1. Speculation
The most readily comprehensible form of activity in a financial market is straightforward speculation. A derivative product may enable an investor to mimic the result of trading on an underlying financial market by entering into an off-market transaction with a financial institution. Therefore, a company can obtain the effect of speculating on the FTSE-100 without actually having to buy shares in companies in the FTSE-100. The advantage of the derivative is therefore administrative convenience: there is no need to accord with exchange market rules, for example. Further, the entry costs to speculation on a derivative are smaller than the cost of speculating on an exchange or other underlying market: there are no registration or other costs involved, nor is the transaction subject to public scrutiny.

2. Hedging
Derivative products can also be used as a shield against market movements. Purchase of a derivative product will enable a market participant to guard against movement in any obligations or exposures which it owes as part of its commercial operations. This form of activity is discussed in

greater detail at para. 1.8 below. At this point it is important to understand only the role of derivatives in managing risk. While they are financial products which create risk and take advantage of risk for speculative purposes, one of their most significant uses between bank and non-banking client is risk management. Where clients have exposures to movements in underlying markets, derivatives hedging strategies seek to control those exposures. As discussed further below, hedging is also used to reduce the risks associated with entering into a derivatives product by seeking, in effect, to "re-insure" that risk with another derivatives product.

3.   Asset Liabilty Management
The growth in mixed portfolio funds has benefitted from the capacity of derivatives to construct mixed hedging and speculation strategies. Where a financial, or other, institution seeks to deal with its portfolio of liabilities, their size and exposure to market movements can be massaged by the use of derivative instruments.

4.   Arbitrage
The use of derivative products makes it possible for market users to take advantage of mismatches in prices or market conditions by speculating on the underlying financial products without the need to undergo the formalities of conventional market trading. An American option to trade on a market, enables the investor to take advantage of price dissonances which occur during the life of the option. Derivatives markets in themselves contain the possibility to generate arbitrage opportunities.

Constructing commercial and legal analysis

The fundamental need and motivation for both financial institution and client to enter into derivatives transactions is either to earn income (by selling or using a derivative) or to manage risk. The use of derivatives products has expanded rapidly in the late 1980s and 1990s because of the increased volatility in world financial markets. During this period of flux, the complex structures have proved themselves able to take advantage of profit-making opportunities and to offer protection against the risk of loss in the underlying financial markets.

The more complex derivative products carry with them the higher profit margins because they call on greater banking expertise in both financial engineering and risk management techniques. As the attention of the global financial, service and industrial communities turns to new marketplaces, the volatility that is encountered increases all the more. The risks are greater and the reliance of clients on financial risk management techniques is all the greater. Therefore, there is an in-built tendency in the system towards ever increasing product complexity.

From the perspective of an investor using derivatives, the products enable access to new or otherwise inaccessible capital markets at a lower funding cost, and enhance the return on the underlying instrument. Alternatively, by enabling a profitable participation in (or emulation of) an underlying market, or by obtaining protection against the movement in the level of a market, the derivative opens new markets to the investor.

Example

The access to capital markets at a lower funding cost can be achieved by the use of a bond which is linked to a market index by an embedded derivative. The derivative element of a debt instrument enables the issuer to come to the market with the confidence that its interest cost will be controlled by an option to pay at a different rate. The protection of the return on the underlying instrument is achieved by selling or buying options which will generate a profit to balance out any loss on the underlying product. Profitable participation in (or emulation of) an underlying market can therefore be achieved by derivative products based on options which generate market simulated return without requiring market participation. Similarly, protection against the movement in the level of a market interest rate or price can be produced by interest rate or other swaps.

Derivatives can also be used for objectives which are not specificially geared to speculative profit or hedging. There are often regulatory or capital adequacy goals in investing in one particular type of derivative instrument rather than owning market instruments or obligations. Similarly, there are often accounting advantages in holding derivative instruments rather than ordinary financial instruments. Under most accounting codes, interest rate swaps or options to enter into currency swaps are not required to be disclosed separately on a company's balance sheet, whereas an underlying loan would be required to be disclosed.

The tremendous volatility in interest rates, stock market indicies and currency rates, drives the demand for derivative products which guard against, or seek to arbitrage, this volatility. It is this volatility which will continue to drive market innovation. However, it can be expected that this innovation will continue to follow the techniques and structures identified as fundamental in this section.

The importance of legal analysis

The market for financial derivatives requires that the complex derivatives products are scrutinised closely. The detail of these products in their rapidly changing markets require the legal professional to consider strategy and structure. While the issues of return, cash flows, obligation and termination are driven by the finance professionals, all of these elements have an impact on the legal analysis of the product.

It is the Risk / Return equation, the theoretical commercial yardstick component of a financing transaction, which governs the finance professional's calculations. Whereas, lawfulness, risk management, documentation, capacity and suitability are the concerns of the lawyer.

Understanding the risk perameters of a derivatives transaction enables the lawyer to comprehend the commercial motivation for the sale of the product and a specific quantification of the potential risks should the counterparty to the transaction default. The primary categories of risk involved are: credit, market, liquidity, settlement, hedging, operational, legal and sovereign risk.

The client buying a derivatives product will be either an investor in a marketplace or an issuer of fund-raising instrument. The financial institution will generally approach the client with an idea for a derivatives structure. This marketing function of the banks is, arguably, the most important commercial activity to them. A derivative will often be a product no-one knew they wanted until they were sold it. Legal structuring of the right form of product becomes an essential part of the marketing process. Similarly, the negotiations between the relevant lawyers, often makes the difference between a deal being transacted and not.

From the perspective of the client, it is essential that all aspects of the transaction are scrutinised before entering into a contract. The legal analysis forms an essential component of the credit management function in ensuring that the deal can be terminated and conducted in the manner anticipated by the parties. While the achievement of a lower funding cost or speculative profit are the commercial aim, a product will not be profitable or viable if it is legally unworkable. While many of the banks' client base are sophisticated users (pension funds, the treasury departments of large multinational corporations, insurance companies, etc) they usually do not have the legal and credit-based knowledge which is located in the financial institutions. Mutual disclosure of information relating to all aspects of the contract will be important to the legal analysis conducted by both parties.

Legal and Credit Concerns

The concern is that the market is growing quickly in volume and sophistication and that additional market losses could occur. The risk is that of systemic risk where the failure of one or more counterparties causes the failure of further counterparties. The aim of this chapter is to create a model to facilitate the understanding of the legal risks and the isolation of the credit risks of complex derivatives, particularly structured options strategies, equity swaps and exotic swaps and options. Understanding the legal and credit related issues will identify the exposures open to a financial institution or client counterparty and give an idea of the losses which might result from counterparty failure.

Most derivative transactions are high risk in nature. In analysing the instruments, it is important to isolate in derivative instruments their credit structures, particularly in complex derivatives where they carry a high risk-equivalent exposure and/or a long maturity profile. This form of product can be generally considered to be unsuitable for counterparties which are of low credit quality. The credit function within financial institutions is usually discharged in a combination of three ways. First, analysis by in-house credit departments who consult publicly available literature on the counterparty (such as annual reports and accounts) and any in-house analysis prepared (such as equity analysts reports). Secondly, the financial institution will seek a meeting with the treasury department of the counterparty to discuss the ramification of the transaction for both parties. Clearly, such an exchange of information becomes important for the spread of financial products (not just derivatives) which the financial institution will seek to sell to its client base. Thirdly, by reference to the independent credit rating agencies analyses of the counterparty, where such a rating has been prepared.

Dealing with counterparties who are of lower credit-worth, is more profitable for the financial institution than dealing with AAA rated companies. Therefore, there is pressure to provide a means of supplying products to clients which are of weaker credit rating. The mechanisms which are most commonly used to facilitate these transactions are:

- collaterialisation
- periodic mark-to-market
- options to terminate in the contractual documentation

All three alternatives require legal input to structure them correctly. Each of these forms of "credit enhancement" is tailor-made for the client. The legal implications of dedicating a given cadre of assets to provide credit support for a derivatives transaction, is a process which should involve legal advice from the outset in any event.

There is also the question of suitability of the transaction for the counterparty which has low credit quality or possibly little experience in the financial markets[2]. Bound up in these issues are also questions of risk reduction; the impact of netting exposures to a low credit counterparty; creating a suitable hedging strategy across the range of products contracted with this counterparty; and portfolio management across counterparties. The task of confronting these issues in detail from a credit perspective is beyond the scope of this book but there is a need to introduce the topic to locate the role of the lawyer.

The primary inter-action of the credit function, and the commercial motivation for the transaction, is to provide a means of valuing the risk being assumed by a party in entering into the deal with the counterparty of a given creditworth. There are two forms of quantifiable risk: market risk and product risk.

Market risk can be defined as the risk of loss resulting from movement in market prices or rates. Market risk exists because interest rates, currency rates, stock prices, index levels or commodity prices governing a given derivatives transaction fluctuate. Derivative products exist to exploit these

---

[2] Discussed at para. 5.2 below.

fluctuations but are also subject to them throughout their lives. The general assumption in entering into a derivatives transaction is that the appropriate market rate will remain within given perameters during the life of the transaction. However, it is also expected that the rates will not remain exactly the same. The result is the in-building of market risk into the price of the product. As the current price level changes, the level of risk exposure, or the amount of loss the party risks if the counterparty defaults, changes as well.

Market risk may be positive or negative through the life of a given derivatives transaction, depending upon market price and rate movements.

Example
When the risk of counterparty default is negative, there is no loss to the counterparty. For example, where X sells Y an interest rate swap and that swap is in-the-money for Y, if Y defaults by becoming insolvent, there is no loss for X at that time. Rather, X loses an unprofitable transaction. The only potential loss that X will suffer is the cost of the hedge it will have bought in the market to balance out the effect of the swap. However, if the swap itself was out-of-the-money, there is a possibility that the hedge (designed to move in inverse direction to the swap) will be in-the-money.

Swaps   1.3

What is a swap?   1.3.1

At root, a swap is an exchange of cash flows. Where one party has an obligation which it does not want, it exchanges it with another party for an obligation it does want. A swap, then, is simply an exchange of the rate of interest that a borrower is paying for a different rate of interest. Company A will agree to pay the interest on the debt it owes to B bank, in return for which Company A will pay a different rate of interest to the Bank C with which it has entered into the swap. This is a simple exchange of cash flows for a fee.

Swaps grew as an instrument to replace parallel loans and back-to-back loans (as required by UK exchange control legislation before 1979). The swap has a number of potential uses connected with the reallocation of a corporation's financial affairs or as a part of the restructuring of their debt.

Sample transaction

A company may wish to fix the rate of interest that it is paying so that it can forecast its future cash flows with confidence. This may be as part of a corporate restructuring or the renegotation of its borrowing limits with its banks. In the past it may only have been able to obtain floating rate funding. The bank will therefore pay the corporate's floating interest rate obligations in return for which it will receive an agreed upon fixed rate of income from the corporate.

Example
    The amount of cash to be paid as this interest rate is calculated by reference to a notional amount of money. For example, where A Ltd has a loan from Y Bank of GB£10mm at floating rate of LIBOR+100 basis points, it may seek to pay a fixed rate of interest at 9 per cent. The reason for this may be to fix its future cash outflows for strategic plannning purposes but it is most probably based upon an expectation that LIBOR will rise, such that LIBOR +100bp will be more than 9 per cent.

Therefore, X Bank will pay A Ltd's obligation of LIBOR +100bp to Y bank. In consideration for X Bank discharging A Ltd's obligation to Y Bank, A Ltd pays a fixed rate of 9 per cent to X Bank.
    A Ltd's gain is the fixing of its interest payments and a profit where LIBOR +100bp exceeds 9 per cent. X Bank makes a profit on any fee it charges for the transaction (which is usually built into the fixed rate of interest which it receives) and also makes a profit where LIBOR +100bp on GB£10mm is less than an interest rate of 9 per cent on GB£10mm.

If interest rates do rise upwards, then the fixed rate of interest will probably be lower than the floating rate of interest that the company would otherwise have been paying. If interest rates do not rise, but actually fall or remain stagnant, then the corporate client will be paying the more for its borrowing than if it had done nothing. This is the level at which even the most conservative funding policy is tantamount to speculation. The interest rate swap necessitates a bet on the future movement of interest rates. If the corporate in this example finds that interest rates have moved against it, it will be forced to enter into another swap transaction to bet the other way.

    This is the vortex that the Hammersmith and Fulham[1a] local authority was caught in. The local authority read the market movements wrongly on a series of occasions and entered into over five hundred separate

---

[1a] *Hazell v. Hammersmith & Fulham* [1991] 1 All E.R. 545.

transactions in an attempt to make good its early losses. Ordinary companies can be caught in this loop, the risks of suffering financial loss are the same for every organisation in the derivatives markets.

In the case of a currency swap, rather than a straightforward swap on interest rates, the floating interest rate that is used is the interest rate attaching to a given currency in the money markets. It is of course possible to have two floating interest rates matched against one another or two currency prices matched against one another where one party takes a view on the likely performance of one floating indicator against another.

Swaps are dependant on the underlying interest rates and currency markets which they mirror. They are therefore subject to the large scale movements in the underlying markets. The reverse is true. Transactions are often contracted depending on the movement in an interest rate over a period of up to 30 years. The opinions that the swaps markets form about interest rate movements with reference to currencies between 3 months and 30 years out, create speculative pressure on the underlying currency markets that is linked only to short term views on those currencies.

There is no realistic way in which the pricing for a 30 year maturity interest rate swap can claim to have any realistic hope of anticipating the interest rate appropriate for the Italian lire, for example. The bank does not concern itself about this inherent inaccuracy because it can always enter into another swap transaction in the future to reverse its exposure. However, while the bank can cover its bet, the underlying lire market will be affected by the speculative pressure that is introduced onto the lire in the short term. A large swap transaction of this type that anticipates a volatile movement in the lire will affect the way in which the markets look at lire rates and therefore will introduce volatility to the spot price.

The Legal Structure   1.3.2

There is no decisive legal literature (whether judicial or academic) to deal with questions surrounding the legal character of swaps transactions. There are a handful of decided cases which give indications as to the classification of the products involved. However, the bulk of decided caselaw deals with questions which belong more accurately with company law or areas of law governing the capacity of certain types of legal person to enter into financial transactions of the complexity of a swap.

The lawyer is in the business of managing legal risk in dealing with derivative products. That there is commercial risk involved in derivatives transactions is not an argument which requires much corroboration in the current market conditions. The lawyer must therefore be Janus-faced: the client is as eager to find clever ways to get away from transactions, as structured ways of getting into them. Therefore, the availability of restitution is the most important issue for any lawyer dealing with the derivatives markets.

What are swaps to a trader?

While the concept of the swap is disarmingly simple (you have an obligation which you do not like, so you swap for one that you prefer), the legal analysis is not so straightforward. Interest rate swaps are calculated with reference to a notional amount of money. In most circumstances this amount of money will not change hands, rather it is used to calculate the amounts of reciprocal interest payments between the parties. Therefore, the interest rate swap is built around the contract that is entered into between the parties to the transaction rather than obligations with reference to any particular sum of money.

The Contract for Differences issue

It is a truism among participants in the swaps markets that their products are not wagering contracts. However, it is not strictly possible to be totally sanguine about the speculative or non-speculative nature of swaps in all circumstances on market trading. There are two main decisions in which the status of the swap has been considered. As Lord Templeman put it in *Hazell v. Hammersmith & Fulham*[3]:

> "The swap market enables a borrower to raise funds in the market to which the borrower has best access but to make interest and principal payments in its preferred form of currency ... Swaps may involve speculation or may eliminate speculation".

An interest rate swap is therefore an exchange of cash flows the size of which will be decided by the movement in two interest rates by reference to a notional amount of a specified currency. However, the speculative nature of the transaction is still potentially at large.

Recently reported English cases has avoided the difficult task of analysing these products more precisely. The question remains important for the lawyer seeking to analyse the obligations which are owed between the parties. In the wake of the Barings collapse and the litigation involving Orange County and Proctor and Gamble in the USA., it can no longer be satisfactory that the products are left in the limbo of imprecise definition.

In *Morgan Grenfell v. Welwyn Hatfield DC*[4], Hobhouse J. considered the restitutionary possibilities in an interest rate swap contract but the further, familiar issues of gaming and *ultra vires* arose. The plaintiff had entered into a 10-year swap transaction with the defendant under which the defendant was to pay a floating rate of interest to the plaintiff in return

---

[3] [1991] 1 All E.R. 545 at 549–550
[4] [1995] 1 All E.R. 1

for a fixed rate. The defendant had entered into a parallel contract with a third party, also a local authority, to pay a fixed rate of interest to the third party in return for a floating rate of interest, also under an interest rate swap contract. Both of the contracts provided that, according to the usual market practice, the amounts of money actually paid between the parties would only be the difference between the two amounts owed.

It was found on the facts that the contracts were entered into by the local authorities as part of their overall budgetting strategies. The purpose of the swaps transactions were that size of the interest payments owed by the local authorities on their debt portfolios could be controlled. As a result of the ruling in *Hazell v. Hammersmith & Fulham*, it became unlawful for local authorities to enter into these transactions.

Hobhouse J. considered, *inter alia*, whether or not swaps contracts are contracts for differences within the meaning of the Gaming Act 1845. In analysing the payments before him, he found the following:-

> "Since they provide for the payment of differences they are capable of being entered into by way of gaming or wagering. They have, at least potentially, a speculative character deriving from the fact that the obligations of the floating rate payer are to be ascertained by reference to a fluctuating market rate that may be higher or lower than the fixed rate at any given time. Such a contract is capable of being entered into by two parties with the purpose of wagering upon future interest rates."[5]

In *Hazell v. Hammersmith & Fulham*[6], Lord Templeman identified the transactions which the local authority was conducting as being with "no other interest than seeking to profit from interest rate fluctuations". As Hobhouse J. pointed out, "[Lord Templeman] rejected the argument that what the council was doing was undertaking a form of insurance and connected that it was more akin to gambling than insurance."[7] However, as Hobhouse J. continues with reference to the contracts before him, "prima facie they are legitimate and enforceable commercial contracts".

As his lordship continues:-

> "The mere fact that there is a provision for the payment of differences does not mean that the contract must be a wagering contract ... If either party was not wagering, the contract is not a wagering contract."

The question remains then: what if there was wagering as part of the transaction? Is it still possible that the transaction could be found to be a wagering contract?

> "If there was an element of wagering in what Islington did, it was merely a

---

[5] *ibid.* at 7
[6] [1991] 1 All E.R. 545 at 549–550
[7] [1995] 1 All E.R. at 8

subordinate element and was not the substance of the transaction and does not affect the validity and enforceability of the transaction."[8]

That was true on the facts of the case but the court is not precluding the possibility that there will be cases in which the activity *is* purely speculative. The comfortable market consensus that there is no contracts for differences problem with interest rate swaps, is, it is submitted, left in an equivocal position by *Morgan Grenfell v. Welwyn Hatfield DC* is some circumstances.[9]

On the facts in the decided cases, it has been held that the particular transactions were not entered into for speculative purposes. The position remains to be seen where the so-called "high octane" swaps transactions are considered. These are transactions where, rather than the return on a particular interest rate being paid to the counterparty is involved, the counterparty pays or receives the return on a given rate^2 [squared]. The return on such a transaction would appear to be difficult to justify as a "quasi-insurance" measure.

Classification of the swaps contract

The further question is whether contracts for interest rate swaps are executory contracts or mutual debt obligations?[10] The form of restitution that is available under a swaps contract depends on the contractual analysis of the product under one of these two headings. The availability of restitution is the most important issue for any lawyer dealing with the derivatives markets as a prophylactic means of advising the client on entering into the transaction.

The "executory contract analysis" maintains that interest rate swaps do not give rise to debts: whether or not ascertained debts and whether or not contingent.

In the mind of the trader, a swap is often analysed as a series of forward transactions. (A "forward" is an obligation to pay an amount of money, on a given date, for a given product calculated by reference to market movements.[11]) A swap contract requires payments of interest on a series of dates, calculated by reference to interest rate movements on a notional amount. On each of the interest payment dates, it could be said, there is a forward payment made. How does the notion of a whole executory contract (looked at across the complete series of payments) fit in with the analysis of a swap as a series of interest rate forwards? It would appear, that they are in opposition to one another. Certainly, if the transaction

---

[8] *ibid.* at 9
[9] See the discussion below at para. 3.1.3 *et seq.*
[10] It should be conceded at the outset that the executory contract analysis is supported by analogy with Foreign Exchange cases: *Re British Continental Bank* (1922) 2 Ch. 575; *Lisser & Rosencranz's Claim* (1923) 1 Ch. 976; *Bank of India v. Patel* (1982) 1 Lloyds Rep. 506.
[11] See Glossary below at p. 333.

were structured explicitly as a series of forward transactions[12], then it would be difficult to argue that the transaction was a composite executory transaction.

The question then is whether a forward itself would be a simple obligation or an executory contract. There would seem to be no reason why a forward should not simply be an obligation to pay a debt calculated by reference to interest rates at a given time. Therefore, the alternative analysis would remain a viable hypothesis. It would therefore be open to interpretation, whether any particular swaps transaction had been envisaged by the parties from the outset to be priced or structured as a number of separate parts making up the whole.

The role of the set-off provision in market standard documentation may affect the executory contract analysis. By catering for the set-off of obligations, there is a presumption raised that each of the series of transactions is a reciprocal debt. The contract specifically approaches the individual transactions as standing separately and being capable of off-setting.

The approach of the documentation is usually to create a master agreement, which operates as an umbrella agreement. Each individual transaction is then expressly incorporated into that master agreement. (This is the scheme in all of the principal market standard agreements.) There are therefore two possibilities. First, the swap is an executory contract which requires elements within it to be off-set to reach the final, payable amount. Secondly, it is a series of reciprocal debts which are individually off-settable under the terms of a central master agreement.

The form of the documentation would therefore suggest that the individual interest rate swaps must be considered to be separate contracts. The question remains whether or not they are individual debts or individual executory contracts. There is no reason in principle, why they should be executory contracts. The more rational solution is that they are reciprocal debts linked by a master agreement for the purposes of set-off. The master agreement requires that money is paid by each of the parties. It does not require that a delivery of money is made by one party for the other to have to make the reciprocal payment. Either party could be sued for a debt on the basis that it fails to make any payment.

The only circumstance in which the payments are linked to one another is in the settlement procedure whereby each party agrees in the master agreement whether or not to set-off amounts owed to one another either on the same day or in the same currency. This is not the same as being reciprocal.

The reciprocity arises from the obligation to pay floating rate being set-off against the fixed rate payment. The issue of debt or executory contract turns on the chose in action. If A fails to pay, B can sue for the payment.

---

[12] With the proviso that there were no features of the performance of the contract which would indicate that it was in fact a sham.

This does not exclude B's obligation to pay A under the parallel leg of the interest rate swap.

It is argued by some commentators that, if the swap contract does create reciprocal obligations to pay debts, it would be for the gross nominal value of the debt owing to it. However, it is not clear why it would be for the gross nominal value rather than a contract for a stream of payments: that is a number of reciprocal debts. The debt analysis turns on there being a chain of debts, grouped in pairs. The gross nominal value is not the defining issue, as indeed it is not in the executory contracts analysis. As explained above, the deciding question is on what basis either party can sue.

The question of which analysis wins out, must properly be decided on the basis of what the documents say. The documents will usually provide for a series of reset dates on which payments are to be made. Alternatively, the better analysis of a particular contract might be one agreement which requires action on a series of dates.

Market standard swaps contracts contain provisions for the early termination of the transaction, either because of the default of one or other of the parties, or as a result of the agreement of the parties. How does this early termination provision affect the definition of the swap contract? Is this the termination of an executory contract or the extinction of a chain of mutual debts? Early termination terminates all of the resulting transactions. This would seem to indicate a composite agreement requiring a series of payments. However, losses or gains flowing from terminated executory contracts would be categorised as ordinary debt. Therefore, there is little practical difference in the two analyses for this purpose.

The answer, it is submitted, will turn on the approach taken by the contracting parties. The intention of the trader is to mimic the forward transaction. If the aim of the parties is to create a series of forward transactions, that would appear to be the most appropriate solution to the issue of whether the interest rate swap is a forward or composite executory contract.

Restitution and Swaps Contracts

Some of the main results following from the preceding analyses are:-

Under an executory contract to exchange money, the prime remedy of a willing party against a repudiating party is for damages equal to the contemplated loss suffered after exercise of the duty to mitigate. The measure of damages would often be any excess cost in replacing the contract in the market plus any special damages. The damages may be pre-determined by liquidated damage clauses, such as those represented by the Master Agreement termination provisions[13], in accordance with normal contractual principles.

---

[13] Discussed below at paras. 2.5.17, 2.5.18 and 2.5.19.

The appropriate remedy of a solvent party in the event of the repudiation by, or insolvency of, the counterparty is to rescind the contract. If the contract represented claims for debts both ways, then unquestionably the solvent party could not cancel its obligation to pay vested debts to the insolvent party and so full, reciprocal rescission would not be possible.

In the event that the executory analysis is followed, rescission would be possible on the basis that the condition precedent to execution, had not been performed. Rescission plainly requires placing the parties in the position they occupied previously.

Where there is only a liability to make payment one way at the date of completion, due to set-off, the availability of reciprocity is altered and it may affect the suitability of rescission. At first blush, rescission is made simpler by the composite executory contract analysis because it makes calculation of the amounts to be repaid more straightforward. However, the incorporation of separate contracts into a single master agreement, makes it equally feasible to achieve rescission across the spread of swaps transactions.

Specific performance is not usually available for an executory contract of this type. This is because damages are invariably an adequate remedy. The authorities with reference to a contract to pay a loan, satisfy the proposition that courts will not exercise their discretion to grant specific performance where damages could satisfy the remedy. Therefore, specific performance will not be appropriate for cash settled deals under the executory contract analysis.

What if physical delivery is appropriate? Physical delivery may be appropriate in foreign exchange transactions where the notional amounts are occasionally paid or in some equities transactions where physical settlement of shares are required. This, it is submitted, is a ground upon which one could distinguish the loan cases and look to specific performance even on an executory contract basis.[14]

However, the mutual debts analysis permits of specific performance of each of the debts. The ideal restitutionary solution might therefore be for rescission or specific performance to be coupled with damages; which would only be possible under a mutual debts analysis.

Insolvency Analysis

The preceding analysis of the availability of restitution ignores the insolvency law analysis. There is no doubt that the advantage of the "executory analysis" of a swaps contract is that it permits of close-out netting of transactions where one of the parties becomes insolvent. The "mutual debts" analysis causes different problems.

Rescission is altered by the insolvency of one of the parties. It is

---

[14] *South African Territories v. Wellington* [1898] A.C. 309; *Astor Properties v. Tunbridge Wells* [1936] 1 All E.R. 531.

clearly impossible to rescind mutually where one of the counterparties has become insolvent. Further to *British Eagle International Airlines v. Air France*[15] divestment of insolvent's assets is against the spirit of the bankruptcy laws. *British Eagle* on its face suggests that executory contracts therefore may not be rescinded on the insolvency of a counterparty, even if there is a clause to that effect in the contract, and provided that no asset has been transferred under the contract from the insolvent party. The only qualification to this argument, under the executory analysis, is that no asset must have passed under the contract to the insolvent.

However, an express clause in a derivatives document providing for rescission, it is suggested, will be valid.[16] In the absence of a rescission clause, the position of the liquidator with reference to undertaking to perform the contract would be different, as in *Re Castle*[17].

Specific performance is not available for executory contracts in most circumstances because damages will be an adequate remedy. In the case of an insolvent counterparty, specific performance would be an impossibility in most practical circumstances in any event.

Set-off is possible even in cases of insolvency. In *Shipton Anderson & Co v. Micks Lambert*[18], a buyer's right to rescind a commodity contract was upheld when the seller ceased payment under an express termination clause.

The tidier analysis from the insolvency point of view is the composite executory contract view. The mutual debts analysis imports complications of performed and unperformed, and separately enforceable obligations.

While none of the preceding analyses can claim to be entirely accurate, the individual lawyer's analytical preference will probably depend upon which party is being represented, how the documentation is arranged and which form of restitution is being sought. The uncertainty in the analysis of these products is, therefore, as much a strength as a weakness in many circumstances.

1.3.3 Interest Rate Swaps

Analysis

The most common form of swap is the interest rate swap. An interest rate swap is an agreement between parties to make periodic payments to the other party in the same currency. The aim, as discussed above, is to obtain funding at a preferential rate of interest or to alter the cost of funding of an existing loan debt.

The earliest interest rate swaps were conducted in circumstances where A and B could obtain differing costs of funding but where the terms of

---

[15] (1975) 2 All E.R. 390 HL
[16] see, *e.g. Ogdens v. Nelson* [1905] A.C. 109
[17] (1917) 2 K.B. 725
[18] (1936) 2 All E.R. 1032

that borrowing did not suit their own commercial circumstances. It became evident that if they could exchange their available credit terms, it would be to their mutual advantage. Therefore, the interest rate swap was entered into between parties with identically reciprocal requirements. Where the banks succeeded in isolating companies with such reciprocal needs and take a fee for this service.

In the modern marketplace, the bank stands as a warehouse for debt obligations and takes the place of the reciprocally configured market counterparty. Therefore, parties will transact with banks and the banks will undertake, where the terms of the transaction are considered to be viable, to meet the obligations of the counterparty.

Structure of a "vanilla interest rate swap"

A "vanilla swap" is the name given to a transaction which has no complicating factors and just involves the reciprocal payment of amounts of interest. What happens with a pure vanilla swap is that each party assumes the other's debt obligations. Thus each party acquires its preferred basis of borrowing. Therefore this follows the examples given above where A pays B a fixed rate of interest in return for a floating rate of interest.

The amount of cash money, which used to be the subject of the parallel or back-to-back loan arrangements, is now not usually transferred between the two parties to an interest rate swap. Hence the amount of principal by reference to which the amounts of interest are calculated is referred to as the notional amount. Where notional amounts are not transferred, the transaction is not a means of acquiring funding *per se*, rather it is a mechanism for acquiring funding at the right price for the particular party.

Example
In the event that A Ltd is unable to obtain fixed rate funding at a rate of interest below 8 per cent, it may enter into a swap whereby, the fixed rate it is paying at 8 per cent is swapped into a floating rate which it expects will remain below 8 per cent. Therefore, while the swap is not used to procure the loan itself, it is used to procure a better cost of funding for that debt obligation.

It might be that A Ltd approaches X Bank to borrow money and is told by X Bank that A Ltd's credit rating will not enable X Bank to lend to it at less than a fixed rate of 8 per cent. However, A Ltd may be able to offer a package in which A Ltd is lent the money at 8 per cent and allowed to swap that interest rate for a given floating rate of interest with X Bank. While there would appear to be a dubious credit logic to this type of transaction, it would make more sense as a structure when not attached to a vanilla swap.

Suppose that A Ltd is seeking to raise debt funding by issuing notes in the bond markets. In such circumstances, X Bank might not be able to procure funding at less than a commitment to pay an 8 per cent coupon to the market. However, by using an embedded swap, it would be possible for A Ltd to swap its obligation to pay 8 per cent to the market into an obligation to pay X Bank a floating rate whereas X Bank would discharge A's obligation to pay 8 per cent to the market.

21

Documentation

The documentation issues are discussed in more detail at paras. 2.4 to 2.6 below. The market standard documentation was framed to deal with swaps transactions before it was adapted to deal with the more exotic derivative products. Therefore, individual interest rate swaps transactions are documented first by a deal ticket and then by the execution of a Confirmation.[19] The confirmation sets out the terms of the transaction, including commencement, payment and maturity dates. It will also specify the relevant currencies, accounts for payments to be made and will, at the discretion of the parties, deal with a number of terms such as termination. However, these more complex terms are generally left to be set down in a master agreement[20]. The relationship between these documents is discussed fully in Part 2. However, the commercial risk management functions of the parties will have to cater for the situation where transactions are conducted in the absence of a fully executed master agreement.

Structuring issues

As discussed above with reference to the legal interpretation and analysis of a swap, the structure of a swap transaction is something which can be interpreted as a series of forward transactions linked together in a single contract.

The question arises, if a swap is a linked series of forwards, what is the effect of these payments not actually being made? It is the precise wording of the documentation that will be important here. Does the documentation provide that, while money is obliged to be paid, such refers to a failure under further forward contracts or that it is a failure to perform under a contract which may have been partially performed.

Further structuring issues are considered below.[21]

1.3.4 Foreign Exchange products

Foreign exchange markets

The foreign exchange markets operate for two purposes in the modern context. The first level is that of the company which uses the market as a bureau de change when looking to buy foreign currency cheaply to enable it to trade in foreign jurisdictions or to manage its reserves of cash. The second is the speculative opportunities offered by the difference between the fortunes of different currencies and their sensitivities to particular

---

[19] Discussed below at para. 2.4.
[20] Discussed below at para. 2.5.
[21] In Part 2.

events. The banks make their money by buying from one another at one price and then selling to their clients at a mark-up to the price at which they acquired the money. In the same way that newsagents pay one price to the publishers for the newspapers that they sell and then charge a higher cover price to the ordinary customer. The difference is a mark-up, or in the financial jargon a "spread".

The big players in the foreign exchange markets are the banks, and some of the larger corporate institutions, who trade currencies among themselves for the purely speculative opportunities that are on offer. The motivations of the financial institutions are mixed between the process of ensuring that the bank has enough liquid cash in the right currencies and also of exploiting the brief mismatches that exist as markets move between the prices of different currencies and the interest rates that attach to them.

Example
It may be that sterling falls but that the French franc rises more slowly against it than the US dollar because of the particular circumstances of the French economy. The speculator can take advantage of the brief anomaly between franc and dollar prices for sterling and move between the currency. These are relatively minor blips but they do require the use of central bank (Bank of England) capital to preserve the price of the currency – they "arbitrage" the differences.

The market players take long term positions on the price of a currency and buy it in large quantities. As with sterling before it was removed from the ERM in September 1992, the rising price of the currency as interest rates rose, enabled the foreign exchange traders to buy large quantities of sterling cheap, sell them at the peak before the withdrawal and then buy them all back in again when the currency reached rock bottom. To protect the currency, the Bank of England is required to buy large amounts of sterling at a high price to maintain the price of the currency. There are plenty of sellers in this situation.

Currency swaps   1.3.5

The currency swap emerged first as a means of eluding UK exchange control. The currency swap continued to be a useful instrument even after the abolition of UK exchange control in 1979 because it enabled domestic borrowers to make use of more advantageous loan terms available to borrowers in a different currency. The factors to be taken into account were whether more advantageous loan terms would still confer an adavantage after the costs of putting the swap transaction into operation had been met.[22]

---

[22] The genesis of the Currency Swap is discussed in greater detail at para. 1.1 above.

Analysis

The structural analysis of the currency swap, follows that of the interest rate swap closely in most of its details. There is a need to consider the differing commercial goals before coming to the issue of structuring.

The currency swap is usually transacted on trading floors where parties seek to exchange with a bank, the entitlement to the currency which they hold, for another currency. There is therefore a difference in a currency swap in that it may involve the physical exchange of currency amounts[23] rather than the payment of an amount of interest calculated by reference to a notional amount. However, there will be circumstances in which the transaction is conducted on the basis of payments of interest calculated by reference to a notional amount of currency and the interest rate attached to the currency in which the payment is made.

The physical delivery currency swap appears to be closer to the executory contract analysis than to the reciprocal debt analysis on the basis of caselaw to do with foreign exchange transactions and also by virtue of the nature of the obligations owed.[24] The obligation owed is to execute an obligation to provide a physical amount of currency calculated by reference to market movements.

Example

Where A Ltd seeks to acquire French francs but is unable to acquire them at a level below FFR/GBP 100, A Ltd may enter into a swap whereby, the fixed amount of sterling is swapped for a floating amount of French francs at a rate which it expects will remain below FFR/GBP 100. The transaction is entered into on the basis that the French franc equivalent of GBP 1.0mm will be delivered to it on the physical settlement date in the confirmation.

It might be that A Ltd approaches X Bank to borrow French francs and is told by French Bank that A Ltd's credit rating in the French banking market will not enable X Bank to lend to it at less than a fixed rate of 8 per cent. However, French Bank may be able to offer a package in which A Ltd is lent the money in sterling at 7.5 per cent because of its better credit approval among UK banking institutions, and then allowed to swap that interest rate in sterling for a given floating rate of interest attached to the French franc, with French Bank. Thus, A Ltd is able to acquire French francs leveraging off its ability to acquire sterling at preferential rates.

---

[23] Or more accurately, their attribution to the other party by accreditation to an electronically controlled account. However, the principle is the same as for physical delivery of equity stock because the payer is required to have the specified amount of currency under its control or in its possession at the date at which the delivery is required under the terms of the contract.

[24] It should be conceded at the outset that the executory contract analysis is supported by analogy with Foreign Exchange cases: *Re British Continental Bank* (1922) 2 Ch. 575; *Lisser & Rosencranz's Claim* (1923) 1 Ch. 976; *Bank of India v. Patel* (1982) 1 Lloyds Rep. 506.

Documentation

The documentation issues are discussed in more detail in Part 2 below. The market standard documentation was framed to deal with swaps transactions before it was adapted to deal with the more exotic derivative products. Therefore, individual currency swaps transactions are documented first by a deal ticket and then by the execution of a confirmation.[25] The confirmation sets out the terms of the transaction, including commencement, payment and maturity dates. It will also specify the relevant currencies, accounts for payments to be made and will, at the discretion of the parties, deal with a number of terms such as termination. However, these more complex terms are generally left to be set down in a master agreement. The relationship between these documents is discussed fully in Part 3. However, the commercial risk management functions of the parties will have to cater for the situation where transactions are conducted in the absence of a fully executed master agreement.

In circumstances where physical amounts of currency are exchanged, the documentary regime is sometimes different for a foreign exchange transaction from that for an interest rate swap. Whereas the documentation published by ISDA most often used for interest rate swaps[26], the IFEMA ("International Foreign Exchange Master Agreement") is more usually the standard document for transactions which involve the physical movement of cash amounts. The differences are in the specificity of the terms in the IFEMA contract to do with events of failure, termination and execution on foreign exchange markets.

Structure

The propagation of a currency swap usually takes place in three stages. The following is the procedure under what is commonly termed a "traditional currency swap".

1. Initial exchange of amounts in different currencies – usually set at a particular exchange rate (normally the spot exchange price on the contract date).
2. Periodic payments by each party to the other in the amounts which each party received under the initial exchange. The precise amounts of the payments being fixed by applying the rate of interest applicable to that particular currency.
3. A final exchange of currency amounts reversing the initial exchange.

Some currency swaps may omit the initial and/or the final exchange of

---

[25] Discussed below at para. 2.4.
[26] As set out in the Appendix.

currency. A currency swap strictly refers to the situation where the rate of interest payable by each party as part of the periodic payments is fixed for both parties. In particular circumstances there may be a "timing mismatch" where payments are made at different times or in relation to different periods by different parties. Therefore some will gain at the expense of others.

The accounting significance of the swap is that it is an off-balance sheet instrument. The obligation to repay back-to-back loans is a balance sheet liability. The obligation to make a payment under a swap is generally expressed to be conditional in the documentation and therefore is off-balance sheet. In the modern era of capital adequacy requirements, banks are keen to reduce their liabilties and engage in off-balance sheet activities. Swaps are often entered into to manipulate these accounting possibilities.[27] Increasing regulation in this area is a probable future concern.

The second benefit of the currency swap, aside from the manipulation and arbitrage of enhanced borrowing facilities available in another currency, is that of hedging currency exchange risk. When, for example, a company wishes to buy a dollar asset when its own assets are in sterling, it will wish to protect itself against fluctuations in dollar-sterling exchange rates. Therefore a currency swap will enable it to borrow on dollar terms, in effect, and thus provide a hedge against the risk of exchange rate loss.

1.3.6 Cross Currency Interest Rate Swaps

Analysis

Cross-currency interest rate swaps are hybrids in which Party A makes payments in one currency at a fixed rate of interest while Party B makes payments in another currency at a floating rate of interest. The genesis of this form of dealing was in bond issues where the purpose of the issue was to enable the issuer to enter into a swap and thus reduce the effective cost of funding. Therefore, it became possible to entice investors to participate in a bond issue where, in the normal run of events, the investment vehicle would not have been able to raise a particular type of funding (e.g.: fixed rate) because of its credit standing.

Example
Where A Ltd is seeking to raise Deutsche mark debt funding by issuing notes in the German bond markets. In such circumstances, X Bank might not be able to procure funding at less than a committment to pay an 8 per cent coupon to the German market. In the UK market, where its credit profile is better known and its branded name products are better known to market analysts, it is able to raise funding at an effective rate of 7.5 per cent. By using an embedded cross-currency interest rate swap, it would be possible for A Ltd to swap its

---

[27] See more generally "accounting derivatives".

obligation to pay 8 per cent to the market into an obligation to pay X Bank a floating rate based on its 7.5 per cent cost of funding in the UK. The result is that A Ltd is able to enter into the debt issue and the investors are prepared to participate on the basis of a coupon of 8 per cent.

Documentation

The market standard documentation was framed to deal with swaps transactions before it was adapted to deal with the more exotic derivative products.[28] Therefore, cross-currency interest rate swaps transactions are documented first by a deal ticket and then by the execution of a Confirmation[29]. The confirmation sets out the terms of the transaction, including commencement, payment and maturity dates. It will also specify the relevant currencies, accounts for payments to be made and will, at the discretion of the parties, deal with a number of terms such as termination. However, these more complex terms are generally left to be set down in a master agreement.[30] The commercial risk management functions of the parties will have to cater for the situation where transactions are conducted in the absence of a fully executed master agreement. There is increased risk in the transactions where there is no master agreement to regulate the dealings between the parties.[31] In circumstances where physical amounts of currency are exchanged, the documentary regime is sometimes different for a foreign exchange transaction from that for an interest rate swap.

Structure

The structure of the product is dependent upon the specific priorities of the bank and the issuer. It will however, follow the pattern set out in the sections dealing with Interest Rate Swaps[32] and Currency Swaps[33], depending on whether the intention is to produce a commercially efficient rate of funding or to provide the client with a specific amount of the foreign currency. The commercial and structuring aspects are as set out above with reference to interest rate and currency swaps.

---

[28] The documentation issues are discussed in more detail at Part 2 below.
[29] Discussed below at para. 2.4
[30] The relationship between these documents is discussed fully in Part 2.
[31] The credit risk and collateral implications are discussed at Part 5 below.
[32] At para. 1.3.3 above.
[33] At para. 1.3.5 above.

1.3.7 Caps, Collars and Floors

(a) Caps

Analysis

Where a client counterparty enters into an interest rate swap or assumes obligations under a loan transaction, the risk that that client bears is that the interest rate which it is required to pay will rise. A cap is a derivative product which places a ceiling on the maximum interest rate which a counterparty will have to pay under a swap. In short it restricts the economic downside of floating interest rates. The cap is purchased for a lump sum which makes the arrangement commercially similar to a lump sum insurance premium.

The bank assumes the risk of paying the client's interest obligation when the interest rate climbs through the threshold level set in the transaction. The willingness of the bank to enter into the transaction is predicated on its belief that rates will not rise beyond the level established in the contract.

Documentation

The documentation issues are discussed in more detail at Part 2 below. The market standard documentation was framed to deal with swaps and "barriers swaps"[34] transactions. Therefore, cap transactions are documented first by a deal ticket and then by the execution of a confirmation[35]. The confirmation sets out the terms of the transaction, including commencement, payment and maturity dates. It will also specify the relevant currencies, accounts for payments to be made and will, at the discretion of the parties, deal with a number of terms such as termination. However, these more complex terms are generally left to be set down in a master agreement. The relationship between these documents is discussed fully in Part 2. However, the commercial risk management functions of the parties will have to cater for the situation where transactions are conducted in the absence of a fully executed master agreement.

Structure

The legal analysis of a cap is that it is an obligation assumed by the financial institution selling it, to pay the interest of the purchaser when that interest climbs above a pre-determined rate. The advantage for the financial institution is the receipt of an upfront payment against a risk,

---

[34] A collective term for swaps transactions which are structured around movements in rates beyond given thresholds.
[35] Discussed below in Part 2.

which is reflected in the pricing of the cap, of that cap rising beyond that given point.

Caps are used to hedge floating interest rate exposures. If the "bet" on the interest rate swap goes wrong, the counterparty is able to ensure that the loss on the swap is restricted from going too far.

Significantly, though, in the marketplace there are other factors which make the combination of "caps" and "floors" attractive. Parties with a low credit worth are entering the derivatives market as it expands to take up the excess desire that the financial institutions have to deal with someone. However there are restictions on the extent to which their credit department will allow them to deal without stricture. The result is the "collar".

For low credit rated parties, the cap offers the ability to control funding costs while the transaction itself does not pose credit risk to the financial institution selling the cap to the extent of rates moving outside the band and thus affect the low rated party's ability to transact. The risk becomes placed in the relative movement in interest rates within the bands and the party's ability to meet payments at that level.

(b) Floors

Analysis

A floor is the same in principal as a cap but it exists to guard against interest rates that fall too low. The risk that that client bears is that the interest rate which it is required to pay will rise. A floor is a derivative product which places a barrier on the minimum interest rate which a counterparty will receive under a swap transaction. In short it restricts the economic downside of floating interest rates. The need to guard against a rate falling too low is more often used in respect of currency swaps where the rate of interest received from holding a particular currency is necessary to maintain a profit margin.

The bank assumes the risk of paying the client's interest obligation when the interest rate falls below the threshold level set in the transaction. The willingness of the bank to enter into the transaction is predicated on its belief that rates will not fall below the level established in the contract.

Documentation

The documentation issues are discussed in more detail at Part 2 below. Floor and "barrier swaps" transactions are documented first by a deal ticket and then by the execution of a Confirmation.[36] The confirmation sets out the terms of the transaction, including commencement, payment and maturity dates. It will also specify the relevant currencies, accounts

---

[36] Discussed below in Part 2.

for payments to be made and will, at the discretion of the parties, deal with a number of terms such as termination. However, these more complex terms are generally left to be set down in a master agreement. The relationship between these documents is discussed fully in Part 2. However, the commercial risk management functions of the parties will have to cater for the situation where transactions are conducted in the absence of a fully executed master agreement.

Structure

The structure for a floor is the precise inverse to the cap transaction. The difference is that the expected movements in rates is different.

(c) Collars

Analysis

Collars are a combination of cap and floor which ensures the investor against the interest rate payable or receivable moving outside the given range of interest rates. This structure might be used, for example, by a company which needs to be able to predict their cost of funding with relative certainty. The cap-floor combination supplies the certainty needed for strategic planning purposes.

The collar, like the other "barrier swaps", is purchased for a lump sum which makes the arrangement commercially similar to a lump sum insurance premium. The bank assumes the risk of paying the client's interest obligation when the interest rate moves outside the range. The willingness of the bank to enter into the transaction is predicated on its belief that rates will not move outside the spectrum established in the contract.

Documentation

The documentation issues are discussed in more detail at Part 2 below. "Barrier swaps" of this type are documented first by a deal ticket and then by the execution of a confirmation.[37] The confirmation sets out the terms of the transaction, including commencement, payment and maturity dates. It will also specify the relevant currencies, accounts for payments to be made and will, at the discretion of the parties, deal with a number of terms such as termination. However, these more complex terms are generally left to be set down in a master agreement. The relationship between these documents is discussed fully in para. 2.4.2. However, the commercial risk management functions of the parties will have to cater

---

[37] Discussed below in Part 2.

for the situation where transactions are conducted in the absence of a fully executed master agreement.

Structure

The structure for a collar is a combination of that for the cap and the floor transaction. The commercial purpose differs slightly.

Alternative analysis of barrier swaps   1.3.8

To continue the analysis of the "barrier swap" a little further, take the example of a cap which lasts for two years. A two year cap can be analysed as a series of European-style put options. Put differently, the buyer has acquired the right to put (or sell to the other party) a succession of interest rate equivalents at given dates.

An interest rate swap has payments made on a series of dates. A cap requires the parties to consider the interest rate on the payment or reset dates identified in the contract and requires the financial institution to make a payment to the counterparty on the appropriate payment date if the interest rate has passed through the threshold level.

The alternative analysis, is that the counterparty had an option to receive an amount of money from the financial institution equal to the excess of the interest rate over the cap level. Therefore, to price the cap, the deal is treated by the trader as a series of put options on each of the payment dates, each of which has a specific value against expected interest rates at that time. The aggregate of these option amounts is then given its present value to ascertain the upfront premium that has to be paid.

Therefore, the alternative means of structuring the cap is as a series of put options. The documentation could be drafted to structure the transaction explicitly as a series of options.

One possible legal analysis of a cap is that it is a contingent obligation to pay an ascertainable amount of money to a counterparty. The contingency is the movement of interest rates through the threshold level. The analysis of the cap as a series of options is not, therefore, a useful legal one. The counterparty that buys the cap is not required to elect to exercise the options for the bank to become obliged to pay out under the cap transaction. That is, unless one interprets the situation as an automatically exercised put option.

The issue then is whether the implicit involvement of options theory in the pricing of the cap has any effect on the *legal* analysis of the parties' relationship. If the matter of pricing is not discussed explicitly between the parties, it is difficult to see that there could be any implied term in the cap transaction that it be treated as an option without it being specifically documented as an option. For example, the implied term that the option is automatically exercised, could be implicitly inferred into the contract.

Similarly, the question would arise whether a cap that was not priced as a series of options, but rather by some other method (*e.g.*: as a series of forwards or bullet swaps) would alter the legal analysis. If a cap *could* be analysed for legal purposes as an option, could that analysis be displaced by evidence that the instrument has been ascertained in another way.

The only conclusion that can be drawn from this discussion is that there is no single analysis which can be said to attach to any particular product but that the documentation is probably the definitive method of deciding the legal effect that is to be used.

1.3.9 Swaptions

Analysis

A swaption is an option to enter into a swap at a future date. The product is structured in a way that is similar to the debt option products described below. The commercial purpose is to provide the investor with the ability to enter into a swaps transaction at a given date should movements in interest or currency rates make that transaction advantageous.

Documentation

The swaption is structured and documented in the same form of master agreement as the interest rate swap. The detail of the confirmation is, however, necessarily different. Instead of a series of payment dates by which payments are calculated as amounts of interest, the swaption entitles the investor to enter into a swap transaction on given terms. Therefore, the documentation is structured to take account of the delivery and calculation method. There is a strike level for the swaption which governs whether or not it can be exercised, whereas an interest rate swap is necessarily effective from the time when it is sold.

1.3.10 Inverse Floater Swaps

Analysis

Inverse floater swaps aim to take advantage of a steep yield curve, that is where interest rates are expected to rise steeply in the future and therefore there is a great difference between short term interest rates and long term interest rates. The inverse floater is structured so that a floating interest rate is paid and a fixed rate less that same floating rate is received.

Example
Suppose that LIBOR has a steep yield curve. X would pay LIBOR to Y and receive a fixed rate (say 15 per cent) less LIBOR. The result is clearly a movement

that is the opposite of LIBOR. As well as guarding against movements in a steep yield curve, the inverse floater swap is a useful hedging tool in guarding against rate movements.

The "leveraged swap" is closely related to the inverse floater swap but involves greater leverage in the size of the transaction. The size of the payment and the credit risk involved is therefore enhanced by the factor which accelerates the movements in market rates to greater payments under the swap transaction. The amount of leverage clearly adds to the speculative nature of these transactions.

Documentation

The documentation for this product is the same as for the other swap products discussed above. Reference should also be made to Part 2 and the analysis of the appropriate documentation there.

Equity Swaps   1.3.11

Analysis

The equity swap is a comparatively recent and highly complex instrument. It uses the idea of the swap to enable two parties to benefit from the different rates of appreciation between two indicators. Typically these products can cover the full range of equity products. It is possible to match the movement in the price of a particular equity, of a given equity index or of a non-equity market indicator.

Example
The structure is usually for the payment of a fixed amount of money by one party to the other in return for a floating amount. For example, X might wish to speculate on the performance of the Nikkei 225 index against LIBOR. Therefore X would seek to pay LIBOR to Yand in return receive from Y the cash equivalent of the performance of the Nikkei 225 over a given period of time. The benefit to X is a receipt of cash flow equal to the performance of the Nikkei 225 without the expense or administrative difficulties of purchasing a range of stocks appearing on the Nikkei 225. Alternatively, X could pay a fixed amount of interest on a notional amount of money in return for a payment from Y equal to the return on the Nikkei 225 from Y.

The permutations are literally endless. The return on any stock or index can be swapped for a fixed amount of interest or even the return on another stock or index. The more complex products, offer a basket of currencies and stocks in emerging markets as the floating rate payment in return for a fixed rate payment or a payment linked to an established market indicator such as LIBOR.

Documentation

There is limited benefit to be gained from in-depth examples of these products at this stage. The more important issue is the legal analysis of their structure. Examples of the documentation which may be used for these products is set out below in the Appendix [at p. 277].

Structure

The credit implications of these products is clearly complex. Added to the risk of counterparty failure, is the risk of trading on a given exchange or against a market indicator. The added risk that is posed is the complexity of the products themselves. In dealing with the so-called exotic markets, there are risks of failure of the market, large movements in the value of the underlying stock and political risk. Equity derivatives often have a long-term maturity structure which is to be compared with the inherent volatility of equity markets over time. These factors have to be included to the risk factors already discussed in this chapter and added to those identified with the given counterparty.

The other commercial issue to be considered is the difficulty of hedging a position effectively with reference to an equity derivative option or swap. The vanilla debt swaps are complex enough to hedge but there is difficulty in establishing a straightforward method of hedging an obligation to pay the cash equivalent on the return on a basket of Pacific Rim stocks, currencies and indicies against the performance of LIBOR.

There are two methods of structuring an equity swap. The swap can be valued at one point in the future or it can be subject to periodic valuation. Interest rate swaps, as we have seen, are generally subject to periodic payments on given dates throughout the life of the transaction. Similarly, many equity swaps have a series of reset dates set down on which payments are to be made under the transaction. Alternatively, some swaps will mature on a single expiration date. The former structure could be structured as a series of linked forward transactions connected to the performance of the underlying equity. This structure might then cater for the recalibration of the index at each of the reset dates.

The credit implications of the two structures are different. The linked forward structure, involves exposure to periodic shifts in the index which are then met by adjustments in the payment calculation mechanism. The "single shot" structure opens the institution to the movement of the underlying market over a longer period of time. The credit implications of this single measurement are more difficult to measure on a one-off basis.

Debt Options 1.4

Options: Introduction 1.4.1

Option theory is one of the jewels of Business School degrees. Both in terms of the options available in terms of management choices and in terms of derivative instruments. A physically settled option gives the buyer the ability either to have delivered to it or to compel another party to purchase the thing which is the subject of the contract. This can be an option to buy or sell shares, commodities, bonds or even the right to be paid or to pay money at a particular rate of interest. The option gives the participant the right to choose whether or not the price is right. As such an option can be a cheap way of guaranteeing the price of a share for example.

A call option gives the purchaser the right, but not the obligation, to call for delivery of the underlying instrument at a given price on a given date (or one of a number of given dates). A put option gives the purchaser the right, but not the obligation, to sell the underlying instrument at a given price on a given date (or one of a number of given dates).

Example
   If an ICI bonds is trading at 100 in May 1996, the buyer of an option might want to acquire the abiltiy to be sold a specific number of ICI bonds at the price of 150 on November 1, 1996. If ICI bonds are trading at 200 pence each on November 1st, then the option offers a great bet for the purchaser. The banks and others who sell options receive the price paid for the option itself.

It is important to note that derivatives offer a cheap form of speculation because the cost of, for example, an option is cheap compared to the potential economic benefit if the speculation underlying the option works out. Therefore a company may pay, for example, £10,000 for an option which may yield £1 million a year afterwards. The risk is that if the speculation goes the wrong way, £10,000 has been wasted. The more this is done, the more money is wasted. Derivatives are cheap when the company exchanges its payment stream for another. It is only when rates move that the corporate is forced to pay more than it would otherwise. The risks only come to fruition when the markets move against the original opinion of the market. The cost of an option is the price of the premium. Therefore the entry level to these products is low.

Bond Options 1.4.2

Analysis

Bond options are options to purchase bonds at a price at a date in the future. There is a clear correlation between an option and a future /

forward, as discussed below. Briefly, a future offers a thing at a price at a time in the future. The difference with an option is that you have the option whether or not to take the thing.

The second difference, importantly, is that bond options do not include an interest rate movement in their price. Rather a bond option enables the holder to benefit from a movement in interest rates against the interest rate that is payable on the bond. To put that another way: a future's price is 100 minus the interest rate applicable. Therefore a movement in interest rates affects the price directly. A movement in interest rates generally makes the interest rate (or coupon) that is payable on a bond, more or less attractive. Therefore, bond options enable the investor to hedge against movements in interest rates by using an instrument which is more or less valuable relative to interest rates, without actually including that rate in its price.

The bond option can therefore be used to speculate on movements in interest rates or to hedge against those movements.

Documentation

The bond option is structured in a way that is similar to debt-based swaps. The documentation of the products is based upon the same master agreements as the interest rate swap. The detail of the confirmation is necessarily different. Instead of a series of payment dates by which payments are calculated as amounts of interest, the bond option entitles the investor to receive or sell an instrument. Therefore, the documentation is structured to take account of the delivery and calculation method. There is a strike price for the option which governs whether or not it can be exercised, whereas an interest rate swap is necessarily effective from the time when it is sold. Examples of documentation are enclosed below in the Appendix [at p. 281].

1.4.3   Currency Options

Analysis

Currency options are options to purchase a given quantity of a currency at a price at a date in the future. The currency option does not include an interest rate movement in its price. Rather a currency option enables the holder to benefit from a movement in the interest rate attached to the relevant currency. The currency option operates as a means of hedging against movements in the underlying currency.

Documentation

The currency interest rate option is structured in a way that is similar to debt-based swaps. The documentation of the products is based upon the same master agreements as the interest rate swap. The detail of the confirmation is necessarily different. Instead of a series of payment dates by which payments are calculated as amounts of interest, the currency option entitles the investor to receive or sell an instrument. Therefore, the documentation is structured to take account of the delivery and calculation method. There is a strike price for the option which governs whether or not it can be exercised, whereas an interest rate swap is necessarily effective from the time when it is sold. Examples of documentation are enclosed below in the Appendix [at p. 285].

Complex Options   1.4.4

There are many circumstances in which a financial institution and its client will want to use more complex derivative structures than those set out above. To illustrate the complexity which the market is introducing, and to demonstrate that all forms of innovation use traditional techniques, it is useful to explore some of the newer option-based derivatives.

Analysis

The use of OTC options are part of complex structures can achieve particular financial goals. Taking positions in put or call options necessitates a view of the market. Positions are either "short" or "long". A short position means that the institution has a committment to supply an asset but does not hold any of those assets. The institution is therefore expecting that the market will fall so that it can buy up the required amount of those assets at a price lower than that currently prevailing in the market.

- A "long call" is a posititition taken where the market is expected to rise. The premium for a long call option is expended in return for the upside potential in the price of the underlying instrument. The economic loss is therefore limited to the amount of premium paid.
- A "short call" is a position taken where the market is expected to fall. The institution's aim is to make premium income. The seller's risk is that of having to deliver under the option. The buyer's risk is that the market price of the underlying instrument falls below the option's strike price.
- A "long put" is the position taken where the market is expected to fall. The buyer's aim is to fix the price at which it can sell the stock where it expects the price of the stock to fall below the strike price.
- A "short put" is the position taken where a market is expected to rise.

These four variations are price driven options strategies taking advantage of market price levels. Long calls and short puts are used by institutions when they are bullish about the markets; short calls and long puts when they are bearish about the markets.

Combining put and call options can create a different form of product which resembles different derivatives structures. It grants the ability to exit and enter markets. One of the most common types of combination option is the Vertical Spread.

Vertical Spreads

Vertical spreads consist of a long and a short position on the same type of option with identical maturity dates. A bullish spread would contain a long call with a low strike price and a short call with a higher strike price.

Example
Let us suppose a long call option with a strike price of 102 where the market price is 100. The short position has a strike price of 105. This implies that the long position is close to the anticipated market price and therefore more expensive. The short position will generally be further from the money – demonstrating that the investor anticipates that the market will move further. The selling institution will realise premium income while the price rests between 102 and 105. From a financial institution credit perspective the risk is controlled while the price rests between 102 and 105.

Example
Where the call options are struck at 95 short and 99 long, where the market is at 100, the financial institution will make premium income where the market falls to 99 but does not have to perform under the short position unless the market falls as far as 95. This would indicate that the financial institution expected that the market would rise or remain at around 100.

Docmentation

The appropriate documentation is as set out for the appropriate form of debt or equity underlying product discussed at paras. 1.4.2 and 1.4.3 respectively.

1.4.5 Barrier Options

The market has developed barrier options which operate with reference to contractually defined thresholds in market prices. Where a market rate moves beyond the prescribed level, but remains below a further level (or vice versa), the client will receive an income from the financial institution. The advantage to the client is a capped level of loss on the movement in a market rate. The institution makes premium income from this instrument. As a speculative instrument, the barrier option enables the client to play the market without requiring it to buy any of the underlying instruments making up the market.

The banded option structure is a popular structure in the modern marketplace. The advantage for the client is a product which will provide the underlying product where the market moves beyond a given level. It might be expected that, where a company had an equity portfolio that was designed to remain at above a level of 96 (where the market price is 100), where it falls outside the banded level, the company can put its equity portfolio at the pre-determined price level.

Volatility Strategies

There are a number of barrier option strategies which aim to take advantage of market volatility rather than specifically of movements in price. These derivatives are created by reference to mathematical formulae which seek to anticipate the movement in the option and the underlying instrument over time. The techniques used in this form of option structure are used in the alteration of option portfolios over time to account for market price and rate movements.

- The Delta coefficient refers to the rate of change in the price of the option for one unit of the underlying instrument. This is a formula used in the Black-Scholes model. The Delta is frequently interpreted as the likelihood that the option will mature in the money. It is therefore related to the volatility attaching to that option, the time to expiry of the option and its intrinsic value.
- The Gamma coefficient measures the rate of change in the Delta and therefore identifies the frequency with which a delta coefficient hedge will have to be recalibrated.
- The Theta coefficient measure the decrease in value of the option as it approaches its maturity. The value of a long option decreases as days pass towards the completion date of the option.
- The Zeta coefficient then measures the change in the value of the option as a unit of the underlying instrument becomes more volatile.

Straddles

Straddles are formed by combinations of puts and calls with equal strike levels and identical maturity dates. A straddle takes advantage in the movement of the gamma coefficient – that is, alterations in the level of volatility of an option. Quite literally, it is made up of two options whose strike prices straddle the perameters within which the market expects the option's price, or that of its underlying instrument, to move. A straddle allows a financial institution to, for example, exercise a call option for delivery of an underlying security where its price moves above or below that anticipated by the market at the time that the option is purchased. A long straddle then turns a profit for the financial institution where the level of volatility of an option is greater than that anticipated by the market price of the option at the time.

Conversely, a short straddle anticipates that the market will not move outside a given price band and will therefore generate profit if the market narrows to within the selected range.

An aggressive form of this instrument is often referred to as a "strangle". This form of strategy will have put and call options with identical expiration dates but different strike prices. The strike prices that are used generally require large market movements rather than the comparatively modest shifts needed for a straddle to become effective. The difference is therefore one of expectation of market movement and the price that is charged for the option.

Ratio Horizontal Spreads

This form of technique also looks to take advantage of volatility in derivative products and their underlying markets. Here the emphasis is on taking advantage of volatility fluctuation over time. A combination of put and call options is acquired. The options are exercised at different times to maximise the effect of the market movement. If the market is expected to rise, the institution will seek to put options at the early maturity and call them at the low strike price when the market rises.

Ratio Vertical Spreads

The Vertical Spread aims to profit from low volatility market conditions. Where an institution buys more close to the money calls than it sells, it is able to benefit from a low volatility market by not paying the upside on these instruments if the market remains unvolatile. It then receives the maximum profit on the calls that it has sold.

Vertical Spreads

A vertical spread is a combination of a long and short put ("put spread") or a long and short call ("call spread"), where the puts or calls have the same expiry dates. In the case of a bullish call spread, the long position is struck closer-to-the-money than the short position, which indicates a net out-flow of premium. A bullish put spread has the short position with a strike price closer to the money, which indicates in turn a net in-flow of premium.

1.4.9 Synthetic Options

It is possible to combine options in a way that in fact creates a different type of option altogether. Where an institution owns a quantity of an underlying instrument and a put option over the same quantity of that instrument, it has something which is a call option in all but name. The put will be in-the-money where the price of the underlying instrument falls below the put strike price; and the underlying instrument will be sold at a profit where its true market value rises. This profit structure is very similar to that of a call option. This combination is a "synthetic call option".

Similarly, if an institution is long a call and short a put where both have the same expiration date, the institution is, in effect, long a synthetic instrument. The use of these synthetic relationships enable clients of financial institutions to maximise their assets in circumstances where they stand exposed solely to an upward or downward movement in a market in the underlying instrument. The aim of the synthetic option is to transform this position into a "heads you win, tails you win" situation.

The relationship between an underlying instrument and an option, where they form a synthetic position, might have an effect on the appropriate hedging strategy: whether it deals with the positions as separate exposures or as a composite risk. However, the legal analysis may well be different from the commercial appraisal, as discussed below.

Bonds with Warrants   1.4.10

The Japanese debt issuers became large players in the Eurobond market in the 1980's by issuing bonds with warrants attached to them. The advantage to the issuer was the low interest that it would be required to pay on the debt portion of the structure due to the attractive nature of the equity warrant. The warrant product is discussed in greater detail below at para. 1.6. The bond with warrant structure is similar, from the lawyer's perspective, to the convertible product discussed below at para. 1.5.6 and generally at para. 1.6.

Covered Warrants   1.4.11

This is a market misnomer for a structure in which a bank issues an instrument which is backed by an option to purchase the underlying security. This area of the market has been growing in popularity during the last decade but is in reality just another form of packaging straightforward call options to cover a variety of underlying instruments.

Covered warrants also came to deal with indexed warrants where the warrant came to offer a return on a market index rather than simply on an individual stock or instrument. These warrants are distinguishable from those discussed above in that it does not entitle the investor to receive an amount of stock – rather the investor typically receives the cash equivalent of the appreciation or depreciation in the level of the index over a designated period of time.

There has also been a growth in bonds linked to indicies in the same way. For example, an equity-linked bond structure would have an issuer sell bonds with attached warrants which would provide funding for the issuer at a low rate of interest and give the investor the opportunity to receive capital gains equivalent to the movement in the underlying index.

1.4.12 Binary Options

Binary options provide discontinuous pay-offs. The investor receives one of a number of payments methods when a given level is reached by the underlyer. Generally, the binary option is a high risk strategy for the bank.

Where the option is in-the-money at expiration, the investor receives a payment which is often equal to the notional amount under the contract. If the option is not in-the-money at expiration, the investor receives nothing. This is often referred to as an "all-or-nothing" mechanism. This structure differs from the equity swap where the payment is still owed to the investor even though it may be netted against a payment the other way. The amounts paid and received may have no direct connection to the intrinsic value of the option but rather are linked to the notional amount of the transaction. This instrument may be used for hedging where the client wishes to guard against an index moving beyond a given level. However, it has most clearly speculative potential.

The credit risk of this form of product is clearly focused on the all-or-nothing nature of the instrument. Where the payment is linked to the notional amount and capped, it is possible to limit the downside – a little like the payment made by a bookmaker on a straightforward bet. The concern for the credit officer is the potential size of the loss and the difficulty of maintaining a watch over the level and likelihood of exposure during the life of the transaction.

1.5 Equity Options

1.5.1 Options: Introduction

The use of derivatives to speculate on equity markets or to manage the risks associated with equity markets is a development which came late to the derivative markets. The early concentration had been upon debt markets and the foreign exchange markets.

An equity-based option gives the buyer the ability either to have delivered to it or to compel another party to purchase the underlying stock which is the subject of the contract. This can be an option to buy or sell shares or to receive / pay the return on the appropriate stock exchange or index.

Example

> If A plc shares are trading at 500 pence in May 1994, the buyer of an option might want to acquire the ability to be sold a specific number of A plc shares at the price of 550 pence on November 1 1994. If A plc's shares are trading at 600 pence each on November 1, then the option offers a great bet for the purchaser. The banks and others who sell options receive the price paid for the option itself. This option, and the rights under it, can be traded. So B Bank might sell an option to C Bank which might in turn sell that option to D. Therefore the option may be a form of security that is capable of being traded on its own account.

It is important to note that derivatives offer a cheap form of speculation because the cost of, for example, an option is cheap compared to the potential economic benefit if the bet underlying the option works out. Therefore a corporate may pay, for example, £10,000 for an option which may yield £1 million a year afterwards. The danger is that if the bet goes the wrong way, £10,000 has been wasted. The more this is done, the more money is wasted. Equity swaps and options are cheap when the company exchanges its interest stream for another. It is only when rates move that the company is forced to pay more than it would otherwise. The risks only come to fruition when the markets move against the original bet. Derivatives start out cheap but end up expensive.

Complex Equity Derivatives

There are many circumstances in which a financial institution and its client will want to use more complex derivative structures than those set out above. To illustrate the complexity which the market is introducing, and to demonstrate that all forms of innovation use traditional techniques, it is useful to explore some of the newer derivatives. The movements of stock prices are considerably more volatile than on many of the usual debt instruments. The purpose of the equity derivative is therefore to match the movements in this exaggeratedly volatile marketplace.

Share Options   1.5.2

Share options fall into two basic categories: cash settlement and physical settlement. The former is predicated on a requirement for the cash equivalent of an option which is in-the-money at the expiration date. The latter entitles the purchaser of the option to receive or to sell (as appropriate) the given quantity of the underlying share.

(a) Cash settled options

Structure

The cash settled option enables the investor to speculate on the move-ments in share prices without the need to buy shares physically on the relevant stock exchange. The obligation on the seller of the option is therefore for a straightforward cash amount. The structure of the trans-action conforms to that of other derivatives products. The option is similar to a forward or a future in that it provides the right to call or put the appropriate cash amount of the underlying share. The principle difference is that there is no obligation to pay under the option if it remains out of the money.

There is a similarity with the structure of an interest rate swap. There are payments of money in both directions. The purchaser pays a premium and, if the option is in-the-money, the seller pays an amount of money which is calculated by reference to the floating performance of the stock index. The transaction could therefore be structured as a swap if the premium were amortised over the maturity of the option. The floating rate leg of the transaction would have to be made contingent on the performance of the indicator or specified to be between a given nominal amount and the in-the-money value.

Documentation

Individual transactions are contracted by confirmation. The docu-mentation for confirmations is complicated by the need to cater for increased market risk and volatility. The transaction of option business is documented by the standard market master agreement, as discussed below at Part 2.

(b) Physically settled options

Structure

Physically settled options involve the complexity of taking delivery of the shares and the requirement of one of the parties (where the option is in-the-money) purchasing those shares on an exchange. The commercial purpose of the transaction is different. There might be a need for the purchaser to satisfy the requirement of another client or simply a long-term speculative goal.

Documentation

Individual transactions are contracted by confirmation. The docu-mentation for confirmations is complicated by the need to cater for increased market risk and volatility. The transaction of option business is documented by the standard market master agreement, as discussed below at Part 2.

(c) Complex share options

The use of OTC options as part of complex structures can achieve particular financial goals. Taking positions in put or call options necessitates a view of the market. Positions are either "short" or "long". A short position means that the institution has a committment to supply an asset but does not hold any of those assets. The institution is therefore expecting that the market will fall so that it can buy up the required amount of those assets at a price lower than that currently prevailing in the market.[38]

- A "long call" is a position taken where the market is expected to rise. The premium for a long call option is expended in return for the upside potential in the price of the underlying instrument. The economic loss is therefore limited to the amount of premium paid.
- A "short call" is a position taken where the market is expected to fall. The institution's aim is to make premium income. The seller's risk is that of having to deliver under the option. The buyer's risk is that the market price of the underlying instrument falls below the option's strike price.
- A "long put" is the position taken where the market is expected to fall. The buyer's aim is to fix the price at which it can sell the stock where it expects the price of the stock to fall below the strike price.
- A "short put" is the position taken where a market is expected to rise.

These four variations are price driven options strategies taking advantage of market price levels. Long calls and short puts are used by institutions when they are bullish about the markets; short calls and long puts when the investor is bearish about the markets.

Combining put and call options can create a different form of product which resembles different derivatives structures. It grants the ability to exit and enter markets. One of the most common types of combination option is the Vertical Spread.

Vertical Spreads

Vertical spreads consist of a long and a short position on the same type of option with identical maturity dates. A bullish spread would contain a long call with a low strike price and a short call with a higher strike price. Let us suppose a long call option with a strike price of 102 where the

---

[38] As can be seen, the discussion of these products is similar in theory and structure to that of the debt options discussed above at para. 1.4.

market price is 100. The short position has a strike price of 105. This implies that the long position is close to the anticipated market price and therefore more expensive. The short position will generally be further from the money – demonstrating that the investor anticipates that the market will move further. The selling institution will realise premium income while the price rests between 102 and 105. From a financial institution credit perspective the risk is controlled while the price rests between 102 and 105.

Where the call options are struck at 95 short and 99 long, where the market is at 100, the financial institution will make premium income where the market falls to 99 but does not have to perform under the short position unless the market falls as far as 95. This would indicate that the financial institution expected that the market would rise or remain at around 100.

1.5.3 Barrier Options

The market has developed barrier options which operate in bands. Where a market rate moves beyond a level but remains below a further level (or vice versa) the client will receive an income from the financial institution. The advantage to the client is a capped level of loss on the movement in a market rate. The institution makes premium income from this instrument. As a speculative instrument, they are something which enables the client to play the market without requiring it to buy into the market.

The banded option structure is a popular structure in the modern marketplace. The advantage for the client is a product which will provide the underlying product where the market moves beyond a given level. It might be expected that, where a company had an equity portfolio that was designed to remain at above a level of 96 (where the market price is 100), where it falls outside the banded level, the company can put its equity portfolio at the pre-determined price level.

Volatility Strategies

There are a number of option strategies which aim to take advantage of volatility rather than specifically of movements in price. These derivatives are created by reference to mathematical formulae which seek to anticipate the movement in the option and the underlying instrument over time. The techniques used in this form of option structure are used in the alteration of option portfolios over time to account for market price and rate movements.

- The Delta coefficient refers to the rate of change in the price of the option for one unit of the underlying instrument. This is a formula used in the Black-Scholes model. The Delta is frequently interpreted as the likelihood that the option will mature in the money. It is therefore related to the volatility attaching to that option, the time to expiry of the option and its intrinsic value.

- The Gamma coefficient measures the rate of change in the Delta and therefore identifies the frequency with which a delta coefficient hedge will have to be recalibrated.
- The Theta coeffiecient measure the decrease in value of the option as it approaches its maturity. The value of a long option decreases as days pass towards the completion date of the option.
- The Zeta coefficient then measures the change in the value of the option as a unit of the underlying instrument becomes more volatile.

Straddles

Straddles are formed by combinations of puts and calls with equal strike levels and identical maturity dates. A straddle takes advantage in the movement of the gamma coefficient – that is, alterations in the level of volatility of an option. Quite literally, it is made up of two options whose strike prices straddle the perameters within which the market expects the option's price, or that of its underlying instrument, to move. A straddle allows a financial institution to, for example, exercise a call option for delivery of an underlying security where its price moves above or below that anticipated by the market at the time that the option is purchased. A long straddle then turns a profit for the financial institution where the level of volatility of an option is greater than that anticipated by the market price of the option at the time.

Conversely, a short straddle anticipates that the market will not move outside a given price band and will therefore generate profit if the market narrows to within the selected range.

An aggressive form of this instrument is often referred to as a "strangle". This form of strategy will have put and call options with identical expiration dates but different strike prices. The strike prices that are used generally require large market movements rather than the comparatively modest shifts needed for a straddle to become effective. The difference is therefore one of expectation of market movement and the price that is charged for the option.

Ratio Horizontal Spreads

This form of technique also looks to take advantage of volatility in derivative products. Here the emphasis is on taking advantage of volatility fluctuation over time. A combination of put and call options is acquired. The options are exercised at different times to maximise the effect of the market movement. If the market is expected to rise, the institution will seek to put options at the early maturity and call them at the low strike price when the market rises.

Ratio Vertical Spreads

The Vertical Spread aims to profit from low volatility market conditions. Where an institution buys more close to the money calls than it sells, it is able to benefit from a low volatility market by not paying the upside on these instruments if the market remains unvolatile. It then receives the maximum profit on the calls that it has sold.

Vertical Spreads

A vertical spread is a combination of a long and short put ("put spread") or a long and short call ("call spread"), where the puts or calls have the same expiry dates. In the case of a bullish call spread, the long position is struck closer-to-the-money than the short position, which indicates a net out-flow of premium. A bullish put spread has the short position with a strike price closer to the money, which indicates in turn a net in-flow of premium.

1.5.4 Synthetic Options

It is possible to combine options in a way that in fact creates a different type of option altogether. Where an institution owns a quantity of an underlying instrument and a put option over the same quantity of that instrument, it has something which is a call option in all but name. The put will be in-the-money where the price of the underlying instrument falls below the put strike price; and the underlying instrument will be sold at a profit where its true market value rises. This profit structure is very similar to that of a call option. This combination is a synthetic call option.

Similarly, if an institution is long a call and short a put where both have the same expiration date, the institution is, in effect, long a synthetic instrument. The use of these synthetic relationships enable clients of financial institutions to maximise their assets in circumstances where they stand exposed solely to an upward or downward movement in an underlying market. The aim of the synthetic option is to transform this position into a "heads you win, tails you win" situation.

The relationship between an underlying instrument and an option, where they form a synthetic position, might have an effect on the appropriate hedging strategy: whether it deals with the positions as separate exposures or as a composite risk. However, the legal analysis may well be different from the commercial appraisal, as discussed below.

1.5.5 Equity Derivatives

While many of the swap structures common in the derivatives market currently are becoming more commoditised (for example, "vanilla" interest rate swaps and currency swaps) the equity derivative market is, by its nature, open to more exotic structures. The plethora of equity products that are traded on a broad range of stock and futures exchanges are more difficult to package into commoditised structures. The structure of debt derivative products is more homogenous than the equity derivative products that are traded and regulated on equities markets. There are more customised features about equity derivatives.

Convertible Bonds   1.5.6

Convertible bonds were the earliest form of instrument which mixed debt and equity features in a form that is reminiscent of a derivative. A standard form convertible bond is a bond used by its investor to enable it to convert the debt instrument it holds into a specified number of shares if a given threshold conversion price is reached. At the time of conversion from debt to equity, the debt instrument is extinguished and replaced by an equity instrument. The bond issuer then issues fresh equity to make good the obligation to the investor. This enables the investor to speculate on the future equity value of the issuer or otherwise to earn interest income on the bond instrument.

A convertible bond which has not been translated into equity has the features of a bond with an option to convert attached or of a bond with an equity warrant attached. The conversion price is similar to the strike price of an option. The diference between a convertible bond and an option is that the convertible bond will actually create new equity when the conversion is exercised.

Alternative structuring arrangements for a convertible bond are to issue them as debentures. It is also common to issue the bond as a zero coupon bond, so that the investor's speculation is focused more clearly on the movement of the underlying equity price of the issuer. The bond is redeemed at its par value on the expiration date if the conversion price is not reached, without the investor being paid interest during the life of the convertible.

Equity Warrants   1.5.7

Equity warrants give the investor the ability to purchase the issuing company's equity at a given strike price within a prescribed time frame. Warrants have two features which distinguish them from OTC derivatives. Warrants are usually listed on an exchange where they are open to be traded. The warrant also requires an issue of new equity by the company where the warrant is in-the-money and the investor chooses to exercise it. It is the company itself which sells the warrant rather than the arranging bank which sells the option on a third party basis to a market counterparty. A call option would simply require one counterparty to buy existing equity in the marketplace and provide to the option buyer at the prescribed strike price.

A well-known warrant structure is used where a company seeks to raise new capital. On the issue of a debt instrument, a warrant would also be issued to entice the investor with the potential of acquiring stock in the issuer in the future, as well as the cash inflow from the debt instrument. The warrants were detachable from the bond and could therefore be stripped and traded themselves in a secondary market.

While the listing and trading is often arranged in advance by an investment bank which has developed the funding deal for the issuer, in theory at least, it must be possible for the warrants to be traded. To preclude trading, or to arrange the sale of the entire warrant issue would be to subvert entirely the listings process. The choice of exchange for the listings process is often dominated by the mixed need to minimise the amount of information required to list the warrants and the extent to which the warrant issue can be pre-sold to a captive market in effect before the issue date. The minimum of listings formalities, as found in the Luxembourg exchange for example, keeps the cost of the issue low. This clearly adds to the attraction of the equity warrant as a funding mechanism for the issuer by reducing the all-in cost of the transaction. Pre-selling is important to the issuer and its advisers so that they can both be certain that the issue will produce the required level of revenue. This is particularly so where the adviser is committed to purchasing any warrants which have not been sold on the market within a given period of time.

There is a growing practice in the market to use the warrant issuing capabilities of a company with a high credit rating to raise funds for an unrated or poorly rated company. These structures are the most complicated in the warrants area and require a greater level of pre-selling to effect them. The issuer will require a fee for the use of its warrant issuing programme, the "hidden issuer" will receive a lower cost of funding and the investment bank in-between makes a fee income. These structured arrangements may also include a swap arrangement to convert the funding raised into another currency. These products are clearly highly customised but importantly, they use an amalgam of well-understood techniques to create innovative products.

1.5.8 Equity Swaps

Structure

The equity swap is a recent and highly complex instrument. It uses the idea of the swap to enable two parties to benefit from the different rates of appreciation between two indicators. Typically these products can cover the full range of equity products. It is possible to match the movement in the price of a particular equity, of a given equity index or of a non-equity market indicator.

Example
The structure is usually for the payment of a fixed amount of money by one party to the other in return for a floating amount. For example, X might wish to speculate on the performance of the Nikkei 225 index against LIBOR. Therefore X would seek to pay LIBOR to Y and in return receive from Y the cash equivalent of the performance of the Nikkei 225 over a given period of time. The benefit to X is a receipt of cash flow equal to the performance of the Nikkei 225 without the expense or administrative difficulties of purchasing a range of stocks appearing on the Nikkei 225. Alternatively, X could pay a fixed amount of interest on a notional amount of money in return for a payment from Y equal to the return on the Nikkei 225 from Y.

The permutations are literally endless. The return on any stock or index can be swapped for a fixed amount of interest or even the return on another stock or index. The more complex products, offer a basket of currencies and stocks in emerging markets as the floating rate payment in return for a fixed rate payment or a payment linked to an established market indicator such as LIBOR.

There is limited benefit to be gained from in-depth examples of these products. The more important issue is the legal analysis of their structure. Examples of the documentation which may be used for these products is set out below in the Appendix [at p. 277].

Credit implications

The credit implications of these products is clearly complex. Added to the risk of counterparty failure, is the risk of trading on a given exchange or against a market indicator. The added risk that is posed is the complexity of the products themselves. In dealing with the so-called exotic markets, there are risks of failure of the market, large movements in the value of the underlying stock and political risk. Equity derivatives often have a long-term maturity structure which is to be compared with the inherent volatility of equity markets over time. These factors have to be included with the risk factors already discussed in this chapter and added to those identified with the given counterparty.

The other issue to take into account is the difficulty of hedging a position effectively with reference to an equity derivative option or swap. The vanilla debt swaps are complex enough to hedge but there is difficulty in establishing a straightforward method of hedging an obligation to pay the cash equivalent on the return on a basket of Pacific Rim stocks, currencies and indicies against the performance of LIBOR.

There are two methods of structuring an equity swap. The swap can be valued at one point in the future or it can be subject to periodic valuation. Interest rate swaps, as we have seen, are generally subject to periodic payments on given dates throughout the life of the transaction. Similarly, many equity swaps have a series of reset dates set down on which payments are to be made under the transaction. Alternatively, some swaps will mature on a single expiration date. The former structure could be structured as a series of linked forward transactions connected to the performance of the underlying equity. This structure might then cater for the recalibration of the index at each of the reset dates.

The credit implications of the two structures are different. The linked forward structure, involves exposure to periodic shifts in the index which are then met by adjustments in the payment calculation mechanism. The "single shot" structure opens the institution to the movement of the underlying market over a longer period of time. The credit implications of this single measurement are more difficult to measure on a one-off basis.

1.5.9 Binary Options

Binary options provide discontinuous pay-offs. The investor receives one of a number of payments methods when a given level is reached by the underlyer. Generally, the binary option is a high risk strategy for the bank. Where the option is in-the-money at expiration, the investor receives a payment which is often equal to the notional amount under the contract. If the option is not in-the-money at expiration, the investor receives nothing. This is often referred to as an "all-or-nothing" mechanism. This structure differs from the equity swap where the payment is still owed to the investor even though it may be netted against a payment the other way. The amounts paid and received may have no direct connection to the intrinsic value of the option but rather are linked to the notional amount of the transaction. This instrument may be used for hedging where the client wishes to guard against an index moving beyond a given level. However, it has most clearly speculative potential.

The credit risk of this form of product is clearly focused on the all-or-nothing nature of the instrument. Where the payment is linked to the notional and capped, it is possible to limit the downside – a little like the payment made by a bookmaker on a straightforward bet. The concern for the credit officer is the potential size of the loss and the difficulty of maintaining a watch over the level and likelihood of exposure during the life of the transaction.

1.6 Warrants

1.6.1 Warrants: Introduction

Options are also bought and sold in respect of baskets of shares or other financial products. A different form of option has been developed: the warrant. A warrant is an obligation on the part of the issuer to provide a pre-determined number of a particular type of share to the investor at the time specified by the warrant. This is similar to an option in that a view is taken on the likely future price of the underlying security and at a particular time, the investor can exchange the option for the security to which it relates. The warrant need not be issued with the consent of the relevant issuing company. There is therefore an element of volatility introduced to the price of the underlying security by the view that is taken by the warrant market covering it.

The fact that a financial institution issues warrants over a share, of itself introduces the expectation that that share will perform well in the market. This can be expected to lead to a rise in the price of the share on the underlying market, when the market becomes aware of the transaction. The danger is that the share has further to fall in the future. Therefore, adverse speculation in the market will affect its perceived credit worth when all that is happening is the market righting itself in the wake of the articifial rise in price caused by the warrant issue. Again speculation in these markets introduces inherent volatility to the underlying security. This in turn can mean that the corporate involved has difficulty in accessing finance to which would otherwise be within easy reach.

Equity Warrants   1.6.2

Equity warrants give the investor the ability to purchase the issuing company's equity at a given strike price within a prescribed time frame. Warrants have two features which distinguish them from OTC derivatives. Warrants are usually listed on an exchange where they are open to be traded. The warrant also requires an issue of new equity by the company where the warrant is in-the-money and the investor chooses to exercise it. It is the company itself which sells the warrant rather than the arranging bank which sells the option on a third party basis to a market counterparty. A call option would simply require one counterparty to buy existing equity in the marketplace and provide to the warrant investor buyer at the prescribed strike price.

A well-known warrant structure is used where a company seeks to raise new debt capital at a low coupon. On the issue of a debt instrument, a warrant would also be issued to entice the investor with the potential of acquiring stock in the issuer in the future, as well as the cash inflow from the debt instrument. The warrants are detachable from the bond and can therefore be stripped and traded in their own right on a secondary market.

While the listing and trading of warrants is often arranged in advance by the arranging investment bank which will have developed the funding deal for the issuer, in theory at least, it must be possible for the warrants to be traded.[39] To preclude trading, or to arrange the sale of the entire warrant issue would be to subvert entirely the listings process. The choice of exchange for the listings process is often dominated by the mixed need

---

[39] The rules for such issues will depend upon the precise regulation of the exchange on which the warrant is issued.

to minimise the amount of information required to list the warrants and the extent to which the warrant issue can be pre-sold to a captive market in effect before the issue date. The minimum of listings formalities, as found in the Luxembourg exchange, for example, keeps the cost of the issue low. This clearly adds to the attraction of the equity warrant as a funding mechanism for the issuer by reducing the all-in cost of the transaction. Pre-selling is important to the issuer and its advisers so that they can both be certain that the issue will produce the required level of revenue. This is particularly so where the adviser is committed to purchasing any warrants which have not been sold on the market within a given period of time.

There is a growing practice in the market to use the warrant issuing capabilities of a company with a high credit rating to raise funds for an unrated or poorly rated company. These structures are the most complicated in the warrants area and require a greater level of pre-selling to effect them. The issuer will require a fee for the use of its warrant issuing programme, the "hidden issuer" will receive a lower cost of funding and the investment bank in-between makes a fee income. These structured arrangements may also include a swap arrangement to convert the funding raised into another currency. These products are clearly highly customised but importantly, they use an amalgam of well-understood derivatives structuring techniques to create innovative products.

1.6.3 Covered Warrants

This is a market misnomer for a structure in which a bank issues an instrument which is backed by an option to purchase the underlying security. This area of the market has been growing in popularity during the last decade but is in reality just another form of packaging straightforward call options to cover a variety of underlying instruments.

Covered warrants also came to deal with indexed warrants where the warrant came to offer a return on a market index rather than simply on an individual stock or instrument. These warrants are distinguishable from those discussed above in that it does not entitle the investor to receive an amount of stock – rather the investor typically receives the cash equivalent of the appreciation or depreciation in the level of the index over a designated period of time.

There has also been a growth in bonds linked to indicies in the same way. For example, an equity-linked bond structure would have an issuer sell bonds with attached warrants which would provide funding for the issuer at a low rate of interest and give the investor the opportunity to receive capital gains equivalent to the movement in the underlying index.

Forwards and Futures   1.7

Forwards: Introduction   1.7.1

Similar to the option, in theory, is the forward markets. There are some forward contracts traded on organised exchanges and others which are the preserve of the OTC markets. The forward is a promise to supply a particular commodity or security at a set price on a set date (often in a set place). In the commodity markets it is usual to buy wheat, for example, at a given price in a given amount at a pre-determined time to be delivered in a given place. In the time it takes for the contract to mature (which might include the wheat to grow, be harvested and shipped) the price of wheat can fluctuate wildly. The contract, that is the right to receive the wheat at a price at a time in the agreed place, can be sold to others at a greater or lower price than that paid for it originally. The same is true, to a greater or lesser extent, of forward contracts entered into between private parties.

It is worth digressing briefly to consider the relationship between swaps, options and forwards. A swap is, by one analysis, a series of forward contracts to pay or to receive an amount of money on a particular date according to the movement in a chosen interest rate. A forward is like two options: one a call option sold to a party to demand payment for a consignment of wheat and on the other hand a put option which entitles the other party to sell the wheat, according to movements in the price of wheat. Therefore, a swap could also be a series of put and call options to receive or to pay an amount of money on a particular date, with reference to a particular interest rate.

The products are all, therefore linked in an essential way. They are, at root, rights or obligations to pay or to receive sums of money according to the movement in a chosen indicator, whether that be an interest rate, a share index, or the price of a bond or commodity index. The analysis of the risks involved with these products should therefore take account of the essential linkage in the bets that are being taken. The concept of a "bet" (or, as the market would prefer to put it, "position") is the most important consideration for the regulator. There are positions which reduce the risk of bigger positions that the market participants are taking and those positions which are simply a bigger form of speculation in themselves.

Commercial structure

A forward conveys the right to purchase or sell a specified quantity of an asset at a fixed price on a fixed date in the future. In exchange traded futures contracts, which are a standardised form of forward contract, the quantity of the underlying asset to be delivered per contract is fixed, as is the underlying financial instrument or index, the minimum price movement for the contract and the life of the contract. In a forward agreement, these elements are at large for negotiation between the parties.

Futures are exchange-traded instruments, the contractual relations are not between the buyer and the seller but between each party and the exchange. This effectively removes counterparty risk from the futures contract for each individual transaction and places it instead in the exchange. The creditworthiness of the exchange is maintained by lodging margin with the clearing house. These margin deposits are then held as collateral against the failure of any participant on the exchange. The precise amount of margin is measured on a daily basis according to the mark-to-market value of the instrument on a daily basis.

Long term futures contracts specify that physical delivery is made at the maturity of the contract. Therefore the right that is being transferred on the purchase of a futures contract is the right to receive a physical thing for a stated price at a stated price in the future. The futures price is the price that the market would pay the notional instrument representing the thing that is to be physically delivered if that thing existed currently. The short term futures contracts generally specify cash settlement rather than physical delivery. Therefore the right that is being transferred on the purchase of such a contract is the right to receive the cash equivalent of the price for that instrument.

The prices are quoted as an amount (100) less the implied interest rate on that instrument. Therefore, the price of a futures instrument moves in inverse correlation to movements in interest rates. This inverse movement against interest rates, makes forwards (and particularly exchange traded futures contracts) the ideal instrument to hedge against movements in interest rates. If interest rates falls and the price of futures therefore rises, there is an inverse correlation that means a movement in one will be compensated by an opposite movement in the other. As a result, one is a useful instrument in hedging a movement in the other.

1.7.2   Documentation

Forward transactions are documented in the same way as the swap products discussed at para. 1.5 above. The individual transactions are contracted by confirmation. The dealings between the parties are conducted with reference to the market standard master agreement, as discussed at para. 2.4 below.

1.8   Hedging

1.8.1   Defining "Hedging"

"Hedging" is the aspect of the derivatives market that is strategic rather than speculative. The typical commercial impetus is as follows. A market participant has a financial instrument which show a profit or a loss depending upon market movements. Therefore that participant wishes to purchase another instrument which will show a profit if the first instrument shows a loss. The second financial instrument, bought to balance the effect of the first, is a "hedge".

It is a little like betting on a two-horse race. You place a bet on the grey horse to win but you are worried that you will lose your stake if the brown horse wins. So you "hedge" your risk by putting a bet on the brown horse that will produce a large enough win to equal the cost of your stake on betting on the grey.

In the financial markets, of course, things are more complex but the principle is the same. If A plc's treasury strategy anticipates that UK base rates will fall, A plc may buy a swap which will be in-the-money if base rates do fall, A plc would be advised to purchase another type of product (perhaps an option indexed to an equity exchange which is expected to move in an inverse direction to UK base rates) which will generate sufficient profit to cover A plc's loss if UK base rates were to rise. The commercial decisions are then as to the likelihood of either rise in UK base rates and the amount that A plc would be likely to lose if UK base rates were to go up.

Potential legal issues   1.8.2

There is no compulsion to hedge. It is fiscally more efficient, in the short term, for A plc not to hedge because A plc would not have to pay a banker's fee for the financial product which comprises the hedge. The decision to hedge is a matter of risk management. What is the likelihood that there is a viable risk and that a hedge would be needed. If A plc does need a hedge, could it cover its exposure with a small hedge or should A plc pay for a hedge which would generate a return equal to the full amount of the exposure.

There have been instances in the 1990's where non-financial institutions have disclosed very large losses in derivatives and swaps trading. Where a company generates a loss in the region of US$ 160 million, as a result of its interest rate swap strategy, by dealing with the interest it was paying on its debt, this must mean that its hedging strategy was small in comparison to the maximum realisable risk.

The important message to take from hedging is that players do not tend to play only once in the market. We have already seen that Hammersmith and Fulham did not swap once, they swapped hundreds of times with lots of different institutions. Similarly, each position is not a one off. A might swap with B but A will want to hedge that swap and so will enter into another transaction with C. B and C will both want to hedge out their liabilities with D and E. In turn D and E will want a hedge with F and with G. In this way, the risk of system failure spreads around the market like a computer virus spreads from one computer disk to another, A's credit risk is spread from one banking institution to another.

This discussion of derivatives might lead us to believe that the way for sovereign borrowers (that is, countries) and all other market players to protect themselves against market movements is to take out a protective hedging position. This does miss the point that to rely on hedging, as the US courts have begun to indicate the financial markets are, is to throw total dependence upon the banks to control our exposure to the crisis that the banks are creating in the first place. Derivative instruments are seen by some as a symptom (to use a tired metaphor) rather than a cure for the disease of market volatility.

The legal issues which arise from hedging, are principally the same issues which arise from the other derivatives products discussed above. There is one further issue which is possibly unique to hedging. If hedging will reduce the risk in A plc, should the directors of A plc necessarily embark on a hedging strategy as part of the prudent financial management of the company? Similarly, does the prudent management structure of a trustee require that the trustee controls the investment portfolio risk of the trust with the use of derivatives. More significantly, can the shareholder or beneficiary under a trust, respectively, sue the fiduciary for failure to use derivatives in the management of financial risk? There is no legal compulsion to enter into hedging strategies currently. However, the products increasing use might lead to the conclusion that reasonable treasury policy requires the minimisation of financial risk with derivatives.

There is the further issue of suitability[40] of the derivatives product used which might find that misuse of derivatives products is something which is equally culpable for the fidiciary. There are two separate issues at law here:-

- breach of fiduciary duty
- negligence

The first issue is whether or not the fiduciary is liable for breach in either failing to use a financial product or for using the wrong product. This might include liability for failing to manage the operations of the person to whom financial strategy decisions are delegated. The delegate may be an employee of the fiduciary or an agent retained for the particular purpose.

The second issue is as to the liability in negligence for a fiduciary who does not indulge in market practice in using the correct form of financial product. It may be that it is market practice to use derivatives to control a particular species of financial risk. The appropriate test might require that the fiduciary do invest in a given form of market product to manage a certain risk.

---

[40] Discussed below at para. 3.14

Part 2

The Markets and their Documentation

Contents

2.1   Exchange Traded Products
2.2   The Primary Markets
2.3   OTC Derivative Contracts
2.4   The Confirmation
2.5   Master Agreements
2.6   The Schedule
2.7   Tax Representations
2.8   Pre-contractual Undertakings and Procedure
2.9   Set-off
2.10 Transferability of Obligations
2.11 Termination

Exchange Traded Products 2.1

While this book does not aim to deal with exchange traded products (because of the voluminous literature that already exists on that subject), it is worth considering the ways in which the exchanges operate, to highlight some of the possible future trends in the regulation of OTC derivative markets and also to give an idea of the full picture relating to derivative products. From the UK perspective, the derivatives which are dealt with on exchanges are principally those futures contracts and options relating to futures on LIFFE. The most important point to consider with reference to exchange traded instruments is that the exchange bears the credit risk of every market participant on the exchange. As such, much of the systemic risk relating to the derivative product is removed. The legal documentation aims to make all the contracts "commoditised" products: that is identical products which conform to certain general patterns and have few customised features that would make them impossible or difficult to inter-change. Examples of the uniformity imposed are standards as to uniform quality of the underlying product or standardised delivery perameters.

The Structure of an Exchange

A corporate body controls the business of the exchange and sets its operating rules. The exchange governs the rules of membership and thereby selects those who can participate in the exchange. The result is a minimum level of credit worth among the market participants. Only those participants who can satisfy the credit worth criteria are able to trade on the exchange. The exchange is then able to control the amount of risk that each member can take. Participants are subject therefore to the rules of the exchange and to the regulatory framework of UK legislation generally.

Individual transactions are then settled with a clearing member, a separate cadre of exchange members who satisfy stricter credit criteria. The clearing members then settle transactions with the clearing house. The credit risk of trading on the exchange is centred on the clearing house, thus minimising the amount of systemic risk.

The marketplace and the clearing house for the exchange are separate legal entities although affiliated one to the other. All trades carried out on the trading floor are then novated to the clearing house at the close of the day's business. Therefore each market participant ends the day with contractual obligations to, and rights against, the clearing house rather than the other exchange participant with whom they dealt ostensibly. All credit risk is therefore centred in the clearing house rather than in the participants. The only counterparty risk that exists is during the day before the close of business and novation to the clearing house.

The clearing house takes "initial margin" from the participants which is a sum of money that enables the clearing house to ensure against risk relating to any of the parties during the day before novation to it. Variation margin is then taken to protect it against future loss on the contract resulting from a failure of any member of the exchange. The amount of margin that is left with the clearing house generally represents any day's worst case scenario loss for the clearing house. All the members of the clearing house are guaranteed against loss by the members of the exchange and the clearing house will generally reinsure itself in the insurance market.

A clearing member of the exchange will clear for members who are not clearing members. This intermediary level of market participation operates as a further level of protection for the clearing house because it only actually clears transactions for the clearing members and does not have to cope with the clearing requirements of all of the members of the exchange. The result is a setting-off of by all clearing members of their exposure to non-clearing members and a further setting-off of all obligations at the level of the clearing house. If a general exemption for the clearing houses from the general restrictions on netting under insolvency laws is provided, then there will be a restricted level of exposure to any one member who goes bankrupt from all the other members of the exchange. This will protect against one of the greatest issues facing the OTC markets, that of failure to set-off obligations if one of the counterparties goes bankrupt.

There is a difficulty with reference to those who are not members of the exchange but who act through agents who are members of the exchange. There is a contract between the clearing house and the agent but not between the principal and the clearing house. Typically the agent will execute a back-to-back transaction with the principal to replicate the contract it has with the clearing house and also with the counterparty to the trade before that trade is novated to the clearing house. The problem that might arise is that the agent becomes insolvent and therefore only the clearing house will have the benefit of any exemption under insolvency law. The clearing house refuses to act with anyone other than its members on the basis that it has privity of contract only with the members of the exchange. Therefore the benefits of netting available to the clearing house and the guarantees that are extended to it by the members, do not provide any relief for the non-member. The other possible view is that the contract is held beneficially for the principal on the basis that the agent has incurred personal liability to the principal.

The detail of these issues is beyond the scope of this text, however, it is important to understand that trading on exchanges in derivatives products, presents dangers in itself.

The Primary Markets   2.2

The Primary Markets are made up of bond or warrant issues which are the primary issues of those products represented by some form of security which are not a private OTC placement. In fact, the distinction from OTC placements is more theoretical that real because many of the primary public placements are restricted to a small number of investors, often simply by the very size and nature of the placement. In the case of warrant issues, for example, there is generally very little liquidity and therefore the section of the public that will be able to invest tends to pre-select itself in any event. The trading of these securities back to the issuer also restricts the size of the class of potential investor.

The legal analysis of these issues is often complicated by the fact that the instrument issued tends to have a hedge implanted in it and therefore the rights of the parties relate to more than one simple security. Many of the securities in the primary markets are linked to indicies in the same way that normal private placement instruments are. The legal implications of this structure are therefore often the requirement of some form of permission from the owner of the index against which the product is to be priced and measured.

The bulk of the legal issues revolve around the fact that warrant issues tend to be cash-settled rather than involving the physical delivery of the underlying product. This is partly because the products themselves are not appropriate for physical settlement; for example, a warrant issued with reference to the underlying shares on an index would require the delivery of a specified quantum of all of the shares in that index. Therefore, the investor is only receiving an amount of money as defined by reference to a defined index. This enables structuring of the products to be tailored to the situation where money is paid and received rather than having to cope with the situation where there is physical delivery and the ability of the lawyer to redefine the obligations and rights of the parties is curtailed.

The use of indices has replaced the use of baskets of shares because the rules of most Stock Exchanges still have more stringent listing requirements for baskets of shares than they do for securities issued against an index. Therefore, baskets of shares are often redefined as share indicies and the method of calculation is altered accordingly. The versatility of the cash-settled instrument thus supports the practical ease of execution.

Documentation for a primary market issue needs to provide for:

- interest;
- payment amounts and dates;
- definition of "business day" to ensure that there are no mismatches of payment days by use of different business day conventions on the primary instrument and the hedging instrument;
- redemption and purchase;
- witholding tax and the ability to gross-up;
- termination event that includes default under the hedge rather than just the primary instrument;
- market disruption, particularly to ensure that the calculation agents for both the hedge and the underlying instrument will not produce a mismatch in calculation methods required by the disruption event.

The warrants issued are usually permanent global warrants. The fact that warrants are not physically issued and delivered to each investor means that contractual rights are not automatically conferred upon such third parties who have invested in the issue. The solution to the problem of privity of contract in this instance is provided by the execution of a deed poll to confer rights to sue under the terms of the global warrant to such third parties.[1]

The structure of a warrant and its exercise is usually structured in the same way as an option.[2] The four most common categories of option exercise are:

European Options:	exercisable only on one day in the future
American Options:	exercisable at any time during the life of the option
Asian Options:	exercisable only on one day in the future but at an average price over the life of the option
Black-out periods:	times during which the option cannot be exercised.

The aim with remedies for failure under an option to deal with an equity-linked security is to put the parties in the position that they would have occupied had they held the security throughout the life of the option.

---

[1] The Law Commission is currently looking at the issue of 3rd party rights under contracts.
[2] The reader is referred to the discussion of equity options above at para. 1.5 and of warrants at para. 1.6.

The difference between warrants and equities or other equity derivatives is the absence of a negative pledge, gross-up provisions, and events of default in warrants. Payments under warrants are not interest payments for UK tax purposes. However, under English law, if the tax is withheld, the full amount due under the contract has not been paid and therefore the payer remains liable for that amount to make up the full value owed under the contract.

It is therefore important to ascertain in advance of a warrant issue whether the issuer's consent is required, whether the Stock Exchange must give its consent and whether the Central Bank of the relevant currency must give its consent.

Is a warrant a debenture?   2.2.1

The benefit of a warrant not being defined as a debenture is that the warrant therefore avoids the listing requirements set out in the Companies Act 1985. Section 744 of the Companies Act 1985 provides that:

> " 'debenture' includes debenture stock, bonds and any other securities of a company, whether constituting a charge on the assets of the company or not".

One definition made of a debenture is "any obligation to pay money" which is often extended to mean that there is a requirement that there be "some element of borrowing" bound up in it. It is thought that on this analysis of the meaning of a debenture, a warrant cannot be a debenture because it does not include (of necessity) any element of borrowing in it. A warrant, as discussed above, requires the issuer of the warrant to issue further equity capital if the warrant is in-the-money. Therefore, there is no a priori involvement of debt. On the contrary, equity share capital is taken to mean any part of the common stock that carries with it a right to participate in a distribution beyond a pre-determined amount.[3]

There is a difference therefore between a bond and a warrant. As discussed[4], a derivative product linked to a bond, is usually intended to improve the cost of funding to the issuer or the bond. The example discussed was that of an embedded swap which might, for example, provide the issuer with a floating rate of interest in connection with the bond which is expected to be a lower rate than that required to be paid to investors under the bond issue.

Alternatively, a convertible bond, is a bond which carries an option, where given contingencies are satisfied, for the bond (a debt instrument) to be converted into equity. A convertible bond is therefore capable of being analysed as a bond with an embedded call option on the issuing company's equity capital. Here the debt instrument does involve an

---

[3] See, e.g. Knightsbridge Estates v. Byrne [1940] A.C. 613.
[4] At para. 1.4.

element debt and equity. The question whether a convertible bond is a debenture could therefore be answered by referring to the inclusion of the word "bond" in the definition of "debenture" in section 744 of the Companies Act 1985, and also by the fact that it necessarily involves the raising of debt.

A warrant is a resaleable instrument which may have the characteristics of a bond in that it can be sold but does not have the characteristics of a bond in that it does not entitle the holder to a cash flow. The investor is not entitled to a stream of interest payments to be made to it. Rather, the investor is entitled to receive an amount of equity capital in the event that the strike price on the warrant is lower or equal to the market price of the stock on the relevant maturity date. Therefore, the payment structure is different from that of a debt and therefore a "vanilla" warrant structure would appear to be something other than a debenture.

Under the terms of the warrant, the exercise of the warrant may require the payment of an amount cash by the investor to the issuer, in excess of the premium, to acquire the appropriate share capital, rather than there being a simple conversion of one form of security for another (that is, debt bond for equity stock). As such a warrant does not entitle the holder to a payment of an interest stream and therefore does not have the charateristics of a debenture, as defined *eusdem generis* with a "bond".

2.3 OTC Derivative Contracts

One of the challenges of derivative products for the lawyer-as-risk-manager is that of rendering the innovations of the market, expressed in the esperanto of the trading floor, into legal documentation that both ensures the maximisation of existing legal concepts and that the antici-pated contractual relations between the parties are sufficiently explained.

As discussed above, there is no currently existing "law on derivatives". This is the result of a lack of coherent statute or regulation.[5] However, there are concepts, cobbled together from other legal disciplines, which form a complete set which could be called "the law affecting derivative products": or, disingenuously, "the law on derivatives". The role of the legal documentation is therefore to capture this complete set of legal concepts and apply them to the transaction at issue.

The second role is that which requires the lawyer to understand the marketplace and to comprehend the range of commercial factors which the traders will and will not have discussed between themselves or even considered. The following sections consider a number of frequently occurring examples of market practice such as the day on which a payment is to be made, whether it is the day specified or whether there

---

[5] This lack is a feature of OTC derivatives in most jurisdictions. See, however, the attempts to introduce coherent litigation in the USA as set out in the Appendix.

is an implied period within which a payment can be made after that date without necessarily causing an event of default. While these concerns are often peripheral to the primary commercial purpose of the transaction, or are points which the lawyer may not consider to be strictly "legal" issues, failure to provide for them explicitly in documentation is one of the more frequent causes of mismatch and conflict between market counterparties. The documentation must therefore be constructed so as to cater for this broad spread of potential events which are the results of market practice rather than anything to do with the operation of law *per se*.

This chapter aims to consider the variety of documents that will typically be required to document a derivatives transaction successfully in the Over the Counter Market. It also explores those provisions which appear to cater for market, rather than legal, events. It is hoped that this chapter will be sufficient to explain to both the market participant and the lawyer the broad range of basic "vanilla" issues which should be dealt with in the documentation.

Structure of the Documentation 2.3.1

The documentation in derivatives contracts between private parties differs from jurisdiction to jurisdiction and also differs from product to product. There are basic similarities between the forms of contract though which are caused by two main factors. As outlined in the introduction, lawyers are dealing in risk management and therefore they are seeking to manage the same sorts of risks in the documentation. There is a broader discussion of the risks involved in the Credit Risks and Collateral chapter[6] but the ensuing discussion of the risks that documentation typically seeks to manage, should indicate the types of occurrence that the lawyer is required to anticipate and cover. The second reason for the basic similarities is that the documentation is attempting to cover products which are, as discussed in the Products section[7] above, rooted in the same basic building blocks of swaps, option and forwards. The fact that these products are of a similar root and that their nature will be substantially the same regardless of the system of law under which they are contracted, ensures that there is a broadly parallel methodology in the completion of a set of swaps, or other derivative documents.

There is a drift towards market standards of documentation. The foremost in this field is the "ISDA" contract (produced by the International Swaps and Derivatives Association) which has slowly adapted to cover the breadth of derivatives contracts which are arranged on an OTC basis. Most of these documents are based upon the English and American systems of law and therefore the civil code jurisdictions, principally France and Germany, have begun to develop their own contracts which

---

[6] Below in Part 5.
[7] Part 1 above.

incorporate their commercial codes in their entirety into the contract. This section shall concentrate on the Anglo-American versions because the aim of the book is to be an English law reference guide and because the breadth of issues covered in the Anglo-American contracts serves to illustrate all of the principal risks which are at large in this area.

There are four aspects of the documentation which are of interest here:

1. the Confirmation;
2. the Master Agreement (usually in a standard form);
3. the Schedule to the Master Agreement;
4. Credit Support documentation.

Derivatives documentation is structured by organising the way in which the parties will deal with one another across all applicable derivatives products, under one Master Agreement. This Master Agreement contains all the important terms about what the parties are to do if one of them defaults, or if tax regulations change, or if there is dispute as to the manner in which amounts owed reciprocally can be set-off against one another, and so forth. The detail of these provisions is set out below. It sets the perameters for all derivatives transactions. To create a metaphor, the Master Agreement sets out the rules of the game which the parties are to play, as those rules are understood by the market place.

Each individual transaction is connected to this Master Agreement by entering into a confirmation (the "Confirmation") which is, as its name suggests, a Confirmation of the trade which two parties have entered into by telephone, fax or telex on the dealing floors. The Confirmation is expressed to be subject to the terms of the Master Agreement. The spread of documentation is therefore inter-linked. The Confirmation sets out the details of each particular match that the parties play with one another. The link to the Master Agreement ensures that the parties are still governed by those over-arching rules of the game.

The Master Agreement is generally in standard form agreed by a trade association and promoted as a market standard. It is in the schedule ("the Schedule") to the Master Agreement that the standard form is modified and it is the negotiation of the Schedule which is the most time-consuming process in the setting in place of the documentation for derivatives.

The Master Agreement, usually in the Schedule, will specify the credit support documentation (usually in the form of guarantees) which will be required as part of the transaction. Credit support documents have become the subject of standardisation initiatives by trade associations but remain negotiated principally on a case by case basis between the parties. The detail of credit considerations and collateral is considered below in Part 5.

The Confirmation   2.4

The Confirmation is, indeed, a confirmation of the trade which two parties have entered into by telephone, fax or telex. The Confirmation is expressed to be subject to the terms of the Master Agreement, as discussed below.

The Creation of a Contract   2.4.1

The creation of a contract and the detailed legal issues which arise, for example "when is the contract formed?" or "who are the parties?", are dealt with in the next section of the book[8]. At this stage I am concerned to communicate the way in which the mechanism works in practice before considering the legal niceties.

The derivative products are completed in the pressure atmosphere of the trading floor by telephone and by fax. Therefore, there is little pre-negotiation of the standard type of forward or option agreement before it is traded. Rather, the traders will be concerned to discuss the financial product which they are buying or selling. It is often only in the case of complex structures that legal advice will be sought or that legal ter-minology will be discussed between the parties.

Typically, the trader will fill out a deal ticket, containing the financial details of the transaction, which will be passed (by hand or by electronic transmission) to the "middle office" where the legal support areas sit. The role of the lawyer is to transform that set of economic terms into a legal document which deals with everything that the parties would require to be expressed, if they knew that the potential problems existed. The trader is often not well acquainted with many of the legal niceties and, frankly, is often not the slightest bit interested.

Therefore, there are a number of sources of potential legal material to evidence the trade in the absence of documentation. There is the tele-phone conversation between the traders in which they will have discussed the detail of the trade and probably dealt with the bulk of the commercial issues between the parties. There are specifically legal issues, such as the choice of governing law, which will be latent between the traders, but the bulk of the "economic terms" will be decided between them.

There is then also the trade ticket which will usually set out the details of the transaction as the trader sees it. This might be evidence of the animus of the trader on entering into the transaction. However, as likely as not, this document will only go to show mistake, in that the traders did not agree with one another as to the economic effect and legal specifics of the transaction from the outset. There is occasionally confusion as to the requirement for credit protection or collateral, for example, in the heat of transacting.

There is a risk of there not being any legal documentation between the

---

[8] At para. 2.5.

time of the trade and the signing of a document. The speed at which the markets move may make the economic and commercial impetus for the transaction moribund before the trading day has finished. Many exotic options, which activate once the market reaches a particular level, will move into the money only hours after they have been transacted on the telephone. Therefore, the transaction will be effectively terminated in the minds of the parties before any documentation has been prepared. However, the paper trail of legal documentation will still require completion to satisfy the financial control centres and the auditors that the deal is being conducted properly and that hedging strategies are being correctly implemented.

Typically it will take a minimum of two to three days to produce a confirmation and to have that agreed by the other party, in a straightforward transaction. There is a pre-settlement risk (discussed in greater detail below in para. 5.2) where an issue arises between the parties between the time of creating an oral contract by telephone and the signing of the legal documentation. The risk is also of failure to perform under the agreement before contracts are agreed. A separate issue then arises of constructing the terms of the agreement from taped telephone conversations and purported agreements between the traders.

Interim confirmations

There are more detailed terms in Master Agreement than in the Confirmation. For example, those provisions to do with close-out netting. The interpretation provision means that the parties can agree to alter the provisions in the Master Agreement with reference to one particular transaction so that they can tailor-make a derivative product without having to re-negotiate a new Master Agreement. However, the credit departments of financial institutions become particularly concerned about the elapse of time, during which a swaps transaction remains undocumented, between the date of the trade and the eventual signing of a Master Agreement. The temptation therefore is to expand the Confirmation to contain many of the provisions that will be found in the Master Agreement. The dangers here are two-fold. It would be easy to allow discrepancies to arise between the Confirmation and the eventual Master Agreement which will complicate the Master Agreement as to supremacy clauses (always presuming that the mismatches are located before the Master Agreement is signed).

One method of countering this risk is to enter into an 'interim confirmation'. This document will set out nothing more than the economic terms of the transaction and the governing law of the contract, to settle any disputes as to the status of the oral contract reached between the traders and the economic terms to which they agreed. At least, on the agreement of an interim confirmation, there is a basis for a comprehensible contract although much of the detail of its terms will remain at large. However, it is the detail of the terms which often takes up most of the negotiation time and yet are of least interest to the contracting parties at the time of the transaction.

The danger is that a full Confirmation will take time to negotiate, thus enlarging the time during which there is no documentary evidence of the economic terms of the trade. It is more important that the prices and maturity dates, and so forth, are evidenced in writing than that the detail of cross default events is worked out. Generally a Confirmation can be signed by both parties by return of fax. In terms of the control of counterparty and systemic market risk, it is submitted that documentation of the economic terms is more important than introducing all of the detailed legal paraphernalia at the outset. Having a fuller Confirmation will not only take longer to negotiate but it will lessen some of the enthusiasm needed to put a Master Agreement in place.

In many ways the most important aspect of a derivative instrument is the understanding of who is to pay what, to whom and when. An interim confirmation will set this out clearly and remove any disagreement between the traders as to amounts, currencies, and so forth. It is also saved from the laborious process of having lawyers agree to form of confirmation. It is invariably the case that a lawyer will be more eager to consider alterations to its own confirmation rather than have to wade through someone else's. The interim confirmation removes the risk associated with lawyers embarking on negotiations which can often last longer than the life of the deal.

Interim Confirmation

Dear :

The purpose of this letter agreement (this "Interim Confirmation") is to confirm the terms and conditions of the transaction entered into between . . . . ("Party A") and . . . . ("Party B") on the Trade Date specified below (the "Transaction"). This Interim Confirmation constitutes a "Confirmation" as referred to in the ISDA Master Agreement specified below.

The purpose of this Interim Confirmation is to confirm such terms and conditions of the Transaction as are set out below. This Interim Confirmation shall be superceded by a full Confirmation entered into between Party A and Party B at a date subsequent to the date of this Interim Confirmation. The terms of this Interim Confirmation shall stand until the creation of such Confirmation.

This Confirmation supplements, forms a part of, and is subject to, the ISDA Master Agreement dated as of [date], as amended and supplemented from time to time (the "Agreement"), between Party A and Party B. If no such Agreement has been entered into between us, then you and we agree to negotiate in good faith to enter into the Agreement (with such modifications

71

as may in good faith be agreed). All provisions contained in the Agreement govern this Confirmation except as expressly modified below.

The terms of the Transaction to which this Interim Confirmation relates are as follows:

General Terms:

Trade Date:	
Option Style:	European / American / Asian
Option Type:	Put / Call
Seller:	Party A
Buyer:	Party B
Index/Price Option:	
Number of Units:	
Strike Price:	
Premium:	
Premium Payment Date:	
Exchange:	
Calculation Agent:	Party A, whose determinations and calculations shall be binding in the absence of manifest error.

Procedure for Exercise:

Exercise Period:	
Expiration Date:	199– or, if that date is not an Index Business Day, the first following day that is an Index Business Day.

Cash Settlement Terms:

Cash Settlement:	Applicable; Seller shall pay to Buyer the Cash Settlement Amount, if any, on the Cash Settlement Payment Date for all Options exercised or deemed exercised.
Cash Settlement Amount:	An amount, as calculated by the Calculation Agent, equal to the Number of Options multiplied by the Strike Price Differential multiplied by one [currency].
Strike Price Differential:	An amount equal to the greater of (i) the excess, as of the Valuation Time on the Valuation Date, of the Strike Price over the level of the Index and (ii) zero.
Cash Settlement Payment Date:	Three Currency Business Days after the Valuation Date.

This Confirmation will be governed by and construed in accordance with the laws of England (without reference to choice of law doctrine).

Please confirm that the foregoing correctly sets forth the terms of our agreement by executing this Confirmation in the space provided below and returning it to us.

Yours sincerely,

Confirmed as of the date
first above written:

PARTY A   **PARTY B**

By: By:
Name: Name:
Title: Title:

The Confirmation and the Master Agreement   2.4.2

The Confirmation stands for all the terms of the contract until a Master
Agreement is put into place. The role of the Master Agreement is to deal
with eventualities affecting the range of dealings between the parties,
such as insolvency. The standard terms of a Confirmation do not extend
to this level of specificity. Therefore the Confirmation must evidence all
the terms of the swaps contract until a Master Agreement is put into place.
It is usual for a Master Agreement to be put into place months after the
first transaction. The Master Agreement will govern the complex legal
terms for all the relevant types of transaction performed between the
parties after it is put in place.

The lawyer must therefore pay particular attention to the credit risks
associated with transactions with particular counterparties in the absence
of a Master Agreement. The credit risk associated with transactions that
do not have a Master Agreement must be taken to increase as a result.

Terms and credit risk   2.4.3

The Confirmation does not specifically take account of credit risk.
Counterparties will work on credit lines approved by the credit departments of each party. The traders will discuss, usually involving the credit
or risk management departments, the requirement for collateral, or margin
arrangements (if any), to secure the transaction in the event that either
party fails to pay.[9]

Given that the Confirmation will normally exist long before the Master
Agreement is put into place, and that it is the Master Agreement which
provides for the necessary credit support documentation, there is need to
consider the credit support position under the transaction as evidenced
by the Confirmation. This is a commercial issue between the parties. It is
usually either solved by the provision of collateral or by the parties simply
accepting one another's credit worth.

It is often the case that there is little likelihood of a Master Agreement
being agreed between the parties. The complicated negotiation process

---

[9] The commercial motivations for these decisions are discussed in Part 5 below.

often militates against the negotiation process being completed at all. Where the parties do not intend to deal with one another on a regular basis, the impetus to complete this documentation is reduced.

2.4.4 The position without a Master Agreement

The vexed question is then, what is done in circumstances where there is no Master Agreement and only a Confirmation. There are a number of implied terms in a Confirmation but most of the events which would cause litigation are those which take the most amount of negotiation on the Schedule. The answer would appear to be that the issues dealt with in the Master Agreement will generally be considered to remain at large in the absence of completed documentation.

However, where the intention of the parties is to enter into a transaction on the basis of the standard documentation, it is likely that the standard terms will be deemed to apply to the contract. The difficulty arises where the conflict surrounds a part of the agreement on which the parties have failed to reach an agreement as opposed to a part of the documentation where there could be shown to be agreement subject only to signing the documents. Clearly, these issues are general points of contract law and the law of evidence. Therefore, there is little to be gained from a detailed discussion here. However, the risks associated with failure to effect all the requisite documentation is apparent.

2.4.5 The Structure of a Confirmation

The Confirmation:

- refers to the general definitions of terms in one of the standard market documents, or a bespoke Master Agreement, and shows that they apply;
- explains that a Master Agreement will be entered into later if it does not exist already and that its terms will govern the contract between the parties;
- if no Master Agreement is entered into, the standard market or bespoke terms may probably still apply.[10]

2. Sets out the terms of the transaction
3. Sets out account details
4. Asks counterparty to check the terms are correct

The Confirmation will usually cover the following points. Examples of specific forms of confirmation for differing forms of derivatives contract are included in the Appendices to this book.

---

[10] See para. 2.4.4

Pro Forma Confirmation

(a)   The Parties

(b)   The purpose of the Confirmation is to set out the Terms and Conditions of the Transaction

(c)   Incorporation of the Master Agreement

(d)   General Terms:

Trade Date:	
Option Style:	European / American / Asian Option
Option Type:	Put / Call
Seller:	Party A
Buyer:	Party B
Index/Price Option:	
Number of Units:	
Strike Price:	
Premium:	
Premium Payment Date:	
Exchange:	
Calculation Agent:	Party A, whose determinations and calculations shall be binding in the absence of manifest error.

(e)   Procedure for Exercise:
    Exercise Period:
    Expiration Date: , 199– or, if that date is not an Index Business Day, the first following day that is an Index Business Day.

(f)   Cash Settlement Terms:
    Cash Settlement:
    Cash Settlement Amount:
    Strike Price Differential:
    Cash Settlement Payment Date:

(g)   Physical Settlement Terms
    Physical Settlement:
    Settlement Date:
    Settlement Price:
    Number of Shares to
    be Delivered:
    Settlement Date:
    Market Disruption Event:

(h)   Index / Instrument Description

(i)   Governing Law

2.4.6 Legal Points to Watch on the Confirmation

Most of the confirmations are standardised and therefore there is only a need to check that the terms are in the usual format.

- ensure that the parties are correct on the titles and in the section before paragraph 1
- ensure that the currency amounts, trade dates and effective dates are the same
- ensure that fixed and floating rate payers are the right way
- check that with reference to dates there are no peculiar conventions chosen
- check the governing law

There are fewer legal points to cater for in the confirmation where (a) the product is a vanilla instrument and (b) where the form of confirmation is a market standard where most of the terms are standardised.

2.4.7 Commercial Points to watch about the Counterparty

- Is the counterparty known ('know your client')?
- Is the counterparty in a jurisdiction in which we can deal?
- Can we deal in the specific product in that jurisdiction?
- Do we need any approvals? (e.g.: central banks, government departments)
- What laws are there restricting capacity to enter into derivatives to which the counterparty is subject?
- Will the counterparty provide documentation to prove its capacity to enter into the transaction?

- Is there a Master Agreement in place with the counterparty?
- If not, what particular legal concerns remain outstanding? Does the confirmation address them?
- Will all transactions be capable of netting on insolvency under this Master Agreement?

- Has the requisite credit survey approved the transaction? ie: will the counterparty be able to pay?
- What credit support is the counterparty willing to provide?
  - ☐ guarantee
  - ☐ cross default
  - ☐ credit event upon merger
  - ☐ cross acceleration of debt
  - ☐ collateral
  - ☐ margin
- What risks have been considered?

☐ Pre-settlement risk
☐ Payment risk
☐ Insolvency / netting risk
☐ Contract risk
☐ Market Risk
☐ Hedging risk
☐ Regulatory risk

Credit Points to Watch   2.4.8

- Which entity is providing the credit support (public debt issuing entity?)

- How will termination payments between the parties be calculated?
- What is the transaction currency?

- What particular contractual requirements are there to protect our own credit possession? Will the counterparty allow us the freedom to include such a clause?

- What tax considerations are there?
    ☐ witholding taxes
    ☐ double tax treaty protection
    ☐ is the counterparty a recognised swaps dealer attracting the coverage of Inland Revenue concessions?
    ☐ are we a recognised swaps dealer in the jurisdiction?

- How quickly will the counterparty provide us with confirmations and other documentation?
- Is the documentation prepared by us or by the counterparty?

The OTC derivative contracts using this form of Confirmation are those derivative contracts executed between 2 parties on a private placement basis. The basic types of product divide between:

- swaps
- options
- forwards

These products are then generally related to either an:

- interest rate
- equity
- currency, or
- commodity

There are a number of commercial considerations which govern the legal advice to be given in respect of derivatives products. Those commercial considerations are dealt with in detail in Part 1 above. The remaining sections of this part 2.4, deal specifically with the most significant provisions of a Confirmation.

2.4.9 Market Disruption

This is usually only found in the equity and commodity derivative instruments where there are underlying markets on which the derivative is based. Therefore interest rate swaps do not usually require a market disruption provision. The only relevant definition of an interest rate swap market disruption event will be a definition of LIBOR and the alternative means of acquiring a rate should the requisite pages of the screen-based information services fail to yield a suitable indicator.

In the equity and commodity markets it is a pre-requisite that there be a functioning market before there will be an index against which the derivative can be priced. Generally there is a provision in OTC equity index confirmations to provide for a market disruption event to be identified half an hour before the close of the index to give the parties a half hour of time to deal with the hedge that is scheduled to run concurrently with the main derivative instrument.

The length of time over which a market disruption event must be identified will depend in many circumstances on the liquidity of the market in question. On some markets, for example the emerging market indicies, a longer period of time is provided for because of the relative illiquidity or relative lack of sophistication of the markets in reacting to a market disruption event. There is clearly a lag between the happening of an event and an alteration to the index or marketplace. These are commercial considerations but will affect the precise detail of the legal documentation that is put in place.

Market disruption will only affect cash settled derivatives if it stops the index being calculated. Otherwise, there should always be sufficient currency to make the contractually required payment. The opposite example would be the physically settled derivatives which require that an amount of the commodity or share be produced and therefore there is clearly risk of the commodity or share being in short supply.

Some exchanges have a maximum price volatility beyond the confines of which trading on the security or commodity is suspended. The question will be then whether any of these events are material market disruptions for the purposes of the particular contract at issue. In some stock exchanges, a movement in a particular share will account for a significant proportion of the volume of the exchange. For example, there might be a particular company which is so important to the economy encompassing that exchange that it accounts for a significant percentage of the size of the equity transacted on that exchange or of the size of a particular index. If that company were to become insolvent, for example, the effect on the index would be very large indeed and arguably contrary to the expectations of both of the parties on entering into the agreement.

There is a further question as to the effect of the change in the trading on the index resulting from the failure of such a significant part of the index. Arguably, the position of the parties would be that the true intention of the contract, to create a synthetic security payments under which mirror the normal movements of that index, had been frustrated by the index itself being all but destroyed by the violent, and unexpected movements of one of the components within it. Clearly there will be a question of degree. The question of the closure or discontinuance of the index is considered below. If the index is completely removed at the instigation of the sponsor which calculates the level of the index (eg: *the Financial Times* in the case of the FTSE 100), then the index itself no longer exists. The consequences for the transaction must be the same as if it were a contract for the transportation of a commodity which is destroyed before the creation of the contract. That is, the contract has been frustrated.

It is a question of fact whether or not the contract is frustrated by the violent movement of one of the components of the index. If the movement is so great as to alter the subject matter of the contract so much that what remains is manifestly contrary to that which was intended by the parties at the time of their contracting, then there must be frustration once again. The question might then be, in any event, whether or not the parties could be said to have received part of that which they contracted for if a certain number of payments have been made under the agreement. If a series of payments have been made and the index does not collapse until the derivative instrument has been in operation for some time, the legal analysis of the instrument will be all important.

The party alleging frustration (presumably on the basis that the instrument is out of the money and therefore wishes a remedy which will terminate the agreement) would argue that each separate payment constitutes a separate option or forward contract. Alternatively, the party for whom the index is in the money will argue that the index should continue as is or that it can be amended such that the instrument can continue in existence. This latter argument must be based on the assertion that the derivative constituted one entire transaction with payments to be made on separate dates, which has been performed in part and which cannot then be subjected to any equitable form of termination. The answer to these vexed questions will clearly turn on the interpretation of the product in question. If the Confirmation and the description of the production by the parties constituted a series of options to receive money or to perform some act, then there must be a separate instrument in respect of each of those events. Alternatively, a warrant that contains a single exercise into share capital would be a single instrument that would have seen some partial performance.

These issues will require an analysis of the particular facts to be resolved in any particular case. The minimisation of market exchange risk, will therefore be alleviated by the correct structuring of the relevant product. As discussed above[11], it is possible to manouevre between levels of risk by altering the composition of the derivative instrument.

2.4.10 Failure to Deliver

'Failure to deliver' under the agreement is a problem which focuses specifically on physically deliverable securities. In the bond market, interest accrues when the investor is awaiting delivery whereas the investor does not have to pay anything to the seller until the bond is actually delivered. Provided there is no counterparty credit risk, the investor will be content to wait until the bond arrives as interest mounts both on the bond and on the money held as its purchase price. Unless there is a back-to-back arrangement planned for the bond, there is no real downside for the investor in late delivery.

The one danger that exists under the single contract approach for derivatives is that the danger of cross default between derivative products arises. The single contract approach, where derivatives are transacted under a single Master Agreement, will generally provide that default under one transaction constitutes a default under all transactions. There is risk, therefore, that default may be triggered for a default which does not go to the heart of all the relevant transactions. As discussed below[12], much depends on the wording of the provision. It is normal for cross default provisions in Master Agreements to provide for automatic termination on the happening of a default. The ideal provision for the defaulting party will provide that there is no automatic termination but rather for the payment of interest or damages for failure to deliver. The non-defaulting party would prefer that the provision gave the option to default or accept late delivery with the payment of appropriate damages or interest. Clearly, then, the investor would rather be able to resist automatic termination so that the spread of derivatives transactions between the parties conducted under a single Master Agreement is not dismantled as a result of the single transaction failure.

2.4.11 Mistake

Market publication error

It is normal for confirmations to provide for mistakes made in the published level of an index or market. Such mistakes may be corrected, with the result that an in-the-money derivative may be out-of-the-money. Therefore, there is one general question with reference to derivatives

---

[11] In Part 1.
[12] Cross-default, para. 2.5.18

connected to indicies or specific markets and that is: in the case of a mistake on the index for which a correction is published 35 days after the initial mistake, what is the position if the contract had provided that mistakes must be proved within 30 days for the alteration of amounts to be paid under the contract?

If the parties had not contracted for that length of time for any reason other than that it was a part of their standard contractual terms, then there is perhaps an argument that it would be a form of unjust enrichment of the party that benefitted from the error to refuse to make payment. In fact, it might be that the parties would agree to make the payment in any event to aright the situation. This is particularly likely if the benefitting party is a financial institution dealing with a valued investment banking client.

The general rule is that the mistake must induce the payment. On these facts, the mistake would be the belief in the correctness of the index. The test is a supposed liability test[13]. The question is whether liability did in fact ever end because, if the terms of the contract are to be decisive, the amount of money paid was actually owed. The correct argument must be that there was a fundamental mistake under the contract that means that the amount paid should not have been paid at all.

Party Error

The primary issue with reference to mistake is that of an error made between the parties when conducting the transaction *ab initio*. This issue is considered in detail in the contract law texts. The position is no different with reference to a derivatives transaction. Where mistake operates so as to nullify consent, there cannot be said to be agreement between the parties.[14] This might apply in circumstances where the stock market over which the parties had sought to contract stock options had, unknown to the parties, ceased to trade. Where there is a fundamental mistake of fact, the contract will be nullified. However, there will not be nullification of a contract where the mistake is one of law.[15] For example, a mistake as to the construction of the contract which the parties negotiate, will not avoid the contract[16], unless there it is a mistake which is fundamental to the subject matter of the contract[17].

Extraordinary Event   2.4.12

The further question is how to deal with the situation in which there is an extraordinary event leading to the merger or nationalisation or liquidation of any relevant entity.

---

[13] *Kelly v. Solari* [1841] 9 M&W 54
[14] per Lord Atkin, *Bell v. Lever Bros* [1932] A.C. 161, 217.
[15] *Gee v. News Group Newspapers, The Times,* June 8, 1990.
[16] *Smith v. Harrison* (1857) 26 L.J.Ch. 412.
[17] *Barclays Bank v. W.J. Sims & Cooke Ltd* [1980] Q.B. 677.

In the case of an option there is a problem as to how the option should be treated if it had yet to expire time to run when the event took place. Let us take the example of a European option. Either the option must be deemed terminated as of the time of the extraordinary event or the option should be allowed to continue in effect under alteration of the pricing structure. The former would apply where the event is equivalent to termination of the contract. The latter would require that the option continue in effect until the appropriate price paid to reflect the value of the option at the time of the extraordinary event is established. Both of these approaches would adequately reflect the 'time value of money' approach of the option theorists, on which it is reasonable to suppose that the options were contracted. However, the provisions of the contract must provide an answer to this question because the choice between the two alternatives would not necessarily be obvious on commercial grounds in all circumstances.

From the lawyer's point of view, the entity over which the investor had the option disappears when the extraordinary event takes place for the purposes of the instrument. Therefore the party should receive the same rights to money as would stem from a termination of the option, where such an extraordinary event can be considered to be similar in effect to events which trigger the termination of the instrument. If the event terminates the ability of the party to perform its obligations under the transaction, it would be appropriate that the option should be treated as though it were terminated.

2.5 Master Agreements

2.5.1 Introduction

The structure of the documentation of derivatives transactions is one of the essential features of the market. The term "derivatives", as discussed above, is one that attempts to define a breadth of products which are not linked on their surface. As has been said, there is an extent to which the broad spread of derivative products have shared characteristics which enable them to be analysed using the same tools. It is the underlying material which differs widely and therefore affects the way in which the derivatives operate in the marketplace.

In legal terms, the documentation adopted by market participants has sought to use single sets of documentation to impose order on the breadth of available products. The use of the Master Agreement structure is the market's attempt to link these products one to another.

The ISDA form of Master Agreement[18] contains the full range of con-

---

[18] A specimen of this agreement is enclosed in the Appendix below. The ISDA form of contract is the most comprehensive of the market attempts at documentation and the discussion in this section therefore follows the scheme of that form of documentation.

tractual terms dealing with what the parties are to do if one of them defaults, or if tax regulations change, or if there is dispute as to the manner in which amounts owed reciprocally can be set-off against one another, and so forth. It sets the perameters for all derivatives transactions. To create a metaphor, the Master Agreement sets out the rules of the game which the parties are to play, as those rules are understood by the market place. Each individual transaction is connected to this Master Agreement by entering into a confirmation ("the Confirmation") which is, as its name suggests, a confirmation of the trade which two parties have entered into by telephone, fax or telex on the dealing floors. The Confirmation is expressed to be subject to the terms of the Master Agreement. The spread of documentation is therefore inter-linked.

Each separate transaction is confirmed, as discussed in the foregoing section, and expressly made subject to the terms of the Master Agreement. The Master Agreement sets out the terms which will be common to all of the derivative contracts which the parties will enter into; including termination, the making of representations and witholding tax issues.

Clearly, the negotiation of the Master Agreement then becomes a matter of importance because it sets the perameters for the derivatives dealings between the parties in the future.

History   2.5.2

The means by which derivatives contracts are documented takes account of the nature of derivatives products and the markets in which they are found. The early derivatives, typically interest rate and currency swaps were documented on a transaction by transaction basis because they were so rare[19]. The market has moved towards increasing commoditisation of derivatives products[20]: now that 'vanilla' swaps have become commoditised products, that is to say they conform to basic structural similarities and have few exotic features, there is often no need to create sophisticated documentation for each transaction. Even with the "value-added" products, there are legal issues which are generic to the products and which do not require separate negotiation and clarification every time a trade is done.

The result has been the development of Master Agreements which govern the most important legal issues between the parties for all of the derivatives transactions that are completed between them. Each separate transaction has its existence as a contract evidenced and its economic terms detailed in Confirmations. The significant legal issues, which are dealt with below in detail[21], are generic for all of the transactions. One of the most important issues is that of setting-off obligations under the variety of transactions that are entered into between two counterparties, some of

---

[19] See the discussion above in Part 1.
[20] On this development, see the discussion at para. 5.2 below.
[21] Specifically in Part 3.

which will be economically beneficial to one party and some to the other. By standardising the documentation between the parties for all derivatives transactions, the risks associated with these legal issues can be managed more efficiently. Most importantly, if one of the parties is unable to meet its payment obligations or is declared bankrupt, the counterparty will be able to activate identical termination provisions in respect of all the relevant derivatives transactions and, depending on the insolvency laws of the relevant jursidiction, set off all amounts owed concerning transactions under the Master Agreement.

Therefore the derivatives markets have begun to develop standard form documents for use with all products in all jursidictions. Unfortunately, the problem of having standard documentation accepted across jurisdicutions has led to a proliferation of standards in France and Germany to rival the Anglo-American ISDA code. The ISDA standard documents are attached in the Appendices. The text will refer cross-references to the appropriate sections of the Master Agreement. These standard documents contain the bulk of the issues which will need to be considered in the contracting of 'vanilla' instruments and many of the exotic structures. Therefore, the following discussion is based upon the structure identified in those standard documents.

2.5.3 Interpretation

The use of a Confirmation to evidence the terms of a transaction runs the risk of contradicting the terms of the Master Agreement. It is therefore necessary to delineate which contractual term shall take precedence over the other. Therefore it is usual for the Confirmation and the Master Agreement to declare that the Confirmation shall take precedence over the Master Agreement should there be any dissonance between the terms of each to do with any particular transaction. This enables any understanding reached in the course of a particular transaction to be given effect.

The interpretation provision means that the parties can agree to alter the provisions in the Master Agreement with reference to one particular transaction so that they can customise a derivative product without having to re-negotiate a new Master Agreement. However, many credit departments in banks worry about the time during which a swaps transaction can remain undocumented between the trade and the eventual signing of a Master Agreement. The temptation therefore is to expand the Confirmation to contain many of the provisions that will be found in the master agreement. One further problem arises here as to the more detailed terms in Master Agreement, for example, to do with close-out netting. The dangers here are two-fold. It would be easy to allow discrepancies to arise between the Confirmation and the eventual Master Agreement which will complicate the Master Agreement as to supremacy clauses (always presuming that the mismatches are located before the Master Agreement is signed).

The second danger is that the Confirmation will take longer to negotiate thus enlarging the time during which there is no documentary evidence of the economic terms of the trade. It is more important that the prices and maturity dates, and so forth, are evidenced in writing than that the detail of cross default events is worked out. Generally a Confirmation can be signed by both parties by return of fax. In terms of the control of counterparty and systemic market risk, it is submitted that documentation of the economic terms is more important than introducing all of the detailed legal paraphenalia at the outset. Having a fuller Confirmation will not only take longer to negotiate but it will lessen some of the enthusiasm needed to put a Master Agreement in place.

Payments   2.5.4

The Master Agreement will specify that the parties are liable to make all payments calculated under the Confirmation and thereby links the obligation under each transaction into the broader web of transactions under the Master Agreement generally.[22] By specifying that all payments calculated by reference to the Confirmation are to be paid as a contractual obligation under the Master Agreement, it becomes easier to set off the amounts whereas the payments might otherwise be thought to be subject to different proper laws.

Condition Precedent

The ISDA Master Agreement specifies that it is a condition precedent of the formation of the contract under either the Master Agreement or the payment of any obligation under a Confirmation, that there is no event of default, actual or potential, has occurred and is continuing at the time any such payment is made. This provison enables the parties to void the contract *ab initio* in the event that there is any hidden defect in the capacity or credit worth of the counterparty.[23]

Netting   2.5.5

There is also a provision for the netting of payments which are either to be made in the same currency or in respect of the same derivatives transaction.[24] The parties' willingness to enter into this provision might be tempered by operational considerations which might make it impossible to net amounts properly across a spread of transactions or of different currencies.

---

[22] ISDA Master Agreement, s. 2(a)(i).

[23] *ibid.* at s. 2(a)(iii).

[24] *ibid.* at s. 2(c).

2.5.6 Witholding Tax

The parties will generally contract to make all payments without deduction of tax. That means that any tax required to be withheld by a party as a result of any withholding tax will have to be paid by that party but also means that the counterparty is still entitled to receive the full amount owed to it. Therefore, in situations where any witholding tax will be liable from the inception of any transaction, the parties may choose to gross up the amounts to be paid.[25]

If a witholding tax is introduced at a later date after entering into the transaction, the party resident within the tax jurisdiction by which the regulation has been introduced (and which will therefore be required to withold the taxable amounts) must provide certificates to the counterparty to evidence the regulation providing for the withholding of tax. Master Agreements include the introduction of a withholding tax as a termination event: the ramifications of this provision are discussed in greater detail below.

2.5.7 Delayed Payments

The Master Agreement should also make provision for the payment of interest by any party which defaults on or delays any payment for whatever reason to make up for the loss of the use of that money to its counterparty.[26]

2.5.8 Representations

A number of substantive legal issues are discussed below but among these are matters such as the capacity of the parties to enter into derivatives transactions. It is usual therefore in a Master Agreement to have the parties make representations as to their competence and as to the formal validity of their entry into the contract.

When dealing with counterparties which are not recognised swaps dealers, careful consideration must be given to the capacity or power of the counterparty to enter into swaps transactions. The capacity of the counterparty normally depends upon the laws under which it was organised and its constitutional documents. If swap transactions are not within the powers of the counterparty, the swap contract may not be enforceable against that counterparty.

Companies in most jurisdictions when organised have specific objects and are given specific powers and are limited to the pursuit of those objects and the exercise of those powers (together with any implied or incidental powers) in order to protect the shareholders of those companies

---

[25] *ibid.* at s. 2(d).
[26] See, *e.g.* the discussion above with respect to Extraordinary Events at para. 2.4.12.

from misuse of company assets by the management. Historically in common law jurisdictions trading companies have had quite limited powers, although the trend of recent decades has been to expand those powers.

Authority 2.5.9

The question of authority is to do with the authority of the signatory to enter into the contract on behalf of the company.[27] This is a sub-division of the capacity of the company to enter into the contract itself, discussed at "Capacity" below[28]. Under normal principles of agency law, an agent (a signatory on a document for example) cannot have a greater capacity to act than the company itself. This principle has been somewhat complicated by the Companies Act 1989, which altered the way in which the *ultra vires* rule works.[29]

The representation which is usually sought is that the signatory, as listed on any signatory register, does have the authority to do what that signatory is purporting to do. Furthermore, it is usual to ensure that the necessary formalities within the company have been performed and that any necessary consents have been obtained.[30]

Capacity 2.5.10

The capacity issue relates to the ability of the company itself to enter into derivatives transactions on the basis of its constitutive documents.[31] The representation is therefore that the entity does have the ability to do what it is purporting to do under the Master Agreement. The fact that a representation is made raises the ability of the party to sue the counterparty making the representation, for a breach of that representation. It would clearly be possible to assert that that representation was a material inducement on the part of the parties to entering into the contract, on the basis that they would not have done so without such assurance. The request for legal opinions and evidence of authority, which are discussed below, raise this representation from the status of being simply a clause in a standard agreement to something upon which the parties were relying in the formation of this contract.

The result of an argument based upon material reliance upon a representation is then that there is some restitutionary remedy resulting from its breach. This is parallel to the arguments in *Westdeutsche Landesbank Girocentrale -v.- London Borough of Islington* which is considered in

---

[27] ISDA Master Agreement, s. 3(a).
[28] At para. 3.5.
[29] See the discussion at para. 2.5.10.
[30] In the wake of issues like the Barings crash and the Proctor and Gamble failure, the issue of internal control and consents can be expected to become ever more important.
[31] ISDA Master Agreement at s. 3(a).

some detail in the section on breach of warranty[32] and restitutionary remedies below. That case provides some authority for the point that there can be restitutionary remedies available in a situation where lack of capacity is the issue preventing enforcability of the derivatives trades. It also demonstrates that there can be no specific efficacy of a representation that the contracting party has the capacity to contract. Therefore, there will be no liability for damages arising from the breach of warranty. The approach of the Master Agreement must therefore be to initiate automatic termination of the contract.

2.5.11   Illegality

Illegality of the contracts could result in any one of a number of situations.[33] Some of the principal examples are given below:

- Where it is illegal to enter into any trade based upon a single type of derivative. For example, it might be illegal to trade in an off-exchange option to go short on a share, after a Master Agreement, entered into to facilitate such transactions, became illegal
- Where it is illegal for a particular type of entity to indulge in a particular form of transaction: e.g. for French investment funds (SICAVs) to enter into derivatives with entities other than French registered banks.
- Where a particular form of activity related to derivatives becomes illegal, eg: by the re-interpretation of a form of Shia law in an Islamic state which would prohibit any dealing to do with interest including interest rate swaps.

The representation sought is that there is no illegality at the inception of the Master Agreement which would make any of these types of contract illegal in any of the places where they are to be performed. There is a question as to where a derivatives contract is performed and also as to what systems of law have an effect on the conduct of the transaction. As is discussed elsewhere, market practice is not to transgress any system of law (for example, with reference to a domestic stock exchange) by dealing on its shares outside the jurisdiction. There are conflict of laws issues here though as to the applicability of a system of law in extending its jurisdiction beyond its geographic boundaries. Illegality in the place of performance and also illegality in another jurisidiction are both points dealt with below in the 'Conflict of Laws'[34] section.

---

[32] At para. 3.13.
[33] ISDA Master Agreement s. 5(b)(i).
[34] At para. 3.6.

Regulatory Approvals 2.5.12

This issue revolves around the required representation that all regulatory approvals to perform the derivatives contract have been obtained.[35] The issue here is clearly very similar to that with illegality, in that the result of a failure to obtain regulatory approval will generally result in an illegality in the performance of a contract.

Legal Validity of Obligations Assumed 2.5.13

The parties attest to the efficacy of the Master Agreement which they have contracted.[36] The representation should include reference to there being no known reason why the contract should not be valid under any system of law relevant to the contracting parties.

Absence of Litigation 2.5.14

The parties represent that there is no outstanding litigation which will prevent the parties from performing their obligations under the Master Agreement or any transaction under it; nor would any such litigation mean that either party would be unable to perform under any of its representations.[37]

Tax Representations 2.5.15

One of the principles on which derivatives transactions are carried out is that there is no witholding or other tax payable by either party. Payment of tax would clearly distort the pricing structure of the derivative product. The use of tax representations aims to ensure that both parties establish both the legal and the factual foundation for there being no withholding tax payable by either party under a derivatives transaction contracted under the terms of the Master Agreement.

The representation only relates to the law as it exists at the time of the creation of the Master Agreement. The issue is then with reference to the introduction of witholding tax after the Master Agreement has been executed. The approach of the ISDA Master Agreement is to use a system of gross-up provisions to allocate the burden of reponsibility for payment of the tax to either the payer or the payee of the payment attracting withholding tax.

Therefore, the general obligation is on the payer to gross up in respect of a sum which it is required to withold where the tax is payable because of a connection with its chosen tax jurisdiction. In all other cases, the payee will suffer the cost of the tax.

---

[35] ISDA Master Agreement s. 4(a).
[36] *ibid.* s. 3(a).
[37] *ibid.* s. 3(a).

There is a different procedure if the liability arises as a result of a change in the tax law of the relevant jurisdiction. Under the ISDA code the Master Agreement becomes terminable at the instance of a party which is required to account for witholding of tax on payments made under a transaction governed by the Master Agreement. This will be a Termination Event only where the requirement to withold arises because of a change in the tax law or as the result of an alteration of the counterparty's corporate structure.

Payee representations are continuous throughout the life of the Master Agreement. There are few jurisdictions which do impose a witholding tax. However, it may be that in some jurisdictions, the payee would be required to provide evidence for the payer that it qualifies for the relevant exemption from witholding tax. The payee will also rely on any relevant tax forms which are provided to it by the payer.

Inability to provide requisite information or to ascertain the tax position of either party, will not necessarily preclude the execution of a Master Agreement nor of the conduct of effective transactions between the parties. However, the tax element is vital to a derivatives transaction and therefore the parties should seek specific advice based on their own tax positions.

The detail of the tax provisions is dealt with in the Tax chapter below at Part 5, para. 5.1.

2.5.16 Accuracy of all Information

Given the importance to the risk management function of the parties, that representations are made as to status, capacity and tax position, it is important that all of the information given is accurate. The failure to provide accurate information or for all the representations to be accurate, is the power to terminate the Master Agreement.

2.5.17 Termination of the Master Agreement

The ISDA Master agreement has a two-tier system of termination.[38] The agreement is differentiated between events which could be said to be the "fault" of one of the parties and events which occur as a result of circumstances beyond the control of the parties.

The first category are called Events of Default in the ISDA Master Agreement and the latter are called Termination Events.

---

[38] *ibid.* at ss. 5 and 6.

Events of Default   2.5.18

Failure to Pay

The most important event is that of a failure to pay by either party. Clearly payment on a timely basis is the essence of the contractual intention of the parties. Generally the term will contain a grace period (subject to the payment of interest as indicated above) to cover for administrative error or another event which might legitimately be said to have interfered with proper payment.[39]

Breach of Contract

Any breach of a material term of the contract is specified as an event which will trigger the termination procedure and removes the need for the parties to rely on the general law of contract.[40]

Failure of guarantee

As a credit related point, the failure of any party specified anywhere in the documentation to provide any guarantee or other form of credit support to the party to the master agreement, will result in the triggering of the termination procedure. This provision should aim to cover the bankruptcy of the guarantor or any other event, such as merger or takeover which effects its ability to continue to meet its obligations under the guarantee. There is a problem of monitoring for the parties involved to ensure that, not only are all of their swaps counterparties still of sufficient credit worth but that all relevant affiliates are as well. Therefore, it is advisable for the contract to provide that the contract will be voidable at the behest of the non-defaulting party within one week of discovering that the event has taken place but that the contract shall be treated as being void from the time of the last netted payment before the credit event took place. This leaves it open to the parties to decide to continue with the transaction or to have a new guarantee put in place by another party or to have collateral provided.[41]

Misrepresentation

To obviate the need to rely on the general law of contract, the parties will tend to provide that in the event of any misrepresentation made by either of the parties, the termination mechanism shall be triggered should the non-defaulting party consider the misrepresentation to be material.[42]

---

[39] *ibid.* at s. 5(a)(i).
[40] *ibid.* at s. 5(a)(ii).
[41] *ibid.* at s. 5(a)(iii).
[42] *ibid.* at s. 5(a)(iv).

Cross Default

The Master Agreement encompasses all the derivatives transactions entered into between the parties which express themselves as being governed by it. The contract may choose to make explicit the inter-linking of these transactions with reference to triggering the termination procedure by expressly including all contracts referencing themselves to the Master Agreement such a default under any one transaction will trigger an event of default in all of the other transactions under the Master Agreement.[43]

Credit Worth

The parties may decide to include within the scope of the events of default, defaults by other group entities in respect of specified types of transaction (whether it be derivatives transactions or term loans or bond coupon payments). This will enable the counterparty to protect itself against a general deterioration in the group's credit worth.

Corporate Restructuring

Alterations in the corporate structure of the parties are events which may alter the counterparty's view of the credit risk of the transaction. Therefore it will prefer to have any form of re-organisation, reincorporation or takeover included among the elective events of default. By maintaining the elective nature of the default, the parties can choose whether or not they wish to activate it: the newly formed entity may be of a suitable credit worth for the transaction to be novated into it.[44]

Bankruptcy

The most straightforward event of default is that of bankruptcy. Clearly, insolvency would make it impossible to perform future obligations under the Master Agreement.[45]

2.5.19 Non-Fault Termination Events

Illegality

The representation (discussed above at paragraph 2.5.11) given by the parties in usual circumstances, is that there is no illegality at the inception of the Master Agreement which would make any of these types of contract

---

[43] *ibid.* at s. 5(a)(vi).
[44] *ibid.* at s. 5(a)(viii).
[45] *ibid.* at s. 5(a)(vii).

illegal in any of the places where they are to be performed.[46] The purpose of including this provision as a Termination Event is to enable the parties to seek a means of negotiating their way out of the illegality situation. Where such avoidance is impossible, it will remain open to the non-defaulting party to terminate the agreement.[47]

Tax Event

One of the principles on which derivatives transactions are carried out is that there is no witholding or other tax payable by either party. The representation only relates to the law as it exists at the time of the creation of the Master Agreement. The representation is made specifically with reference to the tax regulations of the tax jurisdiction through which the representor is acting for the purposes of the relevant transaction. Where a witholding tax is introduced after the Master Agreement has been executed, the Termination provision enables the parties to terminate the contract.[48]

Tax Event Upon Merger

There is similarly provision for termination where a merger or reor-ganisation of a counterparty causes a Tax Event, as discussed.[49]

Credit Event Upon Merger

The provisons dealing with the credit implications of merger are dealt with below at 2.6.7.[50] The events which should be covered with reference to a company include:

- consolidates or amalgamates with another entity; or
- merges with or into another entity; or
- transfers all or substantially all its assets to another entity; or
- reorganises, incorporates, reincorporates as another entity; or
- reconstitutes into or as another entity;
- and, at the time of such consolidation, amalgamation, merger, trans-fer, reorganisation, incorporation, reincorporation, or reconstitution.

The concept of merger should also be extended to cover any entity which is guaranteeing a transaction or providing collateral[51], and also to any applicable affiliated entity of the counterparty. The merger provisions

---

[46] Illegality in the place of performance and also illegality in another jurisidiction are both points dealt with below in the 'Conflict of Laws' section.

[47] ISDA Master Agreement at s. 5(b)(i).

[48] *ibid.* at s. 5(b)(ii).

[49] *ibid.* at s. 5(b)(iii).

[50] *ibid.* at s. 5(b)(iv).

[51] In ISDA, a 'Credit Support Provider'.

ensure that the credit protection afforded by the Master Agreement is replicated in the future when the counterparty may choose to restructure its business. If companies within the group are recapitalised or any guarantor alters its business or asset allocation, the credit decisions made become useless. Therefore, the party is advised to retain the ability to terminate the transaction.

2.5.20 Early Termination

The appropriate Master Agreement will set out the manner in which the Master Agreement shall be terminated as a result of a Termination event or an Event of Default. In the ISDA Master Agreement this is set out at section 6. The mechanism for bringing the contract to a close is then provided at the discretion of the non-defaulting party in the case of a termination event. The usual mechanism is to provide for notice of termination to be provided by the non-defaulting party. This might be obviated by the agreement of the parties where they opt for automatic termination of their contractual relations.

One-way and two-way payments

The issue which has arisen with reference to the evolving ISDA master documentation, has been the method of making payments on closing out the transactions between the parties. One-way payments is the situation where the non-defaulting party is not required to make payments under the master agreement. Under the two-way payment system, both parties are required to make payments contractually due on the happening of an event of default.

2.5.21 Transfer

In the derivatives markets, the transfer clause is becoming more and more important.

There are two arguments which would seem to negate the efficacy of transfer clauses at English law. The first argument is that no transfer can be legally valid unless it is affected with the consent of the other party. The second argument is that a contract to make another contract in the future is invalid at English law.

The first argument is partially correct. It is impossible to transfer one's contractual obligations. It is only possible to vest contractual obligations in another party where both parties to the contract consent to such an assignment. This assignment is therefore in truth a novation of the contract rather than the transfer of contractual obligations.

When this issue arises in the case of master agreements, it is usually with reference to a clause inserted in the schedule which seeks to allow the financial institution, typically, to transfer its swaps books between different entities. If the parties agree to a master agreement with a transfer clause in it, then it can be said that both parties *have* consented to the transfer of the obligations into another entity. There should be care taken at this point in time that a capital gains tax event is not triggered on the basis that a disposal has been made by one party to another for which a deemed value may be imputed to the disponor on the basis that the transfer does not take place at arm's length.

The second argument revolves around the rule that two parties to a contract cannot enter into a contractual term that they will contract about something else in the future. This is the criticism levelled at transfer clauses by some lawyers. What the transfer clause is in fact purporting to do is to provide consent at the time of the formation of the contract that consent is given for the performance of another contractual event in the future. What the clause does not do is commit the parties to create another contract in the future. Rather, the matter is decided at the moment that the contract is formed.

In any event, the efficacy of this rule is not entirely clear in the modern context. A futures contract to buy a commodity at some time in the future for a specified price is no more an invalid contractual term than the transfer clause. Similarly, the older caselaw relating to pre-emption rights over land, such that the freeholder can be committed to offer land for sale to the owner of the pre-emption right.

Miscellaneous   2.5.22

Multibranch Parties

There may be circumstances in which one or other of the parties is seeking to transact through more than one jurisdiction or through more than one branch. There must be consideration given to the potential regulatory, legal and tax effects of dealing through the named jurisdictions and offices.

Expenses

The Master Agreement will deal with the issue of expenses incurred in the event of any dispute arising between the parties. It will also be required to set out the allocation of expenses where transactions are cancelled and there is the cost of acquiring new derivatives or unwinding a hedge, to be considered.

Governing Law and Jurisdiction

The choice of governing law is a central issue in the field of conflict of laws. This book is predicated on the basis that English law will be chosen.

2.6 The Schedule

The Schedule to the documentation is the arena in which the counter-parties seek to control their legal risk. This is the portion of the docu-mentation which is negotiated between the parties. The usual method of negotiating these documents is an exchange between the parties of their own standard form schedules which seek the maximum advantage for the institution involved.

Commercially there are very different impulses behind different types of institution in entering into these transactions. Deposit-taking banks will be eager to remove deposits from the category of liabilities which are taken into account for credit purposes. Corporate entities will seek to have such deposits included within the scope of credit events, given that they constitute accounting liabilities for the deposit taker.

The dilemma for the legal adviser is drawing a line between winning the war of the contracts over a counterparty and managing legal risk effectively.

The major categories of legal risk dealt with in the schedule are:

- Credit risk
- Alteration in corporate structure
- Insolvency
- Default under the terms of the Transaction
- Tax

2.6.1 Credit

The inter-action between legal decisions and credit decisions is important for the management of legal risk. The lawyer is activating, in this section of the contract, commercial decisions made with reference to the perceived credit worth of the counterparty.

2.6.2 The Parties

There are two central questions:
1. which counterparty company should be made a party to the contract?
2. which counterparty group companies should be referred to in the contract for credit control purposes?

The first stage in the documentation is to identify the relevant parties to the transaction. Derivatives business is frequently conducted through special purpose vehicles. In the case of financial institutions this is often to ring-fence derivatives business for regulatory purposes: either to centre transactions on a company which is overseen by a specific regulator or which is beyond the jurisdiction of that regulator.[52]

---

[52] Many American financial institutions conduct much of their derivatives business through offshore institutions to elude the jurisdiction of the CFTC.

From a credit perspective there is a difference between the entity which conducts the derivatives business and the counterparty's most credit worthy company. The ISDA code works on the use of affiliated companies.

The primary risk is that the core company in a group of companies goes insolvent but the derivatives transactions are contracted with a different company. The counterparty would then not be a creditor of the core company. What the counterparty would want to do is terminate the transaction with the contracting party in circumstances where the counterparty's core affiliated company goes insolvent.

Selection of the appropriate counterparty company to make a party to the contract or to incorporate by reference into the credit provisions, is therefore a centrally important credit decision.

The standard ISDA schedule includes these provisions under the 'Part 1 Termination Provisions'; accentuating the focus on the preference of the parties to terminate the contract should the counterparty go bankrupt.

ISDA works by isolating each "Specified Entity" to be incorporated into the contract for the purpose of establishing the counterparties' credit worth. Usually parties will specify either affiliates, or particular group companies with reference to the credit support issues detailed in the ISDA standard form of contract.

The definition of entities which are included for credit support purposes creates the total set of companies whose default in the types of transaction referred to, will initiate a Default. Parties are therefore eager to have as few of their own companies and as many of their counterparty's companies and affiliates listed as possible. This provision refers to default under a Specified Transaction (any derivatives transaction) and is usual to include all relevant group companies in this provision. Clearly, if any company in a group has defaulted under another derivatives transaction, you want to make sure that that constitutes a default under your own. (This type of provision is, however, the very thing which contributes to the likelihood of Systemic Risk discussed below.) (vi) refers to cross default in any form of Specified Indebtedness (virtually any debt, as discussed) and it is in the interests of everyone to see as many companies as possible involved here for their own credit purposes (see below). (vii) refers to bankruptcy other than in a corporate reorganisation: this is such an extreme credit event that all relevant group operating and holding companies should be involved. (iv) refers to misrepresentation made by a provider of credit support and is surprisingly often resisted by counterparties.

2.6.3 Cross Default

Accelerated debt and non-contingent default

The Cross Default provision aims to incorporate a default by a company which, while not a party to the contract, is affiliated to one of the parties. The aim is similar to that discussed at [1] above. Party A seeks to ensure that where Party B's affiliated companies default on some other transaction which affects their cumulative credit worth, Party A will be able to terminate the contract with Party B.

There are a number of alternative means of structuring this provision.

Scope of companies covered

The aim of the provision is for Party A to include any company affiliated to Party B which enters into transactions which impact on the credit of Party B or its ability to make payments under the derivatives contract.

Scope of transactions covered

The second issue is the scope of the transactions which are to be covered. First, it might be that Party A seeks to include any derivatives transaction entered into by Party B's affiliate. This restricts the credit protection available to A to default by B's affiliate in the derivatives field. Alternatively, A might seek to include any debt transaction entered into by B's affiliate. This would include the repayment of any long- or short-term debt.

This provision is regularly included in Schedules to Master Agreements to remove the uncertainty involved in a "Specified Indebtedness" (discussed below) being capable of being declared. It could be that the indebtedness is one that is only capable of being declared if litigation to establish that fact is successful. This is an interpretation that would allow for vexatious claims and would therefore be likely to be dismissed by a court but the aim of this contract is to remove the need for visits to court and therefore it makes sense to remove the provision or rephrase it at this point.

The definition of debt should be made clear in the documentation[53]. As discussed above this definition of debt obligations may relate to all forms of indebtedness or alternatively a limited class. There are occasionally extensions made to this provision in respect of securities and even shareholdings in the corporate or entity counterparty. It seems extraordinary to introduce references to financial instruments which do not create a debt or repayment obligation on the counterparty. The mischief of the expression "Specified Indebtedness" is to capture events where

---

[53] In the ISDA document this is found at s. 14.

parties cannot repay or meet payment or other obligations with reference to any form of debt that they have. It is therefore not the right place to attempt to capture concerns about credit worth or the ability of the company to meet dividend obligations. It becomes a matter of general law as to whether or not a particular form of financial instrument imposes a debt-style payment obligation on the party concerned. As discussed, it is best to consider an extension to the definition of Specified Indebtedness to that effect.

> "Specified Indebtedness shall have the meaning specified in Section 14 with the proviso that "indebtedness" shall include any obligation to pay or provide value in relation to any security or financial instrument that is not made at the discretion of the payer or any Specified Entity listed above."

If the counterparty is a depository institution the following is sometimes added:

> "except that, in respect of Party B, such term will not include deposits received by it in the ordinary course of its banking business" because there are so many deafults on deposit taking business that it would be a great burden on such an institution to have them included."

It may be that the parties do not want to have another currency involved other than US dollars or such other currency as is deemed appropriate by them.

Scope of defaults covered   2.6.4

Default under derivatives transactions, or debt more generally, could include one day's lateness in meeting a payment obligation or it might require the repudiation of a debt / transaction by B's affiliate.

From Party B's point of view, there is an advantage in narrowing the type of obligation that is covered by this provision. Restricting the category of applicable obligations to senior, rated long-term debt is the solution least likely to expose Party B to the risk of having its derivatives contracts terminated as a result of default by its affiliates. A broadly drafted provision which encompasses any late payment of any debt obligation, would make termination more likely.

Credit impact on the counterparty   2.6.5

B will usually prefer not to give such an extension to cover its affiliate. A compromise which is occasionally reached is to restrict the operation of such a provision to circumstances in which there is in fact an impact on B's own credit worth.

Consider the following scenario: B is guaranteed by its parent holding company C. The affiliated entity included in the cross default provision is

D, one of the chief operating entities owned by C. Where C guarantees B, it would be a question whether or not C's own guarantee is of sufficient worth to maintain the credit profile of the transaction between A and B. Where collateral is deposited with A, B might not be in a significantly worse credit position, in the context of the derivatives transaction, than where D had not repudiated its obligations. Therefore, it is possible for A and B to agree on a formulation in which A is enabled to evaluate the credit profile of B (in line with specifically enumerated criteria) before activating its power to terminate the contract.

There is an election between the parties as to the applicability of Cross Default. The parties would generally prefer Cross Default not to apply to them so that the activities of other elements of the same group of companies do not affect their credit standing in respect to the swap transaction. There is always the danger that if ISDA Agreements are negotiated separately with different terms, there will be a greater likelihood of default with reference to one form of ISDA than another. The problem is that most Agreements will have language to the extent that default under one agreement will of itself constitute an event of default under another swap agreement. From a credit perspective, it is preferable to have an event of default that includes Cross Default because it insures you against a worsening credit position in the group as a whole. The only other means of insuring yourself against such a worsening credit profile, that is not caused by the restructuring of the group, is to take out a guarantee from the ultimate group holding company. However, the wording of the guarantee or of the Master Agreement must enable the non-defaulting party to exit the swap transaction where the guarantor's credit worth or that of its associates deteriorates below a given level or at all. Negotiating this form of wording in the Master Agreement will probably be as easy as attempting to do it in a guarantee (given that many parties will not give a parental guarantee). Ultimately this is a decision that must be based on the credit standing of the counterparty and also taken with reference to the maturity of the transactions entered into.

2.6.6   The size of the default

There is clearly a need for a *de minimis* principle in the framing of these provisions. The danger is that a comparatively small failure to make payment will result in the cancellation of a considerably larger derivatives transaction. There are three difficulties here. First, a small default leading to the termination of a large derivatives portfolio. Secondly, the probablility that a small failure to pay by B will not be communicated to A either at all or not until some time after the failure occurred. It may be therefore that A acquires a right to terminate of which it has no knowledge. Thirdly, B's failure might be caused by a clerical or other error which was not envisaged as a default trigger in its derivatives documentation but which gives rise to a prima facie right to terminate nevertheless. The *de minimis* principle is designed to remove these potential anomalies.

The Threshold Amount is the minimum level of financial loss or risk, as appropriate that must be suffered or exposed before any of the default provisions will bite. Clearly, parties of the size that tend to enter into derivatives transactions are constantly exposed to enormous positions which occasionally go wrong. If there were no threshold, an enormous number of swaps and other derivatives would fail as a result of these small blips. The level of the threshold is then a credit decision based on the counterparty. The lower level provides a more sensitive marker but also exposes the party to a reciprocal obligation itself. Mutual shyness tends to set the level quite high.

Alteration of Corporate Structure 2.6.7

This section relates also to credit points with reference to the changed profile of the contracting party (or its affiliates). However, it also includes broader consideration of corporate capacity and insolvency regulation.

The principle commercial issue is the substantial alteration of the constitution of Party B such that Party A is dealing with a materially different entity from that originally contracted with.

Merger / Takeover / Reconstruction 2.6.8

There are three principle forms of corporate alteration in commercial terms:

1. merger: where the counterparty bonds with another entity
2. takeover: where the counterparty is subsumed into another entity
3. reconstruction: where the counterparty radically changes its internal constitution

Merger should also be extended to cover any entity which is guaranteeing a transaction or providing collateral[54], and also to any applicable affiliated entity of the counterparty.

The events which should be covered with reference to a partnership include:

- reconstitution,
- incorporation, or
- admission or withdrawal of a partner

The events which should be covered with reference to a trust structure include

---

[54] In ISDA, a 'Credit Support Provider'.

- reconstitution,
- incorporation, or
- admission or withdrawal of a trustee; or
- dissolution of a pre-ordained amount of the trust fund.

The events which should be covered with reference to a company include:

- consolidates or amalgamates with another entity; or
- merges with or into another entity; or
- transfers all or substantially all its assets to another entity; or
- reorganises, incorporates, reincorporates as another entity; or
- reconstitutes into or as another entity;
- and, at the time of such consolidation, amalgamation, merger, transfer, reorganisation, incorporation, reincorporation, or reconstitution:-
- or where the counterparty effects a recapitalization, leveraged buy-out, or other similar highly-leveraged transaction;
- and substitute in the contract the counterparty (in its new form) or any resulting, surviving, transferee, reorganised, or recapitalised entity.

2.6.9 Merger without assuming obligations of predecessor

The merger without assumption provisions[55] cover the situation in which the counterparty is reconstituted as part of another entity and that new entity does not assume all of the obligations of the counterparty or where any credit support documents do not cover such a new entity. The alteration in the schedule tidies and broadens the scope of the language in the standard terms. The merger event comes to cover a new host of sins. What is not clear is whether or not "reconstitution" covers terms such as re-capitalisation and leveraged buy-out dicussed below. It is to be presumed that they do not, given that lists including leveraged buy-out and re-capitalisation also include terms such as reconstitution and reorganisation. It must be presumed that reorganisation and reconstitution have more precise meanings than would appear to be the case on their face. Therefore it is suggested that this standard form of wording is expanded to cover all possible contingencies listed in the amendments to the schedule that are made below:

"The party or any [guarantor] of such party consolidates or amalgamates with, or merges with or into, or transfers all or substantially all its assets to, or reorganizes, incorporates, reincorporates, or reconstitutes into or as, another entity or X, such [guarantor], or such [specified affiliated entity], as the case may be, effects a recapitalization, highly-leveraged asset restructuring, leveraged buy-out, or other similar highly-leveraged transaction or as another entity and, at the time of such event as listed here:-"

---

[55] In the standard ISDA document contained in s. 5(a)(viii).

Continued Provision of Guarantees 2.6.10

There is then the issue of the continued provision of guarantees and collateral payment by an entity other than one of the contracting parties[56]. The documentation must contain provisions which obtain when materially another entity comes into existence. For example a provision which would operate to replace the contracting counterparty on the event of it undertaking action which:

> "reorganizes, incorporates, reincorporates, or reconstitutes into or as, another entity or X, such [guarantor], or such [affiliated entity], as the case may be, effects a recapitalization, leveraged buy-out, or other similar highly-leveraged transaction"

and substituting in the contract

> "the resulting, surviving or transferee" and "any resulting, surviving, transferee, reorganized, or recapitalized entity".

These suggested amendments will expand upon the usual credit event upon merger provisions, which often do not cover the full gamut of possible forms of corporate alteration. One regularly made amendment is to add the words:

> "or reorganizes, incorporates, reincorporates, or reconstitutes into or as, another entity or X, such guarantor, or such specified affiliated entity, as the case may be, effects a recapitalization, highly-leveraged asset restructuring, leveraged buy-out, or other similar highly-leveraged transaction";

instead of simply "another entity". The effect is to catch any transmutation into another corporate entity and also then to capture the range of financial transactions which might produce a result similar to a re-organisation. The expression "similar highly-leveraged transaction" is vague but attempts to provide a catch-all form of words which covers any attempt to redress the shareholding or asset base in a group of companies by the movement of funds within the group or the assumption of debt, or other form of funding, to perform any such reorganisation.

Creditworth after corporate reorganisation 2.6.11

This provision stipulates, as required by the Master Agreement, whether or not the merger provisions are to apply to the parties or not. It is possible to have them apply to one and not to the other. It is advisable to have these provisions in place even when a short term credit assessment indicates that it is possibly not important. The merger provisions, as

---

[56] In the standard ISDA document contained in s. 5(b)(iv).

discussed above, ensures that the credit protection afforded by the Master Agreement is replicated in the future when the counterparty may choose to restructure its business. If companies within the group are recapitalised or any guarantor alters its business or asset allocation, the credit decisions made become useless. Therefore, the party is advised to retain the ability to terminate the transaction.

2.6.12 Collateral Terms

Subject to the execution of a security agreement (the "Security Agreement") between the parties, the following provisions shall govern the payment and return of collateral hereunder until such time as the Security Agreement is executed and delivered, at which time the Security Agreement shall supercede and replace these provisions. Counterparty shall be the pledgor in respect of such Collateral (the "Pledgor") and GSI shall be a secured party in respect of such Collateral (the "Secured Party"). In order to secure its obligations under this transaction and any Specified Transaction entered into between the parties hereto prior to the date of this Transaction or hereafter (individually referred to as a "Transaction" and collectively referred to as the "Transactions"), the Pledgor hereby grants to the Secured Party a continuing first priority and perfected security interest in, and a lien on, all Collateral (together with all proceeds).

2.7 Tax Representations

The tax treatment of derivative instruments is dealt with in the "Taxation" chapter. The tax representations in Part 2 of the schedule are to do with the parties representing that there are no liabilities to witholding tax that will arise. Further, the parties represent that all relevant filing with tax authorities and so forth has been completed and undertake to furnish one another with all requisite documentation to satisfy their own, municipal taxation authorities.

ISDA Master Agreement form of Tax Representations

Payer Tax Representations

For the purpose of Section 3(e), Party A and Party B will each make the following representation:-

It is not required by any applicable law, as modified by the practice of any relevant governmental revenue authority, or any Relevant Jurisdiction to make any deduction or withholding for or on account of any Tax for any payment (other than interest under Section 2(e), 6(d)(ii) or 6(e) to be made by it to the other party under this Agreement.

In making this representation it may rely on:-

(i)   the accuracy of any representation made by the other party pursuant to Section 3(f).
(ii)   the satisfaction of the agreement contained in section 4(a)(i) or 4(a)(iii) and the accuracy and effectiveness of any document provided by the other party pursuant to Section 4(a)(i) or 4(a)(iii); and
(iii) the satisfaction of the agreement of the other party contained in Section 4(d).

Payee Tax Representations

For the purpose of section 3(f), Party A and Party B will make the representations specified below, if any:

(a) The following representation will apply to Party B but not to Party A:
It is fully eligible for the benefits of the "Business Profits" or "Industrial and Commercial Profits" provision, as the case may be, the "Interest" provision or the "Other Income" provision (if any) of the Specified Treaty with respect to any payment described in such provisions and received or to be received by it in connection with this Agreement and no such payment is attributable to a trade or business carried on by it through a permanent establishment in the Specified Jurisdiction.

If such representation applies, then:

Specified Treaty means the [UK]/[——] Double Taxation Convention.

Specified Jurisdiction means the United Kingdom.

(b) The following representation will/will not apply to Party A and/but will/will not to Party B:

(A)   It is entering into each Transaction in the ordinary course of its trade as, and is, a recognised UK swaps dealer for the purposes of the UK Inland Revenue extra statutory concession C17 on interest and currency swaps dated March 14, 1989, and
(B)   it will bring into account payments made and received in respect of each Transaction in computing its income for United Kingdom tax purposes.

Pre-contractual undertakings and procedure   2.8

In this part of the schedule, the mechanics of the performance of derivatives business between the parties is set out. To continue a simile used earlier in the book, this is one of the parts which sets out the rules of the game, whereas the confirmations will dictate the passage of play in any particular match.

2.8.1 Representations as to Powers

The issue of corporate capacity is one that is discussed elsewhere in this book[57]. This provision seeks to elicit from the parties a respesentation from each of the parties that it has the power to enter into thetransaction and that each individual who signed the agreement has the proper authority of the entity to bind it to the contract.

The representation will usually be to the effect that:

> "the individual(s) executing and delivering the Master Agreement (and any other documentation (including any Credit Support Document) relating to the Master Agreement)[58] are duly empowered and authorized to do so, and it has duly executed and delivered this Agreement and any Credit Support Document to which it is a party."

There are a number of legal issues arising from this representation:

1. Is it a warranty or a condition of the contract?
2. What is the effect of the representation if the entity does not have the authority to contract?
3. What is the effect of the representation if the individual signatory does not have the authority to contract?

2.8.2 Warranty or condition?[59]

There is a distinction in English contract law between a term in a contract that is a warranty that some action will be performed and a condition of the contract itself. A warranty entitles the non-contravening party to damages for its breach. A condition of a contract entitles a non-contravening party to rescind the contract: that is, to annul the contract *ab initio*.

2.8.3 Local Business Day

There is an important danger of a mismatch in circumstances where the parties are obliged, by operation of law or as a result of different jurisdictional business practices, to make payments on different days. Therefore, the scope of the relevant local business days on which the payments are to be made, must be provided for explicitly.

---

[57] At para. 3.5 below.
[58] Specifying perhaps that it is limited to documentation 'to which it is a party or that it is required to deliver as part of the terms of the Master Agreement'.
[59] This issue is discussed in greater detail at para. 3.13 below.

Procedures for Entering into Transactions 2.8.4

Agreement to Deliver Documents

The documents listed in this section are those required to meet the capacity problems dealt with in "Capacity" below. In general they are legal opinions attesting to the capacity of the entity to enter into swaps, documentation to show that all internal procedures have been complied with and copies of the entity's constitutive documentation (articles of association and so forth).

Miscellaneous further provisions 2.8.5

This section will contain the following:

Information Addresses for supplying notices and further documentation, etc. Details of a Process Agent, if applicable.

Multibranch Parties it may be that one or other of the parties wishes to conduct business out of a number of different locations. There may be tax or other legal implications involved in this decision.

Calculation Agent the purpose of this provision is to determine which of the parties will be responsible for all calculations and determinations under the Master Agreement. Such a provision may be made subject to the review and agreement of the other party.

Guarantee and credit support documents details of any Credit Support Document, each of which are incorporated by reference into, and made a part of, the Master Agreement. They are also incorporated by reference into each Confirmation (unless provided otherwise in a Confirmation) as if set forth in full in the Master Agreement or such Confirmation.

Collateral documents this includes margin deposit agreements and deposit of collateral agreements[60]. This provision should also specify any guarantee documentation that is required with reference to the maintenance of collateral levels or the credit worthiness of any collateral that is provided.

Governing Law the Master Agreement will typically be governed by English and New York law.[61] The approach of this book is to assume

---

[60] As discussed in para. 5.5 below.
[61] While this is true of many derivatives master agreements it is not an immutable rule. One exception is the type of agreement which has been developed by the German and French Banking Associations. It is also possible to have the market standard documentation effected under a different governing law, however, there is always the risk of different legal treatment of some of the provisions of the agreement.

English law is the governing law. The provision usually provides: 'This Master Agreement is governed by, and construed and enforced in accordance with English law'.

Jurisdiction the choice if jurisdiction is usually taken to match the Governing Law in transnational contracts. However, the choice of jurisdiction is a commercial one to be made by the parties. This is with reference to the single caveat set out above that the terms of the standard documentation will not necessarily translate to the procedural requirements of all legal jurisdictions. One condition that is frequently specified is that the jurisdiction is the exclusive jurisdiction of the chosen forum.

Netting of Payments it is preferable, for the reasons set out at paras. 2.9 and 3.2, that payments between the parties are set-off one against the other. There are two possible choices here. First, to set-off payments made with reference to a particular type of derivatives transaction carried out on the same day. For many institutions, this will cause logistical problems. Many operations systems cannot deal with netting on this scale across transaction. Secondly, netting can take place across currencies on a particular day. This route is often more possible for operations systems which acquire and pay amounts to market counterparts from a currency liquidity-management system in any event.

2.9 Set-off

The importance of the set-off provisions is set out in the section on netting on insolvency, discussed at para. 3.2 below. The mechanism for ensuring close-out netting is therefore essential. There are two generally used methods of effecting close-out netting. Samples of these methods, culled from those used in market standard documentation, are set out below.

The standard form of set-off provision in the ISDA documentation is in roughly the following format:-

"Any amount ("the Early Termination Amount") payable to one party (the Payee) by the other party (the Payer) [under the Termination Provisions in the Master Agreement], in circumstances where there is [one party which has contravened one of the Automatic Termination Provisions] or [one party in the case where an Automatic Termination Provision] has been contravened, will, at the option of the party ("A") which is not the party which has contravened the Automatic Termination Provisions (and where there has not been prior notice to that contravening party), be reduced by its set-off against any amounts ("the Other Agreement Amount") payable (whether at such time or in the future upon the occurrence of a contingency) by the Payee to the Payer (irrespective of the currency, place of payment or the place where the obligation was entered onto the books of either party) under any other agreement(s) between the Payee and the Payer or instrument(s) or undertaking(s) issued or executed by one party to, or in favour of, the other party (and the Other Agreement Amount will be discharged promptly and in all respects to the extent it is so set-off). A will give notice to the other party of any set-off effected under this provision.

"For this purpose, the Early Termination Amount (or the relevant portion of such Early Termination Amount) may be converted by A into the currency in which the other is denominated at the rate of exchange at which such party would be able, acting in a reasonable manner and in good faith, to purchase the relevant amount of such currency.

"If an obligation is an unliquidated amount, A may in good faith estimate that obligation and set-off in respect of the estimate, subject to the relevant party accounting to the other when the obligation is ascertained.

"Nothing in this provision shall be effective to create a charge or other security interest. This provision shall be without prejudice and in addition to any right of set-off, combination of accounts, lien or other right to which any party is at any time otherwise entitled (whether by operation of law, contract or otherwise)."

An alternative method of producing set-off would be as follows:

"In the event of an Early Termination Date, if the Contravening Party would be owed amounts under this Agreement in respect of the Transactions relating to such designation of an Early Termination Date which are terminated in accordance with the Early Termination Date, the Non-Contravening Party shall be entitled, within its own discretion, to set-off any obligations owed by the Contravening Party or any affiliated entities specified in this Master Agreement to the Non-Contravening Party ("the Obligations"), whether matured, unmatured, contingent, or otherwise, in any currency whatsoever, against the amounts owed under this Agreement by the Non-Contravening Party to the Contravening Party with respect to such terminated Transactions referred to above; and the obligations of the Non-Contravening Party under this Master Agreement in respect of such terminated Transactions shall be deemed satisfied and discharged to the extent of any such set-off. The Obligations, or any part thereof, may be converted in good faith at the applicable exchange rate at the time of such conversion into such currency as may has been designated in this Master Agreement by the Non-Contravening Party.

"The Non-Contravening Party shall have the right, exercisable within its own discretion, to designate any Early Termination Date (where an Automatic Termination Event has occurred) to be the Early Termination Date for any other [derivatives] Transaction entered into between the parties. Such designation shall be made by notice to the Contravening Party. The amount of any sums owed as a result of such designation shall be calculated on a mark-to-market basis by the Non-Contravening Party in good faith and in any event in accordance with the provisions of the Master Agreement.

"The Non-Contravening Party shall not be required to pay to the Contravening Party any amount until the Non-Contravening Party is satisfied that each derivatives Transaction has terminated and all amounts due and payable by the Contravening Party under each derivatives Transaction and generally under the terms of the Master Agreement have been fully and finally paid.

2.10 Transferability of Obligations

2.10.1 Transfer

A transfer clause permits the transfer of the Master Agreement by one party to another company without necessarily requiring the consent of the counterparty. The aim of such a provision is to reflect the modern market practice. As discussed above, there has been a movement towards banks using separately capitalised vehicles to do their derivatives business, primarily so that they are in a better credit position when dealing with large corporates. As such, banks have begun to transfer their "swaps books" (trading operations) to specialist entities. It may also be that these new entities will only want to take part of the swaps business with them (*e.g.*: the ability to do commodity swaps). Therefore there is a preference on the part of the banks to preserve the ability to move the obligations around at will.

There is of course a tension between this and the desire for credit event upon merger clauses which prohibit the transfer of ISDA obligations to new group companies. It might make more sense to provide an alteration to the Credit Event upon Merger clause rather than introduce this separate provision which is seemingly in conflict with the ability to call an event of default when that entity transforms. The comfort offered to the counterparty is usually a parental guarantee that will cover the new entity or a representation as to the credit worth of the new entity.

As discussed above, while the new derivatives vehicles have been AAA rated so that they can deal with the large corporates, the increasing use of deriviatives might change this. As corporates of a lower credit worth use swaps, it is likely that the AAA rating will come under pressure from BBB credits. Therefore, the banks may choose to use vehicles for high rated business and for low investment grade business.

2.10.2 Severability

If any term is held to be invalid or unenforceable (in whole or in part) for any reason, the remaining terms continue in full force and effect as if this Agreement had been executed with the invalid or unenforceable portion eliminated, so long as this Agreement as so modified continues to express, without material change, the original intentions of the parties as to the subject matter of this Agreement and the deletion of such portion of this Agreement will not substantially impair the respective benefits or expectations of the parties to this Agreement provided, however, that this severability provision shall not be applicable if any provision of section 2, 5, 6, or 13 (or any definition or provision in section 14 to the extent it relates to, or is used in or in connection with any such section) shall be so held to be invalid or unenforceable.

Termination

2.11

Automatic termination on default

2.11.1

The issue is whether or not the parties want automatic termination to apply. The risk is that a counterparty may realise that its swap position, possibly with numerous counterparties if it is speculating, is in the money and that it needs to terminate the swap position without incurring unwinding fees. Therefore it may choose to cause a mandatory event of default to be activated so that the swap is compulsorily terminated and payments netted off. By barring this event, the parties achieve a result that is closer to a rolling creditwatch than a speculator's tool.

By precluding automatic termination but retaining the right to terminate, the party to a Master Agreement can balance the decision whether to terminate an unprofitable deal but be safe from the future credit risk, or keep a profitable position alive while taking a strong view on the future credit risk of a defaulting counterparty.

What is not clear is the estoppel position with reference to a party who chooses not to exercise a right of termination but who later chooses to terminate that swap at a time when the counterparty is forced into insolvency by the cost of termination. As a hypothetical situation, it does appear that the party is entitled to call for termination on the happening of a termination event or an event of default. The situation might be different where a party commits a Credit Event upon Merger, for example, and its counterparty chooses not to exercise termination rights. If that Event continues, the defaulting party is probably entitled to believe that the counterparty will not exercise rights of termination in respect of that event in the future and could continue in reliance on that fact. As a result, promissory estoppel would seem to apply.

The question then is whether the non-defaulting party can, on realising that the swap has fallen out of the money, engineer a "new" event of default. This could be done by writing to the counterparty to insist that continued behaviour of the sort specified by the Master Agreement would constitute a new event from that time. The correct view would be that there is no new event unless a different occurrence from that specified has actually taken place.

Payments on Early Termination

2.11.2

These provisions dictate the manner in which payments made as a result of an early termination are to be made.

The ISDA terminology "Market Quotation" will apply where the calculation of those payment amounts is made with reference to price quotations obtained from a given number of market participants who are market makers in the appropriate product. Roughly speaking, "Market Quotation" is the amount which the market would pay on the date of termination. The alternative method is that of "Loss" which requires proof of the loss suffered by the non-defaulting party. The latter method is often easier to police although it does have problems of evidence in terms of loss and also in taking into account the full range of issues which can be included in the scope of loss. The cost of unwinding hedging transactions is one matter which the non-defaulting party would usually seek to include in its calculations.

The remaining question is that of "one-way" and "two-way" payments between the parties.

2.11.3 "Termination Currency"

This provision speaks for itself: it decides in which currency the termination payments are to be made. There may be advantages in paying or receiving in a currency different from the contractual currency.

Part 3

The Legal Issues

Contents

3.1   Interest Rate Swaps
3.2   Netting on Insolvency
3.3   Automatic Termination
3.4   Restitution
3.5   Capacity
3.6   Conflict of Laws
3.7   Capital Adequacy
3.8   Political Risk
3.9   Agents and Fund Managers
3.10 Trusts and Fund Managers
3.11 Transfer Clauses and Novations
3.12 Gaming
3.13 Breach of Warranty
3.14 Suitability
3.15 Regulation

From the point of view of the lawyer, derivatives contain the seeds of greater complication than for even the banker or trader in the marketplace. The complex hybrid (and even the simple) instruments can be analysed in a number of different ways[1], which offers both difficulties and opportunities in identifying and exploiting legal arbitrage possibilities for tax and general regulatory purposes. Altering the structure of a derivative instrument therefore offers possibilities as well as risk.

This chapter considers some of the specifically legal problems which surround the derivatives market. The aim is to highlight issues drawn from other areas of law where the derivative products discussed in Part 1 are particularly susceptible to being rendered void or robbed of some of their legal efficacy. In Part 5 (Credit Risk and Collateral) below, the credit risks associated with derivatives and arising from their structure and commercial effect, are discussed. While this is a subject divorced from strictly legal analysis, there is credit risk associated with legal problems.

It should also be remembered that if a product can be repackaged as a different set of obligations and rights but with the same legal effect, it is possible to charge counterparties a lot more to use it. For example, as discussed, a swap can be analysed as a series of cash-settled interest rate forwards rather than one single agreement to make or receive payments on a series of pre-determined dates. The extension and use of this form of legal analysis in this way demonstrates that hybrid derivative instruments have been in existence for some time in derivatives theory and that they offer possibilities for legal arbitrage.

---

[1] As illustrated above in Part 2.

Example
A convertible security (that is a debt security that can be converted into common stock) can also be analysed as a security with an in-built option to convert into common stock where that option is capable of activation on a prescribed date. There are a number of structuring possibilities contained in these different analyses that make it possible to redefine the obligations between the parties. By altering the legal obligations built into the product, it is possible to arbitrage different commercial objectives in the light of comparative benefits in different financial markets.

As said earlier[2], a derivative is at root either an option or a forward or a swap. A swap can be defined as a series of forwards, as mentioned. A forward can be defined as two options exercisable on the forward date selected: either to put or to call. Therefore a swap could be defined as a series of twin options which are exercisable on a series of dates prescribed in the documentation. The benefits of the available means of *analysing* these products is that it enables the products to be *defined* in a number of different ways.

To avoid creating an option (perhaps for tax purposes it might be efficient to have a different set of obligations) it would be possible to use forward agreements. Similarly, it is possible to create capital or income payments to taste by selecting the form of product which allows for a one-off payment on the exercise of an option or provides for an income stream receivable on any one of a series of pre-determined dates.

The following are the range of the main legal issues which have arisen between market participants from the products discussed in Part 1 and the documentation set out in Part 2.

3.1 Interest Rate Swaps

3.1.1 Defining the Swap[3]

The lawyer is in the business of managing legal risk in dealing with derivative products. That there is commercial risk involved in derivatives transactions is not an argument which requires much corroboration in the current market conditions. The lawyer must therefore be Janus-faced: the client is as eager to find clever ways to get away from transactions, as structured ways of getting into them. Therefore, the availability of restitution is the most important issue for any lawyer dealing with the derivatives markets.

---

[2] See, *e.g.* paras. 1.3.1 and 2.4 above.
[3] "Trading in derivatives is a risky business." John Major, April 1995.

What are swaps to a trader?   3.1.2

The simplest of the derivatives is probably the swap. The concept is
disarmingly simple: you have an obligation which you do not like, so you
swap for one that you prefer. The legal analysis is not so straightforward.
Interest rate swaps are calculated with reference to a notional amount of
money. In most circumstances this amount of money will not change
hands. Therefore, the interest rate swap is built around the contract that
is entered into between the parties to the transaction rather than obligations with reference to any particular sum of money.

The Contract for Differences issue   3.1.3

It is a truism among participants in the swaps markets that their products
are not wagering contracts. That is not strictly the case. There are two
main decisions in which the status of swaps contracts has been considered.

As Lord Templeman put it in *Hazell v. Hammersmith & Fulham*[4], 'The
swap market enables a borrower to raise funds in the market to which the
borrower has best access but to make interest and principal payments in
its preferred form of currency... Swaps may involve speculation or may
eliminate speculation'. An interest rate swap is therefore an exchange of
cash flows the size of which will be decided by the movement in two
interest rates by reference to a notional amount of a specified currency.

Recently reported English cases has avoided the difficult task of analysing these products more precisely. The question remains important for
the lawyer seeking to analyse the obligations which are owed between
the parties. In the wake of the Barings collapse and the litigation involving
Orange County and Proctor and Gamble in the USA, it can no longer be
satisfactory that the products are left in the limbo of imprecise definition.

In *Morgan Grenfell v. Welwyn Hatfield DC*[5], Hobhouse J considered
the restitutionary possibilities in an interest rate swap contract but the
further, familiar issues of gaming and *ultra vires* arose. The plaintiff had
entered into a ten-year swap transaction with the defendant under which
the defendant was to pay a floating rate of interest to the plaintiff in return
for a fixed rate.

The defendant had entered into a parallel contract with a third party,
also a local authority, to pay a fixed rate of interest to the third party in
return for a floating rate of interest, also under an interest rate swap
contract. Both of the contracts provided that, according to the usual
market practice, the amounts of money actually paid between the parties
would only be the difference between the two amounts owed.

It was found on the facts that the contracts were entered into by the
local authorities as part of their overall budgeting strategies. The purpose

---

[4] [1991] 1 All E.R. 545 at 549–550.
[5] [1995] 1 All E.R. 1.

of the swaps transactions were that size of the interest payments owed by the local authorities on their debt portfolios could be controlled. As a result of the ruling in *Hazell v. Hammersmith & Fulham*, it became unlawful for local authorities to enter into these transactions.

Hobhouse J considered, *inter alia*, whether or not swaps contracts are contracts for differences within the meaning of the Gaming Act 1845. In analysing the payments before him, he found the following:

'Since they provide for the payment of differences they are capable of being entered into by way of gaming or wagering. They have, at least potentially, a speculative character deriving from the fact that the obligations of the floating rate payer are to be ascertained by reference to a fluctuating market rate that may be higher or lower than the fixed rate at any given time. Such a contract is capable of being entered into by two parties with the purpose of wagering upon future interest rates.'[6]

In *Hazell v. Hammersmith & Fulham*[7], Lord Templeman identified the transactions which the local authority was conducting as being with 'no other interest than seeking to profit from interest rate fluctuations'. As Hobhouse J pointed out, '[Lord Templeman] rejected the argument that what the council was doing was undertaking a form of insurance and connected that it was more akin to gambling than insurance.'[8] However, as Hobhouse J continues with reference to the contracts before him, 'prima facie they are legitimate and enforceable commercial contracts'.

As his lordship continues:

'The mere fact that there is a provision for the payment of differences does not mean that the contract must be a wagering contract...If either party was not wagering, the contract is not a wagering contract.' The question remains then: what if there was wagering as part of the transaction? Is it still possible that the transaction could be found to be a wagering contract? 'If there was an element of wagering in what Islington did, it was merely a subordinate element and was not the substance of the transaction and does not affect the validity and enforceability of the transaction.'[9]

That was true on the facts of the case but the court is not precluding the possibility that there will be cases in which the activity *is* purely speculative. The cosy market consensus that there is no contracts for differences problem with interest rate swaps, is left in an equivocal position by *Morgan Grenfell v. Welwyn Hatfield DC*.

---

[6] ibid. at 7.
[7] [1991] 1 All E.R. 545 at 549–550.
[8] [1995] 1 All E.R. at 8.
[9] ibid. at 9.

How is a lawyer to analyse swaps? 3.1.4

At a greater level of complexity, are interest rate swaps contracts executory contracts or are they mutual debt obligations?[10] The form of restitution that is available depends on the legal analysis of the product. The availability of restitution is the most important issue for any lawyer dealing with the derivatives markets.

The 'executory contract analysis' maintains that interest rate swaps do not give rise to debts: whether or not ascertained debts and whether or not contingent.

In the mind of the trader, a swap is often analysed as a series of forward transactions. A 'forward' is an obligation to pay an amount of money, on a given date, for a given product calculated by reference to market movements. A swap contract requires payments of interest on a series of dates, calculated by reference to interest rate movements. On each of the interest payment dates, it could be said, there is a forward payment. How does the notion of a whole executory contract (looked at across the complete series of payments) fit in with the analysis of a swap as a series of interest rate forwards? The question then is whether a forward itself would be a simple obligation or an executory contract. There would seem to be no reason why a forward should not simply be an obligation to pay a debt calculated by reference to interest rates at a given time.[11]

The role of the set-off provision in market standard documentation may affect this analysis. By catering for the set-off of obligations, there is a presumption raised that each of the series of transactions is a reciprocal debt. The contract specifically approaches the individual transactions as standing separately and being capable of off-setting.

The approach of the documentation is usually to create a Master Agreement, which operates as an umbrella agreement. Each individual transaction is then expressly incorporated into that Master Agreement. (This is the scheme in all of the principal market standard agreements.) There are therefore two possibilities. First, the swap is an executory contract which requires elements within it to be off-set to reach the final, payable amount. Secondly, it is a series of reciprocal debts which are individually off-settable under the terms of a central Master Agreement.

The form of the documentation would therefore suggest that the individual interest rate swaps must be considered to be separate contracts. The question remains whether or not they are individual debts or individual executory contracts. There is no reason in principle, why they should be executory contracts. The more rational solution is that they are reciprocal

---

[10] It should be conceded at the outset that the executory contract analysis is supported by analogy with Foreign Exchange cases: *Re British Continental Bank* (1922) 2 Ch. 575; *Lisser & Rosencranz's Claim* (1923) 1 Ch. 976; *Bank of India v. Patel* (1982) 1 Lloyds Rep. 506.

[11] Executory contract analysis is supported by analogy with FX cases: *Re British Continental Bank* (1922) 2 Ch. 575; *Lisser & Rosencranz's Claim* (1923) 1 Ch. 976; *Bank of India v. Patel* (1982) 1 Lloyds Rep. 506.

debts linked by a Master Agreement for the purposes of set-off. The Master Agreement requires that money is paid by each of the parties. It does not require that a delivery of money is made by one party for the other to have to make the reciprocal payment. Either party could be sued for a debt on the basis that it fails to make any payment.

The only circumstance in which the payments are linked to one another is in the settlement procedure whereby each party agrees in the Master Agreement whether or not to set-off amounts owed to one another either on the same day or in the same currency. This is not the same as being reciprocal.

The reciprocity arises from the obligation to pay floating rate being set-off against the fixed rate payment. The issue of debt or executory contract turns on the chose in action. If A fails to pay, B can sue for the payment. This does not exclude B's obligation to pay A under the parallel leg of the interest rate swap.

It is argued by some commentators that, if the swap contract does create reciprocal obligations to pay debts, it would be for the gross nominal value of the debt owing to it. However, it is not clear why it would be for the gross nominal value rather than a contract for a stream of payments. The debt analysis turns on there being a chain of debts, grouped in pairs. The gross nominal value is not the defining issue. As explained above, the deciding question is on what basis either party can sue.

The question of which analysis wins out, might be decided on the basis of what the documents say. The documents will usually provide for a series of reset dates on which payments are to be made. Alternatively, the better analysis of a particular contract might be one agreement which requires action on a series of dates.

Market standard swaps contracts contain provisions for the early termination of the transaction, either because of the default of one or other of the parties, or as a result of the agreement of the parties. How does this early termination provision affect the definition of the swap contract? Is this the termination of an executory contract or the extinction of a chain of mutual debts? Early termination terminates all of the resulting transactions. This would seem to indicate a composite agreement requiring a series of payments. However, losses or gains flowing from terminated executory contracts would be categorised as ordinary debt. Therefore, there is little practical difference in the two analyses for this purpose.

The answer, it is suggested, will turn on the approach taken by the contracting parties. The intention of the trader is to mimic the forward transaction. If the aim of the parties is to create a series of forward transactions, that would appear to be the most appropriate solution to the issue of whether the interest rate swap is a forward or composite executory contract.

Restitution and Swaps Contracts   3.1.5

Some of the main results following from the preceding analyses are:

Damages

Under an executory contract to exchange money, the prime remedy of a willing party against a repudiating party is for damages equal to the contemplated loss suffered after exercise of the duty to mitigate. The measure of damages would often be any excess cost in replacing the contract in the market plus any special damages. The damages may be pre-determined by liquidated damage clauses, such as those represented by the ISDA termination provisions, in accordance with normal contractual principles.

Rescission

The appropriate remedy of a solvent party in the event of the repudiation by, or insolvency of, the counterparty is to rescind the contract. If the contract represented claims for debts both ways, then unquestionably the solvent party could not cancel its obligation to pay vested debts to the insolvent party and so full, reciprocal rescission would not be possible.

In the event that the executory analysis is followed, rescission would be possible on the basis that the condition precedent to execution, had not been performed. Rescission plainly requires placing the parties in the position they occupied previously.

Where there is only a liability to make payment one way at the date of completion, due to set-off, the availability of reciprocity is altered and it may affect the suitability of rescission. At first blush, rescission is made simpler by the composite executory contract analysis because it makes calculation of the amounts to be repaid more straightforward. However, the incorporation of separate contracts into a single Master Agreement, makes it equally feasible to achieve rescission across the spread of swaps transactions.

Specific Performance

Specific Performance is not usually available for an executory contract of this type. This is because damages are invariably an adequate remedy. The authorities with reference to a contract to pay a loan, satisfy the proposition that courts will not exercise their discretion to grant specific performance where damages could satisfy the remedy. Therefore, specific performance will not be appropriate for cash settled deals under the executory contract analysis.

What if physical delivery is appropriate? Physical delivery may be appropriate in foreign exchange transactions where the notional amounts *are* occasionally paid or in some equities transactions where physical settlement of shares are required. This, it is submitted, is a ground upon which one could distinguish the loan cases and look to specific performance even on an executory contract basis.[12]

However, the mutual debts analysis permits of specific performance of each of the debts. The ideal restitutionary solution might therefore be for rescission or specific performance to be coupled with damages; which would only be possible under a mutual debts analysis.

In *South Tyneside Metropolitan Borough Council v. Svenska International Plc*[13] the financial institution Svenska had entered into the swap transaction for hedging rather than speculative purposes. The transactions were checked daily to ensure that they would not be exposed to the risk of interest rate movements. Svenska then sought to resist payment, where it had nothing to set against its losses, when the local authority ceased making payments under the swap contract. In following the House of Lords decision in *Hazell v. Hammersmith and Fulham*, Clarke J. would not derogate from the general principle that there was no justification for permitting the bank to rely on its supposition that the contract was valid. Svenska could not argue a defence of estoppel nor did Clarke J. consider it appropriate to allow a defence of change of position to be established here.

3.1.6 The Insolvency Aspect

The preceding analysis of the availability of restitution ignores the insolvency law analysis. There is no doubt that the advantage of the 'executory analysis' of a swaps contract is that it permits of close-out netting of transactions where one of the parties becomes insolvent. The 'mutual debts' analysis causes different problems.

Rescission is altered by the insolvency of one of the parties. It is clearly impossible to rescind mutually where one of the counterparties has become insolvent. Further to *British Eagle International Airlines v. Air France*[14] divestment of insolvent's assets is against the spirit of the bankruptcy laws. *British Eagle* on its face suggests that executory contracts therefore may not be rescinded on the insolvency of a counterparty, even if there is a clause to that effect in the contract, and provided that no asset has been transferred under the contract from the insolvent party. The only qualification to this argument, under the executory analysis, is that no asset must have passed under the contract to the insolvent.

However, an express clause in a derivatives document providing for rescission, it is suggested, will be valid.[15] In the absence of a rescission

---

[12] *South African Territories v. Wellington* [1898] A.C. 309; *Astor Properties v. Tunbridge Wells* [1936] 1 All E.R. 531.
[13] [1995] 1 All E.R. 485.
[14] (1975) 2 All E.R. 390 HL.
[15] See, *e.g. Ogdens v. Nelson* [1905] A.C. 109.

clause, the position of the liquidator with reference to undertaking to perform the contract would be different, as in *Re Castle*[16].

Specific performance is not available for executory contracts in most circumstances because damages will be an adequate remedy. In the case of an insolvent counterparty, specific performance would be an impossibility in most practical circumstances in any event.

Set-off is possible even in cases of insolvency. In *Shipton Anderson & Co v. Micks Lambert*[17], a buyer's right to rescind a commodity contract was upheld when the seller ceased payment under an express termination clause.

The tidier analysis from the insolvency point of view is the composite executory contract view. The mutual debts analysis imports complications of performed and unperformed, and separately enforceable obligations.

Conclusion   3.1.7

None of the analyses has total claim to truth. However, depending on the circumstance, and the detail of the documentation, the individual lawyer's preference will probably depend upon which party is being represented and which form of restitution is being sought.

Netting on Insolvency   3.2

Netting   3.2.1

Netting is as effective (from the credit protection perspective) as taking security if it can be made to work effectively. The question is whether the single contract approach for netting across all transactions is effective. For there to be netting across transactions there must be "connexity" between the claims made. The statement at the beginning of the Master Agreement that all derivatives contracts are linked by expressing them-selves to be confirmations as defined by the Master Agreement and thereby governed by its specific legal terms, creates a connection between the various transactions. In the case of an interest rate swap and a bond option, there would not be any obvious connexity other than that the parties to the transactions were the same. There would not be enough connexity to make a lawyer comfortable without anything further, those two contracts were linked. The creation of the Master Agreement ensures that this connexity is established. In civil law jurisdictions there is a possibility that this approach does not establish connexity because it is a statement of form rather than substantive legal relations. The docu-mentation must therefore be explicitly structured to establish legal

---

[16] (1917) 2 K.B. 725.
[17] (1936) 2 All E.R. 1032.

relations on the basis of a connexity of relations, as discussed above at Part 2.

By creating a contractual right to set-off amounts owed by each party to the other, there does not need to be reliance on the general insolvency rules. The mechanics for set-off are established. Under English law all that is required is a right to terminate on insolvency. It must be a mandatory term of the contract that such set-off take place. To establish set-off, the amounts to be claimed must be liquidated: there must not be any uncertainty as to the amounts required to be set-off. The inclusion of formulae in the confirmations and the termination provisions in the Master Agreement should, between them, make the amounts certain for calculation purposes.

The Basle Committee of the Bank for International Settlements has begun to examine the issue as to whether or not netting should be recognised for capital adequacy purposes. The capital cost of doing derivatives business would be reduced where capital need only be set against a net position with a counterparty rather than the whole amount under each transaction. The one sticking point at the time of writing was whether this netting would include cross-product netting: that is, could banks set-off bond option obligations and interest rate swap obligations with a single counterparty.

The UK draft law

The question is who should bear the burden of making payments to do with the cost of unwinding a swap. In the case of certain events of default or termination events, there is no 'fault' attaching to either party, such as in the event of force majeure or supervening illegality.

Payments due under the Master Agreement will be made by applying set-off: in the case of two-way payments, the ideal system would prevent closure to realise in the money swap transactions. There is no means of netting fairly unless a provision is inserted to cater for instances where either party 'engineers' an event of default. This would prevent cherry-picking as well by allowing termination set-off on the 'genuine' happening of the events leading to termination. There could then be a provision which provides for set-off on the situation of a party choosing to unwind the swap by an alteration of the terms of the confirmation notice.

The Financial Law Panel has published a proposal for the explicit recognition of close-out netting under English insolvency law. It remains to be seen whether or not this statement is adopted into statutory insolvency law.

Executory contract analysis

Where the derivative instrument is analysed as an executory contract, on the insolvent winding up of one of the parties, mutual executory contracts entered into before the insolvency petition can be terminated at market

124

value. Where there is a provision in the Master Agreement to the effect, gains and losses on a series of terminated transactions can be set off. The standard provisions in the ISDA form of Master Agreement will operate to allow for netting on insolvency where there are two-way payments. It is advisable, from an insolvency perspective, that there be a requirement for notice rather than automatic termination under an appropriate event of default in the Master Agreement. One of the difficulties with automatic termination is that of calculating the appropriate amount to be paid as at the termination date.

Contingent debt contracts

The provisions in the ISDA Master Agreement will provide for set off on the insolvency of one of the parties to a derivative instrument which provides for a contingent debt: for example, cash settled options, caps and floors. Where it is the seller of the instrument that goes into insolvency, the value of the claim under the contract will be available for set-off. Where it is the buyer of the instrument that goes into insolvency, it is likely that the value of the instrument at termination will be available for set-off. However, where the value at termination cannot be ascertained or accelerated, it is likely that set-off will still be available provided that the Master Agreement does not attempt to divest the seller of its obligations under the agreement. As above, it is preferable that there be two-way payments and that there be a requirement for notice before termination.

Rescission and Netting   3.2.2

The appropriate remedy of a solvent party in the event of the repudiation by, or insolvency of, the counterparty is to rescind the contract. If the proper analysis of the derivatives contract is that it represented claims for debts both ways, then unquestionably the solvent party could not cancel its obligation to pay vested debts to the insolvent party and so full, reciprocal rescission would not be possible. However, in the event that the executory analysis is followed, rescission would be possible on the basis that the condition precedent to execution, had not been performed.

The exposure on open transactions of the type under consideration is net and not gross on a corporate liquidation. There is as yet no case in which market close-outs have been prohibited by English insolvency law. Where there is only a liability to make payment one way at the date of completion, due to set-off, the availability of reciprocity is altered and it may affect the suitability of rescission.

The peculiarities of the ISDA Master Agreement complicate the picture with reference to close-out netting. There are a number of provisions which are not specifically recognised by English law. There is therefore a need to include a provision in the Master Agreement which provides for ineffective provisions to be deleted and for the remainder of the contract to continue in effect. The complication is clearly that a contract which has a part of its terms removed, will complicate the position as to rescission. Rescission in these circumstances is made simpler by the composite executory contract analysis because it makes calculation of the amounts to be repaid more straightforward. However, the incorporation of separate contracts into a single Master Agreement, makes it equally feasible to achieve rescission across the spread of swaps transactions.

The certainty of the netting position on swaps, collars, forwards and physically-settled options would be enhanced if full-two-way payments is adopted. In the case of caps, floors and cash-settled options, the adoption of full two-way payments is essential. The insolvency law position remains uncertain. There is no authority to suggest that the market standard derivatives contract structures will necessarily be made invalid.

3.2.3   Cherry-Picking and Payment Netting

Cherry-picking

Cherry-picking is the practice of corporate liquidators or receivers seeking to avoid all contracts which require the company to pay money to counterparties, while requiring that moneys owed are paid to the company in liquidation. In short, the selective performance of profitable contracts by the liquidator and the concomitant rejection or disclaimer of unprofitable contracts. If it is possible for the liquidator to pick and choose between the contracts, then it would be impossible for the counterparty to net its exposure to that insolvent party. The exposure to the insolvent company would be the aggregate amount of its losses to the insolvent company.

If netting is available[18], the counterparty would be able to set-off monies owed from monies receivable and pay or receive a net amount. The concomitant effect on market counterparties of a corporate insolvency therefore becomes more manageable.

Example
Therefore if A and B enter into five derivatives transactions, where A owes B GBP 10mm under three contracts and B owes A GBP 7mm under the remaining two contracts. B then becomes insolvent. B's liquidator will seek to cherry pick by giving effect to those three contracts under which A owes B GBP 10mm, while refusing to pay under the two contracts under which B owes A GBP 7mm. The Master Agreement must therefore provide that only net amounts should be paid on insolvency and therefore A would only be required to pay GBP 3mm rather than GBP 10mm.

In the case of an executory contract, there are two requirements to defeat cherry-picking:

---

[18] As discussed at para. 3.2 above.

- the solvent party must be able to rescind all of the transactions on the winding up of the counterparty; and
- the solvent party must be able to set-off all of the losses and gains on all of the transactions in the insolvent winding-up.

In the case of a contract giving rise simply to a debt claim, it must simply be possible to set those debts off on the insolvency of the insolvent party.

Payment netting

There is a risk involved with insolvency where the insolvency occurs in the time between the payment being made and reciprocally received under a derivatives contract. 'Delivery netting' is the situation where the solvent party makes its payment on the appointed day but the insolvent party fails to make its payment as a result of the insolvency. The exposure of the solvent party here is to the gross amount owed by the insolvent party. 'Open contracts' on the market contain the risk of acquiring a replacement contract on the open market. Depending upon the market movements, the potential loss on a 'delivery contract' may be greater or less than that on an 'open contract'. The cost of replacing a contract may rise between the striking of the transaction and the date for payment, such that the cost of replacement is greater than the amount of the money not received from the other party.

Many contracts will therefore contain a provision that amounts to be paid by one party to another on the same day may be paid net rather than gross. That is, the parties will not pay the full amounts to one another, but rather will pay only the net amounts. The issue here is one of the institutions' systems. It is possible that an institution will have the computer capacity to organise these payments where they are to be made in the same currency, where that is passed through a central foreign exchange department. However, different types of derivatives will often be transacted by different departments: *i.e.* commodity derivatives will be conducted in a different department from currency derivatives. Therefore, systems may not be able to net across different products. The lawyer must be aware of these commercial shortcomings and therefore of the legal risk involved in these legal documents. There is a risk of the mismatching of derivatives transactions.

There are possibilities where there is physical delivery that netting of amounts owed by one party to another (a possibility with the increasing use of commodity derivatives and equity derivatives). Under ISDA, the delivery netting takes place on the day that the reciprocal payments fall due and therefore few legal issues are raised.

3.2.4 Insolvency and the Master Agreement

The Master Agreement should seek to guard against the danger of insolvency as far as possible. The legal risks under English law can be managed to the extent set out in the preceding paragraphs. In dealing with other governing laws, it is clearly necessary to consult with local counsel as to the effect of insolvency of one of the parties. Particular attention should be paid to:

- Termination procedure
- Use of cross default language
- Confirmations to be linked under one Master Agreement
- Need to avoid mismatches between contractual terms; *i.e.* difference thresholds for loss
- Non-elective events of default
- Reputation risk caused by insolvency
- Use of English / New York governing law
- Contractual ability to negotiate a termination of an out-of-the money position for a fee

3.3 Automatic Termination

Automatic termination of an agreement preserves the parties from two risks. The first, is that there be a movement in the value of derivatives transactions contracted under a Master Agreement which increases the amount owed to the insolvent party. This position would be complicated if the Master Agreement were contracted under a governing law which did not permit close-out netting. The second danger occurs where neither party (or the solvent party only) do not have notice of the counterparty's insolvency. The insolvent party could continue to trade in derivatives without being able to make good amounts owed. An automatic termination provision ensures that the contract is brought to an end from the time at which the counterparty is effectively insolvent.

Such an automatic termination is possible and lawful under English law. Retroactivity in the relevant clause, does not affect this automatic termination applying. The retrospectivity of the clause could be activated, for example, by the discovered breach of representations made in the Master Agreement as to capacity, legality and absence of litigation.

Restitution

3.4

Rectification of Contracts

3.4.1

The Court of Appeal decision in *Britoil v. Hunt Oil*[19] considered the ability of contracting parties to rectify an agreement on the basis that it did not correctly reflect their common intention. Hunt Oil argued that a provision of the signed agreement failed to reflect the true intention of the parties and that this true intention could be found in an earlier and non-bonding Heads of Agreement letter (which was found to be equivalent to a draft of the final form of the contract) exchanged between the parties. Accordingly, they requested rectification of the signed agreement. The Court of Appeal made several comments about the availability of rectification in denying Hunt Oil's application:

1.   All complex commercial transactions are preceded by draft versions which gradually isolate ambiguities and disagreements between the parties, a court would generally be reluctant – as a matter of policy – to conclude that an informal document should be treated as a superior statement of the parties' agreement than the final and executed document. Any other policy would undermine the certainty that parties expect when they sign final agreements – if "the relevant document is a legally binding document, it is appropriate to hold the parties to the objectively ascertained meaning of the words used".

2.   The only way to obtain rectification is to show that, as a matter of fact, there was a common mistake which resulted in there being no legally binding force to the signed agreement.[20] The claimant bears the burden of proving that there has been a mistake which is common between the parties. The Court of Appeal refused to accept that there was a mistake simply on the basis of a disparity between the wording of the draft letter and the wording of the executed document. It was not enough that there was ambiguity between the wording in the two different documents. The Court of Appeal held that it would be necessary to show something with 'the objective status of a prior agreement', either written or oral, which provides the evidence of a continuing intention clearly different to that of the executed agreement, thereby proving the common mistake.

This decision has ramifications for financial institutions which act as managers of derivatives transactions. In documentation where the manager distributes selling information to investors, stating that the advertising material is not an offering document for the underlying financial product, these will be the only legally binding terms dealing with the constitution of the product, between the parties when the transaction is confirmed by telephone and telex/fax. In the case of warrant transactions, a final offering circular is distributed before the products are sold. There

---

[19] May 25, 1994.
[20] It should be remembered that meeting the standard of proof for this equitable remedy is difficult.

are difficulties in arguing that the initial documentation has the 'objective status of a prior agreement', given that it is stated not to be a binding document at all.

However, this document might constitute a material part of the terms of that agreement. A common mistake must be made by the contracting parties. However, a mistake that involves the manager will not be a common mistake because the manager is not a party to the contract. In the case of warrants, the commercial paper is generally issued through a third party in any event – therefore the manager is kept very much at arm's length. None of the defences[21] open to the manager will be open to the issuer because it is not party to all of the relevant discussions, between it and the investor.

3.4.2 Restitution and Swaps Contracts

(a) Executory Contract Analysis

Some of the main results following from the preceding analyses are:

Damages

Under an executory contract to exchange money, the prime remedy of a willing party against a repudiating party is for damages equal to the contemplated loss suffered after exercise of the duty to mitigate. The measure of damages would often be any excess cost in replacing the contract in the market plus any special damages. The damages may be pre-determined by liquidated damage clauses, such as those represented by, for example, the ISDA Master Agreement termination provisions, in accordance with normal contractual principles.

Under an executory contract to exchange money, the prime remedy of a willing party against a repudiating party is for damages equal to the contemplated loss suffered after exercise of the duty to mitigate. The measure of damages would often be any excess cost in replacing the contract in the market plus any special damages. The damages may be pre-determined by liquidated damage clauses, such as those represented by the ISDA termination provisions, in accordance with normal con-tractual principles.

Rescission

As discussed above, the appropriate remedy of a solvent party in the event of the repudiation by, or insolvency of, the counterparty is to rescind the contract. If the contract represented claims for debts both ways, then unquestionably the solvent party could not cancel its obligation to pay

---

[21] *e.g.* estoppel, which is probably open to the manager during negotiations.

vested debts to the insolvent party and so full, reciprocal rescission would not be possible.

In the event that the executory analysis is followed, rescission would be possible on the basis that the condition precedent to execution, had not been performed. Rescission plainly requires placing the parties in the position they occupied previously.

Where there is only a liability to make payment one way at the date of completion, due to set-off, the availability of reciprocity is altered and it may affect the suitability of rescission. At first blush, rescission is made simpler by the composite executory contract analysis because it makes calculation of the amounts to be repaid more straightforward. However, the incorporation of separate contracts into a single Master Agreement, makes it equally feasible to achieve rescission across the spread of swaps transactions.

Specific Performance

Specific Performance is not usually available for an executory contract: where that is the analysis of the derivatives contract. This is because damages are invariably an adequate remedy. The authorities with reference to a contract to pay a loan, satisfy the proposition that courts will not exercise their discretion to grant specific performance where damages could satisfy the remedy. Therefore, specific performance will not be appropriate for cash settled deals under the executory contract analysis.

What if physical delivery is appropriate? Physical delivery may be appropriate in foreign exchange transactions where the notional amounts *are* occasionally paid or in some equities transactions where physical settlement of shares are required. This, it is submitted, is a ground upon which one could distinguish the loan cases and look to specific performance even on an executory contract basis.[22]

However, the mutual debts analysis permits of specific performance of each of the debts. The ideal restitutionary solution might therefore be for rescission or specific performance to be coupled with damages; which would only be possible under a mutual debts analysis.

(b)   Mutual Debts Analysis

If the claims were reciprocal obligations to pay debts would be for the gross nominal value of the debt owing to it.

Some of the main results following from this analysis are:

---

[22] *South African Territories v. Wellington* [1898] A.C. 309; *Astor Properties v. Tunbridge Wells* [1936] 1 All E.R. 531.

Damages

Under an executory contract to exchange money, the prime remedy of a willing party against a repudiating party is for damages equal to the contemplated loss suffered after exercise of the duty to mitigate.

The mutual debts analysis would follow a similar analysis to that set out under the executory contracts analysis. A debt would have as damage for breach of contract the amount of money required to put the counterparty in the position occupied had the contract been performed. The measure of damages would often be any excess cost in replacing the contract in the market plus any special damages. The damages may be pre-determined by liquidated damage clauses, such as those represented by the ISDA termination provisions, in accordance with normal contractual principles.

Rescission

The appropriate remedy of a solvent party in the event of the repudiation by, or insolvency of, the counterparty is to rescind the contract. If the contract represented claims for debts both ways, then the solvent party could not cancel its obligation to pay vested debts to the insolvent party and so rescission would not be possible.

Rescission requires it to be possible for the parties to be placed in the position they occupied previously. The 'mutual debts analysis' enables a cleaner form of rescission because you only have to cancel one of two debts – in fact the executory contract falls down here because it makes rescission difficult on its own terms. The difference with there being mutual debts only one way at the date of completion is that it alters the availability of reciprocity and it may affect the suitability of rescission.

Specific Performance

Specific performance is not usually available for an executory contract of this type. This is because damages are invariably an adequate remedy. This proposition is satisified with reference to a contract to pay a loan.

3.5 Capacity

3.5.1 Capacity: the issues

The question of capacity is the one which has caused the most vexation in the area of the law affecting derivatives. While the problem may require reference to systems of law other than English law, this section will deal with the position at English law and consider some of the likely issues of

English law that will be raised by companies incorporated outside the UK before looking at some of the conflict of laws issues raised.

There are two problems to distinguish between when considering capacity:

1. can the entity purporting to contract enter into derivatives transactions?
2. does the person entering into the contract on behalf of that entity have the requisite authority?

The real risk of the incapacity of a counterparty is that of having the contract avoided ab initio and of suffering the cost of unwinding a hedge as a consequence. There will be cost involved in reversing a position.

Parties are often restricted to a limited number of types of transaction. Some financial institutions, for example, will be confined to transactions entered into for hedging purposes. Therefore, they will not be allowed to speculate on the movement of interest rates with derivatives.

Parties often attempt to give representations as to their ability to act in a derivatives transaction. These representations of themselves beg the question whether or not the entity has the capacity which it represents. Where a party represents that it believes itself to have capacity to enter into deriviatives transactions or where an agent can represent that she acts as a validly authorised officer of the entity, the question is still at large whether or not that entity can validly enter into the contract and whether that officer has been validly authorised. The vogue for obtaining lawyer's opinions that an entity has acted validly or that an officer is validly authorised, does nothing more than attest to the lawyer's own opinion of the law. The other party then has the benefit of the lawyer's professional insurance but does not necessarily have the comfort that a court will find that the entity and the agent were both able to act at law.

The position with reference to companies under the Companies Act 1985 has been improved from the point of view of the comfort of third parties by the Companies Act 1989, which is discussed below. Representations may serve to evidence the intention of the parties at the time to enter into a particular type of transaction but they would appear to have no greater efficacy than that.

One question which is not decided by the cases is the ability of a party to recover moneys paid as a result of the incapacity of its counterparty. There is a prima facie argument that the payments were made under a mistake of law: that mistake being that the counterparty was legally able to participate in derivatives transactions.

The Master Agreement should therefore contain representations as to the capacity of the parties and of their contracting agents. It should be an automatic termination event under the Master Agreement where any such representation is breached.

3.5.2 Capacity under English Law

When dealing with counterparties which are not recognised swaps dealers, careful consideration must be given to the capacity or power of the counterparty to enter into swaps transactions. The capacity of the counterparty normally depends upon the laws under which it was organised and its constitutional documents. If swap transactions are not within the powers of the counterparty, the swap contract may not be enforceable against that counterparty.

Companies in most jurisdictions when organised have specific objects and are given specific powers and are limited to the pursuit of those objects and the exercise of those powers (together with any implied or incidental powers) in order to protect the shareholders of those companies from misuse of company assets by the management. Historically in common law jurisdictions trading companies have had quite limited powers, although the trend of recent decades has been to expand those powers.

Swaps transactions raise questions of capacity for various reasons. Being a relatively new financial transaction, swaps transactions were not within the contemplation of the drafters of the constitutional documents of those companies and other entities. There is also relatively little case law on swaps, although it is growing.

In addition, swaps are not easily (if at all) classifiable in terms of older, better known transactions. For example, it is not necessarily to argue that because a company has the power to borrow, it has the power to enter into a swap even for hedging purposes, which except in unusual circumstances cannot be characterised as a borrowing. The alternative argument is that the power to enter into a swap is incidental to the power to borrow. This argument may appear particularly persuasive where the swaps transactions are entered into for hedging purposes. However, as the House of Lords held in *Hazell v. Hammersmith & Fulham*, there is no distinction yet drawn by the courts between hedging and speculative swaps transactions.

Finally, the fact that incompetent use of swaps might lead to sizable losses for a company raises the possibility that a shareholder or other interested party will seek to challenge the swap transactions on the grounds that they are not within the powers of the company. The question of capacity attracted much attention in connection with UK local authorities. The House of Lords in *Hazell v. Hammersmith & Fulham* held that all swaps, even those entered into for hedging purposes, exceed the powers of local authorities.

Regarding UK companies in general, the Companies Act 1989 has eliminated much of the problem that a contract for a transaction which is not within the powers of the company is (generally) unenforceable against the company. Some concerns remain in certain circumstances, as discussed at paras. 2.9.1 below. Other UK entities which require special consideration are building societies and insurance companies, discussed at paras. 2.9.2 and 2.9.3 respectively.

The position at English law can be stated with more confidence after the amendment to the 1985 Companies Act and the *Hammersmith and Fulham* decision.

Companies Act companies

3.5.3

s.35 and s.35A Companies Act 1985

s.35A adds a gloss onto the position before 1989 that there was to be some form of ostensible authority for a person who was not duly authorised to bind the company (although the company could ratify the contract. For this ostensible authority to be efficacious from the point of view of a third party, that third party was required to be acting in good faith. The position after the 1989 amendment is that the power of the board of directors, acting validly, was not to be subject to any limitation in the company's constitutive documents in conferring authority on its officers, from the point of view of a third party acting against the company. It should be remembered that the board of directors might only delegate a limited authority to an officer and therefore there is not necessarily carte blanche for any action by any officer of the company. In such a case, recourse must be had to the common law and the old rule of ostensible authority where there is an issue of a limited delegation. There is similarly complication in cases where an authority delegated to a committee of directors is then delegated to a particular officer. It may be that general rules of company law restrict the further delegation that power. It is therefore in the interests of the counterparty to ensure that the correct officer is acting.

Section 35(1) Companies Act 1985, as amended by the Companies Act 1989, provides:

> "The validity of an act done by a company shall not be called into question on the ground of lack of capacity by reason of anything in the company's memorandum."

This section covers transactions between persons dealing with the company and also any third party, or the company itself, invoking the invalidity of a transaction because it is *ultra vires*. Subsection 2 provides that a member of the company can bring proceedings to prevent the doing of an act which is beyond the company's capacity. Subsection 3 provides that it remains the duty of the directors of the company to ensure that the company does not do any acts beyond its constitutional powers.

Section 35A(1) provides:-

> "In favour of a person dealing with a company in good faith, the power of the board of directors to bind the company, or authorise others to do so, shall be deemed to be free of any limitations under the company's constitution."

135

The purpose of the section appears to be to provide that, in favour of a person dealing with the company in good faith, the board of directors shall be deemed to have authority to exercise all the powers of the company, except such as the Act requires to be exercised by some other organ,and to authorise others to do so, notwithstanding any limitations on the company's constitution on the authority of the board of directors.

Section 35a fails to provide adequate protection for the third party who has dealt with a different organ of the company. An organ of the company is probably identified by the company's constitution giving particular powers to a part of the company as a whole. It is not clear whether this would extend to a treasury function empowered separately from the rest of the company. The precise definition of the term "organ" remains unclear.

Under s.35A(2):-

> "(a)   a person "deals with" a company if he is a party to any transaction or other act to which the company is party;
> (b)   a person shall not be regarded as acting in bad faith by reason only of his knowing that an act is beyond the powers of the directors under the company's constitution; and
> (c)   a person shall be deemed to have acted in good faith unless the contrary is proved."

It is clear therefore that a derivatives transaction counterparty would be dealing with a company under this definition.

The Hammersmith and Fulham litigation[23]

It was found on the facts that the contracts were entered into by the local authorities as part of their overall budgetting strategies. The purpose of the swaps transactions were that size of the interest payments owed by the local authorities on their debt portfolios could be controlled. As a result of the ruling in *Hazell v. Hammersmith & Fulham*, it became unlawful for local authorities to enter into these transactions.

Hobhouse J considered, *inter alia*, whether or not swaps contracts are contracts for differences within the meaning of the Gaming Act 1845. In analysing the payments before him, he found the following:

> 'Since they provide for the payment of differences they are capable of being entered into by way of gaming or wagering. They have, at least potentially, a speculative character deriving from the fact that the obligations of the floating rate payer are to be ascertained by reference to a fluctuating market rate that may be higher or lower than the fixed rate at any given time. Such a contract is capable of being entered into by two parties with the purpose of wagering upon future interest rates.'[24]

---

[23] [1991] 1 All E.R. 545 at 549–550.
[24] ibid. at 7.

In *Hazell v. Hammersmith & Fulham*[25], Lord Templeman identified the transactions which the local authority was conducting as being with 'no other interest than seeking to profit from interest rate fluctuations'. As Hobhouse J pointed out, '[Lord Templeman] rejected the argument that what the council was doing was undertaking a form of insurance and connected that it was more akin to gambling than insurance.'[26] However, as Hobhouse J continues with reference to the contracts before him, 'prima facie they are legitimate and enforceable commercial contracts'.

As his lordship continues:

'The mere fact that there is a provision for the payment of differences does not mean that the contract must be a wagering contract...If either party was not wagering, the contract is not a wagering contract.' The question remains then: what if there was wagering as part of the transaction? Is it still possible that the transaction could be found to be a wagering contract? 'If there was an element of wagering in what Islington did, it was merely a subordinate element and was not the substance of the transaction and does not affect the validity and enforceability of the transaction.'[27]

That was true on the facts of the case but the court is not precluding the possibility that there will be cases in which the activity *is* purely speculative. The cosy market consensus that there is no contracts for differences problem with interest rate swaps, is left in an equivocal position by *Morgan Grenfell v. Welwyn Hatfield DC*.

Building Societies   3.5.4

Building societies are governed by a different system of legislation from the Companies Act companies. Section 23(1) Building Society Act 1986 enables a building society to:

"effect contracts of a prescribed description[28] for the purpose of reducing the risk of loss arising from changes in interest rates, currency rates or other factors of a prescribed description which affect its business."

There are three classes of building society:

- those which use derivatives for their full balance sheet;
- those which use derivatives to hedge a part of their balance sheet;
- those for which derivatives are prescribed.

Therefore, the question is whether or not a derivatives transaction is for the reduction of risk. The issue of the form of hedging used is therefore

---

[25] [1991] 1 All E.R. 545 at 549–550.
[26] [1995] 1 All E.R. at 8.
[27] ibid. at 9.
[28] "Prescribed contracts" are defined in the Building Societies (Prescribed Contracts) Order 1993.

important. The full and limited approaches to hedging strategies provide different evidence of corporate intention. A full hedge, is a hedging strategy which seeks to cover the whole of a risk. A limited hedge either covers only a part of the total risk or is only partly aimed at risk coverage. The question for these purposes is to identify the difference between a "hedge" and a "managed open position".

The central issue remains whether the test for the intention behind the hedge is a subjective one, that is dependent upon the declared animus of the building society and its officers, or an objective one, that is an imputed intention derived from all the surrounding indicators of the intention of the building society and its officers. The limited approach demonstrates that a particular class of assets or liabilities are being hedged and therefore it is easier to show the intention contained in dealing with them. The full balance sheet approach looks at the entire scope of assets and liabilities and seeks to manage the whole of those positions. This makes the demonstration of an intention more difficult because of the spread of assets involved and the necessarily different nature of the hedge.

There are two market practice attempts to cover up the risk involved in dealing with Building Societies:

1. Contract of indemnity by deed
2. Legal Opinion

The efficacy of legal opinions has been discussed above and it is evident that there is only a restricted level of protection afforded by having a legal opinion provided. The use of deeds, which create contracts, without the need for consideration to pass, should serve to create a form of collateral promise that will offer comfort to the counterparty. The problem involved with this approach is that the building society is simply attesting to its belief that it can enter into this form of transaction and is therefore simply making further representations. This will clearly depend upon the representation that is made in the deed by the building society which may of itself constituted an agreement which the building society is prevented from executing.

3.5.5 Insurance Companies

Under the Insurance Companies Act 1982 s.16(1):

"...an insurance company......shall not carry on any activities.....otherwise than in connection with or for the purposes of its insurance business".

The issue is therefore as to the freedom of insurance companies to enter into derivatives transactions. Hedging transactions would appear to be "in connection with .... its insurance business" where they manage risks.

However, by analogy with *Hazell v. Hammersmith & Fulham* litigation, there is no means of being entirely sure that hedging transactions will necessarily be separated out from speculative transactions for enforcement purposes.

Section 58 of the Insurance Companies Act 1982 enables courts to amend contracts entered into by insurance companies when those companies are unable to pay their debts, in situations that the court considers to be just.

Section 36 of the Insurance Companies Act, which has yet to be brought into force, provides that contracts entered into by insurance companies are void where the liability owing by the insurance company is uncertain at the time of the formation of the contract is ineffective. This provision has yet to come into effect and there is no timetable for its introduction currently. Therefore, the ability of an insurance company to enter into derivatives contracts, whether for hedging or speculative purposes, must be in question should this provision be activated.

Conflict of Laws   3.6

The question of capacity is one which applies to entities in all jurisdictions. For example in Islamic jurisdictions, the Shia law prohibits the payment and acceptance of interest but many jurisdictions refuse to allow banks to deal with warrants that are index-linked because that is a form of speculation which is also contrary to a strict reading of Shia law. There are laws in every jurisdiction which have the potential to affect the ability of specified types of entity to enter into derivatives transactions. There may similarly be conflict of laws problems with reference to the capacity of an entity to enter into these transactions under a contract whose proper law is English Law. An example might be the situation where the prohibition on action is a result of a penal or revenue law which English law will generally not enforce. There are those organisations, such as EEIB's which do not have a specific system of law governing their incorporation to and therefore the general rule as to allowing the law of incorporation to decide will not operate with reference to these entities which are organised on a supra-national level. It is likely that their constitutive documents will decide but the question is still at large as to which system of law will govern any points of interpretation.[29]

---

[29] There is insufficient space to consider the complexities of Private International Law here. Suffice it to say, that, in a trans-national market place like the OTC derivatives market, there is a need to ensure that choice of law and applicable law questions generally are carefully considered.

3.7 Capital Adequacy

The Committee on Banking Supervision which meets under the auspices of the Bank for International Settlements (the "BIS") issued the 1988 Basle Accord which set out a risk-based capital framework for banks which sets out capital requirements for interest rate and currency exchange rate contracts. The Basle Accord is currently being implemented in stages by the Bank of England.

Capital adequacy requirements increase a bank's cost of entering into swap transactions by limiting the volume of swaps banks can do and therefore exerting downward pressure on the bank's return on equity. The Basle Accord guidelines do not recognise the effect of netting on termination under Master Agreements, as discussed at para. 2.9. However, the regulations do recognise "netting by novation" in some foreign exchange contracts. This means that even though the overall credit exposure of a bank having several swaps with a counterparty may be small or nil, the capital required to support those swaps must be determined separately for each swap and may therefore be high.

However, the Basle Committee has recently proposed changes which would recognise bilateral netting for these purposes where agreed minimum legal requirements are met. Under current proposals, netting would not be permitted where the agreement allows a non-defaulting party to make limited payments or no payments at all to a defaulting party, even where the defaulter is a net creditor. As discussed [one-way or two way payments].

3.8 Political Risk

One significant legal aspect of political risk concerns the situation in which there is a transaction with a particular branch of a financial institution, and then a form of force majeure or general supervening illegality occurs which alters the ability of that branch to perform the terms of the contract as originally intended. It might be that one party is precluded from making payments under the terms of the contract by reason of the force majeure or some legislation which prohibits performance.

In documentation it is therefore desirable to provide that each party is dealing with the whole of the counterparty and not simply with any one branch. The notion that the contract is to be performed with the entire corporate group of the counterparty, obviates the risk that a particular transaction could be interpreted as having taken place with a single within the group or with a branch that does not necessarily constitute a legal person in its own right. In the event of force majeure or supervening illegality, a specific term that the two parties are dealing with the whole of one another's group companies ensures that it is the group to whom the party can look for payment and not simply a single, specified part of the group.

The situation where payments are made to a branch of a counterparty in a jurisdiction which is not the residence of the contracting party.[30] When conditions in the Philippines made it impossible for C to pay out of Manila, it was therefore in technical default under the Master Agreement with W. The documentation specified "C Bank, Manila Branch" as the party to the documentation. C claimed that its swaps documentation with W was limited solely to the Manila branch and not to the entire C group. Therefore, the Philippines entity was prohibited from performance under the contract. W argued that it had contracted with the entirety of C and not simply with the single Manila branch, which was not even incorporated as a separate entity. It was held that C was the legal entity which had contracted and that its Manila branch did not constitute a separate legal entity. Therefore the failure to pay was enforceable against C.

Agents and Fund Managers   3.9

Agents   3.9.1

This chapter focusses specifically on the role of agents acting on behalf of their principals in entering into derivatives transactions. The next chapter looks at a specific form of agent, the trustee, and considers the legal status of the derivatives instrument in the light of the more complex rules that exist for a trustee.

Fund managers pose a particular problem with reference to derivatives instruments. The derivative markets are more and more open to the investing fund managers who are seeking to hedge their positions with derivatives and to use the derivatives to speculate in the bond and equity markets. Fund managers act on behalf of investors who are usually not disclosed by the fund manager to the swaps counterparty, or only to a restricted number of officers of the counterparty. Therefore the counterparty is contracting with an agent and not a principal. As a result, all of the general issues as to capacity and insolvency are at large. From a commercial point of view, the counterparty does not know the credit profile of the investors in the fund.

The largest risk is that the undisclosed principal goes bankrupt and that the trustee in bankruptcy looks to the whole of the fund to meet the claims of creditors, thus leaving the swaps counterparty without recourse to any funds under the derivatives Master Agreement. There is no ability to check the authorisation of the fund manager to act without looking at the terms of the fund and the specific authorisations that have been given to the manager with reference to specific investments. The next chapter shall

---

[30] Such a case is the US case of *Citibank v. Wells Fargo*, unreported.

consider the terms of the trust fund but this chapter is concerned with actions against an agent in contract regardless of the more complex status of its trusteeship.

Hedge funds

There has been a large amount of adverse press about "hedge funds", so called, which are short term investors in the equities and bond markets who are moving more and more into derivatives markets. It is not unknown for the aggressive hedge funds investment strategies to produce 50 per cent to 70 per cent returns at a time when US money markets are producing a 3 per cent return. The crash in world bond markets in March 1994 were blamed on hedge funds taking aggressive stop-loss positions (which are a form of put option that provides that a security be sold once it touches a particular price so as to prevent any loss to the fund). The role of these funds was probably over-emphasised but the possibility of regulation of stop-loss tactics (blamed for the equities crash in 1987) and of hedge funds in general, indicates the commercial unease with which some of these institutions are currently viewed.

There is no knowledge of the underlying asset base of these funds which operate on the basis of movements of large amounts of cash. From the commercial point of view of the banker, or possibly even of the corporate treasurer, the attraction of dealing with the hedge fund is greater than it is for the lawyer. The obtaining of a guarantee of the fund is unlikely given that the principal remains undisclosed. Therefore the obtaining of collateral offers the best form of protection for the counterparty. It is a matter of commercial practice on what terms and for what amount of collateral will be available. The reader is referred to the more specific section on collateral below [at para. 5.5] but some more general comments will be made here with reference to fund managers.

It is important that the assets are held in an account and not subsumed within the fund where it is impossible to establish the priority of security before a tracing remedy is effected. The lawyer needs to be able to identify the security that will make up the collateral. The fund will not be eager to tie up cash assets in a static fund to provide collateral. Therefore the amount will need to be decided with reference to each confirmed transaction. It may be that the fund manager will be able to offer a pool of funds over which the party will have rights of recourse in the event of any default. However, a floating charge will not be able to establish priority of recourse of secured lenders to the fund and the creditors on insolvency of the undisclosed investors.

The importance of fund managers, including well-established pension funds now as well as hedge funds, will mean that there is a market need to regularise the obligations of funds under swaps and other derivatives agreements. The answer suggested elsewhere in this book is for the formation of a clearing house for option and warrant obligations and another specialised clearing house for currency and equity swaps transactions. The obligations of funds can therefore be netted off on a daily basis to reduce the overall outstanding amount left on the market and thereby reducing the systemic risk of the failure of a large fund owing money to corporates and financial institutions.

The introduction of money-laundering legislation to the UK in 1994 is a further reason for the imposition of tighter controls on the contractual obligations of fund managers under derivatives transactions.

Rights of principal against third party 3.9.2

Disclosed principal – generally a disclosed principal can sue the third party[31]. The third party cannot set-off against the principal any debt which the agent may owe to the third party[32] unless the agent has authority to receive payment this way.[33] That custom provides for such set-off is not adequate: rather there must be express permission.[34]

The issue is whether there is any defence of privity of contract where the principal was undisclosed. In the case of an undisclosed principal, the privity of contract doctrine still operates. The ratio for this rule is that, if the principal had been undisclosed, the contract could not have been made with that principal. The principal cannot interefere with such a contract[35] where if you wanted contract with a particular person and no one else, the third party can set-off debt owed by the agent.[36]

Trusts and Fund Managers 3.10

The preceding chapter dealt with the role of fund managers in the global derivatives markets and looked at the contractual obligations that exist between a party to a derivatives transaction, the fund manager and the undisclosed principal. This chapter considers the position of the fund manager as trustee of the fund which it manages.

Trustees are personally liable but can be indemnified from the proceeds of the trust fund, depending on the provisions of the trust fund in most circumstances. There can be no certainty under English law that netting will work in the case of trustees who go bankrupt or whose controlled funds go bankrupt.

There is one argument for regulatory reform that, to avoid the complexity of personal and proprietary remedies in the English law of trusts, trusts which invest in the financial markets should be required to incorporate

---

[31] *Langton v. Waite* (1968) CR 6 Eq 165.
[32] *Pratt v. Willey* (1826).
[33] *Stewart v. Aberdeen* (1838).
[34] *Pearson v. Scott* (1878) 9 Ch. D 198.
[35] *Collins v. Association Greyhound Racecourse* [1930] 1 Ch. 1.
[36] *Cooke v. Eshelby* (1887) 12 App Cas 271.

as investment companies which in turn are required to lodge collateral and/or margin with a centrally established clearing house. In the absence of the creation of a clearing house, the margin should be deposited as collateral in escrow where it can be obtained by the third party in a suit. There would be regulation to ensure the capital adequacy of the investment company to the clearing house or regulator.

The position of trustees under derivatives transactions does not differ from the position with reference to general investment of trustees. The documentation position is therefore complicated by the need to identify the correct contracting party, ensure that there is proper credit protection in place and to ensure that the counterparty is able to sue the relevant fund under the terms of the fund.

3.11   Transfer Clauses and Novations

It has become practice in international swaps market to create special purpose vehicles (SPV's) to conduct the institution's swaps business. This move was prompted by the deteriorating credit worthiness of the banks in the late 1980's and the difficulty they had in satisfying their corporate counterparties as to the financial risk involved in doing business with them. By creating and capitalising SPV's separately from the rest of the bank, it became possible to have a AAA credit rated entity which would satisfy the credit concerns of the corporate counterparties. The result of creating AAA rated entities, is that they cannot deal with counterparties of a credit rating of less than AA without risking the downgrading of their asset quality. Therefore there is likely to be a trend for the use of entities with a lower credit worth (probably AA) which can do business with counterparties of a credit rating lower than AA, without risking its own status.

The result of this manoeuvring is that the banks will need to relocate their swaps books within the group. This necessitates agreement with all the counterparties to the alteration of their contract with the bank. Therefore the banks have begun in many cases to argue that they should be allowed to have "transfer clauses" in their documentation which constitute an agreement between the parties that the bank will be able to transfer its obligations under the contract to another group entity. For commercial purposes, the clauses generally contain representations that the new entity will be of an equal or improved credit worth to that with which the counterparty originally contracted or that the group guarantee will necessarily be extended to the new entity.

There are two legal issues involved:

1. Are such contractual terms to allow relocation of the obligations valid *in se*?
2. To what extent can a party shift its obligations onto another entity?

It is argued that it is impossible to enter into an agreement to agree at English law and therefore that a purported transfer clause will not have any effect.

Gaming
3.12

Prior to the passage of the Financial Services Act 1986 in the United Kingdom, there was some doubt as to whether or not derivatives transactions would be unenforceable gaming contracts. *Morgan Grenfell v. Welwyn Hatfield District Council* (April 1993). Interest rate swap contracts would not, in the absence of other considerations, constitute gaming contracts but were commercial or financial transactions to which the law would give full recognition and effect. In addition, simply because a contract provides for the payment of differences does not mean that the contract will be a gambling contract. Such a provision would raise a rebuttable presumption that the contract was a gaming contract. However, the whole of the contract must be construed – if the whole of the document cannot be construed as having the character of a gambling contract, it will not be found to be a gaming contract.

Morgan Grenfell v. Welwyn Hatfield District Council is authority for the proposition that, provided that the intention of one party to the transaction is not gambling, the validity of the transaction will not be effected. On this analysis, where the intention of a financial institution is other than gambling (that is, that there is a genuine financial and commercial purpose) then the contract will be valid and enforceable.

What is not clear, is whether a genuine financial or commercial purpose will be evidenced only by a transaction which is a hedging transaction, using derivatives to manage risk, or whether it will include speculative activity which is intended to increase profitability. It is a feature of modern business practice that the Treasury departments of large corporate and financial institutions are required to move beyond efficient cash management towards generating profit from cash control activities to bolster the performance of operating units whose margins are being squeezed.

The court in *Morgan Grenfell v. Welwyn Hatfield District Council* found that the purpose of one of the parties was to realise a 'non-speculative profit', in which case the transaction was not gambling. Reference was made to 'dealing on a back-to-back basis with a variation of the terms so as to give it a built-in and assumed element of profit...by taking a turn on the interest rates or as in the present case by a difference in the up-front payment or premium that is provided for'.

3.13 Breach of Warranty

Westdeutsche Landesbank Girocentrale v. London Borough of Islington and *Kleinwort Benson v. Sandwell* raised a point concerning the British Bankers' Association Interest Rate Swap ("BBAIRS") derivatives contract which contained a warranty as to the capacity of the local authority to sign the contract and of the individual signing the contract to act as signatory.

It was held that the authority could not contract and therefore could not warrant its own ability to contract. The authority had mistakenly thought that its general power to borrow extended to speculative swaps transactions. Given that the authority could not itself contract, there could be no valid authority given to its agent which would be a larger authority than that held by the authority itself.

The court provided for a mixed equitable and legal remedy. The court provided for a remedy that was in part equitable tracing and part contractual breach of contractual warranty.

3.14 Suitability

Unfair Contract Terms Act 1977 ("UCTA")

One issue to arise under UCTA is that of financial institutions seeking to rely on their standard documentation when dealing with non-financial institutions. One of the issues to arise from the Proctor and Gamble litigation is that of suitability of derivative products for the clients who used them. Similarly, the documents used to transact 'unsuitable' derivatives may impose unsuitable obligations on counterparties where it is a standard form of documentation that is being used.

The question, however, is whether or not UCTA will be applicable at all. UCTA applies in situations where there is a "business liability" created over someone "dealing as a consumer". There will be a "business liability" where an act is done "in the course of a business". The more problematical part is where a person "deals as a consumer". It is a requirement that the contract is not made in the course of a business. It is difficult to conceive of circumstances where a party to a derivatives transaction would not be acting in the course of its business. Even a party which enters into derivatives only occasionally would appear to be in the course of its business and not as its consumer.

The question is then as to the position under the standard form contracts used to document derivatives transactions generally and specifically with reference to the provisions entered into between the parties as to remedies for specific breaches of the contract and termination events. The issue could be raised by a form of standard document used by a party who regularly enters into derivatives contracts. Many institutions use a standard form of schedule to an industry standard contract, as set out in Part 2. The first issue is whether or not this could be said to constitute a standard form contract of the particular entity in question.

One further question is whether or not section 11 of the UCTA will prohibit any derivatives transactions on the basis that they are extortionate credit bargains. In the main, the courts will find that any relief on the basis that a deal is extortionate, will not be available where the two parties are of equal bargaining power. However, the litigation commencing after the Procter and Gamble losses on 'high octane' derivatives, shows that this is perhaps not as straightforward as would seem to be the case.

The question of 'suitability' has grown up around this species of issue. The corporate client would argue that there is a duty of care on the part of the bank to ensure that the product being sold to it is suitable for it. Is there a duty of care extending beyond that usually owed to one requiring the bank to ensure that the product is appropriate for the particular client? The argument runs on the basis that only the banks know how the products work. There has been assertion in some cases that the banks have provided copies of their bespoke computer programmes to clients when selling them products. These programmes are sophisticated models which estimate the movements of the markets which will underpin the hedging or speculative transaction. What is not clear is whether or not the client is able to operate the model so that it can predict the effect of the product with an expertise that approaches that of the bank.[37]

This is an issue which should be considered in the general terms of business documentation entered into between the parties.

Regulation   3.15

Initially the swaps market was largely unregulated, primarily because the bank and securities regulators in various countries were unaware of the existence of swap transactions. Subsequently, regulators had some difficulty characterising the product for regulatory purposes because there was a lack of clear analogy to older, better known products. As regulators have assimilated themselves to the older products in the market for swaps and other treasury derivatives, newer products continue to be developed, each with potentially different regulatory consequences. For example, the commodity swap, which developed out of the interest rate swap market, initially gave rise to some difficulties with the US Commodities Futures Trading Commission ("CFTC") which had not arisen in connection with interest rate swaps.

Ironically, once the CFTC began considering commodity swaps, it also

---

[37] The truth of course is that, even if the client can operate the programme, the assumptions which underpin it (as to future interest rate movements, etc) are subject to violent change. An unexpected event of the magnitude of the Gulf War, for example, will radically alter any market predictions without being capable of being incorporated into model.

began considering, several years after the development of the US interest rate and currency swaps market, whether it should assert regulatory control over the whole, or at least some significant part, of the market. In July 1989 the CFTC published a statement outlining a "safe harbour" for swap transactions that would not be subject to CFTC regulation. The bulk of swaps products fall within that class of swaps.

In the UK, the primary regulation is conducted under s.48 of the Financial Services Act 1986 ("FSA"), Bank of England regulation of the wholesale money markets and the capital adequacy rules applicable to banks. Issues which had to be considered by lawyers in the early days of the swaps markets included issues arising under the Gaming Acts, the Insurance Companies Acts and other statutes and statutory instruments.

Securities regulation of the swaps market revolves, for the main part, around the FSA control of "listed money market institutions"[38]. One such institution, at least, will generally be a party to a swaps transaction. Provided that the notional amount of a particular swap is greater than £500,000, the listed institution is not generally subject to the requirements of the FSA in respect of such a swap but instead is subject to Bank of England regulation of the wholesale money markets.

---

[38] s.43 of the FSA.

Part 4

Taxation

Contents

4.1 Tax Provisions in Master Agreements
4.2 The Taxation of Financial Derivatives

Tax Provisions in Master Agreements   4.1

One of the principles on which derivatives transactions are carried out is that there is no withholding or other tax payable by either party. Payment of tax would clearly distort the pricing structure of the derivative product. The use of tax representations aims to ensure that both parties establish both the legal and the factual foundation for there being no withholding tax payable by either party under a derivatives transaction contracted under the terms of the Master Agreement.

The representation only relates to the law as it exists at the time of the creation of the Master Agreement. The representation is made specifically with reference to the tax regulations of the tax jurisdiction through which the representor is acting for the purposes of the relevant transaction. The parties will therefore also state the tax jurisdiction through which the transactions will be performed.

The issue is then with reference to the introduction of withholding tax after the Master Agreement has been executed. The approach of the Master Agreement is to use a system of gross-up provisions to allocate the burden of responsibility for payment of the tax to either the payer or the payee of the payment attracting withholding tax. Gross-up provisions require that the party bearing the burden of the tax account for the amount which would have been paid but for the existence of the tax together with the amount of tax due. Where the tax is imposed as a result of a voluntary nexus between the payee of the payment and the tax jurisdiction imposing the withholding tax, the payee will bear the burden of the withholding tax. However, if the tax arises otherwise than by voluntary nexus with the tax-imposing jurisdiction, the payer will be required to bear the burden of the tax.

Example
Where an English payee acting through its New York office receives a payment from a German payer acting through its Paris office, the English payee would receive a grossed up amount from the German payer for a tax imposed on that payment by the German or French tax authorities. This is because the tax is not imposed as a result of the connection between the payee and the taxing jurisdiction. However, if the tax were imposed by the UK or US authorities, that would be as a result of its connection with those authorities and therefore the payee would bear the burden of the tax.

Therefore, the general obligation is on the payer to gross up in respect of a sum which it is required to withhold, where the tax is payable because of a connection with its chosen tax jurisdiction. In all other cases, the payee will suffer the cost of the tax.

The exceptions to the above rule are generally twofold. First, where the payee has made a representation which is not true at the time it is made or which becomes untrue as a result of subsequent events. Secondly, where the payee fails to conform to a provision in the Master Agreement requiring performance of a tax-related obligation.

The parties will have to look to the structure of the tax representations. It is usual for a payer's representation to provide that it will not be required to withhold amounts from payments it makes. This in turn is usually predicated on the giving of reciprocal payee representations by the counterparty. Failure in the efficacy of either representation will therefore be a breach of a contractual term which will attract liability to account for the gross-up to tax.

There is a different procedure if the liability arises as a result of a change in the tax law of the relevant jurisdiction. Under the ISDA code the Master Agreement becomes terminable at the instance of a party which is required to account for withholding of tax on payments made under a transaction governed by the Master Agreement. This will be a Termination Event only where the requirement to withhold arises because of a change in the tax law or as the result of an alteration of the counterparty's corporate structure.

Payer Representations

The relevant jurisdiction will be:

- the jurisdiction in which the payer is resident for tax purposes;
- the jurisdiction where the office through which the payer is acting for the purposes of the transaction, is located;
- the jurisdiction in which the payer executes the Master Agreement; or
- the jurisdiction from or through which the payer makes its payments.

There are few jurisdictions which do impose a withholding tax. However, it may be that in some jurisdictions, the payer would require evidence from the payee that it qualifies for the relevant exemption from withholding tax. The payer will also rely on any relevant tax forms which are provided to it by the payee.

Inability to provide requisite information or to ascertain the tax position of either party, will not necessarily preclude the execution of a Master Agreement nor of the conduct of effective transactions between the parties. However, the tax element is vital to a derivatives transaction and therefore the parties should seek specific advice based on their own tax positions.[1]

The parties will also have to consider the position of tax payments with reference to interest on money held or paid, particularly where there is default interest. Again, this is a matter on which the parties should take specific tax advice.

The ISDA code provides for refusal to provide particular tax forms where it would 'materially prejudice the legal or commercial position' of the payee.

Payee Representations

The relevant jurisdiction will be:

- the jurisdiction in which the payee is resident for tax purposes;
- the jurisdiction where the office through which the payee is acting
- the purposes of the transaction, is located;
- the jurisdiction in which the payee executes the Master Agreement; or
- the jurisdiction from or through which the payee receives payments.

Payee representations are continuous throughout the life of the Master Agreement. There are few jurisdictions which do impose a withholding tax. However, it may be that in some jurisdictions, the payee would be required to provide evidence for the payer that it qualifies for the relevant exemption from withholding tax. The payee will also rely on any relevant tax forms which are provided to it by the payer.

Inability to provide requisite information or to ascertain the tax position of either party, will not necessarily preclude the execution of a Master Agreement nor of the conduct of effective transactions between the parties. However, the tax element is vital to a derivatives transaction and therefore the parties should seek specific advice based on their own tax positions.

Statements of Practice

Corporation tax deductions would usually require that payments made under swaps would be analysed as annual payments, which would require withholding tax under usual principles. The ESC C17 means that recognised swaps dealers do not have to withhold tax.

---

[1] There is a growing development of so-called "tax derivatives" which take advantage of the arbitrage possibilities offered by different jurisdictions' tax codes. The provision of cash flows from or to low-tax jurisdictions between parties whose tax status is clearly understood or requiring complex analysis, may generate cash flows with a net tax saving.

Finance Act 1993 regime

The provisions in the Finance Act 1993 relate specifically to foreign exchange transactions and therefore it is not proposed to deal with them in detail here. The concentration in this section is therefore on the 1994 Finance Act.

4.2 The Taxation of Financial Derivatives

4.2.1 Finance Act 1994 Part IV Chapter II ss. 147–177

This area is of interest to anyone working with financial institutions or companies which have foreign exchange or other sophisticated financial requirements. The derivatives market has grown at a speed which would put many viruses to shame: the current estimated notional size of the market is US$ 14 trillion. Of that US$ 14 trillion, the majority of activity outside the USA is conducted in London or through London-based dealing rooms. English law is the governing for those contracts – their tax analysis is therefore of great importance to the strategic managers of the financial institutions involved.

The taxation of financial derivatives is a confused matter. The bulk of the provisions dealing solely with 'interest rate contracts' and 'currency contracts' are contained in Finance Act 1994 Part IV Chapter II ss.147–177 ("Chapter II"). The restricted definition of the products which are included in Chapter II makes the task of analysing the regime all the more complicated. It is not clear in many circumstances where the general options taxing provisions in the legislation are to come when there is over-lap with the options on products falling within Chapter II.

The aim of this article is to provide a map to the statutory material and to explain how the regulation inter-acts with the broad range of derivatives products.

4.2.2 Summary of Finance Act 1994

All "qualifying contracts", comprising interest rate and currency contracts, entered into by companies will be within the new regime. The definitions judge the qualifying nature of a contract according to the type of payments which may fall to be made under it. An interest rate contract must contain a right or obligation to receive or pay an amount calculated by reference to a variable rate of interest. A currency contract must provide for an exchange of currency at the end of the contract's life. In each case, a number of other payments, including payments by reference to fixed interest rates, termination payments and payments of fees and expenses, are permitted. Options to enter into qualifying contracts or to acquire currency may also be qualifying contracts.

Although the definition leave some uncertainties the intention in that the majority of interest and currency swaps, caps, collars, floors, options and futures should come within the new regime. Contracts relating to equities, commodities and gilts will continue to be subject to the existing regime.

Qualifying contracts will be taxed or relieved in accordance with the amount recognised in respect of them in the company's accounts, provided that the accounts are in accordance with acceptable accounting principles and either adopt a mark-to-market or accruals basis as appropriate to the contract in question. Where the accounts do not meet these requirements, the company can agree an acceptable mark to market or accruals basis with an Inspector of Taxes.

The amounts recognised on the mark to market or accruals basis will be taxed or relieved as income. Case 1 treatment will apply if the contract was into for purposes of a trade and, in other cases, profits or losses will be amalgamated with and treated in the same way as profits and losses under the FA 1993 regime. Where the currency element of the contract is subject to the FA 1993 regime on currency swaps and futures special provisions apply to prevent double charging. All payments can be made gross, regardless of the identity of the counterparty.

There are anti-avoidance provisions which will disallow loss relief in relation to certain contracts which shift value away from the taxpayer, or which are entered into otherwise than on arm's length terms, or where the counterparty is a tax haven entity.

The new rules will automatically take effect in relation to currency contracts in existence on a company's first accounting period beginning after the date the legislation becomes operative but will not take effect for existing interest rate contract until six years later unless the company makes an election to the contrary. If an election is made, it will bind all UK group members. Transitional provisions will apply in relation to existing contracts.

Mismatches may still arise in relation to contracts which hedge debt assets or liabilities because the existing law will continue to apply to the debt itself. The remaining question is therefore whether the Inland Revenue will seek to extend the accruals or mark-to-market treatment to debt instruments.

Qualifying Contracts 4.2.3

An 'interest rate contract or option' or a 'currency contract or option' is a 'qualifying contract' for the purposes of the Act[2].

Qualifying contracts have reference to a 'qualifying company'[3] where

---

[2] s.147(1)
[3] s.147(1), defined in s.154

such a company 'becomes entitled to rights or subject to duties under the contract on or after its commencement day'[4].

Chapter II is to come into operation after the Treasury by order provides that its operation shall begin. For the purposes of Chapter II of the Finance Act 1994, a company falling within the chapter, is treated as becoming entitled or subject to interest rate or currency contracts at 'the beginning of its commencement day'. A 'commencement day' with reference to a company within the chapter is the 'first day of its first accounting period to begin after the appointed day'. The 'appointed day' is a day provided for by the Treasury by order[5].

4.2.4 Contracts which may be qualifying contracts

A company is a qualifying company if its commencement day falls within twelve months of the appointed day.[6] All 'quasi-qualifying contracts' which are held by a qualifying company within 6 years from its commencement day, are to be treated as if that company became entitled to them in the first accounting period after six years from that commencement day.[7] However, the qualifying company is entitled to elect that all such quasi-qualifying contracts became entitled on the commencement day[8]. Such an election is irrevocable.[9] With reference to groups of companies, only the principal company in a group can make the election.[10]

Section 170 of the Taxation of Chargeable Gains Act 1992 (to do with the chargeable gains of groups of companies for capital gains tax purposes) has effect for the purposes of section 148.

4.2.5 'Interest rate contracts' and options

A contract is an interest rate contract if:

a qualifying company is required to pay or can receive a variable rate payment[11]; and
the transfers of money or money's worth for which the contract provides fall within the categories set out at paragraphs [..] below[12].

As the section 149(1) of the TCGA provides: 'A *contract* is an interest rate contract..'[13]. There is a requirement that there be a contract. There is an

---

[4] s.147(1)
[5] s.147(4)
[6] s.148(1)
[7] s.148(2)
[8] s.148(3)
[9] s.148(4)
[10] s.148(6)
[11] Subject to s.149(2).
[12] s.149(1)
[13] My italics

issue as to at what point on the facts is there a contract in the creation of a derivative product in any event.[14]

The condition provided under s.149(2) is that there is a payment or receipt of a variable rate payment. This is so whether or not this is unconditional or subject to conditions being fulfilled.

Noticeably it does not cater for the situation in which the contract is determinable, which may, in itself occasion the generation of losses where contracts have been accounted for and later are not performed.

It may be that some operation of law makes the variable rate payment payable or receivable. That would seem to elude the requirement in the section that there be conditional or unconditional provision for the making of the variable rate payment.

As provided in section 149(2), the qualifying company must become entitled to pay or receive '. . . at a time specified in the contract . . .' The question then is: what time is specified in the contract? Typically, this would be one of the following: the Trade Date, or the date on which the contract is completed, or the date on which the contract is confirmed, whichever is the earlier.

The issue is whether it is a date on which the qualifying company is actually required to pay or whether it is a date on which the company acquires the obligation to make payment. S.149(2) is phrased in terms of the "entitlement" to make or receive payment rather than the payment itself. The manipulation of this effective date of an interest rate contract will enable the company to organise the period in which the contract falls to be taxed and also to manipulate the commencement date referred to above.

The drafting of the provision makes it impossible to incorporate a contractual term that the contract is defeasible and therefore there is no absolute entitlement, by including 'whether . . . subject to conditions . . .'. This would not be the case, it is submitted, with a call or a put option. There is a contingent entitlement in, or obligation over, the party which can be obliged to pay or receive under an option contract. However, this cannot be required to be paid until the option is exercised. It is argued that this is something more than being subject to a condition. Rather the obligation itself does not come into effect until the option is exercised. There is a contract in the formation of an option but that contract does not entitle a company to receive, rather it gives it the right to call for receipt. Therefore, there is a possibility that structures using options or swaptions would fall out with the section 149 test.

With reference to interest rate contracts, it is noticeable that there is nothing in these provisions to cater for the situation in which interest rate payments are made or received other than under what is recognised as an interest rate swap arrangement. It may be then that a contract may provide for the payment of interest rates under a forward arrangement.

---

[14] As discussed above at Part 1, the range of derivative products potentially applicable here.

This would appear to attract a charge to tax even though it is a one-off payment rather than a series of payments.

There is then an issue as to the payment of interest rate swap payments which are organised as a series of separate forwards. Each of these payments is taxable with reference to a different taxable period. It would be possible to transfer many of these payments outside the commencement date period of six years by this method.

While section 149(2) refers to variable rate payments, section 149(3) deals with the situation where fixed rate payments are made and received.[15] As section 149(3) provides:

> "an interest rate contract may include a provision under which, as the consideration for a payment...the qualifying company becomes entitled to make...or to a right to receive, at a time specified in the contract a fixed or fixed rate payment."

The issue then arises: what if there are two fixed rates payable? Or even: what if there are two variable rates? The drafting of the provision is somewhat inelegant in that it provides that an interest contract 'may' include a fixed rate leg. Therefore, section 149 includes the idea that there can be an interest contract with two variable rate legs. In market practice, it is of course, quite possible that there be one interest rate, over deutschemarks for example, paid in exchange for the interest rate over sterling. However, the provision does provide for there to be only one fixed rate payment. It is possible that a contract which provides for two fixed rate payments being exchanged, would not fall within the provision.

The commercial likelihood of this arrangement would turn on the definition of a 'fixed or fixed rate payment'. If the parties were arranging to swap a fixed rate of interest in one currency for an amount of another currency, there is scope for there to be two payments of absolute amounts which would not qualify as an interest rate contract.[16]

A 'fixed payment' is defined as a 'payment of a fixed amount specified in the contract'.[17] Therefore, it does not cater for an amount which is fixed other than in the contract. A payment of an amount which is fixed by reference to some indicator will be a variable rate payment. However, if the amount is fixed by some other method which does not permit of its being variable, outside the contract (say by tender) then it will not fall within the definition of a fixed payment.

A fixed rate payment is defined as a payment 'which falls to be determined (wholly or mainly) by applying to a notional principal amount specified in the contract..a rate the value of which at all times is the same

---

[15] As discussed above at para. 1.3 this is the usual procedure where interest rate swaps are created.

[16] The issue would remain as to whether or not this is a currency contract.

[17] s.149(6)

158

as that of a fixed rate of interest so specified'. Reference for the payment must be to a notional amount, as discussed above[18] with reference to swaps transactions.

A variable rate payment is defined as a payment 'which falls to be determined (wholly or mainly) by applying to a notional principal amount specified in the contract..a rate the value of which at all times is the same as that of a variable rate of interest so specified'. Where one of the rates is actually a stock price, or other similar market instrument, it would not appear to be a variable rate payment. The requirement is one of a payment of interest. Similarly, if the 'notional amount' actually changes hands, as in some foreign exchange or equities transactions, then it would be difficult to define that as being 'notional' at all.[19] There is also the issue of embedded swaps.[20]

Further to section 149(4), where payments fall to be made at the same time and where one payment falls to be made to and the other by a qualifying company:

'. . . it is immaterial for the purposes of this section that those rights and duties may be exercised and discharged by a payment made to or, as the case may require, by the company of an amount equal to the difference between the amounts of those payments.'

In short, this provision deals with the situation in which there may be set-off of any amount by a further payment leading to there being no difference between the two payments. This would appear to countervail netting provisions[21] in the agreement and treat them the same as payments which have not been set-off one against the other.

'Currency contracts' and options   4.2.6

The second category in Chapter II of the Finance Act 1994 is the 'currency contract'.

A contract is a currency contract under section 150 where two conditions are satisfied. The first is satisfied if:

a qualifying company (a) becomes entitled to a right and subject to a duty to receive payment at a specified time of a specified amount of one currency (the first currency), and (b) becomes entitled to a right and subject to a duty to pay in exchange and at the same time a specified amount of another currency (the second currency).[22]

The further requirement in section 150(1) is for there being a currency

---

[18] At para. 1.3
[19] In the case of interest rate transactions where the rates are calculated with reference to foreign exchange, the notional may change hands.
[20] As discussed at para 1.4, where the swaps are embedded in, e.g. a eurobond issue.
[21] See para. 2.9 above
[22] s.150

contract is that the transfers of money or money's worth for which the contract provides. As section 150 provides: 'A contract is a currency contract . . .'. There is a requirement that there be a contract. There is an issue as to what point on the facts is there a contract created in the formation of a derivative product.[23] There is no condition under section 150 that the payments covered are either unconditional or subject to conditions being fulfilled. Rather there is specific provision that there be entitlement to receive or pay amounts in a currency. Therefore, contingent payments are not prima facie caught. However, the provisions explicitly deal with options.

A currency contract includes an instrument which provides that a qualifying company has a right to receive or a duty to pay an amount of currency 'at a specified time of a specified amount' of the other currency, and is subject to reciprocal obligations.[24] Therefore, a forward currency contract requiring mutual payments is caught. However, a contract which does not provide for the amount or the specific date of the payment, will not be caught by these provisions. There is no guidance in the legislation as to the tax effect of such payments which are subject to conditions precedent or which are calculable by reference to a formula in the contract, and therefore not strictly within the legislation. However, it is submitted that any contract may well fall within the *Furniss v. Dawson* 'artificial step' doctrine.

Section 150 does not cater for the situation in which the contract is determinable, which may, in itself occasion the generation of losses where contracts have been accounted for and later are not performed. It may be that some operation of law makes the currency payment payable or receivable. That would seem to elude the requirement in the section that there be conditional or unconditional provision for the making of the variable rate payment.

The issue of time arises again in a different context. Section 150(5) provides that a reference to a time in the contract where the contract itself calculates the amount of currency payable by reference to an interest rate, is a reference to a time earlier than that in the contract.

The question then is: what time is specified in the contract? S.150(2) requires that this is the time of the making of the payment. This is to be contrasted with the variety of possibilities under an interest rate contract: the Trade Date, or the date on which the contract is completed, or the date on which the contract is confirmed, whichever is the earlier. The issue remains, however, whether that date is the date on which the qualifying company is actually required to pay or whether it is a date on which the company acquires the obligation to make payment.

Section 150(2) is phrased in terms of the "entitlement" to make or receive payment rather than the payment itself, for the creation of a

---

[23] As discussed above at para. 1.3
[24] s.150(4)

currency contract. The 'specified time' however, refers to the time of payment.

The manipulation of this effective date of a currency contract will enable the company to organise the period in which the contract falls to be taxed and also to manipulate the commencement date referred to above.

The drafting of the provision makes it possible to incorporate a contractual term that the contract is defeasible and therefore there is no absolute entitlement, by including 'whether . . . subject to conditions . . .'. This would not be the case, it is submitted, with a call or a put option, given what is said below. There is a contingent entitlement in, or obligation over, the party which can be obliged to pay or receive under an option contract.

With reference to currency contracts, there is nothing in these provisions to cater for the situation in which interest rate payments are made or received other than under what is recognised as a currency swap or option arrangement. It may be then that a contract may provide for the payment of interest rates under a forward arrangement. This would appear to attract a charge to tax even though it is a one-off payment rather than a series of payments. It might be possible to transfer many of these payments outside the commencement date period of six years by this method.

Section 150(2) requires that there be two currencies payable reciprocally. The question arises, what if there is a bridging transaction so that two currencies are not payable under one single transaction? If sterling is to be paid by A (a qualifying company) to B (another qualifying company) and B makes payment in deutschemarks to A, there is a qualifying payment. If A pays to B in sterling and receives reciprocal consideration from B in an instrument other than currency or a currency option, the transaction does not fall prima facie within section 150. For the other half of the transaction, B could pay A deutsche marks as part of another, contractually unrelated transaction.

The tax planners issue is then to consider whether this would be an 'artificial step' precluded from tax avoidance by *Furniss v. Dawson*. On its face, that analysis would appear to be incontrovertible.

The analytical problem caused by the legislation differentiation between interest rate contract and currency contracts, is that swaps will frequently be constructed so as to require fixed payments of currency in return for payments of currency calculated by reference to the interest rate attached to a particular currency. Therefore, commercially there is a fusion of the two concepts. In looking to sections 150(3) and (4), this difficulty arises. One further issue which is not dealt with in the legislation is: what if a differential payment of interest rate is made instead of a notional amount?

An option to enter into a currency contract, or an option to enter into such an option, constitutes a 'currency contract' in itself.[25]

---

[25] s.150(6)

An option which would give a qualifying company an entitlement to receive, or a duty to make, a currency payment, constitutes a 'currency contract' in itself.[26] This is so where the payments fall within section 151. Similarly, contracts which are subject to a condition precedent, are to be treated as a currency contract[27] as if the fulfilment of the condition were the exercise of an option in itself.[28]

Where payments may be made at the same time, equal to the difference between the amounts of the payments under the currency contract, such set-off is 'immaterial'. In short, this provision deals with the situation in which there may be set-off of any amount by a further payment leading to there being no difference between the two payments. This would appear to countervail netting provisions[29] in the agreement and treat them the same for tax purposes as payments which have not been set-off one against the other.

4.2.7   Swaptions and options on swaps

Section 149(5) deals specifically with swaptions and options on swaptions where they generate payments falling within section 151. Section 151 sets out those provisions which may be included in the categories of interest rate and currency contracts.

Section 151(1)(a), where a qualifying company acquires a right to receive a payment in consideration of entering into a contract or option (a sale premium) & (b) Where a qualifying company acquires a duty to make a payment in consideration of entering into a contract or option (a purchase premium). The question here is what is meant by 'payment'? Does that require that money is 'held to the account of' or must cash money actually change hands? Much of these instruments will be arranged through cash management systems where sums of money are not physically paid, rather accounts are credited or debited at the end of trading day with the net amounts owed or owing. It would seem in the spirit of the provisions that it is enough for there to be money's worth accredited to the trading account of the relevant party for there to be 'payment'.

An interest rate contract or currency contract (or option in either case) may include provision for any of the following:

(a)   a reasonable fee for arranging the transaction;
(b)   reasonable costs in arranging the transaction;
(c)   a termination or variation payment in respect of the instrument;
(d)   compensation payment for a failure to comply with the contract or option.

---

[26] s.150(7)
[27] s.150(8)(a)
[28] s.150(8)(b)
[29] s.150(9)

Provisions which may be disregarded 4.2.8

This provision is the *de minimis* provision in Chapter II of the Finance Act 1994. Its aim is to remove, for the purposes of the tax analysis, all steps in a contract which are inserted for the purpose of eluding the scope of the Chapter.

Section 152(1) provides that:

'Where – (a) but for the inclusion in a contract or option of provisions for one or more transfers of money or money's worth, the contract would have been a qualifying contract; and
(b) as regards the qualifying company and the relevant time, the present value of the transfers, is small when compared with the aggregate of the present values of all relevant payments,
the contract or option shall be treated for the purposes of section 149 or, as the case may be, section 150 above, as if those provisions were not included in it.'

Therefore there is a two step process.

First, but for the inclusion of specific provisions, providing for transfers of money, prevent the contract being a qualifying contract. What is not clear is whether or not this would enable the Revenue to decide that market standard provisions, which keep the instrument outside the definition of an interest rate or currency contract, can be ignored. The purpose of the section would seem to be to catch only those provisions which operate as 'artificial steps'. The *sine qua non* requirement supports this analysis. Therefore, where a product's structure would of itself be outside the strict terms of sections 149 and 150, section 152 will not operate to bring it within Chapter II.

Secondly, it is not clear what the provisions '... the aggregate of the present values of those transfers ... is small' is to connote. The standard that is to be interpreted from the word 'small' is unclear. It is submitted that this is a term which must be considered in all the circumstances. For example, the time at which the test is applied may lead to very different results. With some derivative products, there is a late accrual of value or, as with long term positions, there is a large accrual of value in the early stages which then falls away over time. Any transfer might then be small in relation to the present value of the instrument. The suggested answer is that, if the value at the time connotes something other than a 'small' portion of the aggregate present value of the instrument, it will not fall within the section. A mark-to-market approach is the only cogent solution.

Similarly, it is not clear what 'present value' means. It may be the mark-to-market value of the instrument, alternatively, it may be the difference between the amount paid for instrument and its then replacement value in the market.

Section 152(2)(a) provides that, within section 152(1), any negative value shall be treated as the 'equivalent positive value'. It is not clear how this is supposed to be made 'equivalent'. Similarly, under section

152(2)(b), 'relevant payments' are to be treated as if an aggregate of those payments. What is not clear is whether this includes netted transaction payments under a single master agreement.

4.2.9 Qualifying companies

Any company is a 'qualifying company' for the purposes of Chapter II of the Finance Act 1994.[30] There is no mention of trusts or partnerships. Unlimited companies organised under the Companies Act 1985 would appear to fall within the provisions. However, 'an authorised unit trust', is not a 'qualifying company'.[31] An investment trust authorised under the Taxes Act 1988 is not a 'qualifying company'.[32]

miles AND ELIZABETH

4.2.10 Calculation of profits and losses

Where a qualifying company holds a qualifying contract, a profit will accrue to that company in accordance with the prescribed formula.[33] Similarly losses accrue according to the formula.[34] The formula provides that the profit or loss is the excess of 'A' over 'B'.[35]

Where the company's profit and loss is calculated on a mark-to-market basis[36], the following tax analysis for the formula is used. 'A' is defined to be the aggregate of the qualifying payment(s) payable to the company in the period and any increase in the value of the contract (on a mark-to-market method).[37] 'B' is defined as the aggregate of qualifying payments payable by the company in the period and any reduction in the value of the contract (on a mark-to-market method).[38]

Where the company's profit and loss falls to be calculated on an 'accruals' basis, the following tax analysis is used. 'A' is defined to be the aggregate of the qualifying payment(s) allocated as being receivable in that period.[39] 'B' is defined as the aggregate of qualifying payments allocated as being payable by the company in that period.[40]

Any amounts which are ignored as a result of section 152, are discounted for the purposes of the formula in section 155[41]. However, where instruments are acquired or disposed of by a company during the

---

[30] s.154(1)
[31] s.154(2), see s.469 of the Income and Corporation Taxes Act 1988.
[32] s.154(3), see s.468 of the Income and Corporation Taxes Act 1988.
[33] s.155(1)
[34] s.155(2)
[35] s.155(1), s.155(4)(a) and (b).
[36] 'Mark-to-market' is defined below at para. 5.5. In short it means a valuation of the instrument in the market at the time of the valuation.
[37] s.155(4)(a)
[38] s.155(4)(b)
[39] s.155(5)(a)
[40] s.155(5)(b)
[41] s.155(6)

accounting period, their value is deemed to be nil immediately before such disposal or immediately after such acquisition.[42] However, where an instrument is disposed of, there is no deeming of a nil value where the contract is discharged by payments, none of which is a qualifying payment within Chapter II.[43] The purpose of this provision is that there should not be any disposal of an interest for a contractual consideration which is not itself susceptible to the tax treatment under Chapter II.

The Basis of Accounting   4.2.11

There is a choice between bases of accounting. Section 156 provides for either the 'mark to market basis of accounting'[44] or an 'accruals basis of accounting'[45]. A mark-to-market basis will be appropriate (a) where it is in accordance with normal accounting practice; (b) all payments are allocated to the accounting period in which they become due and payable; and (c) the method of valuation chosen produces a fair value.[46] For these purposes there is no definition of what constitutes normal accountancy practice nor what constitutes the 'market'. The definition of due and payable will seem to allow the rolling forward of payments so that the payment date is altered.[47]

The further issue is how do you acquire a fair value for transactions (other than from market participants) for contracts which revolve around exotic derivative products. The statutory explanation of "fair value" accounting requires the amount for which the contract could be sold to a knowledgeable and willing counterparty at arm's length.[48]

The accruals basis of accounting operates where (a) where it is in accordance with normal accounting practice; (b) all payments are allocated to the accounting period to which they relate (without regard to the accounting period in which they are made); and (c) where payments relate to more than one period they are apportioned on a just and reasonable basis.

The basis of accounting for linked currency options is a mark-to-market basis. The conditions for currency options to be linked are set out in section 157[49]. There must be a nexus between the parties who can exercise the options.[50] The second condition is that there must be simultaneous exercise of the options.[51]

---

[42] s.155(7)
[43] s.155(8)
[44] s.156(1)(a)
[45] s.156(1)(b)
[46] s.156(3)
[47] Where the contract is renewed and thereby the original contract is terminated and replaced (usual market practice), the analysis of s.155(7)(b) is that a contract has nil value when it is disposed of.
[48] s.156(7)
[49] s.157(3)
[50] s.157(5)
[51] s.157(6)

The difficulty with the accounting methods for these products is that the valuation of derivatives products is a fraught business in any event, as discussed elsewhere in this book. For example, the alteration of an instrument causes difficulties in deciding on the excess amounts to be used in section 155. Where the contracts were speculative in any event, it is difficult to examine where there is a market to measure many of the products. This either relies upon the company measuring its own obligations or in trying to find a measurement among competitors where products might be confidential or where there are few competitors who have a presence in the particular market.

Furthermore, does a hedge move in value when the underlying product moves, or can it have a market value at all? One argument runs that a hedge only has value with reference to the product under which it was created. A swap entered into to hedge the interest rate risk on a loan, for example, has value both as a speculative instrument in itself, and also as the counter-balance to movements in interest rates. The user of the swap has bought it to balance out risk, in this example. Therefore, it would appear sensible to value it on the basis of the risk which it reduces. However, the mark-to-market basis of valuation requires that it be treated as a speculative, market instrument and valued according to that basis.

4.2.12   Termination of qualifying contracts

The termination provision refers to a qualifying contract being terminated, or such a contract being disposed of by the company, or to a contract held by the company being altered such that it is no longer a qualifying contract.[52] In such a case, under the accruals basis of accounting the amount of a payment under a contract which has been included either in A or B for the purposes of s.155, must be entered in B or A respectively in the following accounting period.

4.2.13   Anti-avoidance provisions

There are a range of anti-avoidance provisions. Under section 165, transfers of value by qualifying companies and similarly, under section 166 transfers of value to associated companies are restricted for their tax effect.

The final category is under section 167 transactions otherwise than at arm's length will not obtain any tax advantage under the Act. Under section 167(2), the legal advisor must decide on what basis might a transaction be entered into otherwise than at arm's length between counterparties. The provision, realistically will refer, in most circumstances to arrangements within groups of companies or possibly between a company and a 'principal bank' seeking to arrange advantageous funding. Section 165(9) sets out those matters which are to be

---

[52] s.161(1)

taken into account in deciding whether or not companies are dealing otherwise than at arm's length.

Conclusion   4.2.14

Derivatives are a confusing form of financial product. For the banker and corporate Treasurer, they pose enormous difficulties in measuring and matching complex instruments which predict and hedge market movements. For the legal, accounting or taxation professional, there is the further problem of translation into the language of the professional. The Barings, Proctor & Gamble, and Orange County disaster are the latest in a long line of high-profile derivatives crashes. The potential use of derivatives as hedging instruments is being marred in the minds of the regulators and the public. For the instruments and the markets to calm themselves, there needs to be better professional understanding and control of the problems associated with these products. The legislation in the 1994 Finance Act does not assist the professional in developing that clear understanding and, it is suggested, are in need to reform already. The final word of advice to anyone venturing into the derivatives field, is to walk carefully, with the guidance of those other professionals who have been there and lived to re-tell the tale.

Part 5

Credit Risk & Collateral

Contents

5.1 Introduction
5.2 The Credit Aspect of Derivatives
5.3 The Credit Profile of OTC Options
5.4 The Credit Exposure of Swaps
5.5 Collateral

Introduction   5.1

A number of different entities will use derivative instruments in the current market place. The sophistication of the products has progressed from the deals such as the first swap between IBM and the World Bank where the interest rate and currency swap was established as a one-off transaction between large institutions. Derivatives are used by dealers as a hedging tool and a means of speculation. Borrowers use derivatives as a means of hedging exposure, providing access to a lower cost of funds and providing access to particular types of funding in the first place. Investors who enter the derivative markets use the products as a method of portfolio management, as hedging tools and as a means of speculating.

The central purpose of the derivative is risk management. As financial products and their markets become more and more volatile, the corporate treasurer is expected to be more and more sophisticated. The acquisition of funding at preferential rates is all important. The use of the derivative enables the treasurer to minimise the company's exposure to the risk of movements in interest rates or currency prices. For the institution, the risks involved range from the ecomonic to credit risks on counterparties' default or bankruptcy to the failure of management systems and procedures to cope with the detail of the transactions.

Credit risk divides into settlement risk and counterparty risk. Settlement risk concerns the exposure between entering into the deal and the time when the deal is settled and moneys or documentation exchanged. The risk is that the counterparty will default or fail to act as required by the contract. Credit risk is considered in more detail below but this gives some idea of the types of issues that are envisaged when talking about credit risk.

The risks associated with management are complex and not really the subject matter of a text on the legal issues relating to derivatives but are still something that the lawyer should bear in mind given some of the recent caselaw in the UK and in the USA concerning the reponsibilities of management when dealing with derivatives: there is now not only the issue of negligence but also matters of fiduciary responsibility and even an obligation on the part of directors to minimise financial risk. The problem of management incompetence stretches across the board as systems are put inplace for the first time to deal with new and complicated products. A complicated product clearly requires a competent level of manager to choose the right product and also to ensure that the product is monitored effectively. In effecting a hedging instrument, there are questions of systems control. If a company were to acquire an option to change its position on a certain obligation, the status of that option must be monitored to ensure that it is exercised when it is in the company's favour. The examples are endless.

Therefore, there is an issue as to operating systems being of an adequate standard. Risks need to be measured and reported to the right people in the organisation. Monitoring a risk requires an understanding of the effect of general market events on the product. Therefore effective means of analysing and controlling risk must be created. The concomitant risks are therefore all related to personnel. There is the downside of staff who cannot cope with the subject matter and also the "upside" risk of having staff who understand the products all too well, who are therefore left to control the organisation's systems and who are consequently hired by a competitor.

5.1.1 Inherent Market Risks

One of the much-mooted economic risks associated with the derivatives markets is that they introduce volatility to their underlying markets and affect the performance of corporate investors. It is argued that the derivatives markets constitute not only a possible means of reducing risk, but also a composite US$14 trillion risk to the financial system in themselves.

The derivatives market aims to enable participants to manage their exposure to the risk of movements in interest rates and securities prices. Therefore they operate for both the speculator and the prudent corporate treasurer. In 1994 the bond markets have undergone trauma every bit as dramatic as the stock market crashes in the late 1980's. Commodity prices have been hit by the violence in the run-up to the South African elections and the break-up of the old Eastern Europe. The need to find new products to invest in for the speculator have led to the enormous growth in the swaps markets.

The role of the derivatives salesperson in a bank and the in-house strategists is to forecast movements in the financial markets generally. They take views on interest rates movements up to 30 years into the future and on the shares, bond and commodity markets. As a result of the forecasts that they make they isolate mismatches in the markets which can be manipulated for the benefit of clients. The banks either take a view contrary to their clients or a view contrary to the markets. As such they are speculating on their view being correct and that of everyone else being wrong.

The derivatives markets are relatively new and the products that are being developed are similarly embryonic. What is not clear is the form that national and supranational regulation of the markets will take in the future. It may be that the markets are left to their own devices or the share-based products might come under close scrutiny. If the latter occurs, the products will not meet their objectives.

The other problem is that the products are only designed for the short term in which the predictions upon which they are designed, hold true. Derivatives only work for so long as the markets follow the expected patterns. After that time the user has to pay for more to cater for new market conditions. This process is acceptable only for so long as the use of the products is to manage the risks. Once they develop into speculative positions, then there is unacceptable risk for those institutions which we can identify as being central to the macro-economy.

Systemic Risk   5.1.2

Senior partner at Goldman Sachs, Stephen Friedman, was asked in a newspaper profile what he considered to be the greatest risk to the firm. His predecessor had answered the same question by saying simply: "nuclear war". Friedman considered the real threat to be: "systemic risk". This, more than nuclear war, is the threat to the financial system. Systemic risk is built around the complex web of derivatives deals that was discussed earlier. If one player in the market goes bankrupt, the remainder of the market will then have exposure to the bankrupt entity either directly or indirectly. If this in turn forces other entities into liquidation the exposure of each player in the market to one another intensifies, with the very real possibility that the entire market will collapse. The derivatives markets constitute not only a possible means of reducing risk, but also a composite $14 trillion risk to the financial system in themselves.

Systemic risk is the risk that the whole market falls apart and that many of its participants are driven into bankruptcy, or at best financial difficulty. In the derivatives markets there is a great risk of this caused by the matrix pattern that the need to hedge exposure produces. When a swap is entered into, parties usually hedge out that exposure. That means that every transaction has its roughly equal and opposite sibling. Therefore each institution will tend to deal twice to be hedged. Therefore every party becomes linked to every other party in this web of, literally, double-dealing. The fact that an option is cheap to enter into (there is only the small upfront premium to pay) means that the risk of financial loss does not arise until later when the option is either in or out of the money. The fact that these obligations are held off-balance sheet means that creditors (whether trade creditors or banks) do not know of the other party's exposure. If a party cannot pay its obligations under one transaction, it will mean that it cannot pay its obligations under all of its other trans-actions. Unlike normal bankruptcies or credit events, all the other players in the market are effected because the complex house of cards falls down.

173

Every counterparty in the market is put under pressure in respect of its obligations.

5.1.3 Credit Risk

A derivative product is a financial tool that is derived from another financial product. For example, an option to buy a share at some point in the future is a financial product derived from the underlying share. A swap on an interest rate is a product derived from the underlying loan.

The derivatives markets grew in the 1980's as a result of the need to manage exposure to high interest rates. In the 1990's the volatility in interest rates has increased. The spectre of global recession has continued with the UK showing a marked reluctance to recover from one of the longest recessions ever. Corporates have seen the need to manage their cash flows in ways other than by increasing profit. The 1980's enabled corporates to grow profits sharply with a boom in marketing and public access to credit facilities. In the 1990's, the focus has shifted to maximising profit by controlling expenses. This has meant "downsizing" (unemployment and the increased use of part-time labour) and seeking better working capital management by obtaining better credit terms from buyers and suppliers. At the same time, treasurers have been looking to obtain better use from existing funding capabilties. The deriviatives markets enable the Treasurer to manage the cost of funding more precisely and to control the risks of movements in prices or interest rates.

The major question posed by systems of insolvency law, is the availability of the solvent party to a transaction to enforce the contract against the insolvent party. The notion of liquidity is different from solvency, but the economic risks are similar. The aim of a treasury function within the corporate structure is to provide liquidity without impacting the solvency of the entity in one way or another. Liquidity means matching obligations with ability to pay. Derivatives markets aim to add to this pool of liquidity as well as adding speculative obligations. The risk posed by derivatives concerns the access to, and fear of, a haemorrhaging of liquidity.

The question is then: what to do about those entities whose capacity is not controlled by a system of law within the UK? One solution is to force all institutions entering into transactions in the UK to use a UK entity. This will simply return activity to the Euromarkets.

What reviews are taken of counterparty, (e.g. hedge fund) credit before entering into the transaction? It is only recently that the banks have begun to look at the credit risk involved in these markets. The issue of hedge funds and unknown principals behind other investment funds, means that it is impossible for the counterparty to enter into any due diligence over the entity with which it is contracting.

Legal and Accounting Risk 5.1.4

The control of these risks lie in enforcing a due diligence review in all circumstances of a prospective market counterparty's credit status before signing conduct of business contracts, the taking of collateral and broader use of parental guarantees.

There are credit risks associated simply with the products themselves. The accounting treatment of swaps and derivatives products remain a vexed issue. The strategies of companies entering into derivatives contracts are as risky as the movements in the markets themselves. There is an inherent danger if these products remain off-balance sheet. The markets need to know about the exposure of the counterparties with which they are dealing. Trade creditors need to know whether the company it is supplying can meet its obligations and banks need to know more about the risks involved in the companies to which they are lending money. The following are some of the questions:

- How will we know about a company's interest rate strategy?
- How will we know a company's exposure to an index which might crash?
- How will we know if a company's stock could be affected by being part of a basket of derivative instruments?

Accountancy rules must be altered so that companies are required to publish their interest rate and other derivative strategies. The derivatives entered into and the gains/losses that result, must be made visible on the balance sheet as unrealised assets or liabilities of the company.

Under many systems of insolvency law, an insolvent company will be entitled to receive all monies owed to it but not to pay any monies out. A system of insolvency law that enforces all of the obligations such that X and Y find the difference of all of their transactions and the net amount is paid to the party who is owed it. This ensures that Y does not suffer such a large loss.

The further policy question is then whether the other creditors of the insolvent company should have to allow a bleeding of assets from the insolvent company's balance sheet by operation of a law designed to protect derivatives market participants. The need for English law to tighten up its insolvency code in this respect is discussed at para. 3.7. There remains a spread of legal questions as to whether or not a number of legal persons can enter into these transactions at all. These issues are discussed in the Capacity section at para. 3.8.

The Credit Aspect of Derivatives 5.2

As the use and understanding of derivative instruments has increased, the products have become "commoditized". That is to say, these financial instruments are created in a standard form by financial institutions for their client base. Commoditized products remove the requirement for extensive negotiation and detailed documentation of the derivative. From the lawyer's perspective this means that the legal nature of the product is no different but rather that the parties to the transaction understand better the way in which it operates. From a commercial point of view, these products are easier to construct and market but they carry lower profit margins because a large number of financial institutions are able to create them. The competition in the derivatives market serves to reduce profit margins further. Financial institutions rely upon the commoditized products to ensure a steady cash in-flow.

Given the shift towards commoditization at the end of the 1980's, the financial institutions began to create a series of new instruments and strategies in the 1990s to provide customised types of risk protection and investment opportunities for clients. These new products (the so-called "complex derivatives") attract a higher profit margin because of their complexity, the fact that they are tailor-made for specific clients and because few insitutions are able to supply them.

The complex derivative instruments have their roots in the basic instruments set out above. In many circumstances they are in fact 'derivatives' of the traditional interest rate swaps, options and forwards. Leveraged swaps, inverse floater swaps, differential swaps, and index principal swaps are all examples of complex derivatives (discussed in Part 1) which use the standard swaps structures. The attraction of these products to the financial institutions and their client base is that they offer a means of exploiting markets which had been hitherto untrammelled by the derivatives markets.

In addition to developing these new swaps products, the financial institutions have created alternative risk management and profit-making strategies which rely specifically on structured OTC options. By linking different option strategies with one another, it is possible to generate very specific results. Options strategies can produce unlimited profit with unlimited potential loss, limited profit with limited potential loss, effective hedging of risk with limited profit potential.

There is credit risk to both parties to such a transaction and therefore all products and strategies which depend upon complex derivatives required specific credit concentration.

The primary reason for focusing on OTC derivatives is that that is the area of the derivative markets which has shown the most grown and innovation. The bespoke nature of the products in this market, also mean that they can be tailored to specific clients and sold at a higher rate. It is also in the OTC market that the issues of credit and legal risk management are at the most important: most significantly centred on the risk of the failure of the counterparty to perform. In the case of structured financial arrangements with embedded options or warants, credit risk is centred primarily on the creditworth of the issuer of the bond or convertible. This category of risk is better known as "inventory risk". The risks attributable to counterparty default when holding a bond are increased when there is an embedded derivative forming part of the structure.

There is a broad spectrum of newer derivatives which have not been launched yet by many of the financial institutions but which deserve a mention: tax derivatives, property derivatives, macroeconomic derivatives, credit derivatives, insurance derivatives and inflation derivatives.

The Motivation for Derivatives Transactions   5.2.1

The need and motivation for both financial institution and client to enter into derivatives transactions is either to earn income (by selling or using a derivative) or to manage risk. Derivatives products are used because of the volatility in world financial markets. The complex structures take advantage of profit-making opportunities and offer protection against the risk of loss in the financial markets.

The complex derivatives carry with them the higher profit margins because they require greater expertise in both financial engineering and risk management techniques. Thererfore there is an in-built tendency in the system towards ever increasing product complexity.

From the perspective of an investor using derivatives, the use of derivatives enables access to capital markets at a lower funding cost, or enhances the return on the underlying instrument, or by enabling a profitable participation in (or emulation of) an underlying market, or by obtaining protection against the movement in the level of a market. The access to capital markets at a lower funding cost can be achieved by the use of a bond which is linked to a market index by an embedded derivative. The protection of the return on the underlying instrument is acheived by selling or buying options which will generate a profit to balance out any loss on the underlying product. Profitable participation in (or emulation of) an underlying market is achieved by derivative products based on options which generate market simulated return without requiring market participation. Protection against the movement in the level of a market interest rate or price is produced by interest rate or other swaps.

Derivatives can also be used for objectives which are not specificially geared to speculative profit or hedging. There are often regulatory or capital adequacy goals in investing in one particular type of derivative instrument rather than owning market instruments or obligations. Similarly, there are accounting advantages in holding derivative instruments rather than ordinary products. Under most accounting requirements, interest rate swaps do not appear on a company's balance sheet whereas a loan would be required to be disclosed.

The tremendous volatility in interest rates, stock market indicies and currency rates, drives the demand for derivative products which guard against or arbitrage this volatility. It is this volatility which will continue to drive market innovation. However, it can be expected that this innovation will continue to follow the techniques and structures identified as fundamental in this section.

The market for financial derivatives requires that the complex derivatives products are scrutinised closely. The detail of these products in their rapidly changing markets require the legal professional to consider strategy and structure. While the issues of return, cash flows, obligation and termination are driven by the finance professionals, all of these elements have an impact on the legal analysis of the product. The Risk / Return equation is the profit-loss component which governs the finance professional's calculations. Lawfulness, risk management, documentation, capacity and suitability are the concerns of the lawyer.

Understanding the risk perameters of a derivatives transaction enables the lawyer to comprehend the commercial motivation for the sale of the product and a specific quantification of the potential risks should the counterparty to the transaction default. The primary categories of risk involved are: credit, market, liquidity, settlement, hedging, operational, legal and sovereign risk.

The client of a derivatives product is either an investor or an issuer. The financial instituition will generally approach the client with an idea for a derivatives structure. This marketing function of the banks is the most important commercial activity in the markets. From the perspective of the client, it is essential that all aspects of the transaction are analysed before entering into a contract. The legal analysis forms an essential component of the credit management fucntion in ensuring that the deal can be terminated and conducted in the manner anticipated by the parties. While the achievement of a lower funding cost or speculative profit are the commercial aim, a product will not be profitable or viable if it is legally unworkable. While many of the banks' client base are sophisticated users (pension funds, the treasury departments of large multinational corporations, insurance companies, etc) they do not have the legal and credit-based knowledge which is located in the financial institutions. Mutual disclosure of information relating to all aspects of the contract will be important to the legal analysis conducted by both parties.

The concern is that the market is growing quickly in volume and sophistication and that additional losses could occur. The risk is that of systemic risk where the failure of one or more counterparties causes the failure of further counterparties. The aim of this section is to create a method of understanding the legal risks and isolating the credit risks of complex derivatives, particularly structured options strategies, equity swaps and exotic swaps and options. Understanding the legal and credit related issues will identify the exposures open to a financial institution or client counterparty and give an idea of the losses which might result from counterparty failure.

Most derivative transactions are high risk in nature. In analysing the instruments, it is important to remember that derivative instruments with unaltered credit structures will carry a high risk-equivalent exposure and/

or a long maturity profile. This form of product is therefore generally considered to be unsuitable for counterparties who are of low credit quality. The credit function within financial institutions is usually discharged in a combination of three ways. First, analysis by in-house credit departments who consult publicly available literature on the counterparty (such as annual reports and accounts) and any in-house analysis prepared (such as equity analysts reports). Secondly, the financial institution will seek a meeting with the treasury department of the counterparty to discuss the ramification of the transaction for both parties. Clearly, such an exchange of information becomes important for the spread of financial products (not just derivatives) which the financial institution will seek to sell to its client base. Thirdly, by reference to the independent credit rating agencies analyses of the counterparty, where such has been prepared.

Dealing with counterparties who are of lower credit-worth, is more profitable than dealing with AAA rated companies. Therefore, there is pressure to provide a means of supplying products to clients which are of weaker credit rating. The mechanisms which are most commonly used to facilitate these transactions are:

- collateralisation
- periodic mark-to-market
- options to terminate.

All three alternatives require legal input to structure them correctly. Each of these forms of 'credit enhancement' is tailor-made for the client. The legal implications of dedicating a given cadre of assets to protect a derivatives transaction is a process which should involve legal advice from the outset.

There is also the question of suitability of the transaction for the counterparty which has low credit quality[1]. Bound up in these issues are also questions of risk reduction, the impact of netting exposures to a low credit counterparty, seeking a suitable hedge across the range of products contracted with this counterparty, portfolio management across counterparties. Examining these issues in detail from a credit perspective is beyond the scope of this book but there is a need to introduce the topic to locate the role of the lawyer.

The primary inter-action of the credit function and the commercial motivation for the transaction is to provide a means of valuing the risk being assumed by a party in entering into the deal with the counterparty of a given creditworth. The most significant form of quantifiable risk is market risk.

"Market risk" can be defined as the risk of loss resulting from movement in market prices or rates. Market risk exists because interest rates, currency rates, stock prices, index levels or commodity prices governing a given

---

[1] Discussed at para. 5.2

derivatives transaction fluctuate. Derivative products exist to exploit these fluctuations but are also subject to them throughout their lives. The general assumption in entering into a derivatives transaction is that the appropriate market rate will remain within given bounds throughout the life of the transaction. However, it is expected that the rates will not remain exactly the same. The result is the building of market risk into the price of the product. As the current price level changes, the level of risk exposure, or the amount of loss the party risks if the counterparty defaults, changes aswell. Market risk may be positive or negative through the life of a given derivatives transaction, depending upon market price and rate movements.

When the risk of counterparty default is negative, there is no loss to the counterparty. For example, where X sells Y an interest rate swap and that swap is in-the-money for Y, if Y defaults by becoming insolvent, there is no loss for X at that time. Rather, X loses an unprofitable transaction. The only potential loss that X will suffer is the cost of the hedge it will have bought in the market to balance out the effect of the swap. However, if the swap itself was out-of-the-money, there is a possibility that the hedge (designed to move in inverse direction to the swap) will be in-the-money.

Market risk can then be divided for credit analysis purposes into two categories: "potential market risk" and "actual market risk".

5.2.2   Potential Market Risk

"Potential Market Risk" is the risk exposure which the bank must allocate at the inception of a derivatives transaction to cover the risk of counter-party failure. Potential market risk attempts to quantify future market rate movements which may impact the risk exposure to that counterparty. Potential market risk, quantified in the manner set out briefly below, can be taken to be a 'worst case scenario' which the party faces should the counterparty fail to perform under the contract.

5.2.3   Actual Market Risk

"Actual Market Risk" measures the true value of risk exposure once the trading under a transaction has commenced. It is reasonable to assume that market prices and rates will move between trade date and maturity date. The hope is that those rates will not move more than that estimated by the Potential Market Risk calculations as part of the Risk Equivalency process[2]. The Actual Market Risk is the loss which the party would suffer as a result of counterparty default at a specific point in time. This amount is also known as the replacement cost or mark-to-market risk. It can be viewed as the amount which the party will lose if the counterparty default

---

[2] Discussed below at para. 5.3

actually occurs or the cost to replace the transaction lost and unwind the hedging transaction.

Analysis of both Potential Market Risk and Actual Market Risk are essential parts of the credit review process from the outset. The combination of these two concepts contain the loss potential for the life of the transaction.

Risk Equivalency   5.2.4

"Risk Equivalency" is the process by which the notional amount of a transaction is re-evaluated in the light of its characteristics[3] to yield a figure which most accurately reflects the potential risk of the transaction. This is also referred to as the loan equivalent exposure. Risk equivalency is necessary primarily because the derivative instruments are not funding transactions, like unsecured loans. The process adjusts the notional amount so that the actual and potential risks are appropriately quantified.

Example
An unsecured loan of US$500m represents a potential risk of US$500m. An interest rate swap on a notional of US$500m with anticipated interest payments on current rates of US$5m, represents an actual market risk of US$5m. All that is at risk is the interest payment of US$5m and not the notional amount. The risk equivalency process involves the alteration of the notional amount to yield a risk equivalent exposure which is considered to be a suitable credit risk for the given counterparty.

The Risk Equivalency Factor is then calculated by a twofold process. First, the risk factor is calculated to reflect the underlying movements in the rates or prices which govern the transaction. Calculating the risk factor is a combined process of measuring the underlying products rate movements over time and also the maturity of the proposed transaction. Secondly, that risk factor must be applied to the formula that is being used to calculate the price of the derivative instrument in question. The risk factor must be altered on a continuous basis through the life of the transaction to account for market movements or any added credit risks.

The probabiltiy of counterparty default can be estimated through default probability factors. These factors are generally based on an historical review of counterparty default measured against the frequency of default by counterparties of similar ratings from the external ratings agencies and also any information specific to the profile of the specific counterparty. As discussed above, this information is then garnered from a number of sources within and without the financial institution.

The business of performing these calculations is the subject of complex mathematical texts. Option pricing models such as the Black-Scholes Option Pricing Model and the Binomial Option Pricing Model are widely

---

[3] Whether these characterisitcs are maturity, initial rate, frequency of payments, etc.

used in the derivatives markets and many credit calculation models use these fundamental techniques in quantifying risk factors[4]. All that this author would add is the rider that no model is perfect. Calculation of risk according to a model will never predict earthquakes, political risk or calamities like the effect of asbestosis claims on the insurance market or losses generated by unsupervised traders.

From this example, it would appear that an unsecured loan offers a greater risk than a derivative instrument. However, that is to consider the size of the loss rather than the inherent risk of the instrument. While the loan does offer a larger absolute threat of loss, the amount of that loss is fixed at US$500m. The loss which can be made on a derivative fluctuates with market movements and therefore may grow to be proportionately far larger. Derivative products such as cross-currency swaps, zero coupon swaps, equity derivative options and binary debt options are examples of derivatives with very high risk equivalency exposures. It should also be remembered that institutions enter into more derivatives transactions than they make unsecured loans.

5.3 The Credit Profile of OTC Options

In virtually all OTC Options, risk exposure is one-sided (the only exception being currency options, where the exercise of the option may result in the seller of the option being exposed to delivery risk). In all cases it is the buyer of the option (whether a put option or a call option) who suffers the exposure to credit risk.

The role of the option seller is to provide the buyer with an economic advantage should a given strike price be reached by the option. The seller earns premium income in return for providing this opportunity. When the seller has received its premium, it has no further credit exposure to the buyer. Unless the seller receives its premium, it will not be required to honour the obligation to make good the economic advantage under the option. Therefore, the seller of the option has no credit exposure to the buyer in a simple, one-off option transaction. The only potential cost open to the seller occurs in two ways. The first is clearly the risk that the option will be in-the-money for the buyer and therefore the seller bears the risk that the market will move so as to require it to make good the advantage to the buyer. This is a commercial risk wich is part of the risk/return calculation. The second potential cost is in the circumstance where the option is part of a structure which does not provide for an up-front premium. In circumstances, for example, where there is a swap with an embedded option, it is common for the premium to be paid at the end of the transaction or to be amortised through the life of the transaction.

---

[4] See *e.g. The Credit Risk of Complex Derivatives* by Erik Banks, Macmillan 1994.

Equity Derivatives

While many of the swap structures common in the derivatives market currently are becoming more commoditised (for example, 'vanilla' interest rate swaps and currency swaps) the equity derivative market is, by its nature, open to more exotic structures. The plethora of equity products that are traded on a broad range of stock and futures exchanges are more difficult to package into commoditised structures. The structure of debt products is more homogenous than the products that are traded and regulated on equities markets. There are more customised features about equity derivatives. It is therefore more difficult to set standard credit parameters for equity derivatives than for the more commoditised debt derivatives. However, for this discussion there is a need to divide the products between the most easily recognised equity derivatives and those with exotic features, particularly the embedded option products.

The Credit Exposure of Swaps   5.4

There is no single agreed approach to the management of credit exposure to swaps. This subject must be of concern to legal and compliance officers who are required to correlate the institutions own objectives on credit control with those of the regulatory institutions. There are clearly differences between the requirements which the regulators will place on the institution and the institution's own credit parameters. Risk calculation methods have varying priorities: capital adequacy, pricing, counterparty credit, bank failure, systemic risk, and so forth.

The Bank for International Settlements has set out its two methods of calculating bank exposure to derivatives[5]. The Current Exposure Method ("CEM") concentrates on the replacement cost of the product (or mark-to-market value), together with a factor to account for future credit exposure. The Original Exposure Method ("OEM") focused on the future credit exposure without looking to the mark-to-market value. The mark-to-market value method is the method which is prevalent in the market among the financial institutions. It is also the approach taken in the credit support instruments discussed below.

The BIS has set out the manner in which banks are to allocate capital to cover their exposure to derivatives.

$$\text{Capital Ratio} = \frac{k}{(MTM + (CEM_{factor} \times N)) \times RW}$$

where:
Capital ratio is an institution's target BIS ration
k is the capital required to support a transaction

[5] *International Convergence of Capital Measurement and Capital Standards*; BIS (1988).

CEM$_{factor}$ is the appropriate current exposure method factor
N is the notional amount of the swap
RW is the risk weighting.

There are two potential approaches then to the question of credit exposure arising from swaps transactions.

5.5 Collateral

Collateral is a distinct form of credit protection which throws up a plethora of legal problems of its own. The growing market practice of using collateral has prompted the desire to deal with the subject separately from that specifically of Credit Risk above. There are a number of different ways of managing credit and other risks which are discussed. The market has begun to favour collateral and marginning techiques over the others for reasons which have been developed in the Credit Risk section above. For the time being those coming to this section with commercial and legal questions to do with collateral only, will benefit from an uncluttered discussion of the topic. Those requiring a discussion of collateral compared to other forms of credit enhancement tool (within the scope of this book) should refer to the Credit Risk section above[6].

5.5.1 The purpose of collateral

The purpose of collateral is to secure the obligations of the parties to an OTC derivative in situations where there are credit concerns. Simply put, collateral is property of some sort which is given by X to Y during the life of a derivatives transaction to assuage Y's concerns about X's credit worth.

There are a number of questions, from a commercial point of view, that arise from the outset.

1. The first is the decision whether or not collateral is required at all. The resolution of this issue is based on the form of credit analysis discussed above in the Credit Risk section.
2. The second is measurement of the type of collateral that is required compared to the amount of collateral which the counterparty will be able (i) to acquire and (ii) to render up collateral, without causing itself enormous liquidity problems. The provision of collateral clearly presents problems for the provider in locating suitable liquid assets which are then ring-fenced from other areas of its business.
3. The third question is then as to the type of asset that is required to be provided. There will be a preference for liquid assets such as cash and

---

[6] At para. 5.4

government securities on the part of the party benefitting from the provision of the collateral.

4. The fourth question then concerns the formal and regulatory requirements that govern the manner in which that property is to be provided.
5. The fifth question concerns the rights that Y has in respect of that property including (i) on what basis can Y take absolute possession of the property, (ii) what further recourse can Y obtain in the situation in which the property does not equal the size of the exposure to X if something does go wrong, and (iii) what can Y do with the property while it is being held.
6. The sixth question is as to the agency that will have possession or custody of the property during the life of the derivatives transaction.

Clearly, some of these issues are general commercial issues and some of them are pure legal issues. In the whole though, they are issues which a lawyer must consider and deal with in framing collateral documentation.

This section will first consider the commercial issues covering the provision and taking of collateral. Then it will consider the legal issues surrounding collateral. Finally, it will examine some of the regulatory and inter-party alternatives to *ad hoc* collateralisation, as practised in the market currently, which produce the same credit amelioration effect.

Commercial Issues   5.5.2

Requirement for Collateral

The first question is whether collateral is taken or whether another form of credit enhancement device is used.
The options available are:

- a charge over the counterparty's assets
- the provision of collateral
- the provision of magin credit
- the use of automatic termination clauses

It is a credit issue whether or not collateral is taken. With the growth of the derivatives markets and the introduction of lower credit quality participants (such as the macro hedge funds), the appetite for risk has altered. The use of collateral has grown. The large financial institutions will often require collateral to be provided. Clearly this is, straightforwardly, a credit issue.

The opposite question is therefore whether the institution which is required to produce the collateral will agree to do so. This question is considered below.

Introductory

There are two general points to be made with reference to the taking of collateral. Security will need to be recognised on enforcement by the jurisdiction in which the relevant asset is located. Therefore, the security holder is normally advised to do everything necessary to perfect the security under the laws of the place where the security is held. This may involve documentary formalities and local filings and may also involve making the security documentation subject to the laws of the relevant jurisdiction. For example, where a legal charge is sought over Japanese registered shares it is usually advisable that the charging documentation be governed by Japanese law. Secondly, there is the issue of the appropriate insolvency laws which may apply should the counterparty go into insolvency. The result may be that it is impossible for the collateral or charging agreement to be performed. Therefore, in cases where the insolvency position is important, it is vital that the appropriate insolvency code is investigated.

Measurement

The second issue is then how you measure the likely size of your exposure to the counterparty and, consequently, how much collateral you require. This is very obviously a commercial issue and therefore it is not proposed to deal with the complex subject of collateral measurement here.

Type of Collateral

Collateral comes in a number of forms. The institution could take cash, securities or other forms of transferable property which are of a measurable value. It is a commercial decision what form of collateral is taken. There are some legal issues discussed below which might influence the type of collateral on the basis that the formal requirements for the perfection of some forms of collateral are less stringent than others, and so forth.

5.5.3 Legal Issues

The means of credit enhancement

The most straightforward method of providing security from an OTC derivative transaction, is to deliver cash or liquid securities to the counterparty and to grant that counterparty a charge over the assets delivered. The available routes would be:

- to provide a fixed amount of the relevant assets at the inception of the transaction and agree ther basis on which that level of collateral is increased or reduced over the life of the transaction; or

- to enter into a mark-to-market transaction whereby the appropriate level of collateral is determined by reference to the mark-to-market value of the outstanding obligations owed under the relevant transactions

The mark-to-market method is often used to enhance the credit position with reference to a Master Agreement where it is a pre-requisite for one or other of the parties that there be sufficient collateral available throughout the life of the Master Agreement across the range of all transactions conducted under it.

Which mark-to-market method?

The mark-to-market method is favoured by market participants because it allows for a flexible response to market movements. The calculation agent under the mark-to-market agreement clearly retains a large amount of influence in deciding the present value of the range of transactions captured under the mark-to-market agreement. As a matter of market practice, these calculations are done on a net basis. Mark-to-market agreements are more complicated than a straightforward charge but do reduce the risk of the security holder being unsecured at the time of default.[7]

There are a variety of methods by which the relevant mark-to-market level is determined. It is not always considered necessary that the amount of collateral be equal to 100 per cent of the potential exposure of the security holder. However, this calculation will vary depending upon the volatility of the derivative market in question or its underlying component. Therefore, the value of the security held by the security holder may be as much as 120 per cent of the exposure which the security holder faces at the time of the agreement.

The level of collateral

The amount of Collateral pledged will depend, in some circumstances, on the form of the Collateral itself. The more volatile the value of the Collateral, the greater the risk of the Collateral itself decreasing in value. Therefore, there is a likelihood that a greater proportion of exposure coverage will be required where the Collateral is of lower intrinsic value. A similar consideration arises where cash is pledged as Collateral in one currency to secure an obligation in another currency. There is a risk of foreign exchange movement, leading to the devaluation of the comparative value of the Collateral.

---

[7] This presumes always that the netting process will be legally effective under the Master Agreement.

It is also important to decide whether collateral arrangements need to be two-way or only one way agreements. This decision will usually turn on the comparative credit worth of the two parties. Financial institutions will often seek one-way collateral arrangements from non-financial institutions (of a weaker credit worth than themselves). *Inter se*, comparable financial institutions will either agree two-way collateral arrangements or, as is more common in the markets, will agree to dispense with collateral and concentrate instead on the credit enhancement provisions in the Master Agreement.[8]

Marking to market

The parties must decide how frequently the collateral should be marked to market. Some arrangements will enable the collateral to be marked at any time. Alternatively, the collateral may be marked only on the occurrence of a specified class of events: for example, on credit down grades by a credit ratings agency or a given percentage increase in the size of the security holder's exposure. Collateral agreements will often provide that marking takes place on a daily, weekly, bi-weekly, or monthly basis.

Charge

The principal advantage of taking a fully perfected charge is that, on the insolvency of the counterparty, the chargee is entitled to have the obligations owed to it under the charge satisfied. The excess of any collateral over the size of the obligations will be required to be returned to the liquidator. The principal disadvantage of a charge is that it is required to be registered under section 395 of the Companies Act 1985. The risk is that failure to register the charge makes it void against the liquidator, administrator or other creditor of the insolvent party. Further, under section 395(2), where the charge is void for lack of registration, the money secured by it becomes repayable.[9] The obvious commercial point is that companies will not want to have charges registered against them in many circumstances and therefore may seek an alternative means of credit enhancement.

The means by which the applicability of registration is established is set out in section 396 of the Companies Act 1985. The two most appropriate heads from the point of view of OTC derivatives are:

---

[8] See para. 2.5.
[9] The status of this provision is unclear with reference to non-English or Welsh companies. However, registration is advisable given that, even if registration is refused by Companies House on the basis that the registering entity does not have a place of business in England and Wales, the purported registration satisfies s.395: *NV Slavenburg'sBank v. Interncontinental National Resources*. Similarly, it is not clear whether the renvoi rules under private international law would make this rule applicable between companies whose status is not clear but which have chosen English law as their proper law.

- a charge on book debts
- a floating charge on a company's undertaking of property

The term "book debt" is not defined in the statute. It would appear that debt securities provided by a financial institution as security collateral would be deemed to be 'book debts' owed to it. Therefore, a charge over those securities would lead to a requirement to be registered.

The question of the status of a charge over cash as a 'floating charge' would depend upon the manner in which the charge was established. Whereas a charge might be created as a fixed charge, there are difficulties with the commercial aims of the parties which might make the charge appear to be a floating charge. The possibility of substitution of the assets for other assets would require that it be analysed as a floating charge over a class of assets identified in the agreement. To alter the analysis, the chargee would be required to exercise some control over the assets for which the collateral could be substituted. Where the chargee approves the substitute collateral as a condition precedent of substitution, it would appear that the charge remains a fixed charge. Similarly, the automatic rights for return of collateral based on the movement in mark-to-market values, would make the fixed charge appear to be a floating one. The result of classification of a charge as a floating charge would be that, on insolvency, it would take effect subsequent to fixed, secured creditors.

Guarantees

This work is not large enough to encompass the detail of the law on guarantees. There is no particular aspect of derivatives which requires a different legal or guarantee treatment. The only complications tend to be commercial difficulties which require the lawyer to interpret them into documentation. The credit aspects of finding a company of sufficient credit worth to give the guarantee are not specifically legal problems. The solutions lie either in conducting transactions with the highly credit-rated entity or ensuring that the guarantee forms a credit support agreement under the Master Agreement.

Letter of comfort

The market uses letters of comfort where one or other of the parties is unwilling to provide a full guarantee. The letter of comfort is not a legally binding document but does provide an assurance that the company providing the letter will support the contracting entity in the event of any inability to pay.

Set-off

The availability of effective netting provisions in the Master Agreement and appropriate Confirmations is central to the parties ability to minimise their exposure one to another. Dealing with obligations on a net, rather than a gross, basis is central to the price efficiency of a derivatives transactions.

The position with reference to charges over cash has been complicated by the *Charge Card Case*[10]. The High Court found that it is conceptually impossible for a bank to take a charge over a credit balance which a customer has with it. The *ratio decidendi* was that the charge taken over the deposit would be, in reality, a charge taken over the bank's debt created by the deposit. The nature of a debt is a right against the relevant debtor. A charge therefore would be a right for the bank to sue itself. Therefore, a charge would have to be created with a third party bank.

A possible combination of set-off and taking a security interest

Where set-off is included in the documentation, there is no need for registration of formality of formation under the Companies Act. Furthermore, provision for set-off will avoid the rule in the *Charge Card Case*. Taking a security interest, may also have negative pledge problems. However, the advantage of a security interest is the ability to deal freely with the collateral.

The best solution may therefore be to fuse the set-off and security interest possibilities. Set-off will generally not enable the parties to set-off money rights against other property obligations and vice versa. Therefore, set-off will not work in circumstances where some of the collateral is in cash form and the remainder is in securities or other property. The scope of the set-off method is therefore prone to practical problems where a number of deals are done under one collateral agreement.

The means by which a solution will be reached is therefore to create two types of interest that are capable of being set-off. The best answer seems to be to create a security interest over the property which enables the party beneficially entitled to the collateral on default of the counterparty, to deal with the subject matter freely. This is done by giving the beneficiary rights to deal freely with an obligation to return equivalent securities or cash to the other party. This converts the interest from one in property to one in money: that is the amount of cash which is required to be returned to the other party at the end of the life of the transaction.

---

[10] *Re Charge Card Services Ltd* [1989] Ch. 497.

Sample Documentation

See Structure of Collateral documentation below at para. 5.6.5.

Collateral Terms in Master Agreement   5.5.4

Subject to the execution of a security agreement (the "Security Agreement") between the parties, the following provisions shall govern the payment and return of collateral hereunder until such time as the Security Agreement is executed and delivered, at which time the Security Agreement shall supercede and replace these provisions. Counterparty shall be the pledgor in respect of such Collateral (the "Pledgor") and GSI shall be a secured party in respect of such Collateral (the "Secured Party"). In order to secure its obligations under this transaction and any Specified Transaction entered into between the parties hereto prior to the date of this Transaction or hereafter (individually referred to as a "Transaction" and collectively referred to as the "Transactions"), the Pledgor hereby grants to the Secured Party a continuing first priority and perfected security interest in, and a lien on, all Collateral (together with all proceeds

Potential Tax Problems

There are a number of potential tax problems associated with the taking of collateral. There is the possibility that the giving up of collateral, which is subsequently lost as a result of default under the agreement. Therefore there is a potential for capital gains tax liability for this disposal. There are also potential issues with Manufactured Dividends and Witholding tax on bank interest, as discussed above in Part 4.

Conflict of Law Issues

The issues raised by collateral provisions revolve principally around the enforcability of such arrangements in the locus where the collateral is situated. The issues of (i) governing law; (ii) illegality of the place of performance; and (iii) the locus of a debt. These issues are discussed in greater detail at Part 3.

Structure of Collateral Documentation   5.5.5

The *pro forma* Collateral Agreement included below is intended specifically as a guide to the bulk of the terms which should be included in such an agreement attached to a Master Agreement. The terms are not conclusive and would require further analysis for any given situation. However, they serve to summarise the foregoing discussion.

Pro forma Mark-to-Market Collateral Agreement
One-way agreement attached to Master Agreement

- **Whereas the parties (the "Counterparty" and "A Bank") have entered into a Master Agreement**
- **in consideration of A Bank entering into the Master Agreement**
- **in order to support and secure the obligations of the Counterparty under the Master Agreement**
- **Counterparty agrees to deposit "collateral" with A Bank from time to time.**

A. Definitions

"Collateral" means the aggregate of the following items pledged by Counterparty to A,

The type of collateral that is provided is a matter for negotiation between the parties.

Cash This is the simplest form of collateral. A given amount of cash is deposited and held to the account of the counterparty. The further issue is then who has control over that money and who has the use of that money while it has been hypothecated for the purpose of credit enhancement. Therefore, the question of who collects interest on the cash while it is held in the account. It is usual that the rate of interest is specified according to a standard, benchmark interest rate such as LIBOR.

Government bonds and government obligations generally, as defined by the parties' credit requirements.

Other bearer-form government obligations as rated by Standard & Poor's Corporation ("S&P") or by Moody's Investor Services ("Moody's"); whether US dollar-denominated or in some other currency;[11]

Short term commercial paper as rated by S&P or by Moody's;

Securities issued by a given class of companies which satisfy the requisite credit requirements, or provided by the counterparty itself or its affiliates; or

Other marketable securities acceptable to A Bank, including all interest, dividends, and other income thereon and all proceeds thereof.

---

[11] It is for the parties themselves to decide on the credit rating that they require for the requisite collateral. It is usual to have this measured in accordance with the relevant S& P or Moodys ratings either for the issuing entity or its public debt issues.

Custody of collateral

The Collateral shall be deposited with or maintained by A in a custody account at a commercial bank or other institution acceptable to A.

"Exposure" means that a party is the beneficiary of a conditional or unconditional payment or performance obligation of the other party pursuant to one or more transactions under the Master Agreement.

"Net Exposure" means the point at which the total value of one party's exposure exceeds the total value of the other party's exposure.

"Total Required Collateral" as of any day on which the level of collateral required is to be valued, is to be the fair market value of the Collateral required to be pledged by Counterparty to A Bank under the terms of this agreement.
It is usual to insert a catch-all provision that any terms not defined in the Collateral agreement will have the meaning used in the relevant Master Agreement.

B. Method of Marking to Market

At the close of business on an appropriate calculation day [as defined in the agreement], **A Bank shall in a commercially reasonable manner mark-to-market the parties' respective positions under all outstanding transactions under the Master Agreement so as to determine (i) the amount of any Net Exposure which A Bank has at that time (ii) the value of the Collateral being held by A Bank and (iii) the Total Required Collateral as of such day.**

The Total Required Margin shall be equal to the following:

There are a number of techniques to value the required collateral. The first is to fix on a threshold amount, which, when exceeded, requires the deposit of a fixed amount of collateral:

If A Bank has Net Exposure to Counterparty in an amount less than or equal to GBP x, the Total Required Collateral will be GBP y.

In a situation where there is a level of collateral currently held, the Counterparty may be compelled to add to that pool of collateral to bring it up to the Total Required Collateral figure. Alternatively, collateral may not be held already, in which case, the whole of the Total Required Collateral must be provided. Alternatively, an amount of Collateral may be required to be provided to reduce the exposure to a pre-determined level other than zero.

C. Depositing Collateral

The Total Required Margin must be provided to A by close of business on the [insert number of business days within which collateral must be deposited]

The parties may require notice of such requirement to be given by the calculation agent to the other party before the collateral is required.

Counterparty represents that it will be the legal and beneficial owner of any securities constituting the Collateral at the time of depositing such securities and at any other relevant time, and that the Counterparty represents that it shall be free from all charges, liens, interests and encumbrances whatsoever in relation to the said Collateral and that it will have at any relevant time the free and unencumbered right to transfer those securities in pursuance of the terms of this agreement.

The security holder will require an assurance that it has priority security over the relevant assets. This should extend to substituted assets and potentially any accretions to those assets by way of dividend, coupon or otherwise.

Counterparty grants to A Bank a first priority security interest in and a lien upon the Collateral in conjunction with any proceeds of sale thereof, any accretions of value thereto, any distributions thereon and any property substituted therefore whatsoever, as security for the satisfaction of the obligations of the Counterparty under the Master Agreement.

The purpose of the agreement is to secure the rights of the security holder to the assets proferred as Collateral.

In the event of a default by the Counterparty under this agreement or under the Master Agreement, A Bank shall have the full rights of the legal and beneficial owner of the Collateral.

The more difficult issue during the life of the agreement is whether or not the security holder is to be enabled to use the Collateral or whether the Collateral must be maintained in a custody account until a default under the collateral agreement.

In any event, during the life of this agreement, A Bank shall have the unrestricted right to use or rehypothecate any property included in the Collateral, subject only to its obligation to return such property or suitable equivalent property to the Counterparty at the termination of the agreement.

The further problem arises of the location of the Collateral and the possibility of regulatory interference by the *lex loci situationis*.

> **To the extent that any Collateral is located outside of** [jurisdiction] **at any time during the life of this agreement or before the inception of this agreement, that Collateral shall be pledged to A Bank in accordance with the terms of this agreement in accordance with any applicable law of the place where such Collateral is located.**

D. Return of the Collateral

There are a number of circumstances in which collateral may have to be returned. The first is where the exposure of the security holder falls below the level of Collateral that it held. The second is where the Master Agreement or all relevant transactions under it have come to an end.

> **Where on any business day the value of the Collateral then held by A Bank is greater than the value of the Total Required Margin, A Bank shall return to Counterparty Collateral having a value equivalent to any such excess.**

There may be a *de minimis* level set for the amount which the excess must reach before Collateral must be paid back.

> **Where on any business day there are no transactions outstanding under the Master Agreement and where on any business day all of Counterparty's obligations under this agreement have been performed, then** [within a specified time period] **A Bank shall** [pay to Counterparty an amount of cash having a value equivalent to any Collateral then held by A Bank at that date or return securities and cash of like kind, class and value as then constitute the Collateral].

Governing law
Account detail

There are a number of outstanding issues with reference to Collateral which should be addressed in the documentation.

- any market discounts or "haircuts" on securities held as Collateral, should be included in the calculation of the value of the Collateral;

- any regulatory capital requirements should also be taken into account in Collateral valuation;
- the position under regulatory body guidelines must be considered[12].

---

[12] An example of this is any potential requirement under SFA regulations that the collateral be treated as client money or a safe custody investment.

Part 6

The Regulation of the Derivatives Markets

Contents

6.1   The Derivatives Revolution
6.2   The Foreign Exchange Market
6.3   The Derivatives Markets
6.4   The Products Involved
6.5   Types of Institution Involved
6.6   What are the Risks Involved?
6.7   What are the Policy Motivations?
6.8   Possible Solutions
6.9   Regulation
6.10   Taxation
6.11   Overseas
6.12   Conclusions

Executive Summary

1. The derivatives markets are currently valued at a notional amount of US$14 trillion. The danger of systemic risk to the financial markets threatens to destabilise the world economy and to rest control of the economic tiller from the hands of an incoming national governments. The derivatives markets are the 24 hour markets which churn on perpetually around the world driving economic indicators. They can be conducted from anywhere and are driven by the latest developments in computer / telecommunications technology and mathematical theory.

2. Financial markets have the ability to drive macro-economic policy.

3. The derivatives markets and foreign exchange markets are the cause of volatility in financial markets and can only be controlled by the extension of European co-operation and the move towards the development of cross-border currency protection.

4. The Swaps and Derivatives Markets constitute a revolution in the way financial markets are constituted;

    The real risk is that of systemic risk to these markets which would cause huge financial difficulties to the UK's building societies, pension funds, insurance companies and companies, with a resulting fracturing of the economy;

    These risks can be contained by the creation of Clearing House systems for market risk and a prohibition on certain types of institution from involving themselves in speculative activities. These problems are of great current concern in the US Congress and across the EEC;

    The real risks are only now coming to light: the complexity of the products married to the greed of the market players is introducing exceptional volatility to the national economy.

5. The growth of FX and Derivatives speculation (as opposed to hedging)

199

are symptoms of the malaise of the financial system and not signs of its strength nor its sophistication.

Regulatory Proposals

The creation of a regulatory organisation for derivatives products to achieve the following:

1. The standardisation of the documentation for derivatives products
2. The creation of a clearing house for derivatives
3. The creation of guidelines for collateral for non-clearing house derivatives transactions
4. The creation of capital adequacy guidelines for market participants

Legislation to achieve the following:

1. Permitting only hedging transactions for non-banking institutions
2. Accountancy rules requiring total disclosure on the face of accounts
3. Declaration of hedging strategies in accounting materials
4. Standardisation of marking to market procedures
5. Board level overseeing of all non-banks' derivatives transactions
6. Discouragement of derivatives which introduce artificial levels of volatility in financial markets
7. European Union level action to harmonise regulation and to combat foreign currency speculation.

6.1 The Derivatives Revolution

In true Orwellian fashion, technology is growing at such a pace that economic logic is being left behind. The banks and the financial market speculators are the first to benefit from the computer-driven explosion in room 101. The trading desks have hired armies of maths and science graduates to work the cyber-machines that have made the derivatives and foreign exchange markets possible.

Complex mathematical theories and calculations enable traders to forecast (among other things) the volatility on certain instruments, the probabilities of them rising or falling against an index of a hundred other such products, and the correct price for a bond in thirty years time. Of course, to suggest that most of these long term instruments can be structured with any high degree of certainty is not credible, but companies and their financial advisers are betting billions of pounds, dollars and yen, every day, on the accuracy of these financial models in their short, medium and long-term predictions.

The markets have exploded beyond the bounds of self-control, fuelled by one of the largest cash inflows to a market ever seen in economic history. The result is a web of complicated instruments that stretches from the spot foreign exchange markets through share exchanges and bonds markets to world commodities.

The aim of this chapter is to introduce the reader to the modern (postmodern?) FX markets, and to swaps, options, futures and warrants markets; explaining the risks involved in those markets to the economy and to the companies involved. Finally it will propose ways in which regulation should develop to ensure that it retains control of economic policy and that those market risks are effectively managed.

Economic Priorities

In 1993, Metallgesellschaft, the German industrial giant, lost US$1.3 billion in interest rate swaps. In 1994, Proctor and Gamble announced that it had lost US$160 million before tax on two interest rate swaps with Bankers Trust. In 1995, Barings Securities was forced into a position of near insolvency by its failure to supervise the activities of its trader Nick Leeson.

Losses of this size are probably more common in the swaps markets than anybody knows because the companies who suffer them dare not admit to them because such confessions would bring them near to bankruptcy. No outside party can spot the losses because the bilk of derivatives transactions are not recorded in companies' accounts. No one knows the full extent of the risks because no one fully understands the nature of the beast, but every market player involved is in danger.

US$ 420 million passes through the London and New York derivatives markets every day. Of that amount US$ 330 million passes through London alone. (source: the British Bankers Association). The estimated total amount of the market in notional terms is US 14 trillion in 1994. The size of the market is increasing rapidly all the time. The instruments that are being traded on these markets are new and frightening in their complexity. they are also unnaturally profitable for the banks and therefore there is enormous pressure to encourage more and more corporates to play in the market and more and more pressure on resisting regulation of a speculator's paradise.

As Gavyn Davies, one of the Chancellor's seven "wise men" and Managing Director at Goldman Sachs, said recently in discussing the effect of bond market movements on underlying interest rates:

> "These facts show how easily the financial markets can, if they choose, take domestic monetary conditions into their own hands, and out of the hands of the Chancellor. All that the Treasury can do in co-operation with the central bank is determine the spot rate (today's rate) of interest on very short term assets, perhaps up to three months in duration at most. All other rates, now and in the future, may or may not be affected by the authorities' actions at the short end of the money markets – it depends on how the market reads the runes."[1]

---

[1] *The Independent*, March 28, 1994.

There is a further argument that the financial markets have increased in complexity to the detriment of the political process. The growth of the Euromarkets has meant that national governments are no longer able to control the extent of dealings in their own currency and even over the shares of companies that are incorporated in its jurisdiction. Two of the more important elements in the control of national economies have been removed from the control of the national, political process.

The foreign exchange markets and the derivatives markets are closely linked (as will be explained below). What is also linked into these sci-fi money machines is the risk both that control of the economic process will be taken out of the hands of government and that the companies whose success provides fuel for the economy to grow are at risk of enormous loss from the financial markets speculating against them by using these brand new products.

6.2 The Foreign Exchange Market

The Foreign Exchange markets exist to provide access to liquidity for companies and financial institutions and to provide cash resources for corporates to do business across national borders. The foreign exchange markets have also enabled the financial institutions to offer more attractive and complicated funding packages to their clients. The mismatching of interest rates in different countries over different currencies, means that it is often easier to reduce the cost of funding for any corporate project by borrowing in the international money markets.

The FX markets have also become a home for the international speculator who can make use of the arbitrage possibilities between different currency prices and interest rates. It may be that it is cheaper, for example, to access Deutsche Marks from the Sterling markets than from the US Dollar markets. Therefore, the US borrower might use sterling reserves rather than US dollars to obtain Deutsche Marks for a project in Germany which must be paid for in local currency. In the same way, the speculator, anticipating the mismatch between Sterling-Deutsche Mark and Dollar-Deutsche Mark exchange rates (an opening which might exist for only a few hours or even minutes as the result of major market movements by a particular player), might move into Sterling so as to acquire more Deutsche Marks in the expectation that the German economy will show a short term rise. As a result, the successful speculator will be able to sell these Deutsche Marks for more than they were acquired and thus accumulate more capital to risk of further exchange movements.

The growth of the Euromarkets has meant that there is a limited amount which the national economy can do without resorting to either exchange control or the introduction of a two-tier currency, as in South Africa, where one currency is traded on international markets while its sibling cannot be removed from the issuing country or spent elsewhere.

The issue then returns to the central question: does government wish to control these markets or to retain some of the economic benefits taken by those markets by introducing taxation. It may be that to tax speculators does not control the way in which they massage markets. Rather it holds back simply a little of the wealth that is escaping.

The Derivatives Markets   6.3

The derivatives markets grew in the 1980s as a result of the need to manage exposure to high interest rates. In the 1990s the volatility in interest rates has increased. The spectre of global recession has continued with the UK showing a marked reluctance to recover from one of the longest recessions ever. Corporates have seen the need to manage their cash flows in ways other than by increasing profit. The 1980s enabled corporates to grow profits sharply with a boom in marketing and public access to credit facilities. In the 1990s, the focus has shifted to maximising profit by controlling expenses. This has meant "downsizing" (unemployment and the increased use of part-time labour) and seeking better working capital management by obtaining better credit terms from buyers and suppliers. At the same time, treasurers have been looking to obtain better use from existing funding capabilities. The derivatives markets enable the Treasurer to manage the cost of funding more precisely and to control the risks of movements in prices or interest rates.

What is its economic role?   6.3.1

The derivatives market aims to enable participants to manage their exposure to the risk of movements in interest rates and securities prices. Therefore they operate for both the speculator and the prudent corporate treasurer. In 1994 the bond markets have undergone trauma every bit as dramatic as the stock market crashes in the late 1980s. Commodity prices have been hit by the violence in the run-up to the South African elections and the break-up of the old Eastern Europe. The need to find new products to invest in for the speculator have led to the enormous growth in the swaps markets.

The role of the derivatives salesperson in a bank and the in-house strategists is to forecast movements in the financial markets generally. They take views on interest rates movements up to 30 years into the future and on the shares, bond and commodity markets. As a result of the forecasts that they make they isolate mismatches in the markets which can be manipulated for the benefit of clients. The banks either take a view contrary to their clients or a view contrary to the markets. As such they are betting on their view being correct and that of everyone else being wrong.

203

6.4 The Products involved

6.4.1 Foreign exchange

The foreign exchange markets operate at two levels in the modern context. The first level is that of the company which acts like a holidaymaker in a bureau de change looking to buy foreign currency cheaply. The second is the speculative opportunities offered by the difference between the fortunes of different currencies and the particular sensitivities to particular events. The banks make their money by buying from one another at one price and then selling to their clients at a mark-up to the price at which they acquired the money. This is in the way that newsagents pay one price for the newspapers that they sell to the publishers and then charge a higher cover price to the ordinary punter. The difference is a mark-up, or in the financial jargon a "spread".

The real danger to the economy is caused by the banks, and some of the larger corporate institutions, who trade currencies among themselves. This is a mixed process of ensuring that the bank has enough liquid cash in the right currencies but also of exploiting the brief mismatches that exist between currencies. It may be that sterling falls but that the French franc rises more slowly against it than the US dollar because of the particular circumstances of the French economy. The speculator can take advantage of the brief anomaly between franc and dollar prices for sterling and move between the currency. These are relatively minor blips but they do require the use of central bank (Bank of England) capital to preserve the price of the currency.

The greater danger yet is that of the speculator, or band of speculators, who take long term positions on the price of a currency and buy a large amount of it. As with Sterling before it fell out of the ERM, the rising price of the currency as interest rates rose, enabled Soros, Citibank and others, to buy large quantities of sterling cheap, sell them at the peak before the withdrawal and then buy them all back in again when the currency reached rock bottom. The herd instinct of the currency markets takes hold of a currency in the same way that a violent sea takes hold of a small boat. As the waves of traders move in the same direction, the currency is thrown along. To protect the currency, the Bank of England is required to buy large amounts of sterling at a high price to maintain the price of the currency. There are plenty of sellers in this situation. The result is that the speculator takes money straight out of the treasury and puts it into its own pockets.

The banks are making profits because they do not have to think about the exigencies of macroeconomic policy. The six housing programmes lost to Black Wednesday mean that the country, already in trouble, gets even poorer. The companies looking to borrow money or to ensure that they have enough of a particular currency to meet their payment obligations suddenly find that the underlying tenets upon which they have built their funding requirements, have been torn from under them. The cost is always recovered from the ultimate customer.

Speculation on a currency upsets economic planning. The question is how to mitigate the effects of speculation while allowing UK companies to participate in international markets with currencies other than sterling.

Swaps   6.4.2

A swap is simply an exchange of the rate of interest that a borrower is paying for a different rate of interest. Company A will agree to pay the interest on the debt it owes to B bank, in return for which Company A will pay a different rate of interest to the Bank C with which it has entered into the swap. This is a simple exchange of cash flows for a fee.

A corporate may wish to fix the rate of interest that it is paying so that it can forecast its future cash flows with confidence. This may be as part of a corporate restructuring or the renegotiation of its borrowing limits with its banks. In the past it may only have been able to obtain floating rate funding. The bank will therefore pay the corporate's floating interest rate obligations in return for which it will receive an agreed upon fixed rate of income from the corporate. The bank makes its money by charging the corporate an interest rate spread over the fixed amount paid to it. The corporate benefits by a reduced cost of funds in the medium to long term, if interest rates rise upwards. If interest rates do rise upwards, then the fixed rate of interest will probably be lower than the floating rate of interest that the corporate would otherwise have been paying. If interest rates do not rise, but actually fall or remain stagnant, then the corporate will be paying the more for its borrowing than if it had done nothing. This is level at which even the most conservative funding policy is tantamount to speculation. The interest rate swap necessitates a bet on the future movement of interest rates. If the corporate in this example finds that interest rates have moved against it, it will be forced to enter into another swap transaction to bet the other way.

This is the vortex that the Hammersmith and Fulham local authority was caught in. The local authority bet wrong time after time and entered into over five hundred separate transactions like a gambler at a casino on a losing streak. Corporates can be caught in this loop, the risks of suffering financial loss are the same for them as for every organisation in the markets.

Derivatives are dependant on the underlying markets which they mirror. They are therefore subject to the large scale movements in the underlying markets. The reverse is true. The opinions that the swaps markets form about interest rate movements with reference to currencies between 3 months and 30 years out, create speculative pressure on those currencies that is linked only to short term views on those currencies. there is no way in which the pricing for a 30 year maturity interest rate swap can claim to have any realistic hope of anticipating the interest rate appropriate for the Italian lire, for example. The bank does not concern itself about this inherent inaccuracy because it can always swap again to reverse its exposure. However, while the bank can cover its bet, the lire will be affected by the speculative pressure that is introduced onto the lire in the short term. A large swap transaction of this type that anticipates a volatile movement in the lire will affect the way in which the markets look at lire rates and therefore will introduce volatility to the spot price.

6.4.3 Options

Option theory is one of the jewels of Business School degrees. Both in terms of the options available in terms of management choices and in terms of derivative instruments. An option gives the buyer the ability either to have delivered to it or to compel another party to purchase the thing which is the subject of the contract. This can be an option to buy or sell shares, commodities, bonds or even the right to be paid or to pay money at a particular rate of interest. The option gives the participant the right to choose whether or not the price is right. As such an option can be a cheap way of guaranteeing the price of a share for example. If ICI shares are trading at 500 pence in May 1994, the buyer of an option might want to acquire the ability to be sold a specific number of ICI shares at the price of 550 pence on November 1, 1994. If ICI shares are trading at 600 pence each on November 1, then the option offers a great bet for the purchaser. The banks and others who sell options receive the price paid for the option itself. This option, and the rights under it, can be traded. So Citibank might sell an option to Goldman Sachs who might in turn sell that option to Unilever. Therefore the option may be a form of security that is capable of being traded on its own account.

It is important to note that derivatives offer a cheap form of speculation because the cost of, for example, an option is cheap compared to the potential economic benefit if the bet underlying the option works out. Therefore a corporate may pay, for example, £10,000 for an option which may yield £1 million a year afterwards. The danger is that if the bet goes the wrong way, £10,000 has been wasted. The more this is done, the more money is wasted. Swaps are cheap when the corporate exchanges its interest stream for another. It is only when rates move that the corporate is forced to pay more than it would otherwise. The risks only come to fruition when the markets move against the original bet. Derivatives start out cheap but end up expensive.

6.4.4 Warrants

Options are also bought and sold in respect of baskets of shares or other financial products. A new form of option has been developed: the warrant. A warrant is an obligation on the part of the issuer to provide a pre-determined number of a particular type of share to the investor at the time specified by the warrant. This is similar to an option in that a view is taken on the likely future price of the underlying security and at a particular time, the investor can exchange the option for the security to which it relates. The warrant need not be issued with the consent of the relevant corporate. There is therefore an element of volatility introduced to the price of the underlying security by the view that is taken by the warrant market covering it. The very fact that a financial institution issues warrants over a share, introduces the expectation that that share will perform well in the market. This will lead to a rise in the price of the share. The danger is that the share has further to fall in the future. Therefore, should the corporate be on the brink of announcing a major international bond issue to raise debt financing, it might find that adverse speculation in the market will affect its perceived credit worth when all that is happening is the market righting itself in the wake of the artificial rise in price caused by the warrant issue.

Again speculation in these markets introduces inherent volatility to the underlying security. This in turn can mean that the corporate involved has difficulty in accessing finance to which would otherwise be within easy reach.

Forwards   6.4.5

Similar to the option, in theory, is the forward markets. There are some forward contracts traded on organised exchanges and others which are the preserve of the OTC markets. The forward is a promise to supply a particular commodity or security at a set price on a set date (often in a set place). In the commodity markets it is usual to buy wheat, for example, at a given price in a given amount at a pre-determined time to be delivered in a given place. In the time it takes for the contract to mature (which might include the wheat to grow be harvested and shipped) the price of wheat can fluctuate wildly. The contract, that is the right to receive the wheat at a price at a time in the agreed place, can be sold to others at a greater or lower price than that paid for it originally. The same is true, to a greater or lesser extent, of contracts entered into between private parties.

It is worth digressing briefly to consider the relationship between swaps, options and forwards. A swap is, by one analysis, a series of forward contracts to pay or to receive an amount of money on a particular date according to the movement in a chosen interest rate. A forward is like two options: one a call option sold to a party to demand payment for a consignment of wheat and on the other hand a put option which entitles the other party to sell the wheat, according to movements in the price of wheat. Therefore, a swap could also be a series of put and call options to receive or to pay an amount of money on a particular date, with reference to a particular interest rate.

The products are all, therefore linked in an essential way. They are at route rights or obligations to pay or to receive sums of money according to the movement in a chosen indicator, whether that be an interest rate, a share index, or the price of a bond or commodity index. The analysis of the risks involved with these products should therefore take account of the essential linkage in the bets that are being taken. And the concept of a "bet" is the most important consideration for the regulator. There are bets which reduce the risk of bigger bets that the market participants are taking and those bets which are simply a bigger form of gambling in themselves.

6.4.6 "Hedging"

Hedging is the part that then requires all the mathematical skill of the banker. A market player has a financial instrument and therefore wishes to purchase another instrument which will show a profit if the first instrument shows a loss. It is a little like betting on a two-horse race. You place a bet on the grey horse to win but you are worried that you will lose your stake if the brown horse wins. So you "hedge" your risk by putting a bet on the brown horse that will produce a large enough win to equal the cost of your stake on betting on the grey. In the financial markets of course things are more complex but the principle is the same. If you are betting on UK base rates falling further and so have bought a swap to that effect, you need another type of product (maybe an option indexed to the FTSE-100) which will pay out enough to cover your loss if UK base rates go up. The decisions are then as to the likely rise of base rates and the amount that you are likely to lose should rates go up.

No one is compelled to hedge. It is cheaper, in the short term, not to hedge because you do not have to pay a fee for the hedge. It is all a matter of risk. What is the likelihood that a risk will be needed. And if we need a hedge, can we get away with a small hedge or should we pay for a full hedge. For Proctor and Gamble to have lost US$ 160 million just on the interest it was paying, means that its hedge must have been pathetic in comparison to the real risk which must have been the interest on a debt of about US$1.6 billion. The problem for the regulator is therefore to ensure that full hedging is introduced. This is discussed in more detail below.

The important message to take from hedging is that players do not tend to play once in the market. We have already seen that Hammersmith and Fulham did not swap once, they swapped hundreds of times with lots of different institutions. Similarly, each position is not a one off. ICI might swap with Goldman Sachs but ICI will want to hedge that swap and so will enter into another transaction with Bankers Trust. Goldman Sachs and Bankers Trust will both want to hedge out their liabilities with NatWest and Deutsche Bank. In turn Deutsche Bank and NatWest will want a hedge with Barclays and with Citibank.

This discussion of derivatives might lead us to believe that the way for sovereign borrowers (that is, countries) and all other market players to protect themselves against market movements is to take out a protective hedging position. This does miss the point that to rely on hedging, as the US courts have begun to indicate the financial markets are, is to throw total dependence upon the banks to control our exposure to the crisis that the banks are creating in the first place. Derivative instruments are a symptom, to use the tired metaphor, rather than a cure for the disease of market volatility. It also misses the point that the capitalist system has begun to play complicated games with itself that affect the lives of ordinary people but which have no earthly connection to them.

Types of institution involved   6.5

Having looked at the types of market and product that are available, it as well to look at the types of entity that are involved in the markets. For those who take the view that capitalistic markets should be left to the capitalists to organise themselves, there waits the revelation that these complex markets are being accessed by a number of institutions which are central to aspirant notions of the regeneration of the economy. As shown above, there is the risk of large corporates encountering difficulties and so effecting the fortunes of those entities which supply or buy from them. Of equal concern are the non-industrial services which the population relies on. Local authorities, pension funds, insurance companies and building societies are major players in many of these markets: not just to the extent of managing their cost of funds but also in the realms of pure financial speculation. Those who control our ability to buy and own our homes, those who organise all of our local services, those who ensure that our loved ones will be provided for after we die, those who we rely upon to provide for us in our old age, are playing the financial markets as though they are carefree investment bankers.

Local Authorities   6.5.1

The ability of local authorities to enter into swaps transactions was forbidden retrospectively by the House of Lords in the case of *Hazell v. Hammersmith* and Fulham local authority. The local authority had been seeking to speculate on interest rate movements by entering into a series of swaps transactions. When the initial bets went wrong, the authority entered into more and more until the total numbered more than 500 and the authority was unable to meet the interest payments that it was required to make. The same fate befell a number of local authorities attempting to make the best of the meagre rations given to them by central government and the debt facilities that they were able to access. The authority went to court armed with the argument that it was unable, legally, to enter into these transactions in any event and that all the transactions in which they had become involved were void from the date in which they were entered into. The result was that the authority was liable to make any of the payments required by the contracts.

This fortunate result was due to the court realising that the policy implications of requiring the residents of the local borough to pay increased poll taxes and business rates to make good the shortfall was insupportable. The policy of declaring some forms of entity incapable of entering into some forms of transaction is one that should be considered carefully to prevent organisations such as the borough councils from indulging in these transactions and exposing the essential services which they provide to being withdrawn as a result of financial negligence.

6.5.2 Building Societies

The dream of the home-owning democracy is built around the need to access funding to buy homes. The price of the housing market is too high for all but the richest in society to require secured debt funding to purchase their housing. The modern law of property gives the lender the ability to repossess the property at any time during the life of the mortgage if a single payment is late. The properties are actually owned by the building societies. The true ramifications of this have yet to be understood by the policy markers. The existence of the property-owning democracy myth requires the connivance of the building societies not only to provide the money for the house buying but also to refrain from repossessing properties during the life of the mortgage. If building societies go bankrupt, then their customers, the home-owners, will lose their homes to the creditors of the building society.

There are two recent developments in building society funding that are of note here. The first is asset securitisation (a form of derivative if we stretch our definition to its logical limits) and the second is the use of the swaps markets.

6.5.3 Asset Securitisation

Asset securitisation involves bundling assets together and selling them on as a block to someone who is prepared to deal with each of those assets separately. In the case of building societies this means collecting together all of the cash inflows expected from mortgage payments into a single, larger asset and selling it on to a purchaser. It is a sort of complex factoring, or debt-collection, arrangement. The purchaser will manage the individual cash flows. That means the purchaser acquires the rights to everyone's mortgage payments and, as a corollary, the right to repurchase their houses. There is a possible conflict here between the policy on repossessions of Nice Building Society PLC and Machiavellian Debt Collectors Limited. While the debt collectors will be a large bank or other such institution buying cash inflows at a discount, their repossession policy might be very different. Securitising assets therefore proffers a new threat to the political process in the absence of protection rights for the resident or control of the securitisation markets.

The advantage for the building society is a lump sum for cash flow which it will take many years to filter through. For the purchaser who has a long term view of its need to generate income, such as a pension fund, the cash inflow over time will guarantee that it can meet its payment obligations to the pensioners who have invested in it.

The Swaps Markets 6.5.4

The risks with reference to the swaps and derivatives markets are the same for the building societies as for the local authorities. There is limited restriction on the ability of the building societies to enter into swaps transactions. There remains the essential difference between entering into speculation and entering into transactions which simply hedge existing liabilities. The need for further legislation in this area must be balanced against the importance of the building societies in the national economy and the undesirability of the government having to support the societies at some point in the future.

The last remaining question to be flagged up for discussion later is that of the building society with large financial assets which it will be prevented from putting to use to ease the need for it to retain high interest rates over its customers. Therefore how can the building societies be enabled to mitigate their financial risks in the FX and derivatives markets and also take advantage of the clear speculative opportunities that exist while preventing them from entering into "dangerous" transactions?

Insurance Companies 6.5.5

Insurance companies play a similarly important role to building societies and have the same streams of cash inflows with equivalent risks of default on those payments. They then seek to invest the assets that they have and play the financial markets. The derivatives markets enable them to acquire funds at suitably low prices while also offering speculative opportunities to match their ability to play the stock markets while hedging out their risks.

Pension Funds 6.5.6

The same position obtains for pension funds as for building societies and insurance companies. The extra spice is added by the failure of the Maxwell pension funds debacle and the calls for tighter regulation of the business and control of pension funds. There are risks that operate more broadly than the risk of misappropriation of funds: there is the risk that the pension funds will lose money and therefore have to reduce the amounts that they pay out to their investors. It is perhaps scaremongering on an excessive scale to spread alarm about the risks of pension finds going broke on the basis of stock market crashes. The pension funds are among the largest players in these markets and can generally absorb even large "readjustments" in the markets. What they are not able to absorb is the systemic risk of the derivatives markets crashing such that the pension funds, the insurance companies and the building societies, find themselves owing money to and owed money by entities which have gone insolvent and whose liquidators are entitled to demand repayment. The section on "Systemic Risk" poses the problems in more detail below (and considers some solutions) but it is worth remembering that the special, contractual nature of the derivatives markets makes even the largest players vulnerable.

6.5.7 Hedge Funds

Returning to the issue of enhanced speculation by the derivatives markets, we should consider a particular type of fund: the hedge fund. These funds are termed "hedge funds" as part of a facile illusion that they are averse to risk. In fact hedge funds are highly leveraged entities which seek to take enormous risks in the financial markets to make returns for their investors which outstrip the market return. Some hedge funds report returns of 50 per cent while the markets are playing at about 10 per cent.

A hedge fund is a simple Special Purpose Vehicle, separately capitalised by banks and other institutions to take aggressive positions in financial markets and deliver a large return to its owners. Their appetite for risk is large and they are expendable to some extent in the eyes of their owners. While hedge funds have existed for some time (they were launched in the USA in 1949), it is the "macro hedge funds" which were formed in the early 1990's to maximise return in high risk markets when the US and recessionary European stock markets were offering small returns on capital.

The most important facet of a hedge fund is that it is highly leveraged: that is, the notional principal of the obligations into which it enters, greatly exceed the assets which it owns. Therefore they use the futures, options and other derivative markets because they are only required to pay a small amount upfront. They increase the amount they can bet by posting collateral with banks.

The four largest funds (Tiger, Quantum, Steinhardt and Omega) manage US$25 billion out of a total industry of US$80 billion. These funds have been accused of acting in concert with the effect that the bond markets were destabilised in February 1994. Hedge funds could certainly have started the run on the market even though it required the larger players (the mutual funds, etc.) to follow their lead and cause the real downsizing. Many of the hedge funds seem to have been holding too many US dollars and therefore incurred large losses when the Japanese yen rose unexpectedly against the dollar. Therefore they sold their way out of their bond positions, thus destabilising the market. This is a prime example of the way in which derivatives markets and market players can destabilise the means by which corporates raise their money (in this case the bond markets) without there being any underlying problem associated with that market. This form of risk is termed "cross product risk". Hedge funds take aggressive positions in a number of markets at once, principally by using derivatives which are cheap at the time in which they are entered into and will only become expensive if the bet upon which they are bought goes wrong.

Clearly, these entities are dealing heavily in derivatives to manage the volatility in their portfolios. The February 1994 fall in the bond markets has been blamed by the financial press on the hedge funds taking aggressive positions. There is no way in which the hedge funds could be large enough to cause a crash of the size witnessed in February 1994 but they are large enough and aggressive enough to have sparked a downward spiral in prices which sparked the markets into turmoil.

The danger with hedge funds is that they can spark off volatility that otherwise might not have existed or which might have been confinable. The other problem is that they can cause liquidity problems for those who deal with them if they are under-capitalised. The greatest danger of all, as with all investment funds, from the point of view of those with whom they deal, is that no one need know who is putting up the money. If the fund is simply an agent, the bank dealing with them might not be able to sue the principal for whom the agent is acting. Alternatively, it may be that the principal is subsequently found to be incapable, at law, of dealing in derivatives and the contracts may have to be unwound, at cost to both parties. The problem of the undisclosed principal is a great one and of itself introduces greater risk into the market.

Corporates   6.5.8

The corporates have formed the primary part of the examples used to indicate the types of product used up to now. There are a number of products to do particularly with speculation on shares that affect the ability of companies to access funding because of the perceived volatility in their credit worth that is created. The risks of the corporates entering into the markets as principals are then located in the types of product that they choose to use. The largest fear with reference to corporates is the issuing of warrants and options over a company's shares which can only serve to increase volatility associated with those shares and therefore hamper the corporate's own decisions as to its future funding. An over supply of warrants in the market will make it difficult for the corporate to issue shares itself if the market has already chosen to speculate on a purchase of a particular number of shares at a particular price at a particular time. The corporates may wish to seek protection to enable the economy to operate in isolation from the financial markets.

6.5.9 Banks

The banks are the main beneficiaries from the rise in the derivatives markets because they are a new business for which they can charge premium rates and because they offer speculative opportunities in the game that banks play between themselves. The money to pay for these gains has to come from somewhere. The real cost is met by the central banks and the investors in these markets.

As Dalehas said in his book *The Regulation of International Banking*: "the business of banking is, in a literal sense, a large-scale confidence trick". The point he was making was that of bank's total assets, that means money raised from shareholders and loans made to customers and other moneys due, only 3–4 per cent of total assets are cash received from shareholders. Therefore the remainder of the assets which the financial institutions leverage to fund their forays into the financial markets, are promises to pay money. The markets are therefore relying on the promises made to the financial institutions to back up the financial institutions own promises to pay money. The markets need to have confidence in banks who can only show cash-in-hand for about 4 per cent of the money that it owes into the market at any one time. In short the banks do not have enough money to pay their debts. They have the confidence of their creditors that they will make interest payments on time. The confidence of the markets is their most valuable asset. Derivatives markets in particular require such confidence. While this may sound hysterical, in the 1980's and the 1990's, banks have gone insolvent. In the UK, BCCI has been the largest name. In the USA, First Massachusetts and Continental are among the notable insolvencies. Banks are not cast in iron. Hedge funds do not even pretend to be.

6.6 What are the risks involved?

6.6.1 The risks to the economy

The risks to the economy have been spelled out above. The markets introduce volatility and affect the performance of corporate investors.

6.6.2 Systemic risk

Senior partner at Goldman Sachs, Stephen Friedman, was asked in a newspaper profile what he considered to be the greatest risk to the firm. His predecessor had answered the same question by saying simply: "nuclear war". Friedman considers the real threat to be: "systemic risk". This, more than nuclear war, is the threat to the financial system. Systemic risk is built around the complex web of derivatives deals that was discussed earlier. If one player in the market goes bankrupt, the remainder of the market will then have exposure to the bankrupt entity either directly or indirectly. If this in turn forces other entities into liquidation the exposure of each player in the market to one another intensifies, with the very real possibility that the entire market will collapse. The derivatives markets constitute not only a possible means of reducing risk, but also a composite $7 trillion risk to the financial system in themselves.

Systemic risk is the risk that the whole market falls apart and that many of its participants are driven into bankruptcy, or at best financial difficulty. In the derivatives markets there is a great risk of this caused by the matrix pattern that the need to hedge exposure produces. When a swap is entered into, parties usually hedge out that exposure. That means that every transaction has its roughly equal and opposite sibling. Therefore each institution will tend to deal twice to be hedged. Therefore every party becomes linked to every other party in this web of, literally, double-dealing. The fact that an option is cheap to enter into (there is only the small upfront premium to pay) means that the risk of financial loss does not arise until later when the option is either in or out of the money. The fact that these obligations are held off-balance sheet means that creditors (whether trade creditors or banks) do not know of the other party's exposure. If a party cannot pay its obligations under one transaction, it will mean that it cannot pay its obligations under all of its other transactions. Unlike normal bankruptcies or credit events, all the other players in the market are affected because the complex house of cards falls down. Every counterparty in the market is put under pressure in respect of its obligations.

Netting 6.6.3

Under many systems of insolvency law, an insolvent company will be entitled to receive all moneys owed to it but not to pay any moneys out. Therefore, if X Ltd has four swaps with Y Bank, X can receive its money on the two swaps that have worked in its favour while it does not have to pay out under the two swaps that have gone wrong for it. The result for Y bank, and all of X's other creditors is a large loss. A system of insolvency law that enforces all of the obligations such that X and Y find the difference of all of their transactions and the net amount is paid to the party who is owed it. This ensures that Y does not suffer such a large loss.

The further policy question is this: should the creditors of X Ltd have to suffer a removal of assets from insolvent X by force of a law designed to protect swaps market participants. The answer is probably that it is incumbent on commercial parties to take security for debts owed to them. The swaps obligations are so large that they could destabilise the financial markets and increase the cost of borrowing of individuals and corporates in all jurisdictions. The creditors will be able to right the loss off for tax and therefore the damage will probably be easier to contain than if the risk is allowed to spread into the market generally. There is therefore a need for English law to make certain its insolvency code in this respect.

6.6.4   Liquidity in Access to Funding

The notion of liquidity is different from solvency. The aim of a treasury function is to provide liquidity without impacting the solvency of the entity in one way or another. Liquidity means matching obligations with ability to pay. Therefore the currency and maturity of obligations have to be controlled and matched with assets of similar profiles. This should not affect the business at all. Derivatives and FX markets aim to add to this pool of liquidity as well as adding speculative obligations. the aim of regulation should be to ensure the liquidity of the markets and of the system by requiring that the obligations of all players in the markets are aimed at the production of liquidity in real, rather than invented, obligations. This is the way in which a regulatory system that focuses on hedging can ensure that institutions are involved in "economically safe" forms of activity. The second strand of regulation should then be addressed at activities which are not directed at the reduction of some form of risk associated with a real obligation. The risk with insisting on hedging is that the institutions simply create obligations which are speculative activities but which are presented as moneys owed and hedged on the other side. The way in which this form of avoidance can be obstructed is by altering the capacity of entities to enter into transactions unless they are for a commercial purpose, a test which is used widely in tax legislation.

The question is then: what to do about those entities whose capacity is not controlled by a system of law within the UK? One solution is to force all institutions entering into transactions in the UK to use a UK entity. This will simply return activity to the Euromarkets.

6.6.5   Credit risk

What reviews are taken of counterparty (e.g.: hedge fund) credit before entering into the transaction? It is only recently that the banks have begun to look at the credit risk involved in these markets. The issue of hedge funds and unknown principals behind other investment funds, means that it is impossible for the counterparty to enter into any due diligence over the entity with which it is contracting. The solution to this issue is to delineate between situations where the counterparty can undertake a commercially reasonable due diligence procedure (i.e.: it is aware of the party or the party has been rated by a credit agency) and otherwise. Where there has been no due diligence process, one of two things must happen. The counterparty must either have a guarantee from an entity in respect of which it has performed due diligence or it must have taken a sufficient level of margin (that is collateral in the form of shares or other securities) to cover that risk.

Product risk 6.6.6

What are the credit risks associated simply with the products themselves? How are swaps accounted for? what is the inherent danger if these products remain off-balance sheet?

The swaps markets are relatively new and the products that are being developed are similarly embryonic. What is not clear is the form that national and supranational regulation of the markets will take in the future. It may be that the markets are left to their own devices or the share-based products might come under close scrutiny. If the latter occurs, the products will not meet their objectives. The vast unscrambling procedure which I described as part of the hedging procedure will then have to be carried out for an entire segment of the market place.

The other problem is that the products are only designed for the short term in which the predictions upon which they are designed, hold true. It is the ideal market. In the same way that narcotics create a dependency in the user, once the product no longer works, the user is required to buy more. Derivatives only work for so long as the markets follow the expected patterns. After that time the user has to pay for more to cater for new market conditions. This process is acceptable only for so long as the use of the products is to manage the risks. Once they develop into speculative positions, then there is unacceptable risk for those institutions which we can identify as being central to the macro-economy.

Accounting Information 6.6.7

The markets need to know about the exposure of the counterparties with which they are dealing. Trade Creditors need to know whether the company it is supplying can meet its obligations and banks need to know more about the risks involved in the companies to which they are lending money. The following are some of the questions:

- How will we know about a company's interest rate strategy?
- How will we know a company's exposure to an index which might crash?
- How will we know if a company's stock could be affected by being part of a basket of derivative instruments?

Accountancy rules must be altered so that companies are required to publish their interest rate and other derivative strategies. The derivatives entered into and the gains/losses that result, must be made visible on the balance sheet as unrealised assets or liabilities of the company.

217

6.6.8 Capacity Issues

One of the great unresolved legal questions is whether or not a number of legal persons can enter into these transactions at all. We can be sure about local authorities after Hammersmith and Fulham but not about the extent to which insurance companies and building societies are permitted to stray in the field of derivatives transactions.

One of the regulators' tasks must be to stipulate the entities that can and cannot enter into these transactions and the exact type of transactions that are acceptable.

6.6.9 Political risk / Sovereign risk

The points made with reference to product risk obtain to country risk.

6.6.9/1 Marking to Market

The system of calculating profit is known as marking to market. That means measuring the amount made against the market movement for the day. By comparing amounts made with daily market movements on a three month swap, neither party can calculate accurately the amount that they will or will not receive at the end of three months from the movements in the market on the day that that is entered into. Nor does it compute the cost of doing the transaction and the cost of entering into the hedge. It does not factor in the level of risk involved and the completeness of the cover offered by the hedge. A centrally controlled system of marking to market will be necessary for any regulator seeking to take control of the varying amounts owed in the marketplace.

6.7 What are the policy motivations?

The policy motivations must be:

- To allow corporates and other institutions to protect themselves against the risk of volatility in financial markets
- To ensure that the financial markets which provide employment for the UK are not driven offshore
- To ensure that the financial markets which we wish to regulate are not driven offshore
- To reduce speculation in the FX and derivatives markets so that underlying markets are not made artificially volatile
- To prevent specified institutions from indulging in speculation in markets that are too risky
- To insulate the financial markets on which coroporates and others

rely to raise funding from being polluted by hedge funds and other entities with high risk appetites

Speculation -v- hedging   6.7.1

To control risks is positive. To allow some forms of entity to take large risks is negative.

To allow corporates to dabble in these markets contains risks for the employment prospects of a nation and to the general economic condition of the country. (In Germany in 1993, Metallgesellscahft lost US$ 1.3 billion on oil futures contracts.

Regulation of the large financial markets   6.7.2

Can we afford to let these markets continue uncontrolled? If there are dangers to the economy, should we seek to control them?

The question is how should regulation be introduced so that markets do not shift offshore. In short, the UK should only seek to impose regulation on those assets and markets which fall within its geographical jurisdiction. Therefore the shares and debt instruments issued by UK incorporated entities should be protected from the option and forwards markets.

Stability in the economy   6.7.3

The following appear to be the economic priorities:

- For a managed system of regeneration of the economy, the economy must be stable. We must allow stabilising influences.
- The need to plan in the absence of exceptional volatility
- Derivatives involve exceptional volatility to the economy and exercise even greater. To say that there is less volatility produced by derivatives in the UK is to ignore the point that "some volatility" is too much volatility in any event.

Possible solutions   6.8

Clearing house   6.8.1

The way in which the exchanges control credit risk between parties is by the use of standardised products and clearing houses. With derivatives, it is rare for products to be identical although many of the products are of a vintage that it is only the greed of the banks for ever greater profit that leads them to "add value" to basic structures. By ensuring that everyone is buying the same thing when they buy a swap, for example, will ensure that, in the same way that buying a share gives the investor certainty in what it is receiving, the swap participant can have more confidence in understanding the product up for sale. Proctor and Gamble, previously perceived as a sophisticated client, clearly did not understand what it was being sold by Banker Trust. A standardised product would be preferable for the investor and preferable for creditors of the investor so that they can read a company's accounts and understand better the risks that it is involved in.

Once a standardised form of product is defined, a clearing house is required. A clearing house is a corporation created by the market but regulated by the Bank of England, that acts as a central repository for all the risks in the market. The clearing house has large financial institutions as clearing members. Clearing members deal with smaller financial institutions and with the corporates looking to access the market. The clearing members net-off all the risks owed between those corporates and small financial institutions. The clearing members then account at the end of every day to the clearing house for all the risks that have been netted off by it between non-clearing members. The clearing house then nets off the risks between all of the clearing members.

This guards against much of the systemic risk that exists. Rather than the markets owing money to each other as part of the large web of obligations, amounts are only owed on a net basis after the clearing house has worked out who owed what to whom at the end of the day. The risk of netting on insolvency is thereby removed.

This system can operate for most options, warrants, swaps and many forwards. Separate regulation will be required for those derivatives which are contracted on an off-exchange basis because they do not meet with the exchange's definitions. One important point that should be noted is the shock waves that Proctor and Gamble is causing. Corporates and other non-speculating institutions would welcome an exchange to guard against the enormous risks that face them. P&G was recognised as a "big player" that could take care of itself. If P&G can fall, so can all the other corporates with smaller treasury departments and large swaps positions.

The structure and the rules of a clearing house bear all the credit risk. The clearing house will develop rules for the standardisation of products and standards as to the payment of obligations and the delivery of products (e.g.: commodities). Traders on an exchange deliver deal tickets by computer to the central exchange system. Depending upon the level of membership of the player, that player will only be able to take a given level of financial risk which can be monitored by the computer system. All trades carried out between parties on the exchange are contracts between those parties. At the end of the day those contracts are "novated" (transferred and renewed) to the clearing house. This means that the parties do not contract with one another anymore. Rather they have new contracts with the clearing house so that the clearing house stands between the parties. The whole of the risk is therefore with the clearing house. The clearing house owes money to both parties and both parties owe money to it.

Netting

The clearing house then matches all the receipt and payment obligations it has with each party and the balance is paid over to whoever is owed it. Remember that because the clearing house has the obligations of both sides of every trade it should, at the end of every trading day be able to balance all its receipts and obligations with the result that its owes nobody and is owed by nobody. This is a form of system netting. If a player does go bankrupt, all that risk is balanced out by the exchange. It receives no money from that insolvent entity and similarly does not have to pay any money to it. The debts and credits are balanced off and the loss is absorbed by the clearing house. This loss will be no more than the credit of the player with the clearing house in any event.

Capital adequacy

Capital adequacy rules for participants ensure that only those who can deal with the risks are allowed to play. The markets are allowing the risks to go beyond the capability of the institutions to meet the given level of risk.

- A Capital Adequacy policy requires a number of difference means of satisfying the danger of paying debts. There are three ways of doing this which are appropriate for differing types of investor.
- Absolute Capital levels held in deposit accounts.
- Compulsory insurance
- Government guarantees for depositors

The aim should not be to establish a capital adequacy norm at an absolute amount of equity but rather to operate by means of financial ratios which indicate the entities' ability to meet its obligations. The ratio would require that the level of exposure to the selected markets would not exceed the pre-decided amount.

Collateral

Rather than rely solely on capital adequacy, which can be subjected to accounting arbitrage strategies, the use of collateral with the clearing house ensures that the clearing house has access to sufficient collateral (or margin) to cover the loss caused by the insolvency. The following are the types of regulation necessary for the type of margin deposited:

- margin of the right quality
- margin to take effect on insolvency

The one question of policy here is the balance of the need for the margin to take effect on bankruptcy versus the need for general creditors on insolvency to be protected. In the view of the size of the risk of market collapse, as discussed below, it is this writer's view that creditors will be able to absorb the loss better than the swaps market.

There is an alternative to the Clearing House, which is proposed by some of the banks which is a form of Standardised Collateral Management. This system is a form of clearing house for collateral which has been organised informally by one of the large banks. As such it is a private arrangement and lacks the benefit of being transparent to those outside the market. The benefit of a centrally organised clearing house is that it removes 99 per cent of the risk rather than leaving it to the parties to organise that they deal between themselves with 20–50 per cent of the risk.

6.8.5 Regulatory Authority

The result of the above discussion is that there is a need for a regulatory authority to consider the technical aspects of derivatives. The central proposal of a clearing house also requires that the market participants are performing their own internal controls efficiently. It is not possible to count up the number of contracts you have and know as a result the exposure to that market. Derivatives rely upon the calculation function but for the market to become standardised as to risk and as to documentation, there must be a benchmark for measurement set.

Without a doubt, all market participants will argue that whatever standard is set, it does not agree with *their* best guess. That process of itself will show that there is no common best guess in this market. Therefore, a standard needs to be chosen simply to concentrate the minds of the market on the risk that exists. This will also enable the market to measured from one central point and for the regulator to be able to locate those entities who are transgressing trading limits or capital adequacy or minimum cash flow ratio requirements as a result.

Therefore, as in the proposed legislation in the USA, there must be an authority selected with a time scale of not more than one year to select a method of marking to market derivatives transactions. Market participants will then be required to demonstrate their exposure on an accounting basis in accordance with this method and to demonstrate, by reference to their own models, why they think that they have a lower exposure than the regulatory model. This exercise will produce a benchmark by which those entities which have been identified as vital to the UK economy above, will be prevented by acquiring an over-exposure to these financial products.

6.8.6 Other Control Functions

Calculation on a more reactive basis

- marking to the "model" rather than the "market"
- calculating maximum expected exposure

- use of multiple models
- assessment of movement in major assumptions

Monitoring on a Proactive Basis

- reviewing the quality of transactions
- review of credit support and collateral
- netting broadly
- performance of "stress-testing" and
- computer simulations of market conditions

Other Proposals   6.8.7

- Improve market transparency
- Require board level audit and review functions
- Mandatory internal systems and audit controls
- Daily marking to market/model
- Forecast of cash and funding requirements

Standardisation of products   6.8.8

The standardisation enables the risks to be managed and is essential for a clearing house system. Work on establishing the fundamentals for each type of product is a subject too complex for discussion here. Enough to say that the Bank of England and many other central banks have only very recently begun to consider the issue. An incoming Labour government must convene advisers with a view to putting this standardisation into practice.

FX exchange control (extant and implied)   6.8.9

To return to the question of the FX markets, it is a different type of risk that exists. There is still good argument for requiring that parties post collateral with one another. Here the arguments are centred around the need to protect the currency rather than to prevent market collapse. The question is then how to control the FX markets by regulation?

The following appear to be the central concerns:-

- will it be tantamount to exchange control?
- the flight to Euromarkets
- the need to achieve this on an EEC wide basis

Single EC currency   6.8.9/1

The only solution to the expansion of FX speculation is a single currency. Clearly it is impossible to speculate between currencies when there is only one currency in existence. Given the unlikelihood of this happening before Labour comes to power the question might be: is there scope for the expanded use of the hard ECU?

6.8.9/2 Penal taxation

If regulation will not kill these markets, the question is whether the profits can be redistributed. The difficulty with the introduction of tax on foreign exchange gains is that it will only catch UK corporates with a penal level of taxation. Where those corporations are simply hedging out their FX exposure it seems counterproductive to penalise their treasury function. The real enemies here are the FX speculating banks and hedge funds. If they are taxed at penal levels in the UK they would simply disappear offshore. As a matter of English law, foreign nations' tax laws are not enforced in the UK Similarly, most other jurisdictions would not recognise UK laws which sought to recognise hedge funds resident in the Cayman Islands, etc.

The question of FX is therefore more difficult to answer than derivatives. The distinction discussed elsewhere of distinguishing between speculation and usual commercial activity is the best starting point. This is discussed below.

6.9 Regulation

6.9.1 The case for regulation of banks: a reminder

- Bank deposit liabilities are money which regulators seek to control through the minimum requirements held by banks.
- The role of banks as a channel of liquidity into the economy means that there needs to be control of the manner in which they operate.
- The effect on consumers and small businesses of the gains or losses made by the banks trading on proprietary accounts. The losses made in the seemingly profitable markets of South America and the current vogue for investment in the emerging markets of the Pacific Rim, mean that the core deposits and loan accounts of the small business or individual is affected. The central government attempts to control fiscal policy can be affected by the raising of bank loan rates and a tightening of bank policy on credit terms for individuals. Whether these individual results are thought to be good or bad is irrelevant compared to the fact that governments have lost control of the economy if the banks are able to derail the central economic policy thrusts.

Official concern for the stability of banks and financial markets reflects the danger that multiple failures will lead to a contraction of the money supply and a corresponding dislocation of the real economy.

The distinction between the "real" economy and the financial markets is important. The financial markets play a form of cocaine-fuelled roulette with unreally large amounts of money while the "real" economy concerns the ability of small businesses and individuals to manage their own affairs. Unfortunately, this distinction cannot be drawn too strictly because failures in the financial markets are paid for in the real economy. The failures of the financial markets affect the direction of economic policy and therefore impact on the real economy. The distinction is therefore desirable but not actually the case.

The question with reference to regulation beyond that discussed above is whether or not it is possible to prevent some entities from entering into certain types of transaction at all: that is to deny them the corporate capacity to deal. In the case of FX markets this means that corporates could not speculate as part of their ordinary activities and that they could not become involved in derivatives that are not covered by exchanges and clearing houses.

Permit hedging? 6.9.2

The Bank of England operates at present by requiring that there is a conceptual distinction drawn between Structural and Dealing positions with reference to FX risk. The structural side relates to those FX dealings which have to do with the intrinsic business of the entity whereas the dealing side is to do with those transactions which are entered into purely with an eye to financial gain in themselves.

This distinction should be extended to all forms of derivative activity.

Control speculation through registered SPV's 6.9.3

The next step is then to draw up a list of entities which should be prevented from entering into speculative activities on derivatives markets. As discussed above this should include corporates, insurance companies, pension funds and building societies. These would be "Prescribed Institutions".

Undoubtedly Prescribed Institutions will want to speculate. To ensure that this is done in a controlled way, they should be permitted to speculate only if they form Special Purpose Vehicles which have a rating agency credit rating of AA or better and are separately capitalised from the rest of the group. On consolidating their results into the group accounts it would therefore be disclosed the extent to which the speculator is profitable or not. This would allow the corporate, for example, to swap its interest rate risk on an exchange with the SPV and then allow the SPV to speculate with that risk in the markets. The corporate itself is therefore shielded from the risk.

6.10 Taxation

6.10.1 The need for a systematic approach

The codes introduced by the Finance Act 1993 and in the Finance Bill 1994 are a tangled mess. The problem with this regulation is that it is not working from a policy-orientated outlook.

6.10.2 Do we want to tax or to regulate?

Simple redistribution of some of the money lost does not equal controlling the problem. As discussed above, the problem is one of attempting to tax entities which are not resident in the UK. Tax should be imposed on any entity with an office or any trading presence in the UK on all of its sterling denominated speculative activities or any profits remitted to the UK from any other trading activities. UK resident entities should only be taxed on FX gains and losses on normal corporation tax principles as part of their trading profits to prevent them removing their trading activities to jurisdictions where it is impossible to regulate them efficiently.

6.10.3 Taxing hedging transactions

Incidental gains should be taxed under the CPT rules and incidental losses should be allowed; that is losses should be allowed on an absolute basis.

6.10.4 Taxation speculation differently from hedging?

Is it on this distinction that we want punitive tax rates? How would we classify the managed open position which is supposedly a part of normal business activity but which is taking an aggressive speculative position? How do we impose a standard mark to market procedure? The questions in this area simply serve to highlight the problems that would be encountered in attempting to tax markets which are conducted by computer and telephone line (remember these are the derivatives markets) and which do not need to set foot in the UK to speculate on UK shares or the UK currency.

6.11 Overseas

Many of the points to be made with reference to the non-U..K considerations about FX markets and derivatives generally have already been made but they deserve systematic treatment of their own.

The growth of the Euromarkets means that it is impossible for a national regulatory authority to control speculation on currencies. There is a need for co-operation between national regulatory authorities. Without the certainty of national economic control, the planning of macroeconomic policy becomes more complicated. The particular role of London as an international financial centre requires that regulation does not discourage inward investment and the level of employment that that brings.

There are reasons why the United Kingdom is entrenched as a natural economic centre for international financial markets. The use of English Law has standardised the use of the English markets as the centre for complex transactions. The civil code jurisdictions are not as flexible as the common law countries (such as the United States and the UK). The location of a skilled indigenous workforce means that the financial markets, which are still orientated about the US dollar and the USA, can make use of the English speaking talent that already exists.

The fear of the power of the Euromarkets and the relocation of business to exotic locations has prevented many of the putative Basle accords on the control of international banking business.

One of the ways in which banks can be controlled is by imposing capital reserve requirements on their Eurocurrency exposures. The question is then how important will the offshore hedge funds become? This question is already partly answered. The most powerful of the investment banks are in fact just glorified hedge funds that do not actually invest their own balance sheets in many of the projects that they organise or control. The investment banks make the bulk of their earnings from trading on their own account and not just from the fees they receive for managing other people's money. The investment banks are not really banks at all. Rather they are colossal money-management organisations that rely on their size and their reputations to produce the steady stream of investor income. It is difficult to see the conceptual difference between this process and the separately capitalised hedge funds which play the markets and return a form of dividend income to their investors.

Biting the bullet really comes when the regulator has to try and impose restrictions on the foreign offices of domestic banks and on the foreign offices of non-domestic banks which are seeking to speculate against sterling.

The alternative suggestion would be to create a free international banking zone in London where banks can operate free of all regulation but receive the personnel support that a major financial centre can offer. The question of taxation is raised to the extent that the jurisdiction would need to support itself without discouraging the economic activity that brings employment and wealth to the numerous ancillary businesses that supply major corporations. The problem with such a proposal is that it plays the capitalists' game. They want low taxation centres with minimal regulation because regulation is cost. The argument against regulation is that the markets will impose their own credit controls such that the regulators' worries about the risks incurred by banks would be sorted by the need of the market players to remain solvent. The truth is that banks do not report for their individual so no one knows whether or not individual businesses have made large losses or not. The other argument with reference to the credit control point is amply dismissed by an analysis of the history of the swaps markets. It has taken the grumblings of regulators, a decade after the market became established in its own right, to spur the Group of Thirty banks to consider, let alone control, the risks involved in derivatives transactions. Controls mean costs. To continue the analogy with hedge funds and banks, banks want to keep their costs low, that is their control and back office staffing costs to a minimum. A new credit control or need to meet with a regulatory requirement means extra cost for the banks. they do not want to suffer this extra cost and therefore will not implement processes on their own account to deal with the potential problem.

The other danger of attempting to restrict Euromarket activity by regulation is that the banks will simply use other vehicles to enter into those activities from different geographic markets. The trend would be towards the enlarged use of hedge funds by banking and other institutions. The fear is then of the proliferation of the volatility risk of the hedge funds. If the hedge funds are incorporated under separate names and under separate systems of law from the parent bank, the reputation risk to the bank is reduced and therefore the banks will become more cavalier about the risks that they take through those funds.

6.12 Conclusions

"In environments in which the financial system comes close to collapse, the only recourse of all institutions is to the capability of the authorities to manage the economy out of crisis."[2]

This is the view of many on the manner in which regulators should treat the control of financial markets. In view of the risks to British Economy, there needs to be a more active management of the risks that are there in the economy. The 1980s paradigm that the markets should be left to themselves is clearly misguided. The financial markets have been handed the ability to regulate themselves. The paucity of convictions for the epidemic of insider trading is symptomatic of the inability to control the traders. The manner in which the trading floors of New York, London and Tokyo bounce currencies and base rates of interest as though they were rubber balls, is evidence of the fact that we need to be able to control the financial markets while we get on with the important business of leading the UK out of the pit into which 15 years of misrule has thrown it.

The ultimate conclusion summing up this short treatise on the derivatives markets is that the global economy, as the critics of the markets have long maintained, is linked by a succession of crises which the financial

---

[2] *The Regulation of International Banking* by Richard Dale; Woodhead Faulkner, 1984.

system has to overcome. This strain of thinking has become unpopular in recent years as the economic markets appear to have become more stable: in that inflation is generally low and money supply can manage exchange rates. In fact, the global economy has seen a worsening of the quality of life of a large number of human beings. In the UK, mass unemployment has become a fixture at the same time as low inflation. The welfare state has weakened visibly over time and the ability of those in work to protect their own rights has waned. There has been an underlying crisis in the UK economy since the early 1980s and arguably before even then. The monetarist paradigm has encouraged a mode of thought that ignores the human cost of policies that are driven by economics. The decline of manufacturing industry has walked hand-in-hand with the decline of the family and the worsening of crime rates. Economic policy has manifested itself in terms of technical fiscal measures to balance a budget that is further out of balance than ever before. A current account deficit of £50 billion would have been inconceivable in even the 1970s.

In short there has been a crisis which has not been described as such because prevailing economic theory cannot recognise it and because crises are supposed to come and go rather than hang around for a full decade or more. The FX markets and the derivatives markets, with all the sophistication they involve, do not therefore constitute an advance in capitalist money markets. Rather they demonstrate a deepening in the underlying crisis. Derivative instruments carry with them increased volatility and as such have direct effects on the national economy. They also carry business risks for the organisations which become involved in them because they are speculative as well as controlling risk.

Derivatives are potentially a part of the problem. They constitute an essential element in the deepening of the crisis that has been with us ever since 1981.

Appendices

ISDA®

International Swap Dealers Association. Inc.

MASTER AGREEMENT

dated as of ....

.... and ....

have entered and/or anticipate entering into one or more transactions (each a "Transaction") that are or will be governed by this Master Agreement, which includes the schedule (the "Schedule"), and the documents and other confirming evidence (each a "Confirmation") exchanged between the parties confirming those Transactions.

Accordingly, the parties agree as follows:—

1. Interpretation

(a) **Definitions.** The terms defined in Section 14 and in the Schedule will have the meanings therein specified for the purpose of this Master Agreement.

(b) **Inconsistency.** In the event of any inconsistency between the provisions of the Schedule and the other provisions of this Master Agreement, the Schedule will prevail. In the event of any inconsistency between the provisions of any Confirmation and this Master Agreement (including the Schedule), such Confirmation will prevail for the purpose of the relevant Transaction.

(c) **Single Agreement.** All Transactions are entered into in reliance on the fact that this Master Agreement and all Confirmations form a single agreement between the parties (collectively referred to as this "Agreement"), and the parties would not otherwise enter into any Transactions.

2. Obligations

(a) **General Conditions.**

(i)   Each party will make each payment or delivery specified in each Confirmation to be made by it, subject to the other provisions of this Agreement.

(ii)   Payments under this Agreement will be made on the due date for value on that date in the place of the account specified in the relevant Confirmation or otherwise pursuant to this Agreement, in freely transferable funds and in the manner customary for payments in the required currency. Where settlement is by delivery (that is, other than by payment), such delivery will be made for receipt on the due date in the manner customary for the relevant obligation unless otherwise specified in the relevant Confirmation or elsewhere in this Agreement.

(iii)   Each obligation of each party under Section 2(a)(i) is subject to (1) the condition precedent that no Event of Default or Potential Event of Default with respect to the other party has occurred and is continuing, (2) the condition precedent that no Early Termination Date in respect of the relevant Transaction has occurred or been effectively designated and (3) each other applicable condition precedent specified in this Agreement.

(b)   **Change of Account.** Either party may change its account for receiving a payment or delivery by giving notice to the other party at least five Local Business Days prior to the schedule date for the payment or delivery to which such change applies unless such other party gives timely notice of a reasonable objection to such change.

(c)   **Netting.** If on any date amounts would otherwise be payable:—
  (i)   in the same currency; and

  (ii)   in respect of the same Transaction.

by each party to the other, then, on such date, each party's obligation to make payment of any such amount will be automatically satisfied and discharged and, if the aggregate amount that would otherwise have been payable by one party exceeds the aggregate amount that would otherwise have been payable by the other party, replaced by an obligation upon the party by whom the larger aggregate amount would have been payable to pay to the other party the excess of the larger aggregate amount over the smaller aggregate amount.

The parties may elect in respect of two or more Transactions that a net amount will be determined in respect of all amounts payable on the same date in the same currency in respect of such Transactions, regardless of whether such amounts are payable in respect of the same Transaction. The election may be made in the Schedule or a Confirmation by specifying that subparagraph (ii) above will not apply to the Transactions identified as being subject to the election, together with the starting date (in which case subparagraph (ii) above will not, or will cease to, apply to such Transactions from such date). This election may be made separately for different groups of Transactions and will apply separately to each pairing of Offices through which the parties make and receive payments or deliveries.

(d)   **Deduction or Withholding for Tax.**
  (i)   **Gross-Up.** All payments under this Agreement will be made

without any deduction or withholding for or on account of any Tax unless such deduction or withholding is required by any applicable law, as modified by the practice of any relevant governmental revenue authority, then in effect. If a party is so required to deduct or withhold, then that party ("X") will:—

  (1) promptly notify the other party ("Y") of such requirement:

  (2) pay to the relevant authorities the full amount required to be deducted or withheld (including the full amount required to be deducted or withheld from any additional amount paid by X to Y under this Section 2(d)) promptly upon the earlier of determining that such deduction or withholding is required or receiving notice that such amount has been assessed against Y;

  (3) promptly forward to Y an official receipt (or a certified copy), or other documentation reasonably acceptable to Y, evidencing such payment to such authorities; and

  (4) if such Tax is an Indemnifiable Tax, pay to Y, in addition to the payment to which Y is otherwise entitled under this Agreement, such additional amount as is necessary to ensure that the net amount actually received by Y (free and clear of Indemnifiable Taxes, whether assessed against X or Y) will equal the full amount Y would have received had no such deduction or withholding been required. However, X will not be required to pay any additional amount to Y to the extent that it would not be required to be paid but for:—

(A) the failure by Y to comply with or perform any agreement contained in Section 4(a)(i), 4(a)(iii) or 4(d); or

(B) the failure of a representation made by Y pursuant to Section 3(f) to be accurate and true unless such failure would not have occurred but for (I) any action taken by a taxing authority, or brought in a court of competent jurisdiction, on or after the date on which a Transaction is entered into (regardless of whether such action is taken or brought with respect to a party to this Agreement) or (II) a Change in Tax Law.

(ii) *Liability,* If:—

(1) X is required by any applicable law, as modified by the practice of any relevant governmental revenue authority, to make any deduction or withholding in respect of which X would not be required to pay an additional amount to Y under Section 2(d)(i)(4);

(2) X does not so deduct or withhold; and

(3) a liability resulting from such Tax is assessed directly against X,

then, except to the extent Y has satisfied or then satisfies the liability resulting from such Tax, Y will promptly pay to X the amount of such liability (including any related liability for interest, but including any related liability for penalties only if Y has failed to comply with or perform any agreement contained in Section 4(a)(i), 4(a)(iii) or 4(d)).

(e) **Default Interest; Other Amounts.** Prior to the occurrence or effective designation of an Early Termination Date in respect of the relevant Transaction, a party that defaults in the performance of any payment obligation will, to the extent permitted by law and subject to Section 6(c), be required to pay interest (before as well as after judgment) on the overdue amount to the other party on demand in the same currency as such overdue amount, for the period from (and including) the original due date for payment to (but excluding) the date of actual payment, at the Default Rate. Such interest will be calculated on the basis of daily compounding and the actual number of days elapsed. If, prior to the occurrence or effective designation of an Early Termination Date in respect of the relevant Transaction, a party defaults in the performance of any obligation required to be settled by delivery, it will compensate the other party on demand if and to the extent provided for in the relevant Confirmation or elsewhere in this Agreement.

3. Representations

Each party represents to the other party (which representations will be deemed to be repeated by each party on each date on which a Transaction is entered into and, in the case of the representations in Section 3(f), at all times until the termination of this Agreement) that:—

(a) **Basic Representations.**

(i) **Status.** It is duly organised and validly existing under the laws of the jurisdiction of its organisation or incorporation and, if relevant under such laws, in good standing;

(ii) **Powers.** It has the power to execute this Agreement and any other documentation relating to this Agreement to which it is a party, to deliver this Agreement and any other documentation relating to this Agreement that is required by this Agreement to deliver and to perform its obligations under this Agreement and any obligations it has under any Credit Support Document to which it is a party and has taken all necessary action to authorise such execution, delivery and performance;

(iii) **No Violation or Conflict.** Such execution, delivery and performance do not violate or conflict with any law applicable to it, any provision of its constitutional documents, any order or judgment of any court or other agency of government applicable to it or any of its assets or any contractual restriction binding on or affecting it or any of its assets;

236

(iv)   **Consents.** All governmental and other consents that are required to have been obtained by it with respect to this Agreement or any Credit Support Document to which it is a party have been obtained and are in full force and effect and all conditions of any such consents have been complied with; and

(v)   **Obligations Binding.** Its obligations under this Agreement and any Credit Support Document to which it is a party constitute its legal, valid and binding obligations, enforceable in accordance with their respective terms (subject to applicable bankruptcy, reorganisation, insolvency, moratorium or similar laws affecting creditors' rights generally and subject, as to enforceability, to equitable principles of general application (regardless of whether enforcement is sought in a proceeding in equity or at law)).

(b)   **Absence of Certain Events.** No event of Default or Potential Event of Default or, to its knowledge, Termination Event with respect to it has occurred and is continuing and no such event or circumstance would occur as a result of its entering into or performing its obligations under this Agreement or any Credit Support Document to which it is a party.

(c)   **Absence of Litigation.** There is not pending or, to its knowledge, threatened against it or any of its Affiliates any action, suit or proceeding at law or in equity or before any court, tribunal, governmental body, agency or official or any arbitrator that is likely to affect the legality, validity or enforceability against it of this Agreement or any Credit Support Document to which it is a party or its ability to perform its obligations under this Agreement or such Credit Support Document.

(d)   **Accuracy of Specified Information.** All applicable information that is furnished in writing by or on behalf of it to the other party and is identified for the purpose of this Section 3(d) in the Schedule is, as of the date of the information, true, accurate and complete in every material respect.

(e)   **Payer Tax Representation.** Each represenation specified in the Schedule as being made by it for the purpose of this Section 3(e) is accurate and true.

(f)   **Payee Tax Representations.** Each representation specified in the Schedule as being made by it for the purpose of this Section 3(f) is accurate and true.

4.   Agreements

Each party agrees with the other that, so long as either party has or may have any obligation under this Agreement or under any Credit Support Document to which it is a party:—

(a)   **Furnish Specified Information.** It will deliver to the other party or, in certain cases under subparagraph (iii) below, to such government or taxing authority as the other party reasonably directs:—

(i)   any forms, documents or certificates relating to taxation specified in the Schedule or any Confirmation:

(ii)   any other documents specified in the Schedule or any Confirmation; and

(iii)   upon reasonable demand by such other party, any form or document that may be required or reasonably requested in writing in order to allow such other party or its Credit Support Provider to make a payment under this Agreement or any applicable Credit Support Document without any deduction or withholding for or on account of any Tax or with such deduction or withholding at a reduced rate (so long as the completion, execution or submission of such form or document would not materially prejudice the legal or commercial position of the party in receipt of such demand), with any such form or document to be accurate and completed in a manner reasonably satisfactory to such other party and to be executed and to be delivered with any reasonably required certification,

in each case by the date specified in the Schedule or such Confirmation or, if none is specified, as soon as reasonably practicable.

(b)   **Maintain Authorisations.** It will use all reasonable efforts to maintain in full force and effect all consents of any governmental or other authority that are required to be obtained by it with respect to this Agreement or any Credit Support Document to which it is a party and will use all reasonable efforts to obtain any that may become necessary in the future.

(c)   **Comply with Laws.** It will comply in all material respects with all applicable laws and orders to which it may be subject if failure so to comply would materially impair its ability to perform its obligations under this Agreement or any Credit Support Document to which it is a party.

(d)   **Tax Agreement.** It will give notice of any failure of a representation made by it under Section 3(f) to be accurate and true promptly upon learning of such failure.

(e)   **Payment of Stamp Tax.** Subject to Section 11, it will pay any Stamp Tax levied or imposed upon it or in respect of its execution or performance of this Agreement by a jurisdiction in which it is incorporated, organised, managed and controlled, or considered to have its seat, or in which a branch or office through which it is acting for the purpose of this Agreement is located ("Stamp Tax Jurisdiction") and will indemnify the other party against any Stamp Tax levied or imposed upon the other party or in respect of the other party's execution or performance of this Agreement by any such Stamp Tax Jurisdiction which is not also a Stamp Tax Jurisdiction with respect to the other party.

5. Events of Default and Termination Events

(a) *Events of Default.* The occurrence at any time with respect to a party or, if applicable, any Credit Support Provider of such party or any Specified Entity of such party of any of the following events constitutes an event of default (an "Event of Default") with respect to such party:—

(i) *Failure to Pay or Deliver.* Failure by the party to make, when due, any payment under this Agreement or delivery under Section 2(a)(i) or 2(e) required to be made by it if such failure is not remedied on or before the third Local Business Day after notice of such failure is given to the party;

(ii) *Breach of Agreement.* Failure by the party to comply with or perform any agreement or obligation (other than an obligation to make any payment under this Agreement or delivery under Section 2(a)(i) or 2(e) or to give notice of a Termination Event or any agreement or obligation under Section 4(a)(i), 4(a)(iii) or 4(d)) to be complied with or performed by the party in accordance with this Agreement if such failure is not remedied on or before the thirtieth day after notice of such failure is given to the party;

(iii) *Credit Support Default.*
(1) Failure by the party or any Credit Support Provider of such party to comply with or perform any agreement or obligation to be complied with or performed by it in accordance with any Credit Support Document if such failure is continuing after any applicable grace period has elapsed:
(2) the expiration or termination of such Credit Support Document or the failing or ceasing of such Credit Support Document to be in full force and effect for the purpose of this Agreement (in either case other than in accordance with its terms) prior to the satisfaction of all obligations of such party under each Transaction to which such Credit Support Document relates without the written consent of the other party; or
(3) the party or such Credit Support Provider disaffirms, disclaims, repudiates or rejects, in whole or in part, or challenges the validity of, such Credit Support Document;

(iv) *Misrepresentation.* A representation (other than a representation under Section 3(e) or (f)) made or repeated or deemed to have been made or repeated by the party or any Credit Support Provider of such party in this Agreement or any Credit Support Document proves to have been incorrect or misleading in any material respect when made or repeated or deemed to have been made or repeated;

(v) *Default under Specified Transaction.* The party, any Credit Support Provider of such party or any applicable Specified Entity

239

of such party (1) defaults under a Specified Transaction and, after giving effect to any applicable notice requirement or grace period, there occurs a liquidation of, an acceleration of obligations under, or any early termination of, that Specified Transaction, (2) defaults, after giving effect to any applicable notice requirement or grace period, in making any payment or delivery due on the last payment, delivery or exchange date of, or any payment on early termination of, a Specified Transaction (or such default continues for at least three Local Business Days if there is no applicable notice requirement or grace period) or (3) disaffirms, disclaims, repudiates or rejects, in whole or in part, a Specified Transaction (or such action is taken by any person or entity appointed or empowqered to operate it or act on its behalf):

(vi) **Cross Default.** If "Cross Default" is specified in the Schedule as applying to the party, the occurrence or existence of (1) a default, event of default or other similar condition or event (however described) in respect of such party, any Credit Support Provider of such part or any applicable Specified Entity of such party under one or more agreements or instruments relating to Specified Indebtedness of any of them (individually or collectively) in an aggregate amount of not less than the applicable Threshold Amount (as specified in the Schedule) which has resulted in such Specified Indebtedness becoming, or becoming capable at such time of being declared, due and payable under such agreements or instruments, before it would otherwise have been due and payable or (2) a default by such party, such Credit Support Provider or such Specified Entity (individually or collectively) in making one or more payments on the due date thereof in an aggregate amount of not less than the applicable Threshold Amount under such agreements or instruments (after giving effect to any applicable notice requirement or grace period);

(vii) **Bankruptcy.** The party, any Credit Support Provider of such party or any applicable Specified Entity of such party:—
(1) is dissolved (other than pursuant to a consolidation, amalgamation or merger); (2) becomes insolvent or is unable to pay its debts or fails or admits in writing its inability generally to pay its debts as they become due; (3) makes a general assignment, arrangement or composition with or for the benefit of its creditors; (4) institutes or has instituted against it a proceeding seeking a judgment of insolvency or bankruptcy or any other relief under any bankruptcy or insolvency law or other similar law affecting creditors' rights, or a petition is presented for its winding-up or liquidation, and, in the case of any such proceeding or petition instituted or presented against it, such proceeding or petition (A) results

240

in a judgment of insolvency or bankruptcy or the entry of an order for relief or the making of an order for its winding-up or liquidation or (B) is not dismissed, discharged, stayed or restrained in each case within 30 days of the institution or presentation thereof; (5) has a resolution passed for its winding-up, official management or liquidation (other than pursuant to a consolidation, amalgamation or merger); (6) seeks or becomes subject to the appointment of an administrator, provisional liquidator, conservator, receiver, trustee, custodian or other similar official for it or for all or substantially all its assets; (7) has a secured party take possession of all or substantially all its assets or has a distress, execution, attachment, sequestration or other legal process levied, enforced or sued on or against all or substantially all its assets and such secured party maintains possession, or any such process is not dismissed, discharged, stayed or restrained, in each case within 30 days thereafter: (8) causes or is subject to any event with respect to it which, under the applicable laws of any jurisdiction, has an analogous effect to any of the events specified in clauses (1) to (7) (inclusive); or (9) takes any action in furtherance of, or indicating its consent to, approval or, or acquiesence in, any of the foregoing acts; or

(viii)   **Merger Without Assumption.** The party or any Credit Support Provider of such party consolidates or amalgamates with, or merges with or into, or transfers all or substantially all its assets to, another entity and, at the time of such consolidation, amalgamation, merger or transfer:—

(1)   the resulting, surviving or transferee entity fails to assume all the obligations of such party or such Credit Support Provider under this Agreement or any Credit Support Document to which it or its predecessor was a party by operation of law or pursuant to an agreement reasonably satisfactory to the other party to this agreement; or

(2)   the benefits of any Credit Support Document fail to extend (without the consent of the other party) to the performance by such resulting, surviving or transferee entity of its obligations under this Agreement.

(b)   **Termination Events.** The occurrence at any time with respect to a party or, if applicable, any Credit Support Provider of such party of any Specified Entity of such party of any event specified below constitutes an Illegality if the event is specified in (i) below, a Tax Event if the event is specified in (ii) below or a Tax Event Upon Merger if the event is specified in (iii) below, and, if specified to be applicable, a Credit Event Upon Merger if the event is specified pursuant to (iv) below or an Additional

241

Termination Event if the event is specified pursuant to (v) below—

(i) **Illegality.** Due to the adoption of, or any change in, any applicable law after the date on which a Transaction is entered into, or due to the promulgation of, or any change in, the interpretation by any court, tribunal or regulatory authority with competent jurisdiction of any applicable law after such date, it becomes unlawful (other than as a result of a breach by the party of Section 4(b)) for such party (which will be the Affected Party):—

(1) to perform any absolute or contingent obligation to make a payment or delivery or to receive a payment or delivery in respect of such Transaction or to comply with any other material provision of this Agreement relating to such Transaction; or

(2) to perform, or for any Credit Support Provider of such party to perform, any contingent or other obligation which the party (or such Credit Support Provider) has under any Credit Support Cocument relating to such Transaction;

(ii) **Tax Event.** Due to (x) any action taken by a taxing authority, or brought in a court of competent jurisdiction, on or after the date on which a Transaction is entered into (regardless of whether such action is taken or brought with respect to a party to this Agreement) or (y) a Change in Tax Law, the party (which will be the Affected Party) will, or there is a substantial likelihood that it will, on the next succeeding Scheduled Payment Date (1) be required to pay to the other party an additional amount in respect of an Indemnifiable Tax under Section (d)(i)(4) (except in respect of interest under Section 2(e), 6(d)(ii) or 6(e)) or (2) receive a payment from which an amount is required to be deducted or withheld for or on account of a Tax (except in respect of interest under Section 2(e), 6(d)(ii) or 6(e)) and no additional amount is required to be paid in respect of such Tax under Section 2(d)(i)(4) (other than by reason of Section 2(d)(i)(4)(A) or (B));

(iii) **Tax Event Upon Merger.** The party (the "Burdened Party") on the next succeeding Scheduled Payment Date will either (1) be required to pay an additional amount in respect of an Indemnifiable Tax under Section 2(d)(i)(4) (except in respect of interest under Section 2(e), 6(d)(ii) or 6(e)) or (2) receive a payment from which an amount has been deducted or withheld for or on account of any Indemnifiable Tax in respect of which the other party is not required to pay an additional amount (other than by reason of Section 2(d)(i)(4)(A) or (B)), in either case as a result of a party consolidating or amalgamating with, or merging with or into, or transferring all or substantially all its assets to, another entity (which

242

will be the Affected Party) where such action does not constitute an event described in Section 5(a)(viii);

(iv)   **Credit Event Upon Merger.** If "Credit Event Upon Merger" is specified in the Schedule as applying to the party, such party ("X"), any Credit Support Provider of X or any applicable Specified Entity of X consolidates or amalgamates with, or merges with or into, or transfers all or substantilly all its assets to, another entity and such action does not constitute an event described in Section 5(a)(viii) but the creditworthiness of the resulting, surviving or transferee entity is materially weaker than that of X, such Credit Support Provider or such Specified Entity, as the case may be, immediately prior to such action (and, in such event, X or its successor or transferee, as appropriate, will be the Affected Party); or

(v)   **Additional Termination Event.** If any "Additional Termination Event" is specified in the Schedule or any Confirmation as applying, the occurrence of such event (and, in such event, the Affected Party or Affected Parties shall be as specified for such Additional Termination Event in the Schedule or such Confirmation).

(c)   **Event of Default and Illegality.** If an event or circumstance which would otherwise constitute or give rise to an Event of Default also constitutes an Illegality, it will be treated as an Illegality and will not constite an Event of Default.

6.   Early Termination

(a)   **Right to Terminate Following Event of Default.** If at any time an Event of Default with respect to a party (the "Defaulting Party") has occurred an is then continuing, the other party (the "Non-defaulting Party") may, by not more than 20 days notice to the Defaulting Party specifying the relevant Event of Default, designate a day not earlier than the day such notice is effective as an Early Termination Date in respect of all outstanding Transactions. If, however, "Automatic Early Termination" is specified in the Schedule as applying to a party, then an Early Termination Date in respect of all outstanding Transactions will occur immediately upon the occurrence with respect to such party of an Event of Default specified in Section 5(a)(vii)(1), (3), (5), (6) or, to the extent analogous thereto, (8), and as of the time immediately preceding the institution of the relevant proceeding or the presentation of the relevant petition upon the occurrence with respect to such party of an Event of Default specified in Section 5(a)(vii)(4) or, to the extent analogous thereto, (8).

(b)   **Right to Terminate Following Termination Event.**

(i)   **Notice.** If a Termination Event occurs, an Affected Party will, promptly upon becoming aware of it, notify the other party, specifying the nature of that Termination Event and each Affected Transaction and will also give such other information about that Termination Event as the other party may reasonably require.

(ii)   *Transfer to Avoid Termination Event.* If either an Illegality under Section 5(b)(i)(1) or a Tax Event occurs and there is only one Affected Party, or if a Tax Event Upon Merger occurs and the Burdened Party is the Affected Party, the Affected Party will, as a condition to its right to designate an Early Termination Date under Section 6(b)(iv), use all reasonable efforts (which will not require such party to incur a loss, excluding immaterial, incidental expenses) to transfer within 20 days after it gives notice under Section 6(b)(i) all its rights and obligations under this Agreement in respect of the Affected Transactions to another of its Offices or Affiliates so that such Termination Event ceases to exist.

If the Affected Party is not able to make such a transfer it will give notice to the other party to that effect within such 20 day period, whereupon the other party may effect such a transfer within 30 days after the notice is given under Section 6(b)(i).

Any such transfer by a party under this Section 6(b)(ii) will be subject to and conditional upon the prior written consent of the other party, which consent will not be withheld if such other party's policies in effect at such time would permit it to enter into transactions with the transferee on the terms proposed.

(iii)   *Two Affected Parties.* If an Illegality under Section 5(b)(i)(1) or a Tax Event occurs and there are two Affected Parties, each party will use all reasonable efforts to reach agreement within 30 days after notice thereof is given under Section 6(b)(i) on action to avoid that Termination Event.

(iv)   *Right to Terminate.* If:—
   (1)   a transfer under Section 6(b)(ii) or an agreement under Section 6(b)(iii), as the case may be, has not been effected with respect to all Affected Transactions within 30 days after an Affected Party gives notice under Section 6(b)(i); or
   (2)   an Illegality under Section 5(b)(i)(2), a Credit Event Upon Merger or an Additional Termination Event occurs, or a Tax Event Upon Merger occurs and the Burdened Party is not the Affected Party,

either party in the case of an Illegality, the Burdened Party in the case of a Tax Event Upon Merger, any Affected Party in the case of a Tax Event or an Additional Termination Event if there is more than one Affected Party, or the party which is not the Affected Party in the case of a Credit Event Upon Merger or an Additional Termination Event if there is only one Affected Party may, by not more than 20 days notice to the other party and provided that the relevant Termination Event is then continuing, designate a day not earlier than the day such notice is effective as an Early Termination Date in respect of all Affected Transactions.

(c) **Effect of Designation.**

(i) If notice designating an Early Termination Date is given under Section 6(a) or (b), the Early Termination Date will occur on the date so designated, whether or not the relevant Event of Default or Termination event is then continuing.

(ii) Upon the occurrence or effective designation of an Early Termination Date, no further payments or deliveries under Section 2(a)(i) or 2(e) in respect of the Terminated Transactions will be required to be made, but without prejudice to the other provisions of this Agreement. The amount, if any, payable in respect of an Early Termination Date shall be determined pursuant to Section 6(e).

(d) **Calculations.**

(i) **Statement.** On or as soon as reasonably practicable following the occurrence of an Early Termination Date, each party will make the calculations on its part, if any, contemplated by Section 6(e) and will provide to the other party a statement (1) showing, in reasonable detail, such calculations (including all relevant quotations and specifying any amount payable under Section 6(e)) and (2) giving details of the relevant account to which any amount payable to it is to be paid. In the absence of written confirmation from the source of a quotation obtained in determining a Market Quotation, the records of the party obtaining such quotation will be conclusive evidence of the existence and accuracy of such quotation.

(ii) **Payment Date.** An amount calculated as being due in respect of any Early Termination Date under Section 6(e) will be payable on the day that notice of the amount payable is effective (in the case of an Early Termination Date which is designated or occurs as a result of an Event of Default) and on the day which is two Local Business Days after the day on which notice of the amount payable is effective (in the case of an Early Termination Date which is designated as a result of a Termination Event). Such amount will be paid together with (to the extent permitted under applicable law) interest thereon (before as well as after judgment) in the Termination Currency, from (and including) the relevant Early Termination Date to (but excluding) the date such amount is paid, at the Applicable Rate. Such interest will be calculated on the basis of daily compounding and the actual number of days elapsed.

(e) **Payments on Early Termination.** If an Early Termination Date occurs, the following provisions shall apply based on the parties' election in the Schedule of a payment measure, either "Market Quotation" or "Loss", and a payment method, either the "First Method" or the "Second Method". If the parties fail to designate a payment measure or payment method in the Schedule, it will be deemed that "Market Quotation" or the "Second Method", as the case may be, shall apply. The amount, if any, payable in respect of an Early Termination Date and determined pursuant to this Section will be subject to any Set-off.

(i) **Events of Default.** If the Early Termination Date results from an Event of Default:—

(1) *First Method and Market Quotation.* If the First Method and Market Quotation apply, the Defaulting Party will pay to the Non-defaulting Party the excess, if a positive number, of (A) the sum of the Settlement Amount (determined by the Non-defaulting Party) in respect of the Terminated Transactions and the Termination Currency Equivalent of the Unpaid Amounts owing to the Non-defaulting Party over (B) the Termination Currency Equivalent of the Unpaid Amounts owing to the Defaulting Party.

(2) *First Method and Loss.* If the First Method and Loss apply, the Defaulting Party will pay to the Non-defaulting Party, if a positive number, the Non-defaulting Party's Loss in respect of this Agreement.

(3) *Second Method and Market Quotation.* If the Second Method and Market Quotation apply, an amount will be payable equal to (A) the sum of the Settlement Amount (determined by the Non-defaulting Party) in respect of the Terminated Transactions and the Termination Currency Equivalent of the Unpaid Amounts owing to the Non-defaulting Party less (B) the Termination Currency Equivalent of the Unpaid Amounts owing to the Defaulting Party. If that amount is a positive number, the Defaulting Party will pay it to the Non-defaulting Party; if it is a negative number, the Non-defaulting Party will pay the absolute value of that amount to the Defaulting Party.

(4) *Second Method and Loss.* If the Second Method and Loss apply, an amount will be payable equal to the Non-defaulting Party's Loss in respect of this Agreement. If that kamount is a positive number, the Defaulting Party will pay it to the Non-defaulting Party; if it is a negative number, the Non-defaulting Party will pay the absolute value of that amount to the Defaulting Party.

(ii) **Termination Events.** If the Early Termination Date results from a Termination Event:—

(1)   *One Affected Party.* If there is one Affected Party, the amount payable will be determined in accordance with Section 6(e)(i)(3), if Market Quotation applies, or Section 6(e)(i)(4), if Loss applies, except that, in either case, references to the Defaulting Party and to the Non-defaulting Party will be deemed to be references to the Affected Party and the party which is not the Affected Party, respectively, and, if Loss applies and fewer than all the Transactions are being terminated, Loss shall be calculated in respect of all Terminated Transactions.

(2)   *Two Affected Parties.* If there are two Affected Parties:—

(A)   if Market Quotation applies, each party will determine a Settlement Amount in respect of the Terminated Transactions, and an amount will be payable equal toi (I) the sum of (a) one-half of the difference between the Settlement Amount of the party with the higher Settlement Amount ("X") and the Settlement Amount of the party with the lower Settlement Amount ("Y") and (b) the Termination Currency Equivalent of the Unpaid Amounts owing to X less (II) the Termination Currency Equivalent of the Unpaid Amounts owing to Y; and

(B)   if Loss applies, each party will determine its Loss in respect of this Agreement (or, if fewer than all the Transactions are being terminated, in respect of all Terminated Transactions) and an amount will be payable equal to one-half of the difference between the Loss of the party with the higher Loss ("X") and the Loss of the party with the lower Loss ("Y").

If the amount payable is a positive number. Y will pay it to X; if it is a negative number, X will pay the absolute value of that amount to Y.

(iii)   **Adjustment for Bankruptcy.** In circumstances where an Early Termination Date occurs because "Automatic Early Termination" applies in respect of a party, the amount determined under this Section 6(e) will be subject to such adjustments as are appropriate and permitted by law to reflect any payments or deliveries made by one party to the other under this Agreement (and retained by such other party) during the period from the relevant Early Termination Date to the date for payment determined under Section 6(d)(ii).

(iv)   **Pre-Estimate.** The parties agree that if Market Quotation applies an amount recoverable under this Section 6(e) is a reasonable pre-estimate of loss and not a penalty. Such amount is payable for the loss of bargain and the loss of protection against future risks and except as otherwise provided in this Agreement neither party will be entitled to recover any additional damages as a consequence of such losses.

7. Transfer

Subject to Section 6(b)(ii), neither this Agreement nor any interest or obligation in or under this Agreement may be transferred (whether by way of security or otherwise) by either party without the prior written consent of the other party, except that:—

(a)   a party may make such a transfer of this Agreement pursuant to a consolidation or amalgamation with, or into, or transfer of all or substantially all its assets to, another entity (but without prejudice to any other right or remedy under this Agreement); and

(b)   a party may make such a transfer of all or any part of its interest in any amount payable to it from a Defaulting Party under Section 6(e).

Any purported transfer that is not in compliance with this Section will be void.

8.   Contractual Currency

(a)   **Payment in the Contractual Currency.** Each payment under this Agreement will be made in the relevant currency specified in this Agreement for that payment (the "Contractual Currency"). To the extent permitted by applicable law, any obligation to make payments under this Agreement in the Contractual Currency will not be discharged or satisfied by any tender in any currency other than the Contractual Currency, except to the extent such tender results in the actual receipt by the party to which payment is owed, acting in a reasonable manner and in good faith in converting the currency so tendered into the Contractual Currency, of the full amount in the Contractual Currency of all amounts payable in respect of this Agreement. If for any reason the amount in the Contractual Currency so received falls short of the amount in the Contractual Currency payable in respect of this Agreement, the party required to make the payment will, to the extent permitted by applicable law, immediately pay such additional amount in the Contractual Currency as may be necessary to compensate for the shortfall. If for any reason the amount in the Contractual Currency so received exceeds the amount in the Contractual Currency payable in respect of this Agreement, the party receiving the payment will refund promptly the amount of such excess.

(b)   **Judgments.** To the extent permitted by applicable law, if any judgment or order expressed in a currency other than the Contractual Currency is rendered (i) for the payment of any amount owing in respect of this Agreement, (ii) for the payment of any amount relating to any early termination in respect of this Agreement or (iii) in respect of a judgment or order of another court for the payment of any amount described in (i) or (ii) above, the party seeking recovery, after recovery in full of the aggregate amount to which such party is entitled pursuant to the judgment or order, will be entitled to receive immediately from the other party the amount of any shortfall of the Contractual Currency received by such party as a consequence of sums paid in such other currency and will refund promptly to the other party any excess of the Contractual Currency received by such party as a consequence of sums paid in such other currency if such shortfall or such excess arises or results from any variation between the rate of exchange at which the Contractual Currency is converted into the currency of the judgment or order for the purposes of such judgment or order and the rate of exchange at which such party is able, acting in a reasonable manner and in good faith in converting the currency received into the Contractual Currency, to purchase the Contractual Currency with the amount of the currency of the judgment or order actually received by such party. The term "rate of exchange" includes, without limitation, any premiums and costs of exchange payable in connection with the purchase of or conversion into the Contractual Currency.

(c) **Separate Indemnities.** To the extent permitted by applicable law, these indemnities constitute separate and independent obligations from the other obligations in this Agreement, will be enforceable as separate and independent causes of action, will apply notwithstanding any indulgence granted by the party to which any payment is owed and will not be affected by judgment being obtained or claim or proof being made for any other sums payable in respect of this Agreement.

(d) **Evidence of Loss.** For the purpose of this Section 8, it will be sufficient for a party to demonstrate that it would have suffered a loss had an actual exchange or purchase been made.

9. Miscellaneous

(a) **Entire Agreement.** This Agreement constitutes the entire agreement and understanding of the parties with with respect to its subject matter and supersedes all oral communication and prior writings with respect thereto.

(b) **Amendments.** No amendment, modification or waiver in respect of this Agreement will be effective unless in writing (including a writing evidenced by a facsimile transmission) and executed by each of the parties or confirmed by an exchange of telexes or electronic messages on an electronic messaging system.

(c) **Survival of Obligations.** Without prejudice to Sections 2(a)(iii) and 6(c)(ii), the obligations of the parties under this Agreement will survive the termination of any Transaction.

(d) **Remedies Cumulative.** Except as provided iin this Agreement, the rights, powers, remedies and privileges provided in this Agreement are cumulative and not exclusive of any rights, powers, remedies and privileges provided by law.

(e) **Counterparts and Confirmations.**

(i)   This Agreement (and each amendment, modification and waiver in respect of it) may be executed and delivered in counterparts (including by facsimile transmission), each of which will be deemed an original.

(ii)   The parties intend that they are legally bound by the terms of each Transaction from the moment they agree to those terms (whether orally or otherwise). A Confirmation shall be entered into as soon as practicable and may be executed and delivered in counterparts (including by facsimile transmission) or be created by an exchange of telexes or by an exchange of electronic messages on an electronic messaging system, which in each case will be sufficient for all purposes to evidence a binding supplement to this Agreement. The parties will specify therein or through another effective means that any such counterpart, telex or electronic message constitutes a Confirmation.

(f)   **No Waiver of Rights.** A failure or delay in exercising any right, power or privilege in respect of this Agreement will not be presumed to operate as a waiver, and a single or partial exercise of any right, power or privilege will not be presumed to preclude any subsequent or further exercise, of that right, power or privilege or the exercise of any other right, power or privilege.

(g)   **Headings.** The headings used in this Agreement are for convenience of reference only and are not to affect the construction of or to be taken into consideration in interpreting this Agreement.

10. Offices; Multibranch Parties

(a)   If Section 10(a) is specified in the Schedule as applying, each party that enters into a Transaction through an Office other than its head or home office represents to the other party that, notwithstanding the place of booking office or jurisdiction of incorporation or organisation of such party, the obligations of such party are the same as if it had entered into the Transaction through its head or home office. This representation will be deemed to be repeated by such party on each date on which a Transaction is entered into.

(b)   Neither party may change the Office through which it makes and receives payments or deliveries for the purpose of a Transaction without the prior written consent of the other party.

(c)   If a party is specified as a Multibranch Party in the Schedule, such Multibranch Party may make and receive payments or deliveries under any Transaction through any Office listed in the Schedule, and the Office through which it makes and receives payments or deliveries with respect to a Transaction will be specified in the relevant Confirmation.

11. Expenses

A Defaulting Party will, on demand, indemnify and hold harmless the other party for and against all reasonable out-of-pocket expenses, including legal fees and Stamp Tax, incurred by such other party by reason of the enforcement and protection of its rights under this Agreement or any Credit Support Document to which the Defaulting Party is a party or by reason of the early termination of any Transaction, including, but not limited to, costs of collection.

12. Notices

(a) **Effectiveness.** Any notice or other communication in respect of this Agreement may be given in any manner set forth below (except that a notice or other communication under Section 5 or 6 may not be given by facsimile transmission or electronic messaging system) to the address or number or in accordance with the electronic messaging system details provided (see the Schedule) and will be deemed effective as indicated:—

(i)   if in writing and delivered in person or by courier, on the date it is delivered;

(ii)   if sent by telex, on the date the recipient's answerback is received;

(iii)   if sent by facsimile transmission, on the date that transmission is received by a responsible emplopyee of the recipient in legible form (it being agreed that the burden of proving receipt will be on the sender and will not be met by a transmission report generated by the sender's facsimile machine);

(iv)   if sent by certified or registered main (airmail, if overseas) or the equivalent (return receipt requested), on the date that mail is delivered or its delivery is attempted; or

(v)   if sent by electronic messaging system, on the date that electronic message is received.

Unless the date of that delivery (or attempted delivery) or that receipt, as applicable, is not a Local Business Day or that communication is delivered (or attempted) or received, as applicable, after the close of business on a Local Business Day, in which case that communication shall be deemed given and effective on the first following day that is a Local Business Day.

(b) **Change of Addresses.** Either party may by notice to the other change the address, telex or facsimile number or electronic messaging system details at which notices or other communications are to be given to it.

13. Governing Law and Jurisdiction

(a) **Governing Law.** This Agreement will be governed by and construed in accordance with the law specified in the Schedule.

251

(b) **Jurisdiction.** With respect to any suit, action or proceedings relating to this Agreement ("Proceedings"), each party irrevocably:—

(i) submits to the jurisdiction of the English courts, if this Agreement is expressed to be governed by English law, or to the non-exclusive jurisdiction of the courts of the State of New York and the United States District Court located in the Borough of Manhattan in New York City, if this Agreement is expressed to be governed by the laws of the State of New York; and

(ii) waives any objection which it may have at any time to the laying of venue of any Proceedings brought in any such court, waives any claim that such Proceedings have been brought in an inconvenient forum and further waives the right to object, with respect to such Proceedings, that such court does not have any jurisdiction over such party.

Nothing in this Agreement precludes either party from bringing Proceedings in any other jurisdiction (outside, if this Agreement is expressed to be governed by English law, the Contracting States, as defined in Section 1(3) of the Civil Jurisdiction and Judgments Act 1982 or any modification, extension or re-enactment thereof for the time being in force) nor will the bringing of Proceedings in any one or more jurisdictions preclude the bringing of Proceedings in any other jurisdiction.

(c) **Service of Process.** Each party irrevocably appoints the Process Agent (if any) specified opposite its name in the Schedule to receive, for it and on its behalf, service of process in any Proceedings. If for any reason any party's Process Agent is unable to act as such, such party will promptly notify the other party and within 30 days appoint a substitute process agent acceptable to the other party. The parties irrevocably consent to service of process given in the manner provided for notices in Section 12. Nothing in this Agreement will affect the right of either party to serve process in any other manner permitted by law.

(d) **Waiver of Immunities.** Each party irrevocably waives, to the fullest extent permitted by applicable law, with respect to itself and its revenues and assets (irrespective of their use or intended use), all immunity on the grounds of sovereignty or other similar grounds from (i) suit, (ii) jurisdiction of any court, (iii) relief by way of injunction, order for specific performance or for recovery of property, (iv) attachment of its assets (whether before or after judgment) and (v) execution or enforcement of any judgment to which it or its revenues or assets might otherwise be entitled in any Proceedings in the courts of any jurisdiction and irrevocably agrees, to the extent permitted by applicable law, that it will not claim any such immunity in any Proceedings.

14. Definitions

As used in this Agreement:—

"Additional Termination Event" has the meaning specified in Section 5(b).

"Affected Party" has the meaning specified in Section 5(b).

"Affected Transactions" means (a) with respect to any Termination Event consisting of an Illegality, Tax Event or Tax Event Upon Merger, all Transactions affected by the occurrence of such Termination Event and (b) with respect to any other Termination Event, all Transactions.

"Affiliate" means, subject to the Schedule, in relation to any person, any entity controlled, directly or indirectly, by the person, any entity that controls, directly or indirectly, the person or any entity directly or indirectly under common control with the person. For this purpose, "control" of any entity or person means ownership of a majority of the voting power of the entity or person.

"Applicable Rate" means:—

(a) in respect of obligations payable or deliverable (or which would have been but for Section 2(a)(iii)) by a Defaulting Party, the Default Rate;

(b) in respect of an obligation to pay an amount under Section 6(e) of either party from and after the date (determined in accordance with Section 6(d)(ii)) on which that amount is payable, the Default Rate;

(c) in respect of all other obligations payable or deliverable (or which would have been but for Section 2(a)(iii)) by a Non-defaulting Party, the Non-default Rate; and

(d) in all other cases, the Termination Rate.

"Burdened Party" has the meaning specified in Section 5(b).

"Change in Tax Law" means the enactment, promulgation, execution or ratification of, or any change in or amendment to, any law (or in the application or official interpretation of any law) that occurs on or after the date on which the relevant Transaction is entered into.

"consent" includes a consent, approval, action, authorisation, exemption, notice, filing, registration or exchange control consent.

"Credit Event Upon Merger" has the meaning specified in section 5(b).

"Credit Support Document" means any agreement or instrument that is specified as such in this Agreement.

"Credit Support Provider" has the meaning specified in the Schedule.

"Default Rate" means a rate per annum equal to the cost (without proof or evidence of any actual cost) to the relevant payee (as certified by it) if it were to fund or of funding the relevant amount plus 1% per annum.

"Defaulting Party" has the meaning specified in Section 6(a).

"Early Termination Date" means the date determined in accordance with Section 6(a) or 6(b)(iv).

"Event of Default" has the meaning specified in Section 5(a) and, if applicable, in the Schedule.

"Illegality" has the meaning specified in section 5(b).

"Indemnifiable Tax" means any Tax other than a Tax that would not be imposed in respect of a payment under this Agreement but for a present or former connection between the jurisdiction of the government or

taxation authority imposing such Tax and the recipient of such payment or a person related to such recipient (including, without limitation, a connection arising from such recipient or related person being or having been a citizen or resident of such jurisdiction, or being or having been organised, present or engaged in a trade or business in such jurisdiction, or having or having had a permanent establishment or fixed place of business in such jurisdiction, but excluding a connection arising solely from such recipient or related person having executed, delivered, performed its obligations or received a payment under, or enforced, this Agreement or a Credit Support Document).

"law" includes any treaty, law or regulation (as modified, in the case of tax matters, by the practice of any relevant governmental revenue authority) and *"lawful"* and *"unlawful"* will be construed accordingly.

"Local Business Day" means, subject to the Schedule, a day on which commercial banks are open for business (including dealings in foreign currency deposits) (a) in relation to any obligation under Section 2(a)(i), in the place(s) specified in the relevant Confirmation or, if not so specified, as otherwise agreed by the parties in writing or determined pursuant to provisions contained, or incorporated by reference, in this Agreement, (b) in relation to any other payment, in the place where the relevant account is located and, if different, in the principal financial centre, if any, of the currency of such payment, (c) in relation to any notice or other communication, including notice contemplated under Section 5(a)(i), in the city specified in the address for notice provided by the recipient and, in the case of a notice contemplated by Section 2(b), in the place where the relevant new account is to be located and (d) in relation to Section 5(a)(v)(2), in the relevant locations for performance with respect to such Specified Transaction.

"Loss" means, with respect to this Agreement or one or more Terminated Transactions, as the case may be, and a party, the Termination Currency Equivalent of an amount that party reasonably determines in good faith to be its total losses and costs (or gain, in which case expressed as a negative number) in connection with this Agreement or that Terminated Transaction or group of Terminated Transactions, as the case may be, including any loss of bargain, cost of funding or, at the election of such party but without duplication, loss or cost incurred as a result of its terminating, liquidating, obtaining or reestablishing any hedge or related trading position (or any gain resulting from any of them). Loss includes losses and costs (or gains) i respect of any payment or delivery required to have been made (assuming satisfaction of each appliocable condition precedent) on or before the relevant Early Termination Date and not made, except, so as to avoid duplication, if Section 6(e)(i)(1) or (3) or 6(e)(ii)(2)(A) applies. Loss does not include a party's legal fees and out-of-pocket expenses referred to under Section 11. AQ party will determine its Loss as of the relevant Early Termination Date, or, if that is not reasonably practicable, as of the earliest date thereafter as is reasonably practicable.

A party may (but need not) determine its Loss by reference to quotations of relevant rates or prices from one or more leading dealers in the relevant markets.

"Market Quotation" means, with respect to one or more Terminated Transactions and a party making the determination, an amopunt determined on the basis of quotations from Reference Market-makers. Each quotation will be for an amount, if any that would be paid to such party (expressed as a negative number) or by such party (expressed as a positive number) in consideration of an agreement between such party (taking into account any existing Credit Support Document with respect to the obligations of such party) and the quoting Reference Market-maker to enter into a transaction (the "Replacement Transaction") that would have the effect of preserving for such party the economic equivalent of any payment or delivery (whether the underlying obligation was absolute or contingent and assuming the satisfaction of each applicable condition precedent) by the parties under Section 2(a)(i) in respect of such Terminated Transaction or group of Terminated Transactions that would, but for the occurrence of the relevant Early Termination Date, have been required after that date. For this purpose, Unpaid Amounts in respect of the Terminated Transaction or group of Terminated Transactions are to be excluded but, without limitation, any payment or delivery that would, but for the relevant Early Termination Date, have been required (assuming satisfaction of each applicable condition precedent) after that early Termination Date is to be included. The Replacement Transaction would be subject to such documentation as such party and the Reference Market-maker may, in good faith, agree. The party making the determination (or its agent) will request each Reference Market-maker to provide its quotation to the extent reasonably practicable as of the same day and time (without regard to different time zones) on or as soon as reasonably practicable after the relevant Early Termination date. The day and time as of which those quotations are to be obtained will be selected in good faith by the party obliged to make a determination under Section 6(e), and, if each party is so obliged, after consultation with the other. If more than three quotations are provided, the Market Quotation will be the arithmetic mean of the quotations, without regard to the quotations having the highest and lowest values. If exactly three such quotations are provided, the Market Quotation will be the quotation remaining after disregarding the highest and lowest quotations. For this purpose, if more than one quotation has the same highest value or lowest value, then one of such quotations shall be disregarded. If fewer than three quotations are provided, it will be deemed that the Market Quotation in respect of such Terminated Transaction or group of Terminated Transactions cannot be determined.

"Non-default rate" means a rate per annum equal to the cost (without proof or evidence of any actual cost) to the Non-defaulting Party (as certified by it) if it were to fund the relevant amount.

"Non-defaulting Party" has the meaning specified in Section 6(a).

"Office" means a brabch or office of a party, which may be such party's head or home office.

"Potential Event of Default" means any event which, with the giving of notice or the lapse of time or both, would constitute an Event of Default.

"Reference Market-makers" means four leading dealers in the relevant market selected by the party determining a Market Quotation in good faith (a) from among dealers of the highest credit standing which satisfy all the criteria that such party applies generally at the time in deciding whether to offer or to make an extension of credit and (b) to the extent practicable, from among such dealers having an office in the same city.

"Relevant Jurisdiction" means, with respect to a party, the jurisdictions (a) in which the party is incorporated, organised, managed and controlled or considered to have its seat, (b) where an Office through which the party is acting for purposes of this Agreement is located. (c) in which the party executes this Agreement and (d) in relation to nay payment, from or through which such payment is made.

"Scheduled Payment date" means a date on which a payment or delivery is to be made under Section 2(a)(i) with respect to a Transaction.

"Set-off" means set-off, offset, combination of accounts, right of retention or withholding or similar right or requirement to which the payer of an amount under Section 6 is entitled or subject (whether arising under this Agreement, another contract, applicable law or otherwise) that is exercised by, or imposed on, such payer.

"Settlement Amount" means, with respect to a party and any Early termination DAte, the sum of:—

(a) the Termination Currency Equivalent of the Market Quotations (whether positive or negative) for each Terminated Transaction or group of Terminated Transactions for which a Market Quotation is determined; and

(b) such party's Loss (whether positive or negative and without reference to any Unpaid Amounts) for each terminated Transaction or group of Terminated Transactions for which a Market Quotation cannot be determined or would not (in the reasonable belief of the party making the detrmination) produce a commercially reasonable result.

"Specified Entity" has the meaning specified in the Schedule.

"Specified Indebtedness" means, subject to the Schedule, any obligation (whether present or future, contingent or otherwise, as principal or surety or otherwise) in respect of borrowed money.

"Specified Transaction" means, subject to the Schedule, (a) any transaction (including an agreement with respect thereto) now existing or hereafter entered into between one party to this Agreement (or any Credit Support Provider of such party or any applicable Specified Entity of such party) and the other party to this Agreement (or any Credit Suport Provider of such other party or any applicable Specified Entity of such other party) which is a rate swap transaction, basis swap, forward rate transaction,

commodity swap, commodity option, equity or equity index swap, equity or equity index option, bond option, interest rate option, foreign exchange transaction, cap transaction, floor transaction, collar transaction, currency swap transaction, cross-currency rate swap transaction, currency option or any other similar transaction (including any option with respect to any of these transactions), (b) any combination of these transactiuons and (c) any other transaction identified as a Specified ransaction in this Agreement or the relevant confirmation.

"Stamp Tax" means any stamp, registration, documentation or similar tax.

"Tax" means any present or future tax, levy, impost, duty, charge, assessment or fee of any nature (including interest, penalties and additions thereto) that is imposed by any government or other taxing authority in respect of any payment under this Agreement other than a stamp, registration, documentation or similar tax.

"Tax Event" has the meaning specified in Section 5(b).

"Tax Event Upon Merger" has the meaning specified in Section 5(b).

"Terminated Transactions" means with respect to any Early Termination Date (a) if resulting from a Termination Event, all Affected Transactions and (b) if resulting from an Event of Default, all Transactions (in either case) in effect immediately before the effectiveness of the notice designating that Early Termination date (or, if "Automatic Early Termination" applies, immediately before that Early termination Date).

"Termination Currency" has the meaning specified in the Schedule.

"Termination Currency Equivalent" means, in respect of any amount denominated in the termination Currency, such Termination Currency amount and, in respect of any amount denominated in a currency other than the Termination Currency (the "Other Currency"), the amount in the Termination Currency determined by the party making the relavant determination as being required to purchase such amount of such Other Currency as at the relevant Early Termination Date, or if the relevant Market Quotation or Loss (as the case may be, is determined as of a later date, that later date, with the Termination Currency at the rate equal to the spot exchange rate of the foriegn exchange agent (selected as provided below) for the purchase of such Other Currency with the Termnation Currency at or about 11:00 a.m. (in the city in which such foriegn exchange agent is located) on such date as would be customary for the determination of such a rate for the purchase of such Other Currency for value on the relevant Early Termination Date or that later date. The foreign exchange agent will, if only one party is obliged to make a determination under Section 6(e), be selected in good faith by that party and otherwise will be agreed by the parties.

"Termination Event" means an Illegality, a Tax Event Upon Merger or, if specified to be applicable, a Credit Event Upon Merger or an Additional Termination Event.

"Termination Rate" means a rate per annum equal to the arithmetic mean of the cost (without proof or evidence of any actual cost) to each party (as certified by such party) if it were to fund or of funding such amounts.

"Unpaid Amounts" owing to any party means, with respect to an Early Termination Date, the aggregate of (a) in respect of all Terminated Transactions, the amounts that became payable (or that would have become payable but for Section 2(a)(iii) to such party under Section 2(a)(i) on or prior to such Early Termination Date and which remain unpaid as at such Early Termination Date and (b) in respect of each Terminated Transaction, for each obligation under Section 2(a)(i) which was (or would have been but for Section 2(a)(iii) required to be settled by delivery to such party on or prior to such Early Termination Date and which has not been so settled as at such Early termination Date, an amount equal to the fair market value of that which was (or would have been) required to be delivered as of the originally scheduled date for delivery, in each case together with (to the extent permitted under applicable law) interest, in the currency of such amounts, from (and including) the date such amounts or obligations were or would have been required to have been paid or performed to (but excluding) such Early termination Date, at the Applicable Rate. Such amounts of interest will be calculated on the basis of daily compounding and the actual number of days elapsed. The fair market value of any obligation referred to in clause (b) above shall be reasonably determined by the party obliged to make the determination under Section 6(e) or, if each party is so obliged, it shall be the average of the Termination Currency Equivalents of the fair market values reasonably determined by both parties.

IN WITNESS WHEREOF the parties have executed this document on the respective dates specified below with effect from the date specified on the first page of this document.

....
(Name of Party)   (Name of Party)

By: ....   By: ....
  Name: Name:
  Title: Title:
  Date: Date:

SCHEDULE
to the
MASTER AGREEMENT

dated as of _____, ____

between

_____,
a company incorporated under the law of England and Wales **("Party A")**

and

_____,
a _____ organized under the law of the _____ **("Party B")**.

Part 1. Termination Provisions.

(a) **"Specified Entity"** means in relation to Party A for the purpose of:-

Section 5(a)(v):   _____
Section 5(a)(vi):   _____
Section 5(a)(vii):   _____
Section 5(b)(iv):   _____

and in relation to Party B for the purpose of:-

Section 5(a)(v):   _____
Section 5(a)(vi):   _____
Section 5(a)(vii):   _____
Section 5(b)(iv):   _____

(b) **"Specified Transaction"** will have the meaning specified in Section 14.

(c) (i) Section 5(a)(vi) is hereby amended by deleting in the seventh line thereof the words ", or becoming capable at such time of being declared,".

(ii) The **"Cross Default"** provisions of Section 5(a)(vi) as amended above [will/will not] apply to Party A and to Party B.

To the extent such provisions apply:-

"Specified Indebtedness" will have the meaning specified in Section 14.

"Threshold Amount" means US$.... or its equivalent in another currency[1]

---

[1] [If party B is a depository institution and so requests, add the following: ",except that, in respect of Party B, such term will not include deposits received by it in the ordinary course of its banking business which are not paid when due because of action preventing, prohibiting, or restricting the payment of such deposits provided that such action is not a consequent of, or related to, the Bankruptcy (as defined in Section 5(a)(vii)) of Party B, the legal existence of Party B, or the failure by Party B to comply with any law, rule, regulation, resolution, guideline, policy, judgment, order, writ, decree, or ruling provided, however, that, if any depositor requests repayment of any such deposit, such deposit is paid within one Business Day after the relevant governmental or regulatory authority action preventing, prohibiting, or restricting the payment of such deposit is terminated".]

259

(d) Section 5(a)(vii) is hereby amended by:

(e) Section 5(a)(viii) is hereby amended by:

(f) Section 5(b)(iv) is hereby amended by:

(g) The **"Credit Event Upon Merger"** provisions of Section 5(b)(iv) as amended above [will/will not] apply to Party A and to Party B.

(h) The **"Automatic Early Termination"** provision of Section 6(a) [will/will not] apply to Party A and to Party B.

   (i) **Payments on Early Termination.** For the purpose of Section 6(e):-

     (i) Market Quotation will apply.

     (ii) The First / Second Method will apply.

   (j) **"Termination Currency"** means [. . . . . . .].

Part 2. Tax Representations

Payer Tax Representations

For the purpose of Section 3(e), Party A and Party B will each make the following representation:-

It is not required by any applicable law, as modified by the practice of any relevant governmental revenue authority, or any Relevant Jurisdiction to make any deduction or withholding for or on account of any Tax for any payment (other than interest under Section 2(e), 6(d)(ii) or 6(e) to be made by it to the other party under this Agreement.

In making this representation it may rely on:-

(i) the accuracy of any representation made by the other party pursuant to Section 3(f).

(ii) the satisfaction of the agreement contained in Section 4(a)(i) or 4(a)(iii) and the accuracy and effectiveness of any document provided by the other party pursuant to Section 4(a)(i) or 4(a)(iii); and

(iii) the satisfaction of the agreement of the other party contained in Section 4(d).

Payee Tax Representations

For the purpose of Section 3(f), Party A and Party B will make the representations specified below, if any:-

(a) The following representation will apply to Party B but not to Party A:

It is fully eligible for the benefits of the "Business Profits" or "Industrial and Commercial Profits" provision, as the case may be, the "Interest" provision or the "Other Income" provision (if any) of the Specified Treaty with respect to any payment described in such provisions and received or to be received by it in connection with this Agreement and no such payment is attributable to a trade or business carried on by it through a permanent establishment in the Specified Jurisdiction.

If such representation applies, then:

Specified Treaty means the [UK]/[-----] Double Taxation Convention.

Specified Jurisdiction means the United Kingdom.

(b)   The following representation will/will not apply to Party A and/but will/will not to Party B:

(A)   It is entering into each Transaction in the ordinary course of its trade as, and is, a recognised UK swaps dealer for the purposes of the UK Inland Revenue extra statutory concession C17 on interest and currency swaps dated 14 March 1989, and

(B)   it will bring into account payments made and received in respect of each Transaction in computing its income for United Kingdom tax purposes.

Part 3.   Agreement to Deliver Documents.

In addition to the documents listed in Section 4(a)(iii), other documents to be delivered are:-

Party required to deliver document	Form/ Document/ Certificate	Date by which to be delivered	Covered by
Party A / B	Guarantee / Credit support documentation	At execution of this Agreement	
Party A / B	Annual Statement of Financial Condition of Party A / B	Promptly following demand by Party B	
Party A / B	Evidence of authority and specimen signatures with respect to Party B and its signatories	At execution of this Agreement	
Party B	Certified resolutions of Party A / B's board of directors or other governing body authorizing this Agreement and the signatory to this Agreement	At execution of this Agreement	

Part 4. Miscellaneous.

(a) **Notices.** For the purpose of Section 12(a):-
Address for notices or communications to Party A:-
Address for notices or communications to Party B:-

(b) **Process Agent.** For the purpose of Section 13(c):-
Party B appoints as its Process Agent in England:
  Name:
  Address:
  Attention:
  Telex   Answerback:
  Telephone No.:

(c) **Offices; Multibranch Parties.**
  (i) The provisions of Section 10(a) will be applicable.
  (ii) For the purpose of Section 10(c):-
Party A [is/is not] a Multibranch Party [and, if so, may act through the Offices specified in Annex A hereto.]
Party B [is/is not] a Multibranch Party [and, if so, may act through the Offices specified in Annex A hereto.]

(d) **Calculation Agent.** The Calculation Agent is Party [. . .], unless otherwise specified in a Confirmation in relation to the relevant Transaction.

(e) **Credit Support Document.** Details of any Credit Support Document, each of which are incorporated by reference in, and made part of, this Agreement and each Confirmation (unless provided otherwise in a Confirmation) as if set forth in full in this Agreement or such Confirmation:-
  (i)   Guarantee dated the date hereof by . . . . in favour of Party B as beneficiary thereof.
  [(ii) Collateral Deposit Agreement dated as of the date hereof between Party A and Party B.]
  [(iii) Guarantee dated the date hereof by _____ in favour of Party A as beneficiary thereof.]

(f) **Credit Support Provider.**
  (i) Credit Support Provider means in relation to Party A,
       [Insert Name or Not Applicable]
  (ii) Credit Support Provider means in relation to Party B,
       [Insert Name or Not Applicable].

(g) **Governing Law.** This agreement will be governed by, and construed and enforced in accordance with, English law.

(h) **Jurisdiction.** Section 13(b) is hereby amended by: (i) deleting in the second line of Subparagraph (i) thereof the word "non-"; and (ii) deleting the final paragraph thereof.

(i) **Netting of Payments.** Subparagraph (ii) of Section 2(c) will not apply to Transactions.

(j) **"Affiliate"** will have the meaning specified in Section 14.

Part 5
[Add customised terms]

IN WITNESS WHEREOF, the parties have executed this document on the respective dates specified below with effect from the date specified on the first page of this document.

[Party A..........]

By: _____
   Name
   Title:
   Date:

[Party B..........]

By: _____
   Name:
   Title:
   Date:

"NON-STANDARD" OTC OPTIONS CONFIRMATION/MASTER AGREEMENT
(the "Agreement")

BETWEEN
'A' Bank ("A")

and

("Counterparty")

WHEREAS A and Counterparty have entered into an over-the-counter option contract (the "Option") and

WHEREAS the description of the Options is set out in Section A hereof

NOW THEREFORE the parties agree that the Options shall be subject to and governed by the terms and conditions set out in Section B hereof.

PROVIDED THAT this Agreement shall replace all communications, confirmations and purported contractual terms affected between the parties entered into before the date of this Agreement.

A. Description of Option

Seller:	Counterparty
Buyer:	A
Option Style:	European / American / Asian
Option Type:	Put / Call
[Exercise Price:]	
Underlying Share:	
Number of Options:	
Number of Shares per Option:	One
Strike Price per Share:	
Premium:	
Premium Payment Date:	..... or if that date is not a Currency Business Day, the first following day that is a Currency Business Day.
Exchange:	
Settlement Method:	Cash
[Cash Settlement Amount:	(Exercise Price – Market Price) x Number of Units exercised on the Expiration Date, expressed in Sterling.]

B. Terms and Conditions

1. Definitions

"Calculation Agent" means [. . .].

"Currency Business Day" means any day on which commercial banks are open for business (including dealings in foreign exchange and foreign currency deposits) in the principal financial centre for the [relevant currency].

"Exchange Business Day" means a day that is or, but for the occurrence of a Market Disruption Event would have been, a trading day on the Exchange, other than a day on which trading on the exchange is scheduled to close prior to its regular weekday closing time, first announced on the day of such closing.

"Market Price" shall be as defined at condition 2.3.

"Market Disruption Event" as determined by the Calculation Agent, means the occurrence on any day, during the half-hour period prior to the determination of the Index Level, of (i) the material suspension or material limitation of trading in shares composing 20% or more of the level of the [Index], or (ii) the material suspension or material limitation of trading in options or futures contracts related to the [Index] traded on the [relevant options or futures exchange]; provided that a limitation on the hours and number of days of trading will not constitute a Market Disruption Event if it results from an announced change in the regular business hours of the [relevant exchange].

"Settlement Business Day" means any day on which commercial banks are open for business (including dealings in foreign exchange and foreign currency deposits) in [relevant business centre].

"Settlement Day" means the third Settlement Business Day after the Market Price has been fully calculated by the Calculation Agent.

"Valuation Date" means Expiration Date.

"Valuation Business Day" means a day that is (or, but for the occurrence of a Market Disruption Event, would have been) a trading day on the Exchange on which the Underlying Share is traded.

2. Exercise and Valuation

2.1 The Option is a [American / European / Asian style] option, meaning that the Buyer may exercise the Option by notice to the Seller between the hours of 9.00am and 4.00pm (relevant business centre time) [on the Expiration Date only]. Such notice may be given orally, and will be irreversible.

2.2 The Option will be deemed to be automatically exercised if the Cash Settlement Amount is greater than zero at the close of business in London on the Expiration Date, or, if later, the final Valuation Business Day.

2.3 The Market Price means the value of the Underlying Share on the Exchange as calculated by the Calculation Agent on the Valuation Date, and expressed in [relevant currency].

2.4 If on the Valuation Date the Calculation Agent determines that a Market Disruption Event has occurred and is continuing in respect of the

Underlying Share, then such Valuation Date shall be the next Valuation Business Day on which there is no Market Disruption Event or, if a Market Disruption Event is still continuing on the fifth Valuation Business Day following the Valuation Date, such date shall be the Valuation Date and the Calculation Agent shall calculate the Market Price on that day by reference to the method of calculating the valuation of the Underlying Share last in effect prior to the commencement of the Market Disruption Event and in a commercially reasonable manner as it in its discretion thinks fit, subject to any adjustments required to be made under Condition 2.5 of this Agreement.

2.5   **Market Adjustment:** During the life of the Agreement, if any adjustment is made by the Exchange or its successors (collectively the "Exchange") in the trading on the Underlying Share, an equivalent adjustment shall be made in the terms of the Agreement. Except as provided in the following paragraph, no adjustment shall be made in the terms of the Agreement for any event that does not result in an adjustment to the terms of the trading of the Underlying Share. Without limiting the generality of the foregoing, NO ADJUSTMENT SHALL BE MADE IN THE TERMS OF THE TRANSACTION FOR ORDINARY CASH DIVIDENDS ON THE UNDERLYING SHARE. *[This will require adjustment to take account of options traded on . . . . . in respect of the share]*

2.6   If the price of the Underlying Share published on a given day and used or to be used by the Calculation Agent to determine the Market Price is subsequently corrected and the correction is published by the Exchange or a successor within 30 days of the original publication, either party may notify the other party of (i) that correction and (ii) the amount that is payable as a result of that correction. If not later than 30 days after publication of that correction a party gives notice that an amount is so payable, the party that originally either received or retained such amount shall, not later than three Settlement Business Days after the effectiveness of that notice, pay to the other party that amount, together with interest on that amount at a rate per annum equal to the cost (without proof or evidence of any actual cost) to the other party (as certified by it) of funding that amount for the period from and including the day on which a payment originally was (or was not) made to but excluding the day of payment of the refund or payment resulting from that correction.

3.   Settlement

3.1   Following the exercise of the Option in accordance with the Agreement, the Seller shall pay to the Buyer the Cash Settlement Amount on or before the Settlement Day.

3.2   Seller's obligations to Buyer under this Agreement shall not accrue until Buyer has paid the Premium in full.

4 Representations and Warranties

Each party represents and warrants to the other party that (a) it has full power, authority and legal right to enter into this Agreement; and (b) this Agreement constitutes a valid and binding obligation. Counterparty represents and warrants that it is a market counterparty or non-private customer within the meaning of the rules of [The Securities and Futures Authority Limited ("SFA") / relevant regulatory authority].

5 Default

5.1 Each of the following events shall constitute an event of default (an "Event of Default"), with respect to a party ("the Defaulting Party"):

(a) failure to make payment of any amount due under this Agreement within three Settlement Business Days of having received notice of such failure;

(b) The Seller (i) is dissolved (other than pursuant to a consolidation, amalgamation, reorganisation or merger); (ii) becomes insolvent or fails or is unable or admits in writing its inability generally to pay its debts as they become due; (iii) makes a general assignment, arrangement or composition with or for the benefit of its creditors; (iv) institutes or has instituted against it a proceeding seeking a judgment of insolvency or bankruptcy or any other relief under any bankruptcy or insolvency law or other similar law affecting creditors' rights, or a petition is presented for its winding-up or liquidation, and, in the case of any such proceeding or petition instituted or presented against it, such proceeding or petition (A) results in a judgement of insolvency or bankruptcy or the entry of an order for relief or the making of an order for its winding-up or liquidation or (B) is not dismissed, discharged, stayed or restrained in each case within 30 days of the institution or presentation thereof; (v) has a resolution passed for its winding-up, official management or liquidation (other than pursuant to a consolidation, amalgamation, reorganisation or merger); (vi) seeks or becomes subject to the appointment of an administrator, provisional liquidator, conservator, receiver, trustee, custodian or other similar official for it or for all or substantially all its assets; (vii) has a secured party take possession of all or substantially all of its assets or has a distress, execution, attachment, sequestration or other legal process levied, enforced or sued on or against all or substantially all its assets and such secured party maintains possession, or any such process is not dismissed, discharged, stayed or restrained, in each case within 30 days thereafter; (viii) causes or is subject to any event with respect to it which, under the applicable laws of any jurisdiction, has an analogous effect to any of the events specified in clause (i) to (vii) (inclusive); or (ix) takes any action in furtherance of, or indicating its consent to, approval of, or acquiescence in, any of the foregoing acts;

(c) any representation made or deemed repeated by it under this Agreement proves to have been incorrect or misleading in any material respect when made or deemed repeated;

(d) the Seller or any guarantor of such party consolidates or amalgamates with, or merges with or into, or transfers all or substantially all its assets to, another entity and, at the time of such consolidation, amalgamation, merger or transfer: (i) the resulting, surviving or transferee entity either has a materially weaker creditworthiness or fails to assume all the obligations of such party under this Agreement or of such guarantee under any guarantee agreement to which it is or its predecessor was a party; or (ii) any person or entity acquires directly or indirectly the beneficial ownership of equity securities having the power to elect a majority of the board of directors of such party or any guarantor of such party or otherwise acquires directly or indirectly the power to control the policy-making decisions of such party or guarantor; or (iii) the benefits of any guarantee agreement fail to extend (without the consent of the other party) to the performance by such resulting, surviving or transferee entity of its obligations under this Agreement.

5.2   Upon the occurrence of an Event of Default, the party that is not the Defaulting Party (the "Non-Defaulting Party") may by written notice to the Defaulting Party (except in the case of a default specified under Condition 5.1(b)(i)-(iii), (v), (vii) or (viii) in which case no notice is required and the Early Termination Date shall be deemed to occur immediately before the happening of the relevant event) despatched whilst the Event of Default is continuing and specifying the relevant Event of Default, elect to terminate and settle both Options (but not one only) on the Early Termination Date, being the date specified in and no earlier than the date of the notice.

5.3   If an Early Termination Date occurs (or is deemed to occur under automatically under Condition 5.2), the Non-Defaulting Party shall calculate the Early Termination Amount payable by one party to the other and shall as soon as reasonably practicable given to the Defaulting Party a statement thereof (including details of any relevant Quotation). The Early Termination Amount shall be payable on the Settlement Business Day immediately after notice of its amount is given to the Defaulting Party. The Early Termination Amount shall be such amount calculated by the Non-Defaulting Party using the average of four Quotations received from market makers in the relevant indicies and bonds.

5.4   Set-off

Upon the occurrence of any Early Termination Date, in addition to and not in limitation of any other right or remedy (including any right to set off, counterclaim or otherwise withhold payment) under applicable law:

the Non-Defaulting Party or Non-Affected Party (in either case, "X") may, without prior notice to any person, set off any sum or obligation (whether or not arising under this Agreement, whether matured or unmatured, whether or not contingent and irrespective of the currency, place of payment or booking office of the sum or obligation) owed by the Defaulting Party or Affected Party (in either case, "Y") to X or any Affiliate of X against any sum or obligation (whether or not arising under this Agreement, whether matured or unmatured, whether or not contingent and irrespective of the currency, place of payment or booking office of the sum or obligation) owed by X or any Affiliate of X to Y, and for this purpose, may convert one currency into another. If any sum or obligation is unascertained, X may in good faith estimate that sum or obligation and set off in respect of that estimate, subject to X or Y, as the case may be, accounting to the other party when such sum or obligation is ascertained.

Nothing in this Agreement shall be effective as or deemed to created any charge under English law.

6. Illegality and Impossibility

6.1   If a party is required to gross up, or is prevented or frustrated from performing its obligations for reasons beyond its control with respect to the Option, then such party (the "Affected Party") shall promptly give notice thereof to the other party (the "Non-Affected Party") and either party may, by notice to the other, require the liquidation and close-out of the Option and for this purpose the provisions of Clause 5.3 shall apply mutatis mutandis save that:

(a) references to the Non-Defaulting Party shall be taken to be references to the Non-Affected Party;
(b) in calculating the Early Termination Amount, the Non-Affected Party shall not be entitled to take into account Other Expenses; and
(c) the Early Termination Date for the Option shall be the date of the notice given under Clause 6.1, provided that if such date is not a Valuation Business Day, the Early Termination Date shall be the next following Valuation Business Day.

6.2   If notice is given by the Affected Party under Clause 6.1 as a result of the occurrence of an event which renders it illegal for the Affected Party to perform an obligation or to pay an amount in respect of the Option, the parties shall in good faith endeavour to agree an alternative method of performance of the obligation affected by such illegality, failing which either of the parties may require the liquidation and close-out of the Option in accordance with Clause 6.1.

7 Transfer

Neither party may transfer this Agreement, in whole or in part, without the prior written consent of the other, which consent shall not be unreasonably withheld. Notwithstanding the above, either party may transfer the Option without the prior written consent of the other to a subsidiary or affiliate that is subject to the guaranty of the transferor's Credit Support Provider, provided that such transfer shall not otherwise constitute an Event of Default or an event under clause 6.1 or 6.2.

C   Other Provisions:

(a) Credit Support Documents:
(b) Notice Details:
(c) Account details:
(d) Governing Law
     This Agreement shall be governed by English Law.

Agreed and accepted on   199– by
'A' BANK

By: _____
Name:
Title:

COUNTERPARTY

By: _____
Name:
Title:

SHORT FORM "NON-STANDARD" OTC OPTIONS AGREEMENT
(the "Confirmation")

This Confirmation sets out the terms of the OTC Option contracted between the parties as described below.

1. Description of Option

Trade Date:

Seller: Counterparty ("Counterparty")

Buyer: 'A' Bank

Option Style: European / American / Asian

Option Type: Put / Call

Expiration Date: [..], or otherwise the Option shall expire at the closing of trading on the Exchange on the Expiration Date

Exercise Price:

Underlying Share:

Number of Underlying Shares:

Premium:

Premium Payment Date: .... or if that date is not a Currency Business Day, the first following day that is a Currency Business Day.

Exchange:

Settlement Method: Cash / Physical settlement

[Cash Settlement Amount: (Exercise Price – Market Price) x Number of Underlying Shares exercised on the Expiration Date, expressed in Sterling.]

Calculation Agent:

Market Price: The value of the Underlying Share on the Exchange as calculated by the Calculation Agent on the Valuation Date, and expressed in Sterling.

Automatic Exercise: The Option will be deemed to be automatically exercised if the Cash Settlement Amount is greater than zero at the close of business in London on the Expiration Date.

The terms of this Confirmation shall be subject to the terms and conditions on the reverse of this Confirmation.

Agreed and accepted on   199– by
'A' BANK

By: _____
Name:
Title:

COUNTERPARTY

By: _____
Name:
Title:

2. Exercise and Settlement

2.1 Valuation Date is the business day following exercise but shall be no later than the Expiration Date.

2.2 Following the exercise of the Option in accordance with the Agreement, the Seller shall pay to the Buyer the Cash Settlement Amount on the day on which a trade in the Underlying Shares executed on the Valuation Date would settle under normal market practice.

2.3 Business Day shall mean any day that the Exchange is open for business.

3 Representations and Warranties

Each party represents and warrants to the other party that (a) it has full power, authority and legal right to enter into this Agreement; and (b) this Agreement constitutes a valid and binding obligation. Counterparty represents and warrants that it is a market counterparty or non-private customer within the meaning of the rules of The Securities and Futures Authority Limited ("SFA").

4 Default

4.1 The occurrence at any time of any of the following events constitutes an event of default ("Event of Default") with respect to such party (the "Defaulting Party"):

(a) the Defaulting Party fails to make, when due, any payment or delivery required to be made by it under this Confirmation within [three] Business Days of notice of such failure being given to the Defaulting Party; or

(b) any obligations of the Defaulting Party in respect of (i) any indebtedness for borrowed money, (ii) any over-the-counter derivatives transaction or (iii) any guarantee or indemnity given by the Defaulting Party becomes due and payable prior to its original due date by reason of any default or is otherwise not made when due, where the aggregate amount of such obligations is greater than GBP [. . .];

(c) any described in Section 5(a)(vii) of the 1992 ISDA Master Agreement;

(d) any representation made or deemed repeated by it under this Agreement proves to have been incorrect or misleading in any material respect when made;

4.2 Upon the occurrence of an Event of Default, the party that is not the Defaulting Party (the "Non-Defaulting Party") may by written notice to the Defaulting Party, elect to terminate and settle the Option on the Early Termination Date, being the date specified in and no earlier than the date of the notice.

4.3 In this case, the Non-Defaulting Party shall calculate the Early Termination Amount payable by one party to the other and shall as soon as reasonably practicable given to the Defaulting Party a statement thereof. The Early Termination Amount shall be payable on the Settlement Business Day immediately after notice of its amount is given to the Defaulting Party. The Early Termination Amount shall be such amount calculated by the Non-Defaulting Party using the average of four quotations received from market makers in options on the Underlying Share, for a Replacement Option.

5. Transfer

Neither party may transfer this Agreement, in whole or in part, without the prior written consent of the other, which consent shall not be unreasonably withheld. Notwithstanding the above, A may transfer the Option without the prior written consent of the other to an affiliated entity provided that such transfer shall not otherwise constitute an Event of Default.

6. Other Provisions:

(a) Credit Support Documents:
(b) Notice Details:
(c) Account details:
(d) Governing Law: This Agreement shall be governed by English Law.

LONG-FORM "NON-STANDARD" OTC OPTIONS CONFIRMATION
(the "Confirmation")

This Confirmation sets out the terms of the OTC Option contracted between the parties as described below.

1. Description of Option

Trade Date:	
Seller:	Counterparty ("Counterparty")
Buyer:	'A' Bank ("A")
Option Style:	European / American / Asian
Option Type:	Put / Call
Expiration Date:	[..], or otherwise at the closing of trading on the first day which is a Business Day on the Exchange after Expiration Date
Exercise Price:	
Underlying Share:	
Number of Underlying Shares:	
Premium:	
Premium Payment Date:	...... or if that date is not a Currency Business Day, the first following day that is a Currency Business Day.
Exchange:	
Settlement Method:	Cash / Physically Settled
[Settlement Amount:	(Exercise Price – Market Price) x Number of Underlying Shares exercised on the Expiration Date, expressed in Sterling.]
Calculation Agent:	
Market Price:	The value of the Underlying Share on the Exchange as calculated by the Calculation Agent on the Valuation Date, and expressed in Sterling.
Automatic Exercise:	The Option will be deemed to be automatically exercised if the Settlement Amount is greater than zero at the close of business in London on the Expiration Date.

The terms of this Confirmation shall be subject to the terms and conditions on the reverse of this Confirmation.

Agreed and accepted on   199– by
'A' BANK

By: _____
Name:
Title:

COUNTERPARTY

By: _____
Name:
Title:

2. Exercise and Settlement

2.1 Valuation Date is the business day following exercise but shall be no later than the Expiration Date.

2.2 Following the exercise of the Option in accordance with the Agreement, the Seller shall deliver to the Buyer the Settlement Amount on the day on which a trade in the Underlying Shares executed on the Valuation Date would settle under normal market practice.

2.3 Business Day shall mean any day that the Exchange is open for business.

3 Representations and Warranties

Each party represents and warrants to the other party that (a) it has full power, authority and legal right to enter into this Agreement; and (b) this Agreement constitutes a valid and binding obligation. Counterparty represents and warrants that it is a market counterparty or non-private customer within the meaning of the rules of The Securities and Futures Authority Limited ("SFA").

4 Default

4.1 The occurrence at any time of any of the following events constitutes an event of default ("Event of Default") with respect to such party (the "Defaulting Party"):

(a) the Defaulting Party fails to make, when due, any payment or delivery required to be made by it under this Confirmation within [three] Business Days of notice of such failure being given to the Defaulting Party; or

(b) any obligations of the Defaulting Party in respect of (i) any indebtedness for borrowed money, (ii) any over-the-counter derivatives transaction or (iii) any guarantee or indemnity given by the Defaulting Party becomes due and payable prior to its original due date by reason of any default or is otherwise not made when due, where the aggregate amount of such obligations is greater than GBP [. . .];

(c) any described in Section 5(a)(vii) of the 1992 ISDA Master Agreement;

(d) any representation made or deemed repeated by it under this Agreement proves to have been incorrect or misleading in any material respect when made;

4.2   Upon the occurrence of an Event of Default, the party that is not the Defaulting Party (the "Non-Defaulting Party") may by written notice to the Defaulting Party, elect to terminate and settle the Option on the Early Termination Date, being the date specified in and no earlier than the date of the notice.

4.3   In this case, the Non-Defaulting Party shall calculate the Early Termination Amount payable by one party to the other and shall as soon as reasonably practicable given to the Defaulting Party a statement thereof. The Early Termination Amount shall be payable on the Settlement Business Day immediately after notice of its amount is given to the Defaulting Party. The Early Termination Amount shall be such amount calculated by the Non-Defaulting Party using the average of four quotations received from market makers in options on the Underlying Share, for a Replacement Option

5.   Transfer

Neither party may transfer this Agreement, in whole or in part, without the prior written consent of the other, which consent shall not be unreasonably withheld. Notwithstanding the above, A may transfer the Option without the prior written consent of the other to an affiliated entity provided that such transfer shall not otherwise constitute an Event of Default.

6   Other Provisions:

(a) Credit Support Documents:
(b) Notice Details:
(c) Governing Law: This Agreement shall be governed by English Law.

Pro-forma "Non-standard" Equity Index Swap Confirmation

Date:
Subject: Swap Transaction
                FT-SE Index Swap

Dear

The purpose of this document is to set forth the terms and conditions of the Swap Transaction entered into on the Trade Date speified below (the "Transaction") between A Bank ("A") and ...... ("......"). This telescopy constitutes a "Confirmation" as referred to in the Agreement specified below.

1. The definitions and provisions contained in the 1991 ISDA Definitions (the "Definitions") as published by the International Swap Dealers Association, Inc. ("ISDA") are incorporated into this Confirmation. In the event of any inconsistency between the Definitions and this Confirmation, this Confirmation will prevail.

If you and we are parties to an Interest Rate and Currency Exchange Agreement or a Master Agreement in the form published by ISDA ("an Agreement") this Confirmation supplements, forms a part of, and is subject to such Agreement. If you and we are not yet parties to an Agreement, you and we agree to use our best efforts promptly to negotiate, execute and deliver an Agreement, including our standard form of Schedule attached thereto and made a part thereof, with such modifications as you and we shall in good faith agree. Upon execution and delivery by you and us of an Agreement this Confirmation shall supplement, form a part of and be subject to such Agreement. Until you and we execute and deliver an Agreement, this Confirmation shall supplement, form a part of and be subject to the Master Agreement in the form published by ISDA as if you and we had executed that Agreement (but without any Schedule thereto) on the trade date of this Confirmation.

Each party is hereby advised, and each party hereby acknowledges, that the other party has engaged in (or refrained from engaging in) substantial financial transactions and has taken other material actions in reliance upon the parties' entry into the Swap Transaction to which this Confirmation relates on the terms and conditions set forth below.

Each party will make each payment specified in this Confirmation as being payable by it not later than the date for value on that date in the place of the account specified below, in freely transferable funds and in the manner customary for payments in the required currency.

The Agreement and each Confirmation thereunder will be governed by and construed in accordance with English Law.

In this confirmation "Party A" means ...... and "Party B" means ......

2. The terms of this Swap Transaction are as follows:

(a) General:
   Trade Date:
   Effective Date:
   Termination Date:
   No. of Contracts:
   Initial Index Level:
   Reference Dates:

(b) Party A Payment Details:
   Payment for initial
   Calculation Period:
   Payments: No. of Contracts x Spot Index Level for that Calculation Period x Floating Rate Option

   Floating Rate Option:
   Designated Maturity
   Spread:
   Payment Dates: The Second Business Day following each Reference Date

   Day Count Fraction:
   Business Day: London
   Calculation Agent: [A], with all calculations and determinations hereunder to be provided on request to ......
   Reset Dates: The Reference Date preceding each Calculation Period.

(c) Party B Payment Details:
   Payments: [Index] Price Return
   Payment Dates: The second Business Day following each Reference Date
   Reset Dates: The Reference Date preceding each Calculation Period.

3. Definitions and Other Provisions relating to the [Index] Price Return:

(a) **[Index]** means the [.... Index], an index of [...] shares currently sponsored by the Sponsor (or any successor index using, in the determination of the Calculation Agent, the same formula for, and method of calculation used in, the [Index].

(b) **Index Price Return** means the amount (which may be negative) calculated and determined by the Calculation Agent in accordance with the following formula:
   [Insert appropriate formula]

(c) **Index Day** means a day on which each of the [relevant options and futures exchanges] is (or, but for the occurrence of a Market Disruption Event, would have been) open for business.

278

(d) **Index Level** on any day means the value determined by the Calculation Agent to be the [... Settlement Price] of the [Index] on that day, as calculated and publically announced by the Sponsor, adjusted if necessary in accordance with paragraph 4 hereof.

(e) **Sponsor** means the [....] Exchange

4. Adjustment Provisions:

(a) **[Index] Adjustment:** In the event that the value of the [Index] is not calculated and publically announced by another person or entity acceptable to the Calculation Agent (the "Third Party"), the Index Level shall be calculated by reference to the information so calculated and announced by the Third Party. However, in the event that on or prior to the final Reference Date, the Sponsor or a Third Party;

(i) changes the formula for, or the method of calculation of, the [Index] or in any other way modifies the [Index] (other than modifications prescribed in the formula for, or the method of, calculation to maintain the [Index] in the event of changes in constituent stocks, capitalization events, and other routine events), the Calculation Agent shall adjust the Index Level so that it shall be as near as practicable to that which would have been calculated and publicly announced had such change or modification not taken effect.

(ii) shall have ceased calculation and public announcement of the [Index], either temporarily or permanently, the Calculation Agent shall calculate the Index Level using (subject to the provisions in (i) and (ii) above) the formula for, and the method of, calculating such information employed immediately prior to such cessation so that the Index Level shall be as near as practicable to that which would have been calculated and publicly announced by the Sponsor or the Third Party had such party not ceased its calculation and public announcement of such information.

(b) **Market Disruption Event,** as determined by the Calculation Agent, means the occurrence on any day, during the half-hour period prior to the determination of the Index Level, of (i) the material suspension or material limitation of trading in shares composing [..%] or more of the level of the [Index], or (ii) the material suspension or material limitation of trading in options or futures contracts related to the [Index] traded on the [options exchange]; provided that a limitation on the hours and number of days of trading will not constitute a Market Disruption Event if it results from an announced change in the regular business hours of the relevant exchange.

(c) **Reference Date Adjustment:** A Reference Date will be postponed if it would fall on a day (i) which is not an Index Day, or (ii) on which a Market Disruption Event is occurring. In either such case the Reference Date will be postponed until the next following Business Day which is an Index Day and a day on which a Market Disruption Event is not occurring.

However, a Reference Date will not be postponed for more than five Busienss Days following the date which would, but for the events in (i) or (ii) above, otherwise have been the Reference Date. In this event such fifth Business Day will be deemed to be the Reference Date and, if necessary, the Calculation Agent shall adjust the Index Level to take into account, as nearly as practicable, the effect of such Market Disruption Event on the Index Level.

5. Other Provisions

(a) The following Credit Support Documents will be provided:
(b) Account details:
     Payments to Party A:
     Payments to Party B:

Please indicate your agreement to the terms contained herein by completing and signing as indicated below, and immediately returning a copy of the executed Confirmation.

We are delighted to have entered into this Transaction with you.

'A' BANK

By: _____
Name:
Title:

We agree that this Confirmation correctly sets out the terms of our agreement to the Transaction described therein.

[COUNTERPARTY]

By: _____
Name:
Title:

Pro-forma Mark-to-Market Collateral Agreement
One-way agreement attached to Master Agreement

Whereas the parties (the "Counterparty" and "A Bank") have entered into a Master Agreement ... in consideration of A Bank entering into the Master Agreement, ... in order to support and secure the obligations of the Counterparty under the Master Agreement ... Counterparty agrees to deposit "collateral" with A Bank from time to time.

A. Definitions

"Collateral" means the aggregate of the following items pledged by Counterparty to A,
The type of collateral that is provided is a matter for negotiation between the parties.

Cash. This is the simplest form of collateral. A given amount of cash is deposited and held to the account of the counterparty. The further issue is then who has control over that money and who has the use of that money while it has been hypothecated for the purpose of credit enhancement. Therefore, the question of who collects interest on the cash while it is held in the account. It is usual that the rate of interest is specified according to a standard, benchmark interest rate such as LIBOR.

Government bonds and government obligations generally, as defined by the parties' credit requirements.

Other bearer-form government obligations as rated by Standard & Poor's Corporation ("S&P") or by Moody's Investor Services ("Moody's"); whether U.S. dollar-denominated or in some other currency;[30]

Short term commercial paper as rated by S&P or by Moody's;

Securities issued by a given class of companies which satisfy the requisite credit requirements, or provided by the counterparty itself or its affiliates; or

Other marketable securities acceptable to A Bank, including all interest, dividends, and other income thereon and all proceeds thereof.

Custody of collateral

The Collateral shall be deposited with or maintained by A in a custody account at a commercial bank or other institution acceptable to A.

"Exposure" means that a party is the beneficiary of a conditional or unconditional payment or performance obligation of the other party pursuant to one or more transactions under the Master Agreement

"Net Exposure" means the point at which the total value of one party's

---

[30] It is for the parties themselves to decide on the credit rating that they require for the requisite collateral. It is usual to have this measured in accordance with the relevant S&P or Moody's ratings either for the issuing entity or its public debt issues.

exposure exceeds the total value of the other party's exposure.

"Total Required Collateral" as of any day on which the level of collateral required is to be valued, is to be the fair market value of the Collateral required to be pledged by Counterparty to A Bank under the terms of this agreement.

It is usual to insert a catch-all provision that any terms not defined in the Collateral agreement will have the meaning used in the relevant Master Agreement.

B. Method of Marketing to Market

At the close of business on an appropriate calculation day [as defined in the agreement], A Bank shall in a commercially reasonable manner mark-to-market the parties' respective positions under all outstanding transactions under the Master Agreement so as to determine (i) the amount of any Net Exposure which A Bank has at that time (ii) the value of the Collateral being held by A Bank and (iii) the Total Required Collateral as of such day.

The Total Required Margin shall be equal to the following:

There are a number of techniques to value the required collateral. The first is to fix on a threshold amount, which, when exceeded, requires the deposit of a fixed amount of collateral:-

If A Bank has Net Exposure to Counterparty in an amount less than or equal to GBP x, the Total Required Collateral will be GBP y.

In a situation where there is a level of collateral currently held, the Counterparty may be compelled to add to that pool of collateral to bring it up to the Total Required Collateral figure. Alternatively, collateral may not be held already, in which case, the whole of the Total Required Collateral must be provided. Alternatively, an amount of Collateral may be required to be provided to reduce the exposure to a pre-determined level other than zero.

C. Depositing Collateral

The Total Required Margin must be provided to A by close of business on the [insert number of business days within which collateral must be deposited]

The parties may require notice of such requirement to be given by the calculation agent to the other party before the collateral is required.

Counterparty represents that it will be the legal and beneficial owner of any securities constituting the Collateral at the time of depositing such securities and at any other relevant time, and that the Counterparty represents that it shall be free from all charges, liens, interests and encumbrances whatsoever in relation to the said Collateral and that it will have at any relevant time the free and unencumbered right to transfer those securities in pursuance of the terms of this agreement.

The security holder will require an assurance that it has priority security over the relevant assets. This should extend to substituted assets and potentially any accretions to those assets by way of dividend, coupon or otherwise.

Counterparty grants to A Bank a first priority security interest in and a lien upon the Collateral in conjunction with any proceeds of sale thereof, any accretions of value thereto, any distributions thereon and any property substituted therefore whatsoever, as security for the satisfaction of the obligations of the Counterparty under the Master Agreement.

The purpose of the agreement is to secure the rights of the security holder to the assets proferred as Collateral.

In the event of a default by the Counterparty under this agreement or under the Master Agreement, A Bank shall have the full rights of the legal and beneficial owner of the Collateral.

The more difficult issue during the life of the agreement is whether or not the security holder is to be enabled to use the Collateral or whether the Collateral must be maintained in a custody account until a default under the collateral agreement.

In any event, during the life of this agreement, A Bank shall have the unrestricted right to use or rehypothecate any property included in the Collateral, subject only to its obligation to return such property or suitable equivalent property to the Counterparty at the termination of the agreement.

The further problem arises of the location of the Collateral and the possibility of regulatory interference by the lex loci situationis.

To the extent that any Collateral is located outside of [jurisdiction] at any time during the life of this agreement or before the inception of this agreement, that Collateral shall be pledged to A Bank in accordance with the terms of this agreement in accordance with any applicable law of the place where such Collateral is located.

D. Return of the Collateral

There are a number of circumstances in which collateral may have to be returned. The first is where the exposure of the security holder falls below the level of Collateral that it held. The second is where the Master Agreement or all relevant transactions under it have come to an end.

Where on any business day the value of the Collateral then held by A Bank is greater than the value of the Total Required Margin, A Bank shall return to Counterparty Collateral having a value equivalent to any such excess.

There may be a de minimis *level set for the amount which the excess must reach before Collateral must be paid back.*

Where on any business day there are no transactions outstanding under the Master Agreement and where on any business day all of Counterparty's obligations under this agreement have been performed, then [within a specified time period] A Bank shall [pay to Counterparty an amount of cash having a value equivalent to any Collateral then held by A Bank at that date or return securities and cash of like kind, class and value as then constitute the Collateral].

Governing law

Account details

Heading for Letter[1] _____
[Letterhead of Party A]

[Date]

Bond Option Transaction

[Name and Address of Party B] _____

Heading for Telex[1]
Telex
Date:
To: [Name and Telex Number of Party B]
From: [Party A]
Re: Bond Option Transaction _____

Dear   :

The purpose of this [letter agreement/telex] (this "Confirmation") is to confirm the terms and conditions of the Transaction entered into between us on the Trade Date specified below (the "Transaction").

[This Confirmation constitutes a "Confirmation" as referred to in, and supplements, forms a part of and is subject to, the ISDA Master Agreement dated as of [date], as amended and supplemented from time to time (the "Agreement"), between you and us. All provisions contained in the Agreement govern this Confirmation except as expressly modified below.][1]

The terms of the Transaction to which this Confirmation relates are as follows:

1. General Terms:

Trade Date:	[ ]. 199[ ]
Option Style:	[American] [European]
Option Type:	[Put] [Call]
Seller:	[Party A] [Party B]
Buyer:	[Party A] [Party B]
Bonds:	[Insert full title of the Bonds, including maturity and full legal name of the issuer of the Bonds and any other identification number or reference for the Bonds]
Number of Options:	[ ]
Bond Entitlement:	[ ] of nominal amount of the Bonds per Option.
Partial Exercise:	Applicable[2]

---

[1] Include if applicable.

[2] Specify the Partial Exercise is inapplicable if Buyer is not permitted to exercise less than all Options at a time, and specify that multiple exercise is inapplicable if Buyer is permitted to exercise an American style option only once (even if less than all Options are then exercised).

285

Option Strike Price:	[ ]
Premium per Option:	[ ][3]
Total Premium:	[ ][3]
Premium Payment Date:	[ ], or, if that date is not a Currency Business Day, the first following day that is a Currency Business Day.
Seller Business Day:	Any day on which commercial banks are open for business (including dealings in foreign exchange and foreign currency deposits)[4] in [ ].[5]
Exchange Business Day:	Any day that is a Seller Business Day and is a trading day on [insert relevant exchange] other than a day on which trading on such exchange is scheduled to close prior to its regular weekday closing time.
Currency Business Day:	Any day on which commercial banks are open for business (including dealings in foreign exchange and foreign currency deposits) in [ ].[6]
Local Business Day:	Any day on which commercial banks are open for business (including dealings in foreign exchange and foreign currency deposits) in the city specified in the address for notice provided by the recipient.
Calculation Agent:	[ ], whose determinations and calculations shall be binding in the absence of manifest error.[7]

2. Procedure for Exercise:

   Exercise Period: [The Expiration Date][8] [Any Seller Business Day from and including [   ] to and including

---

[3] The premium may be stated as an amount of currency, in basis points or as a percentage of yield.

[4] If Seller is not a commercial bank and is located in a city in which commercial bank holidays may differ from local securities exchange holidays, add "and which is a scheduled trading day on local securities exchanges".

[5] Specify the city in which Seller is located for the purpose of receiving notices.

[6] Specify the principal financial center for the relevant currency. If the payment currency for the premium is not the same as the payment currency for the Cash Settlement Amount, the parties may wish to specify a principal financial center in respect of each payment currency.

[7] If the Calculation Agent is a third party, the parties will want to consider any documentation necessary to confirm its undertaking.

[8] Include if European style option.

	the Expiration Date][9] between 9:00 a.m. and [4:00 p.m.][10] (local time in [ ]).[11]
Exercise Date:	The Seller Business Day during the Exercise Period on which the Option is or is deemed to be exercised.
Expiration Date:	[ ], or, if that date is not an Exchange Business Day, the first following day that is an Exchange Business Day.
Notice of Exercise and Written Confirmation:	Buyer must deliver irrevocable notice to Seller (which may be delivered orally, including by telephone) of its exercise of any right granted pursuant to an Option during the hours specified above on a Seller Business Day in the Exercise Period. [The notice given in respect of an Exercise Date shall specify the number of Options being exercised on that date.][12] [Buyer may exercise the unexercised number of Options on one or more Seller Business Days during the Exercise Period.][13]

If the notice of exercise is delivered after [4:00 p.m.] on a Seller Business Day, then that notice will be deemed delivered on the next following Seller Business Day, if any, in the Exercise Period.

If a notice of exercise is delivered orally, Buyer will execute and deliver a written confirmation confirming the substance of that notice and account details within one Seller Business Day of that notice. Failure to provide that written confirmation will not affect the validity of that oral notice.

Limited Right to Confirm Exercise:	If an Option has not previously been exercised, Seller may, immediately prior to, at or after the last time for exercise on the Expiration Date (the "Expiration Time"), request (which request may be oral, including by telephone) Buyer to

---

[9] Include if American style option.

[10] For American style options on certain bonds, such as Gilts, parties may wish to specify that the latest time Buyer may exercise its option on the Expiration Date is different from the latest time Buyer may exercise on any other Seller Business Day during the Exercise Period.

[11] Specify city in which Seller is located for purposes of receiving notices.

[12] Delete if Partial Exercise is inapplicable.

[13] Include if the Option is American style and Buyer may exercise more than once.

confirm its intent to exercise the Option. Buyer will reply immediately to any such request. [If Buyer confirms its intent to exercise at or before the Expiration Time, then Physical Settlement shall be applicable.][14] If Buyer confirms its intent to exercise after the Expiration Time or if Seller has made no request and Buyer notifies Seller of its intent to exercise after the Expiration Time but not later than 10 Seller Business Days after the Expiration Date, then the Option shall be deemed to have been exercised at the Expiration Time [and, notwithstanding Section 3 below, Cash Settlement shall be deemed to apply.][15] Otherwise, the Option shall be deemed to have expired at the Expiration Time.

Telephone, Telex and/or Facsimile Numbers and Contact Details for Notices:

Seller:

Buyer:

3. Settlement Terms:

Settlement: [Cash] [Physical]

Settlement Date: [   ][16] days following the relevant Exercise Date [, subject to adjustment for a Settlement Disruption Event][17].

[Physical Settlement Terms:][18]

Physical Settlement: On the Settlement Date, Buyer shall [pay to Seller the Bond Payment][19] [deliver to Seller the Bonds to be Delivered][20] and Seller shall [deliver to Buyer the Bonds to be Delivered][21] [pay to

---

[14] Include if Physical Settlement is specified to apply.

[15] Include if Physical Settlement is specified to apply.

[16] If cash settled, specify the number of Currency Business Days in which transactions in the relevant currency are settled, and, if settled by physical delivery, specify the number of days as is customary for the Clearance System.

[17] Include if Physical Settlement is specified to apply.

[18] Include if Physical Settlement is specified to apply. Otherwise, include only Cash Settlement Terms.

[19] Include if Call Option.

[20] Include if Put Option.

[21] Include if Call Option.

Buyer the Bond Payment][22], in each case, through the Clearance System at the accounts specified below, [on a delivery versus payment basis][23].

If there is a Settlement Disruption Event that prevents settlement on a day that but for the occurrence of that Settlement Disruption Event would have been the Settlement Date, then the Settlement Date shall be the first succeeding day on which that settlement can take place through the Clearance System, unless a Settlement Disruption Event prevents settlement on each day that the Clearance System is (or, but for the Settlement Disruption Event, would have been) open for business during the period ending 30 calendar days after the original date that, but for the Settlement Disruption Event, would have been the Settlement Date. If a Settlement Date does not occur during such 30 calendar day period, the party required under this Transaction to deliver Bonds shall use best efforts to deliver the Bonds to be Delivered promptly thereafter in a commercially reasonable manner outside the Clearance System on a delivery versus payment basis.

Split
Tickets:[24]

[The party required to deliver Bonds may divide the Bonds to be Delivered into such number of lots of such size as such party desires to facilitate its delivery obligations. Such party shall notify the party to receive the Bonds of its delivery intentions upon exercise of the Option.]

Bonds to be
Delivered:

The nominal amount of Bonds equal to the number of Options exercised on the relevant Exercise Date multiplied by the Bond Entitlement.

Bond

The product of (a) the sum of (i) the Option Strike

---

[22] Include if Put Option.

[23] If it is agreed that settlement will be other than on the basis of delivery vs. payment, specify the relevant details.

[24] Delete this paragraph if "split ticket" settlement is not acceptable to the parties.

289

Payment: Price [multiplied by the Bond Entitlement][25] plus (ii) accrued interest, if any, on the Bond Entitlement computed in accordance with customary trade practices employed with respect to the Bonds multiplied by (b) the number of Options exercised on the relevant Exercise Date.

Clearance System: [   ]

Settlement Disruption Event: An event beyond the control of the parties as a result of which the Clearance System cannot clear the transfer of the Bonds.

Failure to Deliver: Failure by a party to deliver, when due, Bonds under this Option shall constitute an Event of Default only if on or before the third Local Business Day after notice of the failure is given to the party it does not (a) remedy such failure or (b) provide such security or such other assurances to the other party as such other party, acting in good faith but in its sole discretion, deems adequate.

Buy-in: In addition to any requirement that a party provide security or assurances as a result of its failure to deliver the Bonds to be Delivered, the other party may at any time, and not later than 45 calendar days after such failure (absent an Event of Default) shall endeavour to, exercise a buyer's right to buy-in such Bonds in accordance with Section 450 of the International Securities Market Association's Rules and Recommendations, as amended from time to time.[26] Any buy-in settlement shall be settled without any delay and, in any event, not later than [ ][27] Currency Business Days following the date of the buy-in.

---

[25] Include if the Option Strike Price is stated as a percentage of the nominal value of the Bonds (*e.g.*, 103% of par), but delete if the Option Strike Price is stated as an amount in the relevant currency. If the Option Strike Price is stated as a yield, the formula should be adjusted accordingly.

[26] If a party to the Transaction is not an ISMA member or if the underlying bonds are not "international securities", further consideration should be given to the appropriateness of the Section 450 procedures. In such circumstances, the parties may, among other things, (i) choose to disregard any requirements that copies of notices relating to the buy-in procedures be sent to the ISMA secretariat and (ii) agree on alternative qualifications for selecting a buy-in agent.

[27] Specify the number of Currency Business Days in which transactions in the relevant currency are settled.

Cash
Settlement
Terms:

    Cash
    Settlement:

[If under the Limited Right to Confirm Exercise, any Option is deemed to have been exercised and Cash Settlement applies,][28] Seller shall pay to Buyer the Cash Settlement Amount, if any, on the Settlement Date for all Options exercised or deemed exercised.

    Cash
    Settlement
    Amount:

An amount, as calculated by the Calculation Agent, equal to the number of Options exercised on the relevant Exercise Date multiplied by the Strike Price Differential.

    Strike Price
    Differential:

An amount equal to the greater of (a) the excess of [the Option Strike Price [multiplied by the Bond Entitlement][29] over the Spot Price][30] [the Spot Price over the Option Strike Price [multiplied by the Bond Entitlement][31]][32] and (b) zero.

    Spot Price:

The price as of [   ][33] on the relevant Exercise Date (or, if that date is not an Exchange Business Day, the next following Exchange Business Day) for Bonds equal in amount to the Bond Entitlement, as determined in good faith by the Calculation Agent.

    Conversion:[34]

If the issuer of the Bonds irreversibly converts the Bonds into other securities, this Transaction shall continue as set forth in this Confirmation except that (a) the "Bonds" shall mean such other securities and (b) the Calculation Agent shall, in good faith, adjust the Option Strike Price, the Number of Options and/or the Bond Entitlement as the Calculation Agent determines appropriate to preserve the theoretical value of

---

[28] Include if Physical Settlement is specified to apply.
[29] Delete if the Option Strike Price is stated as an amount in the relevant currency.
[30] Include if Put Option.
[31] Delete if the Option Strike Price is stated as an amount in the relevant currency.
[32] Include if Call Option.
[33] Describe the relevant fixing or otherwise specify a valuation time.
[34] If the issuer of the Bonds is not a government or a governmental entity, the parties may wish to consider providing for adjustments in respect of the merger, liquidation or nationalization of the issuer.

this Transaction to the parties immediately prior to such conversion.

Dispute
Resolution:

If a party objects to a determination by the Calculation Agent of the Spot Price or an adjustment in respect of a Conversion within two Exchange Business Days of notice of that determination, then Buyer and Seller shall negotiate in good faith to agree on an independent third party that shall determine the Spot Price or that adjustment, as the case may be, and, if they cannot so agree within three Exchange Business Days, each of Buyer and Seller shall promptly choose an independent third party and instruct the parties so chosen to agree on another independent third party that shall determine the Spot Price or that adjustment, as the case may be. The determination of an independent third party shall be binding in the absence of manifest error. The costs of such independent third party shall be borne equally by Buyer and Seller.

4. Account Details:
    Account
    Details of
    Buyer:

    Account
    Details of
    Seller:

5. Other Terms:[35]
    [Additional
    Representation
    and
    Agreement:][36]

[A party required to deliver Bonds represents and agrees that it will convey good title to the Bonds to be Delivered, free and clear of any lien, charge, claim or encumbrance.]

---

[35] Consider whether any additions or deletions relating to any applicable jurisdiction or regulatory, tax, accounting, securities exchange or other requirements should be made in this Confirmation if these are not addressed in a related master agreement. For an indication of further issues that the parties may wish to consider when documenting transactions that settle by physical delivery under a 1992 ISDA Master Agreement, *see* Section VI of the *User's Guide to the 1992 ISDA Master Agreements*, 1993 Edition (as published by the International Swap Dealers Association, Inc.).

[36] Include if Physical settlement is specified to apply.

[Transfer:][37]   [Neither party may transfer any Option or any interest in or under this Transaction without the prior written consent of the non-transferring party and any purported transfer without such consent will be void.]

Margin: [Applicable][38] [Inapplicable]

This Confirmation will be governed by and construed in accordance with the laws of [   ] [(without reference to choice of law doctrine)].[39]

Closing for Letter[40]

Please confirm that the foregoing correctly sets forth the terms of our agreement by executing the copy of this Confirmation enclosed for that purpose and returning it to us or by sending to us a letter or telex substantially similar to this letter, which letter or telex sets forth the material terms of the Transaction to which this Confirmation relates and indicates your agreement to those terms.

Yours sincerely:
[PARTY A]
By: _____
      Name:
      Title:

Confirmed as of the
date first above written:
[PARTY B]
By: _____
      Name:
      Title:

Closing for Telex[40]

Please confirm that the foregoing correctly sets forth the terms of our agreement by sending to us a letter or telex substantially similar to this telex, which letter or telex sets forth the material terms of the Transaction to which this Confirmation relates and indicates agreement to those terms, or by sending to us a return telex substantially to the following effect:

Re:

We acknowledge receipt of your telex dated [   ] with respect to the above-referenced Transaction between [Party A] and [Party B] with a Trade Date of [   ] (reference number [   ]) and an Expiration Date of [   ] and confirm that such telex correctly sets

---

[37] Delete if this Confirmation is part of an ISDA Master Agreement.
[38] Parties should specify the margin provisions, if any, that will apply to the Option.
[39] Delete if this Confirmation is part of an ISDA Master Agreement.
[40] Include if applicable.

forth the terms of our agreement relating to the Transaction described therein. Very truly yours, [Party B], by [specify name and title of authorized officer]."

Yours sincerely,
[PARTY A]
By: _____
    Name:
    Title:

Heading for Letter[1]

[Letterhead of Party A]

[Date]

Transaction

[Name and Address of Party B]

Heading for Telex[1]

Telex

Date:

To: [Name and Telex Number of Party B]

From: [Party A]

Re: Bond Option Transaction

Dear   :

The purpose of this [letter agreement/telex] (this "Confirmation") is to confirm the terms and conditions of the Transaction entered into between us on the Trade Date specified below (the "Transaction"). [This Confirmation constitutes a "Confirmation" as referred to in the ISDA Master Agreement specified below.][1]

[The definitions and provisions contained in the 1991 ISDA Definitions (as published by the International Swap Dealers Association, Inc.) are incorporated into this Confirmation. In the event of any inconsistency between those definitions and provisions and this Confirmation, this Confirmation will govern.][1]

[This Confirmation supplements, forms a part of, and is subject to, the ISDA Master Agreement dated as of [date], as amended and supplemented from time to time (the "Agreement"), between you and us. All provisions contained in the Agreement govern this Confirmation except as expressly modified below.][1]

The terms of the Transaction to which this Confirmation relates are as follows:

General Terms:

Trade Date:	[ ]. 199[ ]
Option Style:	[American] [European] Option
Option Type:	[Put] [Call]
Seller:	[Party A] [Party B]
Buyer:	[Party A] [Party B]
Index/Price Option:	[ ]
Number of	[ ][2]

---

[1] Include if applicable.

[2] In addition, include a Multiplier if it is intended that the Cash Settlement Amount will be based on a percentage (*e.g.*, 50% or 200%) of the performance of the Index.

Options:	
Multiple Exercise:	[Applicable/Inapplicable]
[Minimum Number of Options:][3]	[ ]
[Maximum Number of Options:][3]	[ ]
[Options Must be Exercised in Integral Multiples of:][3]	[ ]
Strike Price:	[ ][4]
Premium:	[ ]
Premium Payment Date:	[ ], subject to adjustment in accordance with the Following Business Day Convention.
Index Business Day:	A day that is a Seller Business Day and is (or, but for the occurrence of a Market Disruption Event, would have been) a trading day on [each of] the Exchange [and [insert relevant Option and Future Exchanges]] other than a day on which trading on [any] such exchange is scheduled to close prior to its regular weekday closing time.
Seller Business Day:	Any day on which commercial banks are open for business (including dealings in foreign exchange and foreign currency deposits)[5] in [ ].[6]
Currency Business Day:	Any day on which commercial banks are open for business (including dealings in foreign exchange and foreign currency deposits) in the principal financial center for the relevant currency.
Exchange:	[ ]
Calculation Agent:	[ ], whose determinations and calculations shall be binding in the absence of manifest error.[7]

---

[3] Include if an American style option providing for multiple Exercise Dates.

[4] The parties may insert a number representing an index level as the strike price or a formula from which the strike price will be determined.

[5] If the Seller is not a commercial bank and is located in a city in which commercial bank holidays may differ from local stock exchange holidays, add "and which is a scheduled trading day on local stock exchanges".

[6] Specify city in which Seller is located for the purpose of receiving notices.

[7] If the Calculation Agent is a third party, the parties will want to consider any documentation necessary to confirm its undertaking.

Procedure for
Exercise:

    Exercise
    Period:

[The Expiration Date][8] [Any Seller Business Day from, and including, [   ] to, but excluding, the Expiration Date between 9:00 a.m. and [4:00 p.m.] (local time in   )][9]

    Expiration
    Date:

[   ] or, if that date is not an Index Business Day, the first following day that is an Index Business Day.

    [Notice of
    Exercise and
    Written
    Confirmation:][10]

[Applicable, except in the case of automatic exercise.[11] If the notice of exercise is delivered after [4:00 p.m.] on a Seller Business Day, then that notice will be deemed delivered on the next following Seller Business Day, if any, in the Exercise Period.][12]

    Automatic
    Exercise:

[If not previously exercised,][13] an Option shall be deemed automatically exercised on [the Seller Business Day immediately preceding the Expiration Date][13] [the Expiration Date].[14]

    Seller's
    Telephone or
    Facsimile
    Number and
    Contact Details
    for Purpose of
    Giving Notice:

[   ]

    Exercise Date
    for an Option:

The Seller Business Day during the Exercise Period on which that Option is or is deemed to be exercised.

Valuation:

---

[8] Include if European style option.

[9] Include if American style option. Specify city in which Seller is located for purposes of receiving notices.

[12] If an American style option providing for multiple Exercise Dates, add "Buyer must specify in that notice the Number of Options being exercised on that Exercise Date" and, as a new paragraph, "Buyer may exercise all or less than all the unexercised Options on one or more Seller Business Days during the Exercise Period, but, except in the case of automatic exercise as provided below, on any Seller Business Day may not exercise less than the Minimum Number of Options or more than the Maximum Number of Options and that number of Options must be an integral multiple of the amount specified above."

[10] Include if American style option.

[11] Alternatively, specify: "Except in the case of automatic exercise, Buyer must deliver irrevocable notice to Seller (which may be delivered orally, including by telephone) of its exercise of any right granted pursuant to an Option during the hours specified above on a Seller Business Day in the Exercise Period. If the notice of exercise is delivered orally, Buyer will execute and deliver a written confirmation confirming the substance of that notice within one Seller Business Day of that notice. Failure to provide that written confirmation will not affect the validity of that oral notice."

[13] Include if American style option.

[14] Include if European style option.

Valuation Time: At [the close of trading on the Exchange] [:00 a.m./p.m. (local time in   )[15]].

Valuation Date [in Respect of Each Exercise Date][16]:   [The Exercise Date][17] [The Index Business Day next following the Exercise Date],[18] unless there is a Market Disruption Event on that day. If there is a Market Disruption Event on that day, then the Valuation Date shall be the first succeeding Index Business Day on which there is no Market Disruption Event, unless there is a Market Disruption Event on each of the five Index Business Days immediately following the original date that, but for the Market Disruption Event, would have been the Valuation Date. In that case, (i) that fifth Index Business Day shall be deemed to be the Valuation Date, notwithstanding the Market Disruption Event, and (ii) the Calculation Agent shall determine the level of the Index as of the Valuation Time on that fifth Index Business Day in accordance with (subject to "Adjustment to Index" set forth below) the formula for and method of calculating the Index last in effect prior to the commencement of the Market Disruption Event using the Exchange traded price (or, if trading in the relevant security has been materially suspended or materially limited, its good faith estimate of the Exchange traded price that would have prevailed but for that suspension or limitation) as of the Valuation Time on that fifth Index Business Day of each security comprising the Index.

Market Disruption Event: The occurrence or existence on any Index Business Day during the one-half hour period that ends at the Valuation Time of any suspension of or limitation imposed on trading (by reason of movements in price exceeding limits permitted by the relevant exchange or otherwise)[19] on [(i)] the Exchange in securities that comprise 20% or

---

[15] Specify city in which the Exchange is located, if applicable.
[16] Include if multiple exercise American style option.
[17] Include if European style option.
[18] Include if American style option.
[19] Certain exchanges impose different types of limitations on trading to regulate price movements in individual contracts or securities. The parties should consider whether any such limitations should be ignored by the Calculation Agent in determining whether a material suspension or material limitation imposed on trading has occurred (e.g., whether only limitations on maximum intra-day price movements should be considered in order to avoid the frequent Market Disruption Events which would otherwise occur on some exchanges).

more of the level of the Index [or (ii) [   ][20] in options contracts on the Index or (iii) [   ][20] in futures contracts on the Index] if, in the determination of the Calculation Agent, such suspension or limitation is material.

For the purpose of determining whether a Market Disruption Event exists at any time, if trading in a security included in the Index is materially suspended or materially limited at that time, then the relevant percentage contribution of that security to the level of the Index shall be based on a comparison of (i) the portion of the level of the Index attributable to that security relative to (ii) the overall level of the Index, in each case immediately before that suspension or limitation.

The Calculation Agent shall as soon as reasonably practicable under the circumstances notify the [parties] [other party] of the existence or occurrence of a Market Disruption Event on any day that but for the occurrence or existence of a Market Disruption Event would have been a Valuation Date.

Adjustment to Index:	If the Index is (i) not calculated and announced by the agreed sponsor[21] but is calculated and announced by a successor sponsor acceptable to the Calculation Agent or (ii) replaced by a successor index using, in the determination of the Calculation Agent, the same or a substantially similar formula for and method of calculation as used in the calculation of the Index, then the Index will be deemed to be the index so calculated and announced by that successor sponsor or that successor index, as the case may be.

If (i) on or prior to any Valuation Date the Index sponsor makes a material change in the formula for or the method of calculating the Index or in any other way materially modifies the Index (other than a modification prescribed in that formula or method to maintain the Index in the event of changes in constituent stock and

---

[20] Specify the relevant exchange, if applicable.
[21] Consideration should be given to whether a sponsor to an Index should be identified as such in the relevant Confirmation.

capitalization and other routine events) or (ii) on any Valuation Date the sponsor fails to calculate and announce the Index, then the Calculation Agent shall calculate the Cash Settlement Amount using, in lieu of a published level for the Index, the level for that Index as at that Valuation Date as determined by the Calculation Agent in accordance with the formula for and method of calculating the Index last in effect prior to that change or failure, but using only those securities that comprised the Index immediately prior to that change or failure (other than those securities that have since ceased to be listed on the Exchange).

Correction of Index:

If the level of the Index published on a given day and used or to be used by the Calculation Agent to determine the Cash Settlement Amount is subsequently corrected and the correction published by the Index sponsor or a successor sponsor within 30 days of the original publication, either party may notify the other party of (i) that correction and (ii) the amount that is payable as a result of that correction. If not later than 30 days after publication of that correction a party gives notice that an amount is so payable, the party that originally either received or retained such amount shall, not later than three Currency Business Days after the effectiveness of that notice, pay to the other party that amount, together with interest on that amount at a rate per annum equal to the cost (without proof or evidence of any actual cost) to the other party (as certified by it) of funding that amount for the period from and including the day on which a payment originally was (or was not) made to but excluding the day of payment of the refund or payment resulting from that correction.

Cash Settlement
Terms:
   Cash
   Settlement:

Applicable; Seller shall pay to Buyer the Cash Settlement Amount, if any, on the Cash Settlement Payment Date for all Options exercised or deemed exercised [in respect of that date].[22]

Cash
Settlement
Amount:
An amount, as calculated by the Calculation Agent, equal to the [Number of Options][23] [number of Options exercised on the relevant Exercise Date][24] multiplied by the Strike Price Differential multiplied by one [   ],[25]

Strike Price
Differential:
An amount equal to the greater of (i) the excess, as of the Valuation Time on the [relevant][24] Valuation Date, of [the Strike Price over the level of the Index][26] [the level of the Index over the Strike Price][27] and (ii) zero.

Cash
Settlement
Payment Date:
Three Currency Business Days (each of which is a Seller Business Day) after the [relevant][28] Valuation Date.

Transfer:
Neither party may transfer any Option, in whole or in part, without the prior written consent of the non-transferring party.

Account Details:
Payments to
Seller:
Account for
payments:
Payments to
Buyer:
Account for
payments:

This Confirmation will be governed by and construed in accordance with the laws of [   ] [(without reference to choice of law doctrine)].[29]

---

[22] Include if multiple exercise American style option.
[23] Include if European style option or single exercise American style option.
[24] Include if multiple exercise American style option.
[25] Specify the currency unit of the county in which the Index is compiled or the currency unit to which the underlying values comprising the Index are converted for purposes of compiling the Index (e.g., ECU for Eurotrack 200). If a Multiplier has been specified in this Confirmation, add "multiplied by the Multiplier."
If a currency conversion is contemplated, parties may wish to provide for how, when and by whom the relevant exchange rate is to be determined.
[26] If the transaction is a Put Option.
[27] If the transaction is a Call Option.
[28] Include if multiple exercise American style option.
[29] Consider whether any additions or deletions relating to applicable jurisdiction or regulatory, tax, accounting or other requirements should be made in this Confirmation if these are not addressed in a related master agreement.

Closing for Letter[30]

Please confirm that the foregoing correctly sets forth the terms of our agreement by executing the copy of this Confirmation enclosed for that purpose and returning it to us or by sending to us a letter or telex substantially similar to this letter, which letter or telex sets forth the material terms of the Transaction to which this Confirmation relates and indicates your agreement to those terms.

Yours sincerely,
[PARTY A]
By: _____

Name:
Title:

Confirmed as of the date
first above written:
[PARTY B]
By: _____

Name:
Title:

Closing for Telex[30]

Please confirm that the foregoing correctly sets forth the terms of our agreement by sending to us a letter or telex substantially similar to this telex, which letter or telex sets forth the material terms of the Transaction to which this Confirmation relates and indicates agreement to those terms, or by sending to us a return telex substantially to the following effect:

"Re:

We acknowledge receipt of your telex dated [   ] with respect to the above-referenced Transaction between [Party A] and [Party B] with a Trade Date of [   ] and an Expiration Date of [   ] and confirm that such telex correctly sets forth the terms of our agreement relating to the Transaction described therein. Very truly yours, [Party B], by [specify name and title of authorized officer]."

Yours sincerely,
[PARTY A]
By: _____

Name:
Title:

---

[30] Include if applicable.

Heading for Letter[1]

[Letterhead of Party A]

[Date]

Transaction

[Name and Address of Party B]

Heading for Telex[1]
Date:
To: [Name and Telex Number of Party B]
From: [Party A]
Re: Equity Option Transaction

Dear   :

The purpose of this [letter agreement/telex] (this "Confirmation") is to confirm the terms and conditions of the Transaction entered into between us on the Trade Date specified below (the "Transaction"). [This Confirmation constitutes a "Confirmation" as referred to in the ISDA Master Agreement specified below.][1]

[This Confirmation supplements, forms a part of, and is subject to, the ISDA Master Agreement dated as of [date], as amended and supplemented from time to time (the "Agreement"), between you and us. All provisions contained in the Agreement govern this Confirmation except as expressly modified below.][2]

The terms of the Transaction to which this Confirmation relates are as follows:

General Terms:
Trade Date:	[ ], 199[ ]
Option Style:	[American] [European]
Option Type:	[Put] [Call]

---

[1] Include if applicable.

[2] Include if applicable. If the parties have not yet executed, but intend to execute, an ISDA Master Agreement include, in lieu of the above paragraph, the following: "This Confirmation evidences a complete binding agreement between you and us as to the terms of the Transaction to which this Confirmation relates. In addition, you and we agree to use all reasonable efforts promptly to negotiate, execute and deliver an ISDA Master Agreement (Multicurrency-Cross Border), with such modifications as you and we will in good faith agree. Upon the execution by you and us of such a Master Agreement (the "Agreement"), this Confirmation will supplement, form a part of, and be subject to the Agreement. All provisions contained or incorporated by reference in the Agreement upon its execution will govern this Confirmation except as expressly modified below. Prior to execution of the Agreement the provisions of the ISDA Master Agreement (Multicurrency-Cross Border) are deemed to be incorporated by reference in and form a part of this Confirmation. In the event of any inconsistency between those provisions and this Confirmation, this Confirmation will govern."

Seller:	[Party A] [Party B]
Buyer:	[Party A] [Party B]
Shares:	[Insert full title, class and/or par value of the Shares and any other identification number or reference for the Shares] of [insert full legal name of the issuer of the Shares] (the "Issuer").
Number of Options:	[ ]
Share Entitlement:	[ ] Share(s) per Option
Multiple Exercise:	[Applicable/Inapplicable]
[Minimum Number of Options:][3]	[ ]
[Maximum Number of Options:][3]	[ ]
[Options must be Exercised in Integral Multiples of:][3]	[ ]
Strike Price per Share:	[ ][4]
Premium:	[ ]
	[(Premium per Option: [ ])]
Premium Payment Date:	[ ], or, if that date is not a Currency Business Day, the first following day that is a Currency Business Day.
Seller Business Day:	Any day on which commercial banks are open for business (including dealings in foreign exchange and foreign currency deposits)[5] in [ ].[6]
Currency Business Day:	Any day on which commercial banks are open for business (including dealings in foreign exchange and foreign currency deposits) in the principal financial center for the relevant currency.
Exchange:	[ ][7]
Exchange Business Day:	A [day that is a Seller Business Day and is a] trading day on the Exchange other than a day on which trading on the Exchange is scheduled to close prior to its regular weekday closing time.
Clearance System:	[ ], or any successor to or transferee of such clearance system. If the Clearance System

---

[3] Include if an American style option providing for Multiple Exercise.

[4] The parties may insert an amount or a formula from which the Strike Price per Share will be determined and the adjustments, if any, that dividend payments would occasion.

[5] If Seller is not a commercial bank and is located in a city in which commercial bank holidays may differ from local securities exchange holidays, add "and which is a scheduled trading day on local securities exchanges".

[6] Specify city in which Seller is located for the purposer of receiving notices.

[7] Insert the name of the principal exchange on which the Shares are traded.

ceases to clear the Shares, the parties will negotiate in good faith to agree on another manner for delivery.

Clearance System Business Day: Any day on which the Clearance System is (or, but for the occurrence of a Settlement Disruption Event, would have been) open for the acceptance and execution of settlement instructions.

Calculation Agent:[8] [   ]. Whenever the Calculation Agent is required to act, it will do so in good faith, and its determinations and calculations will be binding in the absence of manifest error.

Procedure for Exercise:

Exercise Period: [The Expiration Date][9] [Any Exchange Business Day from, and including, [   ] to, and including, the Expiration Date][10] between 9:00 a.m. and [(a) [4:00 p.m.] (local time in   )[11] on any Exchange Business Day during the Exercise Period that is not the Expiration Date and (b)][12] the Expiration Time [on the Expiration Date].[12]

Expiration Date: [   ] or, if that date is not an Exchange Business Day, the first following day that is an Exchange Business Day.

Expiration Time: [   ] [a.m./p.m.] (local time in   )[13] on the Expiration Date.

Notice of Exercise and Written Confirmation: Except when automatic exercise applies, Buyer must give irrevocable oral notice to Seller (which will be given by telephone) of its exercise of any right granted pursuant to an Option. Buyer will execute and deliver a written confirmation confirming the substance of that notice, within one Seller Business Day of that notice. Failure to provide that written confirmation will not affect the validity of that telephonic notice. If the notice of exercise is given after the latest permitted time on an Exchange Business Day, then that notice will be deemed given on the next following

---

[8] If the Calculation Agent is a third party, the parties will want to consider any documentation necessary to confirm its undertaking.
[9] Include if European style option.
[10] Include if American style option.
[11] Specify city in which Seller is located for the purpose of receiving notices or, alternatively, specify city in which the Exchange is located.
[12] Include if American style option.
[13] Specify city in which Seller is located for the purpose of receiving notices or, alternatively, specify city in which the Exchange is located.

Exchange Business Day, if any, in the Exercise Period.[14]

Seller's Telephone Number and Telex and/or Facsimile Number and Contact Details for Purpose of Giving Notice:

[   ]

Exercise Date for an Option:

The Exchange Business Day during the Exercise Period on which that Option is or is deemed to be exercised.

Automatic Exercise:

[If not previously exercised][15] an Option will be deemed to be automatically exercised at the Expiration Time if at such time the Option is In-the-Money, as determined by the Calculation Agent, unless:

(a) the Buyer notifies the Seller (by telephone or in writing) prior to the Expiration Time that it does not wish automatic exercise to occur; or

(b) the Reference Price necessary to determine that the Option is In-the-Money cannot be determined at the Expiration Time (in which case automatic exercise will not apply).

In-the-Money:

An Option will be In-the-Money if the Reference Price is equal to or [greater than 101][16] [less than 99][17] percent of the Strike Price per Share.

Reference Price:

The official closing price per Share on the Exchange on the Expiration Date if the Expiration

---

[14] If an American style option providing for multiple Exercise Dates, add "Buyer must specify in that notice the number of Options being exercised on that Exercise Date" and, as a new paragraph, "Buyer may exercise all or less than all the unexercised Options on one or more Exchange Business Days during the Exercise Period, but (except as set forth below) on any Exchange Business Day may not exercise less than the Minimum Number of Options or more than the Maximum Number of Options and that number of Options must be an integral multiple of the amount specified above. Except as set forth below, any attempt to exercise more than the Maximum Number of Options on any Exchange Business Day will be deemed to be an exercise of the Maximum Number of Options. Buyer may exercise (a) more than the Maximum Number of Options if the Exercise Date is the Expiration Date and (b) less than the Minimum Number of Options if on the Exercise Date the Options it exercises are all the unexercised Options."

[15] Include if American style option.

[16] Include if Call Option. The parties may adjust the percentage as they deem appropriate.

[17] Include if Put Option. The parties may adjust the percentage as they deem appropriate.

Time is at or after the close of trading on the Exchange and, otherwise, the [highest bid][18] [lowest offer][19] price per Share on the Exchange at the Expiration Time as determined by the Calculation Agent based on independent commercially available information.[20]

Settlement Terms:

Physical Settlement: Applicable; on the Settlement Date, Buyer will [pay to Seller the Settlement Price][21] [deliver to Seller the Number of Shares to be Delivered][22] and Seller will [deliver to Buyer the Number of Shares to be Delivered][23] [pay to Buyer the Settlement Price].[24] Such payment and such delivery will be made through the Clearance System at the accounts specified below [on a delivery versus payment basis].[25]

Settlement Date: The first day on which settlement of a sale of Shares executed on the Exercise Date customarily would take place through the Clearance System, unless a Settlement Disruption Event prevents settlement on that day. If a Settlement Disruption Event does prevent settlement on that day, then the Settlement Date will be the first succeeding day on which settlement can take place through the Clearance System unless a Settlement Disruption Event prevents settlement on each of the 10 Clearance System Business Days immediately following the original date that, but for the Settlement Disruption Event, would have been the Settlement Date. In that case, (a) if the Shares can be delivered in any

---

[18] Include if Call Option and bid prices are available.
[19] Include if Put Option and offer prices are available.
[20] The parties may specify that the Reference Price will be determined by reference to another stock exchange or quotation system and as of a different time on the Expiration Date.
[21] Include if Call Option.
[22] Include if Put Option.
[23] Include if Call Option.
[24] Include if Put Option.
[25] If settlement cannot or will not be on the basis of delivery vs. payment, specify the relevant details.
Where the Shares do not settle (or the parties otherwise do not wish to settle the Shares) through a clearance system, the settlement procedures will need to be specified and the definitions of Physical Settlement, Settlement Date, Settlement Disruption Event and Dividends and Expenses may have to be modified to take into account such settlement procedures.

other commercially reasonable manner, then the Settlement Date will be the first day on which settlement of a sale of Shares executed on that 10th Clearance System Business Day customarily would take place using such other commercially reasonable manner of delivery (which other manner of delivery will be deemed the Clearance System for purposes of delivery of the relevant Shares), and (b) if the Shares cannot be delivered in any other commercially reasonable manner, then the Settlement Date will be postponed until delivery can be effected through the Clearance System or any other commercially reasonable manner.[26]

Settlement Price: The Strike Price per Share multiplied by the Number of Shares to be Delivered.

Number of Shares to be Delivered: The number of Shares equal to the number of Options exercised on the relevant Exercise Date multiplied by the Share Entitlement, rounded down to the nearest whole Share.[27]

Settlement Disruption Event: An event beyond the control of the parties as a result of which the Clearance System cannot clear the transfer of the Shares.

Adjustment Events:
[Adjustments.[28] Following each adjustment to the strike price or the share entitlement of options on the Shares traded on [insert name of options exchange] (the "Options Exchange"), the Calculation Agent will adjust correspondingly the Strike Price per Share, the Number of Options and/or the Share Entitlement, which adjustment will be effective as of the date determined by the Calculation Agent to be the effective date of the corresponding adjustment made by the Options Exchange. If such options are no longer traded on the Options Exchange, the Calculation Agent will make such adjustment, if any, to the Strike

---

[26] The parties may wish to consider specifying, in advance, the allocation between them of any additional costs associated with delivering the Shares outside of the Clearance System as a result of a Settlement Disruption Event or otherwise.

[27] Where the Shares are traded only in specified numbers (for example, in Japan, 1000 share lots) the parties may wish to specify that the Number of Shares to be Delivered will be rounded to the nearest specified number.

[28] Include if relying on options exchange adjustments.

Price per Share, the Number of Options and/or the Share Entitlement as the Calculation Agent determines appropriate to account for the diluting or concentrative effect of any event that, in the determination of the Calculation Agent, would have given rise to an adjustment by the Options Exchange.]

[Adjustments:[29] Following each Potential Adjustment Event, the Calculation Agent will determine whether such Potential Adjustment Event has a diluting or concentrative effect on the market value of the Shares and, if so, will (a) calculate the corresponding adjustment, if any, to be made to the Strike Price per Share, the Number of Options and/or the Share Entitlement as the Calculation Agent determines appropriate to account for that diluting or concentrative effect and (b) determine the effective date of that adjustment. The Calculation Agent may (but need not) determine the appropriate adjustment by reference to the adjustment in respect of such Potential Adjustment Event made by an options exchange to options on the Shares traded on that options exchange.

Potential Adjustment Event:[30] The declaration by the Issuer of the terms of any of the following:

(a) a subdivision, consolidation or reclassification of Shares, or a free distribution of any Shares to existing holders by way of bonus, capitalization or similar issue;

(b) a distribution to existing holders of the Shares of (i) Shares or (ii) other share capital or securities granting the right to payment of dividends and/or the proceeds of liquidation of the Issuer equally or proportionately with such payments to holders of Shares or (iii) securities, rights or warrants granting the right to a distribution of Shares or to purchase, subscribe or receive Shares, in any case for payment (cash or other) at less than the prevailing market price per Share as determined by the Calculation Agent;

(c) a dividend or other distribution (whether in

---

[29] Include if not relying on options exchange adjustments.
[30] The parties are advised to review the relevant corporate law and practice applicable to the Issuer to determine whether the Potential Adjustment Events are appropriate for the Shares of the Issuer.

cash or Shares); or

(d) any other similar event that may have a diluting or concentrative effect on the market value of the Shares.

[Extraordinary Events:[31]

Consequences of Merger Events:

Following each Merger Event:

(a) if the consideration for the Shares in the Merger Event consists (or, at the option of the holder of the Shares, may consist) solely of shares, upon exercise of an Option the deliveror will deliver such number of such shares to which a holder of the number of Shares equal to the Share Entitlement would have been entitled upon consummation of the Merger Event (and such new number will be deemed the "Share Entitlement" and such shares and their issuer will be deemed the "Shares" and the "Issuer", respectively) and, if necessary, the Calculation Agent will adjust the Strike Price per Share proportionately;

(b) if the consideration for the Shares in the Merger Event consists solely of cash or any other securities or assets other than shares, the Options will be cancelled and Seller will pay to Buyer an amount determined by the Calculation Agent as set forth below; and

(c) if the consideration for the Shares in the Merger Event consists of both (i) shares and (ii) cash or any other securities or assets other than shares, then the consideration will be deemed to be shares. If the sum of the cash and the fair market value (as determined by the Calculation Agent) of any securities or assets other than shares to which a holder of a Share would have been entitled is less than the Strike Price per Share, the adjustments described in paragraph (a) above will be made after reduction of the Strike Price per Share by an amount equal to that sum. If that sum equals or exceeds the Strike Price per Share, [each Option upon exercise will entitle the deliveree to receive (without payment of any Settlement Price) (A) cash equal to the

---

[31] Two alternative approaches to addressing Extraordinary Events are set forth in this form of Confirmation. The parties may elect either the approach that starts on this page or the other approach, which starts on page 313.

product of (1) the excess, if any, of that sum over the Strike Price per Share (before giving effect to the adjustment to the Strike Price per Share described in paragraph (a) above) and (2) the number of Shares in the Share Entitlement (before giving effect to the modification to those terms contemplated in paragraph (a) above) and (B) the number of Shares equal to the Share Entitlement (after giving effect to the modification to those terms contemplated in paragraph (a) above)][32] [the Strike Price per Share will be reduced to zero].[33]

Merger Event: As of the date upon which holders become bound to transfer the Shares held by them, any (a) reclassification or change of the Shares (other than a change in par value, if any, as a result of a subdivision or combination), (b) consolidation, amalgamation or merger of the Issuer with or into another corporation (other than a consolidation, amalgamation or merger in which the Issuer is the continuing corporation and which does not result in any such reclassification or change of Shares) or (c) other takeover offer for the Shares that results in a transfer of all the Shares (other than the Shares owned or controlled by the offeror) on or before the Expiration Date.

Nationalization or Liquidation: If (a) all the Shares or all the assets or substantially all the assets of the Issuer are nationalized, expropriated or are otherwise required to be transferred to any governmental agency, authority or entity or (b) by reason of the liquidation, winding-up or dissolution of the Issuer (i) all the Shares are required to be transferred to any trustee, liquidator or other similar official or (ii) holders of the Shares become legally prohibited from transferring them, then, in the case of (a) or (b), the Options will be cancelled, and Seller will pay to Buyer an amount determined by the Calculation Agent as set forth below.

Payment upon Certain Extraordinary Events: Payment by Seller to Buyer of the amount referred to in Consequences of Merger Events and Nationalization or Liquidation as provided above will be made not later than three Currency

---

[32] Include if Call Option.
[33] Include if Put Option.

Business Days following the determination by the Calculation Agent of such amount in the currency of the Strike Price per Share unless the parties specify otherwise.

Such amount will be determined by the Calculation Agent and based on quotations sought by it from [four leading market dealers] [Reference Marketmakers]. Each quotation will represent the quoting dealer's expert opinion as to the fair value to the Buyer of an option with terms that would preserve for the Buyer the economic equivalent of any payment or delivery (assuming satisfaction of each applicable condition precedent) by the parties in respect of the Transaction that would have been required after that date but for the occurrence of the Option Value Event. Each quotation will be calculated on the basis of the following information provided by the Calculation Agent (and such other factors as the quoting dealer deems appropriate):

(a) a volatility equal to the average of the Option Period Volatility of the Shares for each Exchange Business Day during the two-year historical period ending on the Announcement Date of the Option Value Event;

(b) dividends based on, and payable on the same dates as, amounts determined by the Calculation Agent to have been paid in respect of gross ordinary cash dividends on the Shares in the calendar year ending on the Announcement Date; and

(c) a value ascribed to the Shares equal to the consideration, if any, paid in respect of the Shares to holders of the Shares at the time of the Option Value Event.

If more than three quotations are provided, the amount will be the arithmetic mean of the quotations, without regard to the quotations having the highest and the lowest values. If exactly three quotations are provided, the amount will be the quotation remaining after disregarding the highest and the lowest quotations. For this purpose, if more than one quotation has the same highest or lowest value, then one of such quotations will be disregarded.

If two quotations are provided, the amount will be the arithmetic mean of the quotations. If one quotation is provided, the amount will equal the quotation. If no quotation is provided, the amount will be determined by the Calculation Agent in its sole discretion.

For purposes of determining the amount, "Option Value Event" means the Merger Event or the Nationalization or Liquidation, as the same may be; "Option Period Volatility" means, in respect of any Exchange Business Day, the volatility (calculated by referring to the closing price of the Shares on the Exchange) for a period equal to the number of days between the Announcement Date and the Expiration Date; and "Announcement Date" means, in respect of a Merger Event or a Nationalization, the date of the first public announcement of a firm intention, in the case of a Merger Event, to merge or to make an offer and, in the case of a Nationalization, to nationalize that (whether or not amended or on the terms originally announced) leads to the Merger Event or the Nationalization, as the case may be, and, in respect of a Liquidation, the date of the first public announcement of the institution of a proceeding or presentation of a petition or passing of a resolution (or other analogous procedure in any jurisdiction) that leads to the Liquidation, in each case as determined by the Calculation Agent.]

[Extraordinary Events: Consequences of Merger Events:

Following each Merger Event:

(a) if the consideration for the Shares in the Merger Event consists mandatorily of (i) shares, (ii) cash, (iii) any other securities or assets other than shares or (iv) any combination of (i), (ii) and (iii), then from the date of the Merger Event upon exercise of an Option in accordance with the terms of the Transaction the deliveror will deliver such consideration to which a holder of the number of Shares equal to the Share Entitlement would be entitled upon consummation of the Merger Event (the "Merger Consideration") (and any shares included in the Merger Consideration and their issuer will be deemed the "Shares"

313

and the "Issuer", respectively, and the number of such shares will be deemed the "Share Entitlement") and, if necessary, the Calculation Agent will adjust the Strike Price per Share accordingly; and

(b) if a holder of Shares can elect the Merger Consideration, then upon exercise of an Option in accordance with the terms of the Transaction, the deliveror will deliver such Merger Consideration (as elected by the deliveree) to which a holder of the number of Shares equal to the Share Entitlement (before giving effect to the modification to those terms contemplated in paragraph (a) above) would be entitled upon consummation of the Merger Event and, if necessary, the Calculation Agent will adjust the Strike Price per Share accordingly. Any such election by the deliveree must be made at or prior to the last time a holder of Shares may make its election of consideration, and the deliveree's election must be made in accordance with the procedures for giving notice of exercise. If the deliveree does not make such election, the other party will, in its sole discretion, make such election.

Merger Event: As of the date upon which holders become bound to transfer the Shares held by them, any (a) reclassification or change of the Shares (other than a change in par value, if any, as a result of subdivision or combination), (b) consolidation, amalgamation or merger of the Issuer with or into another corporation (other than a consolidation, amalgamation or merger in which the Issuer is the continuing corporation and which does not result in any such reclassification or change of Shares) or (c) other takeover offer (including a Nationalization with compensation) for the Shares that results in a transfer of all the Shares (other than the Shares owned or controlled by the offeror) on or before the Expiration Date.

Nationalization Without Compensation or Liquidation: If (a) all the Shares or all the assets or substantially all the assets of the Issuer are nationalized, expropriated or are otherwise required to be transferred to any governmental agency, authority or entity or (b) by reason of the liqui-

314

dation, winding-up or dissolution of the Issuer (i) all the Shares are required to be transferred to any trustee, liquidator or other similar official or (ii) holders of the Shares become legally prohibited from transferring them, then, in the case of (a) or (b), Seller or Buyer will, upon becoming aware of such event, notify the other party of such event and Seller will promptly quote a price, if any, at which it would be prepared to offer to repurchase the Option from Buyer.]

Miscellaneous:
Dividends and Expenses:

Following exercise of an Option, all dividends on the relevant Shares to be delivered will be payable to and all expenses of transfer of the Shares on delivery (such as any stamp duty or stock exchange tax) will be payable by, the party that would receive such dividend or pay such expenses, as the case may be, according to market practice for a sale of the Shares executed on the Exercise Date to be settled through the Clearance System.

Representation and Agreement:

The party required to deliver the Shares represents and agrees that it will convey good title to the Shares it is required to deliver, free and clear of any lien, charge, claim or encumbrance (other than a lien routinely imposed on all securities in the Clearance System).

[Failure to Deliver:

Failure by a party to deliver, when due, Shares under the Transaction will not constitute an Event of Default if the party is unable to deliver the requisite number of Shares due to illiquidity in the market for the Shares and if that party (a) notifies the other party within one Clearance System Business Day of the Exercise Date to that effect and (b) delivers on the Settlement Date such number of Shares, if any, as it can deliver on that date. In such case,

(i) the party's failure to deliver will constitute an Additional Termination Event with that party the sole Affected Party and the Transaction (after consideration of any partial delivery) the sole Affected Transaction,[34] and

---

[34] If American style option providing for multiple Exercise Dates, add "or if less than all Options have been exercised (or deemed exercised) on the relevant Exercise Date, the Termination Event will occur in respect of a Transaction (after consideration of any partial delivery) consisting of the exercised Options only".

315

(ii) irrespective of the payment measure elected by the parties, Loss will be deemed to apply for the purpose of determining if any payment will be made in respect of the Transaction.][35]

[Transfer:[36]

Neither the Transaction or any Option nor any interest or obligation in or under the Transaction or any Option may be transferred (whether by way of security or otherwise) by either party without the prior written consent of the other party, except that a party may make such a transfer of the Transaction pursuant to a consolidation or amalgamation with, or merger with or into, or transfer of all or substantially all its assets to, another entity. Any purported transfer that is not in compliance with this paragraph will be void.]

[Default Interest:][37]

[If, prior to the occurrence or effective designation of an Early Termination Date in respect of this Transaction, a party defaults in the performance of any obligation required to be settled by delivery, it will indemnify the other party on demand for any costs, losses or expenses (including the costs of borrowing the Shares, if aplicable) resulting from such default. A certificate signed by the deliveree setting out such costs, losses or expenses in reasonable detail will be conclusive evidence that they have been incurred.]

Account Details:
  Payments to Seller:
  Account for
  payments:
  Payments to Buyer:
  Account for
  payments:
  Delivery of Shares
  to deliveree:
  Account for
  delivery:
This Confirmation will be governed by and construed in accordance

---

[35] Include if subject to an ISDA Master Agreement.

[36] Delete if this Confirmation is part of an ISDA Master Agreement.

[37] For a brief discussion regarding default interest for transactions that settle by physical delivery under a 1992 ISDA Master Agreement, *see* Section VI of the *User's Guide to the 1992 ISDA Master Agreements*, 1993 Edition.

with the laws of [   ] [(without reference to choice of law doctrine)].[38]

Closing for Letter[39]

Please confirm that the foregoing correctly sets forth the terms of our agreement by executing the copy of this Confirmation enclosed for that purpose and returning it to us or by sending to us a letter or telex substantially similar to this letter, which letter or telex sets forth the material terms of the Transaction to which this Confirmation relates and indicates your agreement to those terms.

> Yours sincerely,
> [PARTY A]
> By: _____
>
> Name:
> Title:

Confirmed as of the date first above written:
[PARTY B]
By: _____

Name:
Title:

Closing for Telex[40]

Please confirm that the foregoing correctly sets forth the terms of our agreement by sending to us a letter or telex substantially similar to this telex, which letter or telex sets forth the material terms of the Transaction to which this Confirmation relates and indicates agreement to those terms, or by sending to us a return telex substantially to the following effect:

"Re:

We acknowledge receipt of your telex dated [   ] with respect to the above-referenced Transaction between [Party A] and [Party B] with a Trade Date of [   ] and an Expiration Date of [   ] and confirm that such telex correctly sets forth the terms of our agreement relating to the Transaction described therein. Very truly yours, [Party B], by [specify name and title of authorized officer]."

> Yours sincerely,
> [PARTY A]
> By: _____
>
> Name:
> Title:

---

[38] Consider whether any additions or deletions relating to any applicable jurisdiction or regulatory, tax, accounting, securities exchange or other requirements should be made in this Confirmation if these are not addressed in a related master agreement. For an indication of further issues that the parties may wish to consider when documenting transactions that settle by physical delivery under a 1992 ISDA Master Agreement, see Section VI of the *User's Guide to the 1992 ISDA Master Agreements*, 1993 Edition.

[39] Include if applicable.

[40] Include if applicable.

SECTION-BY-SECTION
DERIVATIVES SUPERVISION ACT OF 1994
TITLE I – FEDERAL DERIVATIVES COMMISSION

SEC. 101. DECLARATION OF PURPOSE.

This title establishes the Federal Derivatives Commission to establish principles and standards for the supervision by Federal financial institutions regulators of financial institutions engaged in derivatives activities.

SEC. 102. DEFINITIONS.

(1) "Federal financial institutions regulators" means the OCC, Federal Reserve, FDIC, OTS, SEC and CFTC.

(2) "Commission" means the Federal Derivatives Commission.

(3) "Federal banking agencies" has the same meaning as section 3 of the FDI Act.

(4) "Financial institution" means any institution subject to section 402(9) of FDICIA, any government sponsored enterprise, or any other institution (including any type of end-user of derivatives) as determined by the Commission.

(5) "Government sponsored enterprise" has the same meaning as in section 1404(e) of FIRREA.

(6) "Qualified financial contract" has the same meaning as in section 11(e)(8)(D) of the FDI Act, except that the commission may determine any similar agreement to be a qualified financial contract for purpose of this title.

(7) "Derivatives activities" means activities involving qualified financial contracts, including those activities determined by the Commission to be qualified financial contracts for the purposes of this title.

SEC. 103. FEDERAL DERIVATIVES COMMISSION.

The Commission shall consist of: the Chairman of the Board of Governors of the Federal Reserve System; the Comptroller of the Currency; the Chairman of the Board of Directors of the Federal Deposit Insurance Corporation; the Director of the Office of Thrift Supervision; the Chairman of the Securities Exchange Commission; the Chairman of the Commodity Futures Trading Commission; and the Secretary of the Treasury. The chairman of the Commission shall be the Chairman of the Board of Governors of the Federal Reserve System.

SEC. 104. COSTS AND EXPENSES OF COMMISSION.

One-sixth of the costs and expenses of the Commission shall be paid by each of the Federal financial institutions regulatory agencies.

SEC. 105. FUNCTIONS OF COMMISSION.

(a) ESTABLISHMENT OF PRINCIPLES AND STANDARDS.—

(1) The Commission shall establish principles and standards related to capital, accounting, disclosure, suitability, or other appropriate regulatory actions for the supervision of financial institutions engaged in derivatives activities.

(2) Each regulatory agency shall issue substantially similar regulations governing derivatives activities to implement the Commission's standards, unless it finds that implementation of such regulations is not necessary or appropriate.

(3) Any financial institution not subject to supervision by a Federal banking agency or the CFTC shall be supervised by the SEC to the extent of their derivatives activities, except as otherwise provided by the Commission.

(b) RECOMMENDATIONS REGARDING SUPERVISORY MATTERS.—

(1) In establishing principles and standards under subsection (a), the Commission shall consider and make recommendations for comparable regulatory action by the Federal financial institutions regulators in other matters related to financial institutions engaged in derivatives activities, such as, but not limited to, the need to establish principles and standards for:

(A) strong capital requirements (with particular attention to a leverage ratio where appropriate) to guard generally against risks at financial institutions, including added risks that may be posed by derivatives activities;

(B) discouraging active trading in derivatives markets by financial institutions, particularly those with access to federally insured deposits, unless management can demonstrate that the institution has adequate capital and technical capabilities;

(C) joint regulatory examinations by the federal banking agencies of insured depository institutions that are derivatives dealers and any affiliates;

(D) board of director responsibility with respect to the oversight of derivatives activities, including specific written policies regarding internal controls and risk management approved by the board of directors of institutions engaged in derivatives activities;

(E) guidelines for the prudent use of collaterial by counterparties to derivatives transactions;

(F) the appropriate parameters, models and simulations for the purposes of evaluating an institution's credit and market risk posed by derivatives activities;

(G) guidelines as to the appropriate credit risk reserves in connection with derivatives activities;

(H) increased standardization of documentation and use of such documentation by all market participants;

319

(I) minimum prudential practices for municipalities and pension funds that may use derivatives;

(J) enhanced disclosures to mutual fund customers of the risks that may be posed to mutual funds that are end-users of derivative products;

(K) guidelines related to legal risk, including, but not limited to, foreign legal risk; and

(L) regulations to protect against systemic risk.

(2) When an applicable regulatory agencies finds a recommendation of the Commission unacceptable, that agency must provide a written statement to the Commission explaining its objections, and such statement shall be published in the Federal Register.

(c) DEVELOPMENT OF UNIFORM REPORTING SYSTEM.—The Commission shall develop reporting systems for financial institutions engaged in derivatives activities.

(d) TRAINING FOR EXAMINERS AND ASSISTANT EXAMINERS.—The Commission shall sponsor training programs concerning derivatives activities for Federal examiners. The programs shall also be open to state examiners, employees of the Federal Housing Finance Board, and employees of the Department of Housing and Urban Development.

(e) EFFECT ON FEDERAL REGULATORY AGENCY RESEARCH AND DEVELOPMENT OF NEW FINANCIAL INSTITUTIONS SUPERVISORY METHODS.—Nothing in this title shall be construed to limit or discourage Federal financial institutions regulatory agency research and development of new financial institutions supervisory methods related to derivatives activities.

(f) ANNUAL REPORT.—The Commission shall prepare an annual report.

SEC. 106. STATE LIAISON.

The Commission shall establish a liaison committee composed of three representatives of state agencies which supervise financial institutions, which shall meet at least twice a year with the Commission.

SEC. 107. ADMINISTRATION.

The Chairman of the Commission is authorized to carry out and to delegate the authority to carry out the internal administration of the Commission. The Commission may also utilize personnel and facilities of the regulatory agencies, may appoint employees, and may obtain the services of experts and consultants.

SEC. 108. RISK MANAGEMENT TRAINING.

The Commission shall develop training seminars in risk management techniques related to derivatives activities for employees of both regulatory agencies and financial institutions.

SEC. 109. INTERNATIONAL NEGOTIATIONS.

The Chairman of the Board of Governors of the Federal Reserve, in consultation with the members of the Commission, shall encourage governments, central banks, and regulatory authorities of other industrialized countries to work toward maintaining, and, where appropriate, adopting comparable supervisory standards and regulations, particularly capital standards, for financial institutions engaged in derivatives activities.

SEC. 110. CREDIT UNIONS.

Insured credit unions shall be supervised for purposes of derivatives activities by the National Credit Union Administration under standards no less stringent than standards under which Federal depository institutions are supervised by the Federal banking agencies.

TITLE II – SUPERVISORY IMPROVEMENTS

SEC. 201. UNSAFE OR UNSOUND BANKING PRACTICES.

Failure of an institution-affiliated party engaged in derivatives activities to have adequate technical expertise may be deemed to constitute an unsafe or unsound banking practice within the meaning of section 8 of the FDI Act.

SEC. 202. INTERNAL CONTROLS.

Standards for safety and soundness prescribed by the Federal banking agencies, in accordance with section 132 of FDICIA, should include internal controls for derivatives activities.

SEC. 203. FOREIGN BANK SUPERVISION.

The International Banking Act of 1978 is amended to require that when evaluating the adequacy of supervision of a foreign bank engaged in derivatives activities by its home country, the Federal Reserve determine whether such country has comprehensive supervision and regulation for derivatives activities. In making any determination under this paragraph, the Federal Reserve shall consider whether the home country maintains comprehensive supervision and regulation of derivatives activities, including capital and disclosure standards, not less stringent than US standards.

TITLE III – FINANCIAL INSTITUTION INSOLVENCY REFORMS

SEC. 301. CONFORMING DEFINITIONS.

This section expands the FDI Act with conforming amendments to the

Bankruptcy Code to include derivatives products currently being used in the market and to accommodate future growth in the derivatives products industry.

SEC. 302. FAILED AND FAILING INSTITUTIONS.

This section alleviates the uncertainty about the scope of the automatic stay for the FDIC when it is a counterparty, as this section clarifies that insolvency and bankruptcy proceedings should not delay or limit the FDIC's rights to repudiate, terminate and net qualified financial contracts involving an insolvent or bankrupt party or counterparty.

This section also requires that the FDIC, in consultation with the other regulatory agencies, prescribe regulations requiring expanded record-keeping for qualified financial contracts by insured depository institutions that are undercapitalized.

SEC. 303. QUALIFIED FINANCIAL CONTRACT TRANSFERS.

This section amends the FDI Act to provide that if the FDIC as receiver of a depository institution notifies a party to a qualified financial contract by the close of business on the business day following its appointment as receiver that all qualified financial contracts between the depository institution and that person or its affiliates were transferred to another depository institution in accordance with 11(e)(9)(A), the provisions of 11(e)(8)(A) allowing the party to terminate or liquidate the contract will not apply. This section also allows the FDIC to extend the notice period up to 5 days if the FDIC determines that the extension may maximize the return on the contract.

This section also amends the FDI Act to explicitly provide that the FDIC may transfer qualified financial contracts to a bridge bank or to analogous types of conservatorships.

SEC. 304. CLARIFYING AMENDMENTS.

This section amends the Bankruptcy Code to require a master agreement governing multiple transactions be treated as one swap agreement in bankruptcy. This swap agreement shall be exempt from the stay, regardless of product type or contract type.

SEC. 305. TECHNICAL AMENDMENTS.

This section makes technical amendments to the FDI Act.

TITLE IV – MISCELLANEOUS

SEC. 401. SAVINGS PROVISION.

The provisions of this Act shall be in addition to and not in derogation of any existing authority of a Federal financial institution regulatory agency to supervise or regulate derivatives activities provided under any other applicable law.

103d CONGRESS   **H.R. 3748**
2nd Session

To provide an enhanced framework for Federal financial institution regulation of derivatives activities.

IN THE HOUSE OF REPRESENTATIVES
January 26, 1994

Mr Leach introduced the following bill; which was referred to the Committee _____

A BILL

To provide an enhanced framework for Federal financial institution regulation of derivatives activities.

Be it enacted by the Senate and House of Representatives of the United States of America in Congress assembled,

SEC. 1. SHORT TITLE.

This Act shall be cited as the "Derivatives Supervision Act of 1994."

TITLE I – FEDERAL DERIVATIVES COMMISSION

SEC. 101. DECLARATION OF PURPOSE.

It is the purpose of this title to establish a Federal Derivatives Commission which shall establish principles and standards for the supervision by federal financial institution regulators of financial institutions engaged in derivatives activities and make recommendations to promote uniformity in the supervision of these financial institutions. The Commission's actions shall be designed to promote consistency in regulatory practices and to insure progressive and vigilant supervision.

SEC. 102. DEFINITIONS.

As used in this title—

(1) the term "Federal financial institutions regulatory agencies" means the Office of the Comptroller of the Currency, the Board of Governors of the Federal Reserve System, the Federal Deposit Insurance Corporation, the Office of Thrift Supervision, the Securities and Exchange Commission, and the Commodity Futures Trading Commission;

(2) the term "Commission" means the Federal Derivatives Commission;

(3) the term "Federal banking agency" has the same meaning as in section 3 of the Federal Deposit Insurance Act (12 USC 1813);

(4) the term "financial institution" means any institution described in section 402(9) of the Federal Deposit Insurance Corporation Improvement Act of 1991, any government sponsored enterprise, or any other institution (including any type of end-user) as determined by the Commission;

(5) the term "government sponsored enterprise" has the same meaning as in section 1404(e) of the Financial Institutions Reform, Recovery, and Enforcement Act of 1989;

(6) the term "qualified financial contract" has the same meaning as in section 11(e)(8)(D) of the Federal Deposit Insurance Act (12 USC 1821(e)(8)(D)), except that the Commission may determine any similar agreement to be a qualified financial contract for purposes of this title; and

(7) the term "derivatives activities" means activities by a financial institution involving qualified financial contracts or any similar agreements that the Commission determines are qualified financial contracts for purposes of this title.

SEC. 103. FEDERAL DERIVATIVES COMMISSION.

(a) ESTABLISHMENT; COMPOSITION.—There is established the Federal Derivatives Commission which shall consist of—

(1) the Chairman of the Board of Governors of the Federal Reserve system,

(2) the Comptroller of the Currency,

(3) the Chairperson of the Board of Directors of the Federal Deposit Insurance Corporation,

(4) the Director of the Office of Thrift Supervision,

(5) the Chairman of the Securities and Exchange Commission,

(6) the Chairman of the Commodity Futures Trading Commission, and

(7) the Secretary of Treasury.

(b) CHAIRMANSHIP.—The Chairman of the Commission shall be the Chairman of the Board of Governors of the Federal Reserve System.

(c) DESIGNATION OF OFFICERS AND EMPLOYEES.—The members of the Commission may, from time to time, designate other officers or employees of their respective agencies to carry out their duties on the Commission.

(d) COMPENSATION AND EXPENSES.—Each member of the Commission shall serve without additional compensation but shall be entitled to reasonable expenses incurred in carrying out his official duties as such a member.

SEC. 104. COSTS AND EXPENSES OF COMMISSION.

One-sixth of the costs and expenses of the Commission, including the salaries of its employees, shall be paid by each of the Federal financial institutions regulatory agencies. Annual assessments for such share shall be levied by the Commission based upon its projected budget for the year, and additional assessments may be made during the year if necessary.

SEC. 105. FUNCTIONS OF COMMISSION.

(a) ESTABLISHMENT OF PRINCIPLES AND STANDARDS.—

(1) The Commission shall establish principles and standards related to capital, accounting, disclosure, suitability, or other appropriate regulatory actions for the supervision of financial institutions engaged in derivatives activities by the Federal financial institutions regulatory agencies.

(2) Each Federal financial institutions regulatory agency shall issue substantially similar regulations governing derivatives activities for the purposes of implementing paragraph (1), unless it finds that implementation of substantially similar regulations is not necessary or appropriate in the public interest.

(3) Any financial institution not subject to supervision by a Federal banking agency or the Commodity Futures Trading Commission shall be supervised by the Securities and Exchange Commission to the extent of their derivatives activities, except as otherwise provided by the Commission.

(b) RECOMMENDATIONS REGARDING SUPERVISORY ACTIONS.—

(1) In establishing principles and standards under subsection (a), the Commission shall consider and may make recommendations for comparable regulatory action by the Federal financial institution regulatory agencies in other matters related to financial institutions engaged in derivatives activities, such as, but not limited to, the need to establish principles and standards for:

(A) strong capital requirements (with particular attention to a leverage ratio where appropriate) to guard generally against risks at financial institutions, including added risks that may be posed by derivatives activities.

(B) discouraging active trading in derivatives markets by financial institutions, particularly those with access to federally insured deposits, unless management can demonstrate that the institution has both adequate capital and technical capabilities;

(C) joint regulatory examinations by the federal banking agencies of insured depository institutions that are derivatives dealers and any affiliates;

(D) board of director responsibility with respect to the oversight of derivatives activities, including specific written policies approved by the board of directors to be in place for dealers and end-users of derivatives setting prudential standards for management of the risks

325

involved in derivatives activities and establishing a framework for internal controls;

(E) guidelines for the prudent use of collateral by counterparties to derivatives transactions;

(F) the appropriate parameters, models and simulations for purposes of evaluating a financial institution's credit and market risk posed by derivatives activities;

(G) guidelines as to appropriate credit risk reserves in connection with derivatives activities;

(H) increased standardization of documentation and the use of standard documents by all market participants;

(I) minimum prudential practices for municipalities and pension funds that may use derivatives;

(J) enhanced disclosures to mutual fund customers of the risks that may be posed to mutual funds that are end-users of derivative products;

(K) guidelines related to legal risk, including, but not limited to, foreign legal risk. Such guidelines may address the steps a financial institution should take to obtain adequate assurances of legal enforceability of derivatives contracts, including the assurances of legal enforceability of netting provisions that should be obtained before an institution relies on such netting provisions;

(L) regulations to protect against systemic risk.

(2) When a recommendation of the Commission is found unacceptable by one or more of the applicable Federal financial institutions regulatory agencies, the agency or agencies shall submit to the Commission, within a time period specified by the Commission, a written statement of the reasons the recommendation is unacceptable and such statement shall be published in the Federal Register.

(c) **DEVELOPMENT OF UNIFORM REPORTING SYSTEM.**—The Commission shall develop uniform reporting systems for financial institutions engaged in derivatives activities. The authority to develop uniform reporting systems shall not restrict or amend the requirements of section 781(i) of title 15 of the United States Code.

(d) **TRAINING FOR EXAMINERS AND ASSISTANT EXAMINERS.**— The Commission shall sponsor training programs concerning derivatives activities for examiners and assistant examiners employed by the Federal financial institutions regulatory agencies. Such training programs shall be open to enrollment by employees of State financial institutions supervisory agencies and employees of the Federal Housing Finance Board and the Department of Housing and Urban Development's Office of Federal Housing Enterprise Oversight under conditions specified by the Commission.

(e) **EFFECT ON FEDERAL REGULATORY AGENCY RESEARCH AND DEVELOPMENT OF NEW FINANCIAL INSTITUTIONS SUPERVISORY METHODS.**—Nothing in this title shall be construed to limit or discourage

Federal financial institution regulatory agency research and development of new financial institutions supervisory methods and tools related to derivatives activities, nor to preclude the field testing of any innovation devised by any Federal financial institution regulatory agency.

(f) **ANNUAL REPORT.**—Not later than April 1 of each year, the Commission shall prepare a report covering its activities during the preceding calendar year.

SEC. 106. STATE LIAISON.

To encourage the application of uniform examination principles and standards by State and Federal supervisory agencies, the Commission shall establish a liaison committee composed of five representatives of State agencies which supervise financial institutions which shall meet at least twice a year with the Commission. Members of the liaison committee shall receive a reasonable allowance for necessary expenses incurred in attending meetings.

SEC. 107. ADMINISTRATION.

(a) **AUTHORITY OF CHAIRMAN OF COMMISSION.**—The Chairman of the Commission is authorized to carry out and to delegate the authority to carry out the internal administration of the Commission, including the appointment and supervision of employees and the distribution of business among members, employees, and administrative units.

(b) **USE OF PERSONNEL, SERVICES, AND FACILITIES OF FEDERAL FINANCIAL INSTITUTIONS REGULATORY AGENCIES.**—In addition to any other authority conferred upon it by this title, in carrying out its functions under this title, the Commission may utilize, with their consent and to the extent practical, the personnnel, services, and facilities of the Federal financial institutions regulatory agencies, with or without reimbursement therefor.

(c) **COMPENSATION, AUTHORITY, AND DUTIES OF OFFICERS AND EMPLOYEES; EXPERTS AND CONSULTANTS.**—In addition, the Commission may—

(1) subject to the provisions of title 5 relating to the competitive service, classification, and General Schedule pay rates, appoint and fix the compensation of such officers and employees as are necessary to carry out the provisions of this title, and to prescribe the authority and duties of such officers and employees; and

(2) obtain the services of such experts and consultants as are necessary to carry out the provisions of this title.

SEC. 108. RISK MANAGEMENT TRAINING.

The Commission shall develop training seminars in risk management techniques related to derivatives activities for employees of the Federal financial institution regulatory agencies and the employees of financial institutions.

SEC. 109. INTERNATIONAL NEGOTIATIONS.

The Chairman of the Board of Governors of the Federal Reserve System, in consultation with the members of the Commission, shall encourage governments, central banks, and regulatory authorities of other industrialized countries to work toward maintaining and, where appropriate, adopting comparable supervisory standards and regulations, particularly capital standards, for financial institutions engaged in derivatives activities.

SEC. 110. CREDIT UNIONS.

Insured credit unions (as defined in section 101(7) of the Federal Credit Union Act) shall be supervised for purposes of derivatives activities by the National Credit Union Administration under standards no less stringent than standards under which Federal depository institutions (as defined in section 3(c) of the Federal Deposit Insurance Act) are supervised by the Federal banking agencies.

TITLE II – SUPERVISORY IMPROVEMENTS

SEC. 201. UNSAFE OR UNSOUND BANKING PRACTICES.

(a) IN GENERAL.—Failure of an institution-affiliated party engaged in derivatives activities to have adequate technical expertise may be deemed by the appropriate federal banking agency to constitute an unsafe or unsound banking practice within the meaning of section 8 of the Federal Deposit Insurance Act (12 USC 1818).

(b) RULE OF CONSTRUCTION.—This section shall be in addition to and not in derogation of the authority of any appropriate Federal banking agency under section 8 of the Federal Deposit Insurance Act to determine unsafe or unsound banking practices.

SEC. 202. INTERNAL CONTROLS.

Section 39(a)(1)(A) of the Federal Deposit Insurance Act (12 USC 1831p–1(a)(1)(A)) is amended by striking "internal controls" and inserting "internal controls (including internal controls for derivatives activities)".

SEC. 203. FOREIGN BANK SUPERVISION.

Section 7(d)(2)(A) of the International Banking Act of 1978 (12 USC 3105(d)(2)(A)) is amended after "country" by inserting, "including, in the case of a foreign bank engaged in derivatives activities, comprehensive supervision and regulation for derivatives activities (as that term is defined in the Derivatives Supervision Act of 1994). In making any determination under this paragraph, the Board shall consider whether the home country maintains comprehensive supervision and regulation of derivatives activities, including capital and disclosure standards, not less stringent than United States standards".

TITLE III – FINANCIAL INSOLVENCY REFORMS

SEC. 301. CONFORMING DEFINITIONS.

(a) Section 11(e)(8)(D)(vi) of the Federal Deposit Insurance Act (12 USC §1821(e)(8)(D)(vi)) is amended—

(1) by striking "purchase" each time it appears; and

(2) after "currency option" inserting, "equity derivative, equity or equity index swap, equity or equity index option, bond option, spot foreign exchange transaction".

(b) Section 101(55) of the Bankruptcy Code (11 USC §101(55)) is amended—

(1) in paragraph (A), by inserting "any qualified financial contract within the meaning of 12 USC §1821(e)(8)(D)(i)" after "currency option,"; and

(2) in paragraph (C) by inserting "and transactions documented thereunder." after "supplements".

SEC. 302. FAILED AND FAILING INSTITUTIONS.

Section 11(e)(8) of the Federal Deposit Insurance Act (12 USC §1821(e)(8)) is amended by adding the following new subparagraphs:

"(F) PREEMPTION.—Notwithstanding any other provision of law, no automatic stay, injunction, avoidance, moratorium, or other restraint, whether issued or granted by a bankruptcy court or any other judicial body, any administrative body, or whether created by statute or otherwise, shall limit or delay the ability of the Corporation, in any capacity, to exercise its authority, rights or powers in accordance with section 11(e)(8) of this Act. This provision shall not limit any other right, power or authority of the Corporation in any capacity.

"(G) UNDERCAPITALIZED INSURED DEPOSITORY INSTITU-TIONS.—The Corporation, in consultation with the appropriate federal banking agencies, shall prescribe regulations requiring expanded record-keeping for qualified financial contracts (including market valuations) by insured depository institutions that are undercapitalized as defined in section 38 of the Federal Deposit Insurance Act (12 USC 1831o)."

SEC. 303. QUALIFIED FINANCIAL CONTRACT TRANSFERS.

Section 11(e)(10) of the Federal Deposit Insurance Act, (12 USC §1821(e)(10)), is amended by adding the following new sub-paragraphs:

"(C) EFFECT OF NOTICE.—If a person who is a party to a qualified financial contract is notified by the Corporation as receiver of a depository institution by the close of business (Eastern Standard Time) on the business day following its appointment as receiver that the Corporation has transferred all qualified financial contracts between the depository institution and such person or its affiliates pursuant to subparagraph (9)(A), then the provisions of subparagraph (8)(A) shall not apply. For the purposes of this subparagraph, the Corporation as receiver shall be deemed to have notified a person if it has taken steps reasonably calculated to provide notice to such person."

"**(D) NOTICE EXTENSION.**—The Corporation may extend the notice period described in paragraph (C) for a reasonable period not to exceed 5 days, if the Corporation determines that such an extension may maximize the net present value return from the sale or disposition of such qualified financial contracts."

"**(E) TREATMENT OF BRIDGE BANKS.**—Neither a bridge bank nor an institution organized by the Corporation and immediately placed into conservatorship or placed into conservatorship at the time of a purchase and assumption transaction with the receiver of a failed depository institution for which the Corporation has been appointed receiver shall be considered a depository institution in default for purposes of this paragraph, paragraph 8 and paragraph 9 of this section."

SEC. 304. CLARIFYING AMENDMENTS.

Section 11(e)(8)(D)(vii) of the Federal Deposit Insurance Act (12 USC 1821(e)(8)(D)(vii)) is amended to read as follows:

"(vii) Notwithstanding any other provision of law, any master agreements for contracts or agreements described in clauses (ii), (iii), (iv), or (vi), together with all supplements to such master agreement shall be treated as 1 swap agreement for the purposes of this Act and title 11 of the United States Code.".

SEC. 305. TECHNICAL AMENDMENTS.

(a) Section 11(e)(8)(D) of the Federal Deposit Insurance Act (12 USC 1821(e)(8)(D)) is amended—

    (1) in clause (i) by inserting "spot contract," after "swap agreement,".

    (2) in clause (iv) by striking "(24)" and inserting "(25)";

    (3) in clause (v) by striking "101(41)" and inserting "101(47)".

(b) Section 11(e)(8)(E)(i) of the Federal Deposit Insurance Act (12 USC 1821(e)(8)(E)(i)) is amended by striking ";" and inserting "," other than a default based solely upon the appointment of a conservator.

TITLE IV – MISCELLANEOUS

SEC. 401. SAVINGS PROVISION.

The provisions of this Act shall be in addition to and not in derogation of any existing authority of a Federal financial institution regulatory agency to supervise or regulate derivatives activities provided under any other applicable law.

Glossary

A

American option
An option which can expire on any one of a number of dates within a given range at the behest of the purchaser of the option, where the option is in-the-money.

Arbitrage
The use of derivative products makes it possible for market users to take advantage of mismatches in prices or market conditions by speculating on the underlying financial products without the need to undergo the formalities of conventional market trading. Derivatives markets in themselves contain the possibility to generate arbitrage opportunities.

Asian option
An option which can expire either on one of a number of dates within a given range; being a hybrid between an American and a European option.

B

Barrier options
An option which moves into the money or out of the money by crossing a price threshold. The option is only in-the-money if the market price of the underlying instrument is within the range identified by the barrier option.

Binary options
Similar to a barrier option, an option which is either in or out of the money when it crosses a given threshold on a specified date. Often, there is only a requirement for payment of a premium should the option be in-the-money.

Bond options
Bond options are options to purchase bonds at a price at a date in the future. There is a clear correlation between an option and a future / forward, as discussed below.

Bonds with warrants
Bonds with warrants are debt instrument with the capability of being converted into equity on reaching a given strike price.

C

Call option
A 'short call' is a position taken where the market is expected to fall. The

institution's aim is to make premium income. The seller's risk is that of having to deliver under the option.

Cap

A cap is a ceiling put on the maximum interest rate which a counterparty will have to pay under a swap. In short it restricts the downside of floating interest rates climbing too high. The cap is purchased for a lump sum. The legal analysis of a cap is that it is an obligation assumed by the financial institution selling it, to pay the interest of the purchaser when that interest climbs above a pre-determined rate.

Capacity

The legal capability (*vires*) of a counterparty to enter into a given transaction or to perform a given act.

Capital Adequacy

Currently the creature of European legislation, the level of asset and equity capital required to be maintained against the institution's liability portfolio. The level of capital required to be set against the exposure to derivatives transactions.

Cherry-picking

On the insolvency of one or other of the parties to a transaction, the insolvent party seeks to enforce those transactions which are in profit and to repudiate those transactions which are not.

Collars

Collars are a combination of cap and floor which guarantees that the interest rates will not move outside the chosen band. This might be important, for example, in the case of corporates which want to be able to predict their cost of funding with relative certainty in advance of entering into a deal.

Collateral

An asset pledged to a lender until the loan is repaid. In most circumstances, where the borrower defaults in repayment of the loan, the lender has the legal right to seize the collateral and sell it to discharge the amount of the loan.

Commoditized

Where a derivative product becomes so commonplace that it is reproduced in a number of transactions, it is said to have become a commodity in itself and therefore "commoditized".

Contract for Differences

A contract where benefit is provided to one or other of the parties on the happening of a given event, as defined in the Financial Services Act 1986.

Convertible bonds
A bond which is capable of being converted into equity on the happening of defined events relating to the price of the equity and time.

Complex options
Options which are combinations of option strategies designed to achieve more specific goals than vanilla option products.

Counterparty
The other party in a derivatives transaction.

Counterparty risk
The risk that the counterparty will fail to pay under its obligations under the contract, or that it will fail to perform any of its obligations under the contract, or that the counterparty will become insolvent and therefore be able to perform any of its obligations under the contract.

Cross-currency interest rate swaps
These swaps are hybrids in which Party A makes payments in one currency at a fixed rate of interest while Party B makes payments in another currency at a floating rate of interest.

Currency option
An option to purchase or to sell an amount of a currency at a given price at a given time in the future.

Currency swaps
A transaction is which cash flows in different currencies are exchanged between counterparties, enabling a party to obtain amounts of foreign currency at a lower funding rate.

D

Debentures
As defined in s.744 Companies Act 1985 includes "debenture stock, bonds and any other securities of a company, whether constituting a charge on the assets of the company or not".

Delta coefficient
The Delta coefficient refers to the rate of change in the price of the option for one unit of the underlying instrument. The Delta is frequently interpreted as the likelihood that the option will mature in the money.

E

Equity swaps
The structure is usually for the payment of a fixed amount of money by one party the other in return for a floating amount. For example, X might wish to speculate on the performance of the Nikkei 225 index against LIBOR. Therefore X would seek to pay LIBOR to Y and in

return receive from Y the cash equivalent of the performance of the Nikkei 225 over a given period of time. The benefit to X is a receipt of cash flow equal to the performance of the Nikkei 225 without the expense or administrative difficulties of purchasing a range of stocks appearing on the Nikkei 225.

Equity warrants
A form of issued instrument in the primary markets which bears similarities to an equity option but which is issued by the company itself and requires the company to issue new equity on its exercise.

European option
An option which matures on a single, given date and which cannot mature on any other date (except possibly by termination of the transaction).

F

Financial risk
The risk that the underlying or relevant derivative market will move with the result that the derivative product moves out-of-the-money.

Floors
A floor is the same in principal as a cap but it exists to guard against interest rates that fall too low. The floor is purchased for a lump sum and is an obligation on the part of the seller to make good any interest lost by the rate floating too low.

Forwards
The forward is a promise to supply a particular commodity or security at a set price on a set date (often in a set place). In the commodity markets it is usual to buy wheat, for example, at a given price in a given amount at a pre-determined time to be delivered in a given place. In the time it takes for the contract to mature (which might include the wheat to grow be harvested and shipped) the price of wheat can fluctuate wildly. The contract, that is the right to receive the wheat at a price at a time in the agreed place, can be sold to others at a greater or lower price than that paid for it originally. The same is true, to a greater or lesser extent, of contracts entered into between private parties.

Fund managers
A market participant which manages large portfolios of investments for clients or fungible portfolios of investments for groups of clients.

Futures
A forward conveys the right to purchase or sell a specified quantity of an asset at a fixed price on a fixed date in the future. In exchange traded futures contracts, which are a standardised form of forward contract, the quantity of the underlying asset to be delivered per contract is fixed, as is

the underlying financial instrument or index, the minimum price movement for the contract and the life of the contract.

Futures price
The price that the market would pay the notional instrument representing the thing that is to be physically delivered if that thing existed currently. The pricing for these instruments feels a little counter-intuitive at first meeting. The prices are quoted as an amount (100) less the implied interest rate on that instrument. Therefore, the price of a futures instrument moves in inverse correlation to movements in interest rates.

G

Gamma coefficient
The Gamma coefficient measures the rate of change in the Delta and therefore identifies the frequency with which a delta coefficient hedge will have to be recalibrated.

H

Hedging
A strategy used to offset market risk. The use of derivatives to hedge financial risk, involves investment in a derivative instrument in which market movements will offset movements in the primary investment.

Hedge funds
A form of low capitalised, highly-leveraged mutual fund which uses hedging techniques as an important part of their trading activities to control financial risk and to enable greater leverage on capital resources to fund market speculation.

I

Index (share, bond, commodity)
Statistical composite which measures the performance and change in a financial market.

Index options
Index options are put or call options derived from an index which allow the investor to trade on an index without having to buy the individual stocks on it.

Inverse floater swaps
Inverse floater swaps aim to take advantage of a steep yield curve, that is where interest rates are expected to rise steeply in the future and therefore there is a great difference between short term interest rates and long term interest rates.

Interest rate swaps
An interest rate swap is an agreement between parties to make periodic

payments to the other party in the same currency. Where A and B can obtain different costs of funding which may not suit their own commercial circumstances, if they can exchange their available terms to their mutual advantage, this is a useful way for them to do business.

In-the-money
Where the strike price of an underlying share under an option is less than the market price on a date when the option is capable of being exercised.

L

Leveraged swaps
The 'leveraged swap' is closely related to the inverse floater swap but involves greater leverage in the size of the transaction. The size of the payment and the credit risk involved is therefore enhanced by the factor which accelerates the movements in market rates to greater payments under the swap transaction.

Long option
A 'long call' is a position taken where the market is expected to rise. The premium for a long call option is expended in return for the upside potential in the price of the underlying instrument.

M

Margin
Collateral provided by a party to its counterparty to cover the counterparty risk arising from a derivatives transaction. Where the exposure of the party providing margin increases it will usually be required to add to the amount of margin deposited with the counterparty.

Mark-to-market
The process of measuring exposures on derivatives products against their value in the market if exercised at the time of measurement.

Maturity
The time at which the derivative product expires. The maturity of a European option is its expiration date.

N

Netting
The process of setting off obligations under transactions one against another so that payments between parties are made net rather than gross. One of the most important issues facing the derivatives lawyer is the availability of netting in the event that one of the parties to a derivatives transaction becomes insolvent.

Notional amount
The notional amount by which the size of payments made under a swap transaction are calculated.

O

OTC derivatives
Derivatives which are transacted privately between parties rather than traded on an exchange.

P

Physical delivery
Physical delivery of an option requires that, when the option is exercised, the underlying financial product is delivered to the counterparty rather than its cash equivalent.

Put option
An instrument granting the purchaser the right, but not the obligation, to sell the underlying instrument to the counterparty at a given price on a given date.

R

Ratio Horizontal Spreads
The aim is to take advantage of volatility fluctuation over time. A combination of put and call options is acquired, with the options being exercised at different times to maximise the effect of the market movement.

Ratio Vertical Spreads
The Vertical Spread aims to profit from low volatility market conditions. Where an institution buys more close to the money calls than it sells, it is able to benefit from a low volatility market by not paying the upside on these instruments if the market remains unvolatile.

Risk Management
The process of assessing and controlling credit risk in financial institutions. The Risk Management procedure involves a combination of credit risk evaluation and portfolio management.

S

Securitised options
The process of securitisation of assets has grown as a market product. Securitisation involves the bundling together of financial instruments which are then sold. Option products are capable of being turned into securities in this way and sold as a single asset.

Stock options
A put or call option with reference to underlying shares traded, in most circumstances, on an exchange.

Straddles
Straddles are formed by combinations of puts and calls with equal strike levels and identical maturity dates. A straddle takes advantage in the movement of the gamma coefficient.

Swaps
A swap is simply an exchange of the rate of interest that a borrower is paying for a different rate of interest. Company A will agree to pay the interest on the debt it owes to B bank, in return for which Company A will pay a different rate of interest to the Bank C with which it has entered into the swap. This is a simple exchange of cash flows for a fee.

Swaptions
An option to enter into a swap transaction. Usually purchased by a client to provide protection against future movements in interest rates by enabling the client to initiate a swap transaction at a given rate for a given maturity.

Synthetic options
A combination of financial products, including options, to produce the effect of another option product.

Systemic risk
The risk that failure of one market participant will cause a knock-on failure in the market resulting in a failure of the derivatives market system.

T

Tax derivatives
A form of derivative product using swap and option techniques to reduce the client company's exposure to tax. The product's aim is to restructure the client's cash flow to produce a more tax efficient form of cash flow. The term "tax derivative" is therefore something of a misnomer, being a complex derivative adapted for a particular purpose.

Theta coefficient
The Theta coefficient measure the decrease in value of the option as it approaches its maturity. The value of a long option decreases as days pass towards the completion date of the option.

V

Vertical Spreads
Vertical spreads consist of a long and a short position on the same type of option with identical maturity dates. A vertical spread is a combination

of a long and short put ('put spread') or a long and short call ('call spread'), where the puts or calls have the same expiry dates.

Volatility Strategies

There are a number of option strategies which aim to take advantage of volatility rather than specifically of movements in price.

Z

Zeta Coefficient

The zeta coefficient then measures the change in the value of the option as a unit of the underlying instrument becomes more volatile.

Index

Accounting information, 217
Accounting risk, 175
Actual market risk, 180–181
Agents, 141–143
  rights of principal against third party, 143
Agreement to deliver documents, 107
Arbitrage, 7
Asset liability management, 7
Asset securitisation, 210–211
Automatic termination, 128

Bankruptcy
  master agreement, and, 92
Banks, 214
  regulation, 224–225
Barrier options, 38–40, 46–48
  ratio horizontal spreads, 40, 47
  ratio vertical spreads, 40, 48
  straddles, 39–40, 47
  vertical spreads, 40, 48
  volatility strategies, 39, 46–47
Barrier swaps
  alternative analysis, 31–32
Binary options, 42, 52
Bond options, 35–36
  analysis, 35–36
  documentation, 36
Bonds with warrants, 41
Breach of warranty, 146
Building societies, 210
  capacity, 137–138

Capital adequacy, 140
  aim of rules, 221
Capacity, 132–139
  building societies, 137–138
  Companies Act companies, 135–136
    Hammersmith and Fulham litigation, 136–137
    s.35 and s.35A Companies Act 1985, 135–136
  conflict of laws, 139
  English law, 134–135
  insurance companies, 138–139
  issues, 132–133
Capacity issues, 218
Caps, 28–29
  analysis, 28
  documentation, 28
  structure, 28–29
Cherry picking, 126
Clearing house
  control of risk, 219–221

Collars, 30–31
  analysis, 30
  documentation, 30–31
  structure, 31
Collateral, 169–196
  charge, 188–189
  commercial issues, 185–186
  conflict of law issues, 191
  custody, 193–196
  definitions, 192
  depositing, 194–195
  guarantees, 189
  legal issues, 186–196
  letter of comfort, 189
  level, 187–188
  mark-to-market method, 187
  marking to market, 188
  meaning, 184
  means of credit enhancement, 186–187
  measurement, 186
  method of marking to market, 193
  possible combination of set-off and taking security interest, 190
  potential tax problems, 191
  pro forma agreement, 192
  purpose, 184–185
  regulation, 221–222
  requirement for, 185–186
  return of, 195–196
  sample documentation, 191
  set-off, 190
  structure of documentation, 191–192
  terms in master agreement, 191
  type, 186
Companies
  capacity, 135–136
Complex equity derivatives, 43
Complex options, 37–38
  analysis, 37–38
  documentation, 38
  vertical spreads, 38
Complex share options, 45–46
  vertical spreads, 45–46
Confirmation, 69–82
  commercial points to watch, 76–77
  creation of contract, 69–73
  credit points to watch, 77–78
  credit risks, and, 73–74
  extraordinary event, 81–82
  failure to deliver, 80
  interim, 70–73
  legal points to watch, 76
  market disruption, 78–80
  market publication error, 80–81
  master agreement, and, 73
  mistake, 80–81

Confirmation—*cont*
  party error, 81
  position without master agreement, 74
  pro forma, 75
  structure, 74–75
  terms, 73–74
Conflict of laws, 139
Contract
  creation, 69–73
  rectification, 129–130
Contract for differences
  legal issues, 117–118
Contract for differences issue, 14–16
Convertible bonds, 49
Corporate restructuring
  master agreement, and, 92
Corporates, 213
Covered warrants, 41–42, 54
Credit aspect of derivatives, 175–177
Credit risk, 169–196
  confirmation, and, 73–74
  growth of derivatives markets, and, 174
  reviews, 216
  types, 171
Cross currency interest rate swaps, 26–27
  analysis, 26–27
  documentation, 27
  structure, 27
Cross default, 98–99
  accelerated debt, 98
  non-contingent default, 98
  scope of companies covered, 98
  scope of transactions covered, 98–99
Currency contracts
  taxation, 159–162
Currency options, 36–37
  analysis, 36
  documentation, 37
Currency swap, 4–5, 23–26
  analysis, 24
  documentation, 25
  structure, 25–26

Damages
  interest rate swaps, and, 121
Debenture, 65–66
  meaning, 65
Debt options, 35
Derivative markets, 203
  economic role, 203
Derivative strategies, 6–11
Derivatives
  meaning, 6
  commercial analysis, 7–8
  credit concerns, 9–11
  legal analysis, 7–9
    importance, 8–9
  legal concerns, 9–11
Derivatives revolution, 200–202
  economic priorities, 201–202

Equity derivatives, 48–49
Equity options, 42–52
  complex equity derivatives, 43
  example, 43
Equity swaps, 33–34, 50–52
  analysis, 33
  credit implications, 51–52
  documentation, 34
  structure, 34, 50–51
Equity warrants, 49–50, 53–54
Euromarkets
  growth of, 202–203
Exchange traded products, 61–63
  clearing house, 62
  initial margin, 62
  marketplace, 62
  structure, 61–63

Failure to deliver, 80
Floors, 29–30
  analysis, 29
  documentation, 29–30
  structure, 30
Foreign exchange
  speculation, 204–205
Foreign exchange markets, 22–23, 203–203
Foreign exchange products, 22–23
Forwards, 55–56
  commercial structure, 55–56
  documentation, 56
  nature of, 207
Fund managers, 141–144
  trusts, and, 143
Futures, 55–56
  commercial structure, 55–56
FX exchange control
  extant, 223
  implied, 223

Gaming, 145
Guarantees, 189

Hedge funds, 142–143, 212–213
Hedging, 6–7, 56–58, 208–209
  defining, 56–57
  legal liability, 57–58
  potential legal issues, 57–58

Illegality
  master agreement, and, 92–93
Inherent market risks, 172–173
Insolvency
  master agreement, and, 128
Institutions, 209–214
Insurance companies, 211
  capacity, 138–139

Interest rate swaps, 20–22, 116–123
  analysis, 20–21
  analysis by lawyer, 119–120
  contract for differences, 117–118
  damages, 121
  documentation, 22
  insolvency aspect, 122–123
  legal issues, 116–123
  rescission, 121
  restitution, and, 121–122
  specific performance, 121–122
  structuring issues, 22
  vanilla, 21–22
Interim confirmation, 70–73
Inverse floater swaps, 32–33
  analysis, 32–33
  documentation, 32–33
ISDA contract, 67–68

Legal issues, 113–148
Legal risk, 175
Letter of comfort, 189
Liquidity in access to funding, 216
Local authorities, 209–210

Market disruption, 78–80
  effect on contract, 79–80
  length of time, 78
Market risk
  actual, 180–181
  meaning, 179–180
  potential, 180
Markets, 59–112
  documentation, 59–112
Marking to market, 218
Master agreements, 82–95
  absence of litigation, 89
  accuracy of all information, 90
  authority, 87
  capacity, 87–88
  collateral terms in, 191
  condition precedent, 85
  confirmation, and, 73
  credit event upon merger, 93–94
  delayed payments, 86
  early termination, 94
    one-way payments, 94
    two-way payments, 94
  events of default, 91–92
    bankrupty, 92
    breach of contract, 91
    corporate restructuring, 92
    credit worth, 92
    cross default, 92
    failure of guarantee, 91
    failure to pay, 91
    misrepresentation, and, 91
  expenses, 95
  governing law, 95

history, 83–84
  illegality, 88, 92–93
  insolvency, and, 128
  interpretation, 84–85
  jurisdiction, 95
  legal validity of obligations assured, 89
  multibranch parties, 95
  netting, 85
  non-fault termination events, 92–94
  payments, 85
  regulatory approvals, 89
  representations, 86–87
  scope, 82–83
  tax event, 93
  tax event upon merger, 93
  tax representations, 89–90
  termination, 90
  transfer, 94–95
  withholding tax, 86
Misrepresentation
  master agreement, and, 91
Mistake
  confirmation, and, 80–81
Motivation for derivatives transactions,
      177–180
  clients, 178
  suitability of transaction, 179
  volatility in interest rates, 177–178

Netting
  master agreements, and, 85
  nature of, 215
  rescission, and, 125–126
  system, 221
Netting on insolvency, 123–128
  contingent debt contracts, 125
  executory contract analysis, 124–125
  netting, 123–124
  rescission, and, 125–126
  UK draft law, 124
Novations, 144–145

Options
  theory, 206
OTC derivatives contracts, 66–68
  documentation, 68
  structure, 67–68
OTC options
  credit profile, 182–183
    equity derivatives, 183

Payment netting, 127
Penal taxation, 224
Pension funds, 211–212
Policy motivations, 218–219
  stability in the economy, 219
Political risk, 140–141, 218
Potential market risk, 180

Pre-contractual undertakings and
    procedure, 105–108
  agreement to deliver documents, 107
  local business day, 106
  procedures for entering into
    transactions, 107–108
  representations as to powers, 106
  warranty or condition, 106
Primary markets, 63–66
  documentation, 64–65
  legal analysis, 63–64
Product risk, 217
Products, 1–57, 204–209
  historical development, 4–5

Rectification of contracts, 129–130
Regulation of derivatives markets, 147–
    148, 197–229
  banks, 224–225
  control functions, 222–223
  control of speculation through
    registered SPVs, 225
  executive summary, 199–200
  hedging, 225
  overseas, 226–228
  proposals, 200, 223
  taxation, 226
Regulation of large financial markets, 219
Regulatory authority, 222
Rescission
  interest rate swaps, and, 121
Restitution, 129–132
  executory contract analysis, 130–131
    damages, 130
    rescission, 130–131
    specific performance, 131
  mutual debts analysis, 131–132
    damages, 132
    rescission, 132
    specific performance, 132
  rectification of contracts, 129–130
  swaps contracts, and, 130
Risk equivalency, 181–182
Risks, 214–218
  economy, and, 214

Schedule, 96–104
  alteration of corporate structure, 101
  collateral terms, 104
  continued provision of guarantees, 103
  credit, 96
  credit impact on counterparty, 99–100
  creditworth after corporate
    reorganisation, 103–104
  cross default, 98–99
  entities, 97
  merger, 101–102
  merger without assuming obligations of
    predecessor, 102

parties, 96–97
  reconstruction, 101–102
  scope of defaults covered, 99
  size of default, 100–101
  takeover, 101–102
Set-off, 108–109
Share options, 43, 46
  cash settled, 44
    documentation, 44
    structure, 44
  complex, 45–46
    vertical spreads, 45–46
  physically settled, 44–45
    documentation, 44–45
    structure, 44
Speculation, 6
Swaps, 11–22
  classification of contract, 16–18
  contract for differences issue, 14–16
  example, 12
  insolvency analysis, 19–20
  legal analysis, 14
  legal structure, 13–14
  meaning, 11
  restitution, and, 18–19
  sample transaction, 11–13
Swaptions, 32
  analysis, 32
  documentation, 32
Synthetic options, 40–41, 48
Single EC currency, 223
Sovereign risk, 218
Specific performance
  interest rate swaps, and, 121–122
Speculation v hedging, 219
Standardisation of products, 223
Suitability, 146–147
  Unfair Contract Terms Act 1977, 146–
    147
Swaps, 205–206
  credit exposure, 183–184
Swaps markets, 211
Systematic risk, 173–174, 214–215

Tax representations, 104–105
  ISDA Master Agreement, 104–105
  payee, 105
Taxation, 149–167
  Finance Act 1993 regime, 154
  hedging transactions, 226
  need for systematic approach, 226
  payee representations, 153
  payer representations, 152–153
  provisions in master agreements, 151–
    154
  regulation, and, 226
  speculation, 226
  statements of practice, 153
Taxation of financial derivatives, 154–167
  anti-avoidance provisions, 166–167

basis of accounting, 165–166
calculation of profits and losses, 164–165
contracts which may be qualifying, 156
currency contracts, 159–162
  meaning, 159–160
Finance Act 1994 Part IV, 154
interest rate contracts, 156–159
  fixed payments, 158–159
  fixed rate payments, 158–159
  variable rate payment, 159
options on swaps, 162
provisions which may be disregarded, 163–164
qualifying companies, 164
qualifying contracts, 155–156
summary of Finance Act 1994, 154–155
swaptions, 162
termination of qualifying contracts, 166
Termination, 111–112

automatic on default, 111
  early, payments on, 111–112
Termination currency, 112
Transfer clause, 94–95, 144–145
Transferability of obligations, 110–111
  severability, 110–111
  transfer, 110
Trusts
  fund managers, and, 143–144

Vanilla interest rate swap, 21–22
  structure, 21

Warrants, 52–54
  covered, 54
  debenture, whether, 65–66
  equity, 53–54
  nature of, 206–207